HANS POELZIG: REFLECTIONS ON HIS LIFE AND WORK

JULIUS POSENER

HANS POELZIG

Reflections on His Life and Work

Edited by Kristin Feireiss

The Architectural
History Foundation, Inc.
New York, New York

The MIT Press
Cambridge, Massachusetts,
and London, England

© 1992 by the Architectural History Foundation and the Massachusetts Institute of Technology
Printed and bound in the United States of America.

No parts of this book may be reproduced in any form or by any means, electronic or mechanical, including photocopying, recording, or by any information storage and retrieval system, without permission in writing from the publishers and the editor.

Library of Congress Cataloging-in-Publication Data

Posener, Julius.
    Hans Poelzig : reflections on his life and work / Julius Posener; edited by Kristin Feireiss [translated by Christine Charlesworth].
        p.   cm.
    Includes bibliographical references and index.
    ISBN 0-262-16127-3
    1. Poelzig, Hans, 1869–1936. 2. Architects—Germany—Biography. 3. Architecture, Modern—20th century—Germany.
I. Feireiss, Kristin.   II. Title.
NA1088.P6P64   1992
720'.92—dc20
[B]
                                           91-39637
                                             CIP

The Architectural History Foundation is a publicly supported, not-for-profit foundation. Directors: William Butler, Colin Eisler, Elizabeth G. Miller, Victoria Newhouse, Annalee Newman, Adolf K. Placzek, Adele Chatfield-Taylor. Editorial Board: David G. De Long, University of Pennsylvania; Christoph L. Frommel, Bibliotheca Hertziana, Rome; William H. Jordy, Brown University, Emeritus; Barbara Miller Lane, Bryn Mawr College; Henry A. Millon, CASVA, National Gallery of Art, Washington, D.C.; Marvin Trachtenberg, Institute of Fine Arts, New York City

Julius Posener has made major contributions to the history of modern German architecture in his books, articles, and lectures. He has taught at schools of architecture in Britain, Kuala Lumpur, and Berlin, where he lives at present.

Translated by Christine Charlesworth
Designed by William Rueter

Frontispiece: Hans Poelzig, 1930

Contents

FOREWORD, by VICTORIA NEWHOUSE   vii
PREFACE   xii

ONE
Developments in German Architecture During Poelzig's Lifetime   3
Documentation   19
  Walter Gropius, address to the "Exhibition for Unknown Architects," 1919
  Bruno Taut, address to the "Exhibition for Unknown Architects," 1919
  Erich Mendelsohn, address to the Working Council for Art, 1919
  Hermann Finsterlin, *Casa Nova*, 1924

TWO
Hans Poelzig, the Person, the Artist: Breslau 1900–1916   22
Documentation   46
  Heinrich Lauterbach, reminiscence of Hans Poelzig, 1951
  Hans Poelzig, "The Modern Factory," 1911
  Theodor Heuss, on Poelzig's paintings, 1939
  Theodor Heuss, on Poelzig's personality, 1939

THREE
Poelzig at Work: Breslau 1904–1916   53

FOUR
A Final Word on Breslau   96
Documentation   100
  Hans Poelzig, "Fermentation in Architecture," 1906

FIVE
Departure into the Unknown: Dresden 1916–1920   102
Documentation   117
  Theodor Heuss, Introduction, *The House of Friendship*, 1917

SIX
Transition from Dresden to Berlin: The Grosses Schauspielhaus   119

Documentation 129
   Arnold Zweig, "Theater, Mass, Individual," 1920
   Hans Poelzig, address to the Werkbund, 1919

SEVEN
The Festival Theater for Salzburg 135
Documentation 150
   Theodor Heuss, on Poelzig as set designer, 1939
   Hans Poelzig, "Festival Theater in Salzburg," 1921

EIGHT
A New Beginning: Berlin 157

NINE
Success 171
Documentation 180
   Hans Poelzig, "On Architecture in Our Time," 1922
   Walter Riezler, "Do Technical Forms Become Outdated?" 1922
   Hans Poelzig, "The Architect," 1931

TEN
Works 1924–1931 197

ELEVEN
The Final Years 1932–1936 245
Documentation 255
   Theodor Heuss, on Poelzig's final years, 1939

TWELVE
The Late Designs 1932–1936 256

THIRTEEN
Reflections 263

POSTSCRIPT 269
LIST OF BUILDINGS AND DESIGNS BY HANS POELZIG 271
NOTES 276
INDEX 281

Foreword

FROM 1926 TO 1929 Julius Posener studied with Hans Poelzig in Berlin. Posener's life was profoundly influenced by this relationship, the memory of which forms the nucleus of the present book. A decade of personal contact, beginning with the twenty-two-year-old student and his fifty-seven-year-old teacher, is the obvious justification for Posener's memoir. But, there is perhaps another, less obvious, motivation.

Throughout a lifetime of writing, Posener has referred to Poelzig as "a lone wolf" who "never could stand any group for long."[1] This is not surprising, since Poelzig represented two diametrically opposed tendencies among architects of the early twentieth century: "fantasy and pure reason."[2] Although he is often lumped together with the small group of so-called German Expressionists—Bruno Taut, Erich Mendelsohn, Otto Bartning, the Brothers Luckhardt—Poelzig was not of their generation (he was older). Nor did he view Expressionism in terms of new forms as they did, but rather as a natural development of history.

By the same token, Posener himself is also "a lone wolf," a modernist who positions himself resolutely outside the classical modern movement, open at the same time to the Eclecticism of Schinkel and Muthesius, the Expressionism of Poelzig, and the modernism of Le Corbusier and Mies van der Rohe.

Posener is a "lone wolf" in a more personal sense as well. In 1935, when Poelzig made his abortive attempt to live in Istanbul, Posener had already left Germany (in 1933). His was to be a twenty-eight-year absence. As a German Jew, Posener was an outsider in National Socialist Germany, and never completely at home in the places where he took refuge: Paris, Jerusalem, England, and Malaysia. This feeling of apartness that was shared by the two men—Poelzig's chosen professional independence, Posener's enforced political exile and subsequent antinationalism—makes Posener a particularly apt biographer of his teacher.

Julius Posener's father, Moritz, was a painter; his mother, Gertrud Oppenheim, a musical prodigy. Both parents came from wealthy Jewish families who considered themselves totally integrated with Berlin's intellectual and artistic communities. Born in 1904, Julius was the youngest of three brothers, following after Ludwig (1902) and Karl (1898). In his recently published autobiography, *Fast so alt wie das Jahrhundert* (Almost As Old As the Century), Posener describes the idyllic life of his large family circle, referring to it as "the family as a work of art."[3] With the outbreak of World War I, the idyll ended. Posener's brother Karl volunteered for the army—out of patriotism and because, as a Jew, he did not want to stand on the sidelines. German anti-Semitism was the single most profound influence on Posener's own life. In his autobiography, he describes its deep roots in the German psyche: the conviction that Jews were so different from Germans that they could never understand German culture. It was a repugnant idea for a man who defined himself in terms of German culture.

Posener's passion for English architecture is well known, especially the country houses introduced to Germany early in the century by the architect and family friend, Hermann Muthesius. It is touching to learn that his first knowledge of things English came from a childhood romance with his neighbor Kittie, aged twelve, when he was fifteen. (Posener's first wife, Charmian Middleton, whom he married in 1948, was English.) That first love prepared the way for Posener's rigorous intellectual involvement with England is very much in keeping with his personality.

After graduating from the German equivalent of high school, Posener decided to study architecture. To this end, in 1923 he entered the Technische Hochschule Berlin in Charlottenburg, where he put up with what he describes as two very dull first years. The only architects who captured his imagination were Muthesius and Mendelsohn, and in 1926 he came to Poelzig's design course not because of any particular interest in the architect's work, but rather to avoid the teachers he disliked.

Posener was immediately captivated by the man he was to refer to for the rest of his life as "my Master."[4] In this book, Posener describes Poelzig's method: "He was of the opinion that it was impossible to teach art. What he tried to teach were the technical, social, practical, the cultural aspects of architecture."[5] In retrospect, Posener claims he "studied architecture under the wrong idea that I had the necessary talent, which I didn't. Poelzig must have thought that I was not altogether without talent, because he passed me in my final exams."[6]

These exams took place shortly before the stock market crash of October 1929. With the profession at a standstill in Germany, Posener investigated job possibilities in Paris. He worked briefly there as a draftsman with Charles Siclis and André Lurçat, then with Jean-Charles Moreaux. But his writing for the German architecture magazines *Die Bauwelt* and *Die Baugilde* soon replaced drafting. At the end of the year he met Marcel-Eugène Cahen who invited Posener to join the new journal he was planning, *Construire*.

Cahen died within a few months of that meeting, but on 1 September 1930 the journal he had planned appeared as *L'Architecture d'Aujourd'hui*, edited by Pierre Vago. Posener was its first salaried employee. He immediately wrote to every important German architect of the time: Peter Behrens, Mendelsohn, Taut, Poelzig. All answered the young unknown by offering him full cooperation. The result was a series of articles on each.

L'Architecture d'Aujourd'hui was supposed to be a "centrist" journal whose pages would be open equally to different schools of architecture — contradiction was to be a given.[7] From his very first articles, Posener made his preferences abundantly clear. Of Le Corbusier's Savoye House he states: "It's a summer house for an artist, you can't expect it to answer all the economic conditions of a modern city dwelling. It would be quite costly to heat it and quite complicated to clean it." Despite its nonfunctionalism, he admits that in a "noneconomic sense, it is perfect and likeable."[8] Mendelsohn's "canon" of renewed forms is contrasted with Gropius's generalizations, which treat each form as symbolic of a theory.[9] In reviewing the exhibition, "Sun, Air, the House for Everyone" that took place in Berlin the summer of 1932, Posener devotes as much space to political, economic, and social considerations for these "expandable houses" as he does to the respective merits of the designs.[10] Dismissing aesthetics, the young critic observes that with few exceptions, the "eminent architects" participating in the exhibition offer nothing "that could make life pleasant."[11] It is a profoundly humanitarian approach, retained by Posener to this day, that certainly owes its bias to the example of Poelzig and is quite different from the perspective of many of the contemporary adherents to the International Style. In the open-minded spirit of *L'Architecture d'Aujourd'hui* itself, in 1936 he was to appreciate even the neo-conservatism of Third Reich architects such as Heinrich Tessenow and Paul Schmitthenner.[12]

Posener lived in Paris in 1929 and in 1930 he returned to Berlin where he took a nonpaying job with Mendelsohn. The latter was clearly much admired by Posener, who writes repeatedly about the "charm" of different aspects of Mendelsohn's work.[13] It is an apt adjective coming from the pen of a man who is charm itself. To this day, he refers to the "fun" of some new discovery, with impish enthusiasm and energy that belie his age.

By 1933, Posener had returned to Paris. Even in Paris, Posener had at that time to face certain anti-Semitic tendencies. In order to keep his job at *L'Architecture d'Aujourd'hui* he was forced to write under the pseudonym of Julien Lepage. Within a year, Albert Laprade, a well-known architect and member of *L'Architecture d'Aujourd'hui*'s *Comité de Patronage* (a consulting committee), objected to what he described as Lepage's impudence in writing about French architecture, "about which he knows nothing," because "*L'Architecture d'Aujourd'hui* will be considered an organ of the Judéo-Soviéto-Boche conspiracy that is trying to ruin French crafts in favor of Germany."[14] In any event, shortly after arriving in Paris, Posener had decided that France should not be the final aim of his emigration. Motivated by his strong Zionist feelings at the time, in 1935 he emigrated to Jerusalem where he was joined by his brother Ludwig. He worked briefly in the office Mendelsohn had set up there the preceding year. During this period, Posener built a house for refugees who had settled north of Tel Aviv. He describes it apologetically as a "terribly German-looking house." It was his last attempt at architectural practice.

In 1941, Posener joined the British army, becoming an officer in the Royal Engineers. Despite strong opposition from both of his brothers, he remained with the occupying forces in Germany, in the military intelligence, until the end of 1946. The postwar years were difficult for him. Eight years in London, where he taught at the Brixton School of Building (1948–56), and five years in Kuala Lumpur (1956–61), where he founded a school of architecture, failed to provide a solution to the question of where he would make his life.

Thinking that the newly formed state of Israel might provide an answer to that question, in 1961 Posener accepted a professorship at Haifa University. He changed his mind when he and his wife learned of the religious and political strictures that would be imposed on their lives. Upon accepting the job at Haifa, Posener had turned down a professorship in Berlin; he reversed this decision and returned permanently to his native city.

There are rare individuals whose professional lives become meaningful only after middle age. One of the most striking examples of this phenomenon is Louis Kahn, whose Yale Art Gallery—completed when Kahn was fifty-two—was his first building to receive major attention. Posener is another. At the age of fifty-seven, he returned to Berlin revitalized.

It was a strange time to come to Berlin. In 1961 the Cold War was at its bleakest; the Berlin Wall was going up, and there was a clear movement away from a city in which life had become intolerable for many people (including Posener's wife, who divorced him in 1965; Posener was remarried, in 1970, this time to a German). In addition to the inclement political climate, Posener was initially disappointed by the fact that his new teaching position at the Hochschule der Bildenden Künste (School of Fine Arts), at present the Hochschule der Künste, was restricted to architectural history rather than design. Posener soon found himself in the midst of a group of architects whom he had met in the early 1930s when he was writing for *L'Architecture d'Aujourd'hui*, among them Hermann Finsterlin, Hans Scharoun, Max Taut, and his former fellow-student in Poelzig's seminary, Claus Müller-Rehm, to whom he attributes his return to Berlin.[15]

Posener soon adapted to the idea of teaching a subject he had never studied, deciding that history had been his true vocation all along.

Trying to find himself in a divided and much altered Berlin, Posener looked back to the prewar years of his childhood, which he refers to as his "lost paradise,"[16] and to the historic garden-suburb houses he so admired then. Passing by bus one day an example of his beloved Muthesius's more famous buildings, the Cramer House, Posener was shocked to see that it had been partially damaged by fire and was being demolished. He subsequently learned that the city authorities were planning to replace the Cramer House with a housing development. Posener's successful protest in West Berlin's leading newspaper, the *Tagesspiegel*, marked the beginning of a series of articles in that paper that have contributed to making him into what one of his former students, Fritz Neumeyer, describes as a "one-man institution: His concern for the world in which he lives has engendered an extraordinary engagement. It ranges from helping to protect all kinds of historic buildings to the more socially oriented issues of the urban community and personal support for groups and individuals."[17]

Rediscovering Berlin's turn-of-the-century architecture, Posener became convinced that the city's modern architecture was prefigured in the age of Wilhelm II, an idea that he set forth in a series of lectures, published in 1964 (reprinted in *From Schinkel to the Bauhaus: Five Lectures on the Growth of Modern German Architecture*, in German, Die Anfänge des Funktionalismus, 1972), and developed into his landmark book on this neglected period, *Berlin auf dem Wege zu einer neuen Architektur: Das Zeitalter Wilhelms des Zweiten* (Berlin on the Way Toward a New Architecture: The Age of William II), 1979. The articles were followed in 1975 by a book on individually planned one-family houses, his contribution to the revised edition of the standard series *Berlin and Its Buildings* (Berlin und seine Bauten, edited by Ernst Heinrich). These are but the most renowned of a number of books, not to mention the innumerable articles, produced by Posener between 1961 and 1990.

Posener also left his mark on the Hochschule der Bildenden Künste. Following in the footsteps of his mentor Poelzig, who in 1931 referred to the "fruitlessness"[18] of contemporary art education, Posener actively supported the student movement of the late 1960s. With the help of his colleague, Hardt Waltherr Hämer, he succeeded in extensively transforming the department's methodology. Posener was delighted with his students' switch away from the right-wing attitudes he associated with his own student days and from the general apathy he had encountered in 1961. He enthusiastically endorsed the student revolt:

> I loved it, I loved the students and I accepted my eldest son Alan's word and called myself a communist, though I must confess, that Alan conscientiously read his Karl Marx, while I had rather vague ideas.[19]

In 1971, Posener had to leave the Hochschule der Bildenden Künste because of its mandatory retirement rule. He was immediately invited by Hermann Mattern, a well-known landscape architect and one of Posener's closest friends, to teach at his own school. Posener also taught at his alma mater, the Technische Hochschule (now the Technische Universität), lecturing there once a week until 1978 and devoting his last five semesters to the period 1750–1933. These lectures—which soon became so popular that they had to be moved to a larger auditorium—encompassed the ideas Posener had been formulating for years. Starting with Ledoux and Boullée, they included discussions of Schinkel, John Ruskin, William Morris, Norman Shaw, W. R. Lethaby, and Le Corbusier. Posener describes them as covering the period "from the beginning of a change in what people considered architecture to be, up to the end of modern architecture in Germany."[20] Nikolaus Kuhnert, the editor of *Arch +*, published the five lecture courses in five issues of the journal (1980–83), which are still being sold. (In 1983 the issues were offered together in a slipcase under the title: *Julius Posener Vorlesungen zur Geschichte der Neuen Architektur [1750–1933]*). This publication has proven to be the most popular of Posener's writings to date. A relatively high percentage of the students who attended the original lectures — Hartmut Frank, Fritz Neumeyer, Wolfgang Schäche, Hartwig Schmidt — have become well-known teachers and authors in their own right.

Posener continues to explore the themes he introduced in these lectures, citing the present study of Poelzig as a direct result of them. As Schinkel faced the lack of a common denominator in the architecture of his time, so did Poelzig. Whereas for Schinkel, this lack was stylistic, for Poelzig it consisted of the existence of new technical possibilities that upset the old order. Poelzig challenged a younger generation that included Gropius and Mies with his own solutions, which are set forth so lucidly in the following pages by Julius Posener.

VICTORIA NEWHOUSE

I am indebted to the late Richard Pommer for the insights he provided into Julius Posener's relationship to Modernism, to Barbara Miller Lane for her correction of contextual facts, and to Posener, himself, for his stimulating collaboration.

Preface

I KNEW HANS POELZIG. He was my teacher. And I might add, by the way, that at the time—in the twenties—I had certain reservations about him. For me, Poelzig stood for this new confusing architecture, which was being called modern, dynamic, "expressionist"; and all this was still way above my head then. It was, therefore, with certain reservations that I went into his design studio. To my astonishment I found that his own work played no part in what went on in his studio; there was no evidence of it there at all. It would have been possible for someone to come to Poelzig knowing practically nothing about his work (as was, in fact, the case with me)—it did not matter. Poelzig obviously did not want to be considered by his students as someone to be followed, and he most certainly did not want to point toward any particular architectural direction. The last thing he wanted was to be taken for the prophet of an architectural credo that he would preach to those who subjected themselves to his influence. There are teachers who do that. Mies van der Rohe was one of them. When you went into his studio in Crown Hall in Chicago you would see on the walls and drawing boards only designs that reflected Mies's attitude. It was the same story in Auguste Perret's school in Paris or, to get back to Berlin, in Heinrich Tessenow's class at the Technische Hochschule—which, incidentally, was right next to Poelzig's studio; the designs one saw there were just like Tessenow's, right down to the style of drawing. By contrast, in Poelzig's class there was a hotchpotch of different styles, philosophies, drawing techniques, and it is quite possible that none of these works resembled any of Poelzig's buildings.

There are teachers who believe they are the only ones who can put their students on the straight and narrow. They see themselves as masters and philosophers. They are advocates of a particular doctrine. Mies, Perret, Tessenow, to mention but a few, were teachers of this kind. Poelzig, however, had no doctrine to offer to those who came to him and he most certainly did not want them to model themselves on him. If a student ever mentioned a building of his, Poelzig would say: "But we are not talking about the Capitol Cinema." It is possible to speak of the "Mies School" or the "Tessenow School," but there was no "Poelzig School."

When I was a student of Poelzig's, between 1926 and 1929, the Expressionist movement in architecture had already died out. Maybe Poelzig had taught differently when Expressionism was still a source of hope. But I have spoken to people who were students of his in the years before the First World War, when he was teaching in Breslau, and what they told me rang true. Convincing his students of a single theory to end all theories was always the thought farthest from his mind. He never spoke of what architecture might need at a particular time, even less of what architecture is. He talked about the position of the dining area in relation to the kitchen, about comfortable and uncomfortable staircases, about the structure of roofs with large spans, about how different spaces with different functions could be made to relate to each other. He attached great importance to the basic facts of daily life and how one should build for them. I do not want to suggest that he attached no importance to form, simply that he refused to recommend a particular form. He also avoided referring to the artistic quality of a student's work. If he liked it, he would say, "There is music in that." I only heard him use the word "genius" once, when referring to a construction solution a student had found. He was of the opinion that it was impossible to teach art. What he tried to teach were the technical, social, practical, the cultural aspects of architecture. Art was something different. He did not speak about art, I mean not in words. Without words, he certainly did; he also often spoke about it when referring to quite different things. He spoke about life as one who loves life. He could also talk about aesthetics occasionally, the occasions being when he talked about something one should avoid. A student once explained how he had positioned a building in such a way that it looked particularly magnificent from the road leading up to it. He claimed it formed a "border" to the road, thus using an expression coined by the romantic or picturesque school of urban design. "Aha," said Poelzig, "he designs with the camera." Such a brief comment sufficed to put us off this kind of urban design once and for all!

So far, I have approached Poelzig, the subject of this book, by evoking my own memories of "the Master," that is, by way of autobiography. Understandable, the reader may say, in one whose whole mental development has been, up to this day, strongly influenced by this one man, his teacher, yet hardly sufficient as an introduction to a rather detailed study of an architect of this century. Let me mention, therefore, how I have come to write this study, which, by the way, is not the first I have written on this particular architect. A few years ago, while teaching temporarily at Columbia University, I received from the Architectural History Foundation in New York the commission to write a book on Poelzig. I was asked to prepare a study on Poelzig, as an Expressionist architect, Expressionism having, in recent years, gained significance again in interested circles in the United States. I accepted the commission with mixed feelings, asking myself if I could fully agree with the view that Hans Poelzig had been one of those architects who, like Bruno Taut and certain others, passed after the First World War through a phase determined by the Expressionist movement. The more I thought about it, the less easy I found it to agree to the proposed title, "Poelzig, an architect of Expressionism." He was, I felt, more—and less—than just that. It is quite possible to talk of a latent *expressionism* in his work, but at the same time Poelzig never belonged to any of the Expressionist groups of artists that emerged right after the war. He was, to begin with, older than those artists, having produced a considerable *oeuvre* which was considered of equal importance to that of his near contemporary Peter Behrens. It is true that his work—like that of Behrens—passed through several phases during those years of change preceding and following the war. Yet, and this is the point, Hans Poelzig never went so far as to follow those changing fashions without reserve, as Behrens did. His work, though passing through those different stages, always retained that character which was his own. It was, first and foremost, the architecture of Hans Poelzig.

This is what has fascinated me: the unity of an *oeuvre* that incorporated different movements in architecture: the early years of the Werkbund—1900 to 1914; the postwar years —until 1925; and the architecture known as Modern or International, which was the work of the avant-garde between 1925 and 1933. As I have mentioned, Poelzig took part in these and yet remained different. This unity within change, and the strongly expressive character of his architecture, from beginning to end, are the themes of this study.

The documentation that I have added to the chapters of this book is intended to show the various influences that affected Poelzig's work at different times. If I have treated Poelzig in the text as someone who up to the First World War, and in fact until 1916, adhered to the Werkbund doctrine of the time (before the war), who went through an Expressionist phase between 1916 and 1922 and then became involved in a new confrontation with the possibilities that were open to architecture, I must admit that this interpretation is a simplification of what really happened. It remains for me to broaden my description of his development and to make clear that Poelzig before the war was not exclusively a Werkbund disciple; that his Expressionism was not in the same vein as that of the younger architects Taut, Finsterlin, or Bartning; and that after 1922 he tried to analyze in his own way the problem of what would become of architecture in the face of new structural possibilities and increasing standardization. In short, I wish to make clear that Poelzig was in a class by himself; that not only was it impossible to categorize him as an Expressionist, it was impossible to categorize him at all. The contemporary documents that I have selected help us to come closer to the truth. I will add my comments to these documents in order to show their relevance for Poelzig's development.

HANS POELZIG: REFLECTIONS ON HIS LIFE AND WORK

CHAPTER ONE
Developments in German Architecture During Poelzig's Lifetime

WHAT WAS POELZIG'S ATTITUDE to the different currents in architecture that succeeded each other during the course of his life? Expressionism in the true sense of the word is only one of them. We have seen that it did not last very long, some ten years, from 1914 to 1924. Poelzig was born in 1869. When his career began, between 1895 and 1901, the Jugendstil—or Art Nouveau—was at its zenith. Peter Behrens, who started to do his own work earlier than Hans Poelzig did, first made a name for himself as a Jugendstil painter, then as an applied artist (Fig. 1). Finally he became known as an architect; he taught himself architecture. Hans Poelzig, on the other hand, studied architecture at university and then worked for several years in the building department of the Prussian civil service. Behrens's Jugendstil works were extreme Jugendstil and in a very short time came to be considered absurd. Behrens, who as late as 1901 had built a Jugendstil house on the Mathildenhöhe in Darmstadt (Fig. 2), turned very decisively away from the Jugendstil. Only two years later his Obenauer House was built in Saarbrücken, the first example of a Neo-Classicism that sought to discover the basic elements of architecture and use them appropriately (Fig. 3). In the plan of the Obenauer House the square plays a part (Fig. 4); within only a few years it was to become an omnipresent element in Behrens's decoration (as seen, for example, in the Crematorium in Hagen and the Concert Hall at the arts and crafts fair in Dresden in 1906 (Figs. 5, 6). He took elements from the vocabulary of Classical architecture and used them in an abstract, unsensuous way, as the embodiment of ordering forces, an elementary Classicism that led to what will remain Behrens's contribution to history—the factories for A.E.G. (Allgemeine Elektrizitäts-Gesellschaft) in Berlin (1909–12; see Figs. 19, 20, 22, 23).

Hans Poelzig, who had not done any work of his own before he was thirty, just caught the tail end of the Jugendstil. I personally know of only one work of his that could be classified as Jugendstil: a design in 1902 for wood paneling for the organ of the University of Breslau (Fig. 7). Poelzig began working at the time of the reaction against the Jugendstil, a reaction which by then had become general. Even though Jugendstil ornaments continued to be produced until the war, the style had been abandoned by architects and by many applied artists. It would be better, they thought, to devote their attention to the circumstances of life, which the applied arts, crafts, and architecture had to come to terms with if they wanted to have any kind of significance. One of the most

4   Hans Poelzig: Reflections on His Life and Work

1   Peter Behrens. Lamp in the Jugendstil (Art Nouveau style).

2   Peter Behrens. Own house in Darmstadt, Mathildenhöhe, 1901.

3   Peter Behrens. Obenauer house at Saarbrücken, 1903.

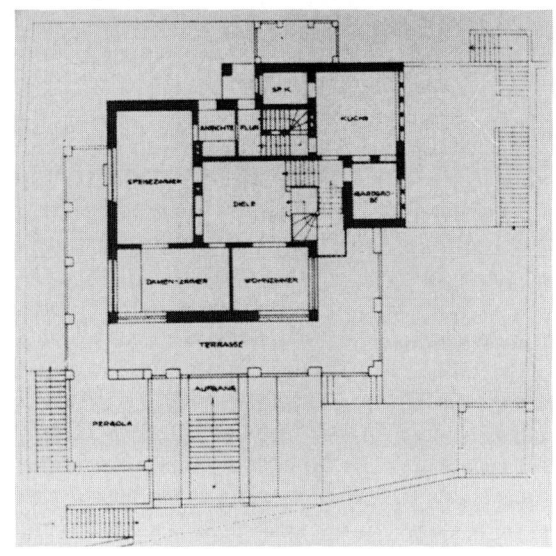

4   Peter Behrens. Obenauer house. Plan.

German Architecture During Poelzig's Lifetime 5

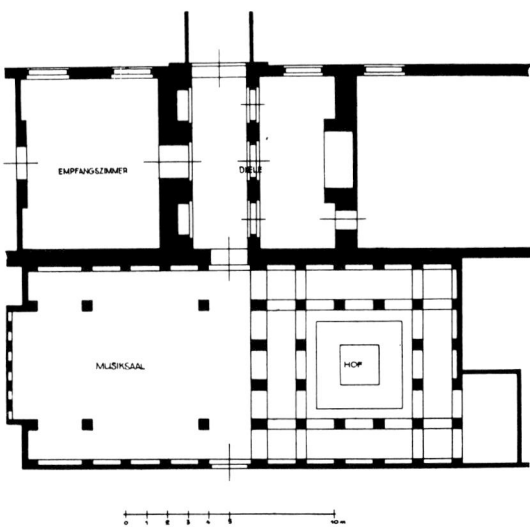

5 (left) Peter Behrens. Concert hall at the Exhibition of Applied Art, Dresden, 1906. Courtyard.

6 (above) Peter Behrens. Concert hall at the Exhibition of Applied Art. Plan.

7 Hans Poelzig. Organ. Breslau University chapel, 1902. Project.

important of these circumstances was thought to be industry and with it technology. This attitude was expressed in the activities of a group of artists and craftsmen who, in the autumn of 1907, got together in Munich with industrialists and other interested parties to form the Deutsche Werkbund. Peter Behrens was a member from the very beginning, one of twelve artists and twelve members of other professions who founded the Werkbund. In the artist group the architects were in the majority.

Let us state here, very briefly, the aims of the Deutscher Werkbund. It was, on the one hand, a German version of William Morris's Arts and Crafts movement. Founded at a time when Morris's aim to ignore, even to abolish, industry had become obsolete, the Werkbund and its driving force — indeed, its "father" — Hermann Muthesius, faced the challenge of industry by actually designing for mass production. One might say that this was the moment when what we call "industrial design" came into being. It must be remembered, however, that the Werkbund tried to develop both industrial design *and* a return to true craftsmanship as understood by Morris. The Werkbund aimed at giving to the products of industry (mass production), as well as to those of handicraft, simple, practical shapes, avoiding any kind of decoration and, indeed, of "style."

Poelzig joined the Werkbund early on. Everything he wrote in those years — like everything Behrens, Theodor Fischer, and Richard Riemerschmid wrote — exuded the spirit of the Werkbund. Strange to say, soon after it had been founded, the Werkbund was called "the association of the most intimate enemies," and it is true that personal quarrels, petty rivalries, power struggles, and also objective differences of opinion never ceased in the Werkbund. Nevertheless, the consensus on fundamental issues must have been very strong in the early years, between 1907 and 1914. One can look at any text one chooses and find a common attitude. It was first expressed in a rejection of the Jugendstil, which they all shared.[1]

8 Hermann Muthesius. De Burlet house, Berlin-Schlachtensee, 1911.

This reaction against the Jugendstil lasted from the beginning of the century to the outbreak of the war. The English simplicity of the first country houses built by Hermann Muthesius caused a sensation (Fig. 8). People came to the garden suburbs to look at the "houses in the new English country house style" — of course it had to be a "style."

Peter Behrens's Neo-Classicism provoked an equally strong reaction. Did people get as excited about Poelzig's work? I don't really think so. It is true that his buildings were a contrast to what had been built before the turn of the century: a contrast not only to the Jugendstil but also to the historicism, the eclecticism that the Jugendstil had been reacting against. The trends in architecture that followed each other in close succession after about 1890 repudiated each other in that each new trend saw its predecessor as an inadequate attempt to overcome the difficulties that architecture had been in since the mid-nineteenth century. There was, however, complete agreement on these difficulties and no one wanted to return to historicism. The Jugendstil artists considered themselves at one with the artists of the Werkbund movement in the protest against historicism, which had been under way since the turn of the century. While Poelzig rejected the Jugendstil, he rejected his-

9 Hans Poelzig. Extension of the town hall, Löwenberg (Silesia), 1903–6.

toricism even more strongly. Both had in common, he said, the fact that they were looking for *the* style; both believed that what distinguished a work of architecture from a simple building was that it was decorated, that it wore ornaments and architectural paraphernalia, be it pilasters or cornices, niches or windows with pointed arches, or finally the new curved forms of Art Nouveau. John Ruskin put it in a nutshell: A castle, he said, remains simply a building until the owner has the idea of giving it a profile. *Then* the building is transformed into a work of architecture. That was the way people thought in the nineteenth century. Even during the Jugendstil period people still thought like that. The fact that the Werkbund took the aims of William Morris and his followers in the English Arts and Crafts movement and developed them further, seeing machine production as equal to production by the human hand, is only an extension of this concept of architecture: The intention was to abolish the difference between a work of architecture and a building. Everyday buildings became the subject of architecture. Of course, this reversal in thought did not begin in 1900. Morris had said that any work that was worth doing was art— Everyman's art and art for Everyman—and this might have led him on to the idea that it was not possible to dismiss the machine as the maker of simple useful objects. But he avoided this train of thought and took up arms against the machine. Each person makes only one step forward and Morris already had taken a large one; acceptance of the machine would have been the next step. Morris occasionally realized that the revival of crafts was not the answer to the problems of his time. He once remarked to a friend who asked him about his work:

I am making a chair with the sweat of my brow—a perfectly simple chair which will be so expensive that only the richest people will be able to afford it.

It was this very problem that the Werkbund took up: how to produce articles that were good, well made, and beautiful and that *ordinary people* could afford.

Poelzig was quite definitely a Werkbund man, but his interest was not in the machine that produced objects. What is known as "industrial design" was alien to him. For him the new age, the industrial age, was about construction methods. Yet he never joined in the call to "bring industry to the building site." He never used prefabricated elements; he found them unpleasant. One could perhaps express his attitude as follows: *Let us take the new means of construction for granted, let us use them alongside craft methods, in conjunction with craft methods, so that they open up new possibilities for craftsmanship and in that sense change it.* Poelzig was concerned to maintain continuity. This also explains why his work had a less sensational effect than that of Behrens or even Muthesius. He extended a medieval town hall in the small town of Löwenberg in Silesia and the extension he built was greeted as tactful, yet fresh and lively (Fig. 9; see Figs. 29, 35–37; 76–78).[2] He built a church in the village of Maltsch, which was meant to be a real village church. Again, like Löwenberg, it was tactful, fitted in with the village, and yet used new forms (Fig. 10; see Figs. 60–66). This was the direction his early work took, this was how it was viewed at the time, and it was received positively. He worked like this, in the spirit of the Werkbund, conserving and innovating, until the First World War, or to be more precise, until 1916.

The outbreak of the war suddenly made the idea of optimistic reform as advocated by the Werkbund seem over and done with, like one of the things of yesteryear that have been trampled on by hard times. This was the beginning of the

10   Hans Poelzig. Village church at Maltsch (Silesia), 1906.

period of expressionism in architecture.

Let us try here to explain that tendency in art that called itself "expressionism." The word itself was meant to denote opposition to the preceding tendency of impressionism. In art, impressions were no longer to be taken seriously. It was, on the contrary, the inner meaning that required expression; the surrounding world had to be transformed into symbolic shapes denoting that inner meaning. The roots of this attitude are to be found in the work of certain masters of the last century, such as Van Gogh and Cézanne. German Expressionist painters—Kirchner, Schmidt-Rottluff, Pechstein, and others—came together in a group called Der Blaue Reiter (The Blue Rider). Architecture had to change into something rather close to abstract sculpture. Just as in poetry, where the grammatical context was to be neglected, Expressionist architects turned away from building technique. I would say that Hans Scharoun's evocations of new shapes belonged to this kind of Expressionism (Fig. 11), while certain other architects, Erich Mendelsohn among them, based their architecture upon what they understood to be the technique appropriate to that new "fluid" material, concrete.

In architecture, the most striking realization was without doubt Bruno Taut's famous "glass

German Architecture During Poelzig's Lifetime

11 Hans Scharoun. Sketch, 1919.

12 Bruno Taut. Glass Pavilion at the Werkbund Exhibition, Cologne, 1914. The upper space.

13 Bruno Taut. Sketch from "Alpine Architecture," 1917.

pavilion" at the Cologne Werkbund Exhibition of July 1914 (Fig. 12), which, together with other outstanding buildings of that unique show of new tendencies in architecture, was unfortunately removed when war broke out. (Hans Poelzig, though an early member of the Werkbund, did not exhibit in Cologne.) Taut's pavilion must have been difficult to build. It certainly was not — nor was it meant to be — a demonstration of construction, although with it Taut introduced certain elements that later were to become quite common in building, such as glass bricks. Glass and metal were the materials that dominated; even the staircases in the pavilion had glass steps. Taut and his friend, the poet Paul Scheerbart, infused glass with mystical qualities that were supposed to liberate mankind. Scheerbart inspired Taut's architecture with verses such as the following.

> Without a glass palace
> life becomes unbearable.
>
> *Ohne einen Glaspalast*
> *Ist das Leben eine Last.*

On the Russian front Erich Mendelsohn sketched Utopian designs. During the war Bruno Taut sketched "City Crown" and "Alpine Architecture" (Fig. 13). Taut wanted to erect the greatest monument to peace conceivable by filing down mountains in the Alps, shaping them, and decorating them with glass flowers. The two cycles of sketches are hymns to peace and the fellowship of man. In this re-

14 Hans Poelzig. "House of Friendship," Constantinople (Istanbul), 1916, competition design.

spect they anticipate the Expressionist poems that Kurt Pinthus published in 1920 under the title *Menschheitsdämmerung* (The twilight of mankind).

Whenever people spoke at the time of Expressionist architecture, they mentioned Hans Poelzig. His design for a "House of Friendship" in Constantinople (Fig. 14; see Figs. 155–166) and his sketches for public buildings in Dresden in 1916 (see Figs. 141–144, 150, 151) were the clearest demonstrations of his Expressionist leanings. But they were not hymns to peace and the fellowship of man. The "House of Friendship" was not meant to be dedicated to all men: It was a German cultural center to be set up during the war in the capital of Germany's Turkish "friends." It was the result of a competition between twelve Werkbund architects (the Werkbund favored the number twelve). I have called Poelzig's design Expressionist. It is. But it is a different kind of Expressionism from that of Bruno Taut or Erich Mendelsohn. Here, no new world is conjured up, neither Taut's world of fellowship nor Mendelsohn's world of new forms of construction. What is new in Poelzig's work refers to architecture, which is an art, not a philosophy. We will see, however, that Poelzig's new architecture is both new and old; that is, it is not without a link to history. We have already pointed out that the change that takes place when a new age in architecture begins can never encompass *everything*. Alongside the new, other tendencies remain in force that continue the earlier phase. If we look at Poelzig's designs we find that his relationship to history did not change greatly: At least in the beginning, what

15 Erich Mendelsohn. Sketch of an industrial building, 1915.

attracted him was the *history* of construction forms. This is what distinguishes his designs from Mendelsohn's sketches: Mendelsohn dreamed of *new* forms of construction (Fig. 15).

The age of Expressionism is the age of great unbuilt projects. This also applies to Poelzig's work; in fact it applies particularly to Poelzig's work. It was not the "House of Friendship" that was built, nor any of the public buildings for Dresden, nor even the Festspielhaus for Salzburg, the "favorite child" of those years. What he was allowed to build was only a conversion: the Grosses Schauspielhaus in Berlin (see Chapter 5). (Karl Scheffler said of this theater that the stage decoration began in front of the curtain.)[3]

Not very much was being built at this time in any case. The Expressionist architecture as shown in the sketches of Bruno Taut and Hans Scharoun was meant to be visionary; these sketches are not meant to be built. There were, however, some important office buildings designed in what was then called "Expressionist" style.[4]

A prominent example is Fritz Höger's Chilehaus in Hamburg of 1922–23, which uses certain ornaments known as Expressionist (Fig. 16). One may say of the Chilehaus that the whole building is "dynamic," to use a favorite term of those years.

The waning of Expressionism in Germany was without doubt connected with the stabilization of the German economy. After the economic collapse of 1918, some people saw a grim future ahead for German industry, an idea that was not unpopular with the Expressionists, including Poelzig. But when inflation

16 Fritz Höger. Chilehaus, Hamburg, 1922–23.

came to an end and industry made a forceful reappearance, that idea lost credibility. Gropius, who in 1918 had proclaimed, "Architects, sculptors, painters, we must all return to craftsmanship,"[5] now spoke about a "machine that creates types." He called this machine "an effective means for using mechanical aids (steam and electricity) to free the individual from his own physical work and provide him with standard products that can be manufactured better and cheaper than by hand."[6]

A new development began. It came after the Bauhaus and was called the International Style, or quite simply *modern architecture*. This development was the work of younger architects. Poelzig had to get used to it, which may not have been easy for him because essentially he was not a technologically minded man. He acknowledged technology, he made use of it, but

17 Hans Poelzig. I.G. Farben administration building, Frankfurt-am-Main, 1928–30.

18 Bruno Taut. Terraced houses, Onkel Tom estate, Berlin-Zehlendorf, 1929.

he did not see technology as a formative agent. He always fought against the claim of modern architects that technology would produce its own style. And yet this very period was the time when most of his work was built, including his largest building, the administration building for I.G. Farben in Frankfurt-am-Main (1928–30; Fig. 17; see Figs. 231, 290–302).

Poelzig was at the height of his fame when this movement, modern architecture, gave way to another. The architecture of National Socialism began before the seizure of power (1933). A battle was fought as early as 1927 about the roof—flat or pitched—when an estate of small houses with pitched roofs (which, incidentally, Poelzig also had a part in) was built as a provocation next to the "Onkel Tom" housing estate in Zehlendorf, Berlin, one of the major works of modern architecture, designed by Taut, Häring, and Salvisberg (Fig. 18; see Fig. 308). The pitch of the roof would not have interested Poelzig particularly, but the return to craftsmanship as seen in the work of architects such as Paul Schmitthenner, who also built part of the estate, and Schmitthenner's rejection of "the technology on the building site," cannot have been unwelcome to Poelzig (see Fig. 219). What Poelzig did not welcome was the type of Nazi propaganda whose attacks—or rather harassments—he suffered on occasion (to the extent that in 1936 he started making arrangements to emigrate to Turkey).

During Poelzig's lifetime German architecture passed through a rapid succession of different phases. And although in retrospect we can say that the change caused by each phase was not quite as radical as it seemed to be to contemporaries, each phase was lively enough to challenge the great architects of the time to react. I have tried to give a sketchy outline of these phases and to indicate how Poelzig reacted to them. It is important at the outset to have some idea of the context of Poelzig's work.

At the beginning of this short summary I spoke of how Poelzig reacted very differently from Behrens, his contemporary. Behrens was a Jugendstil artist, Poelzig was not. But as early as 1903 Behrens had turned his back on Jugendstil and found the way to elementary Classicism. To conclude this chapter we shall compare some well-known industrial buildings designed by these two architects:

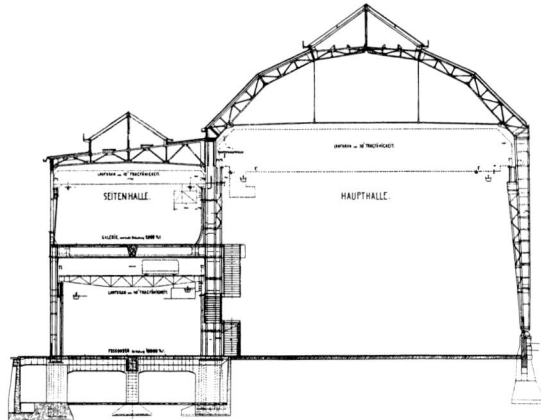

19 Peter Behrens. A.E.G. Turbine Factory, Berlin-Moabit, Berlichingenstrasse, 1909. Section.

20 Peter Behrens. A.E.G. Turbine Factory, Berlin-Moabit. Exterior.

21 C.L.F. Dutert. Galérie des Machines, Paris international exposition, 1889.

Behrens's A.E.G. Turbine Factory in Moabit, Berlin, and Poelzig's industrial buildings in and around Posen. Both belong to the early period of the Werkbund and were built at almost exactly the same time, 1909 and 1911.

Behrens's factory buildings are the culmination of his elementary Neo-Classicism. Walter Gropius, who worked in Behrens's office around this time, called them "truly monumental."[7] They were. The Turbine Factory has a three-hinged girder-arch structure (Fig. 19). Behrens shows the hinge at the foot of the girder on the side facade of the building (Fig. 20). This was a daring thing to do, since the three-hinged girder arch, resting on a pin, a roller bearing, contradicted the ideas people still had around 1900 about the rigidity of a structure. The Belgian engineer, Arthur Jules Vierendeel, who himself invented a new girder system, said of the three-hinged girder arch used in the Galérie des Machines at the Paris Exhibition of 1889: "The frame is not balanced, it has no supports" (Fig. 21).[8] But it was possible to see the whole frame, with the top hinge and both bottom hinges. The frame stood exposed inside the great hall. One could see that it tapered down toward the hinges. This may have been contrary to ideas current at that time concerning construction as something to be based solidly on the ground, but it offered the possibility of comprehending the new way of

23 Peter Behrens. A.E.G. Turbine Factory, Berlin-Moabit. Gable.

22 Peter Behrens. A.E.G. Turbine Factory, Berlin-Moabit. Bottom joint of the three-jointed arch.

construction, which resulted in a kind of floating frame.

In contrast, the only part of the three-hinged girder arch Behrens shows us is the bottom hinge on the outside of the building (Fig. 22). Above the hinge the vertical part of the frame rises up as strong as a pillar. But all that one sees is the covering for the lightly trussed frame, which is the actual structure. The "pillar" "carries" an "entablature." I have written these terms in quotation marks because the pillar is not a pillar, it does not carry anything, and the entablature is pure decoration and has nothing to do with the structure. The impression made is particularly convincing, however, because the angle of the very large glass surfaces between the pillars reveals more of the pillar the higher up it goes, culminating in the deep shade-giving entablature. The ancient temple is evoked. The polygonal tympanum of the gable strengthens this reference (Fig. 23). The gable projects beyond the structure, is quite separate; it looks as if two concrete pylons in the corners which slope at the same angle as the glass surfaces are carrying the concrete tympanum. In fact the concrete surfaces one sees are thin walls, serving the sole purpose of enclosing space. The tympanum is in front of a light Polonceau (triangulated) roof truss which is carried by the frame of the large central window. The effect produced by this structural game is both "truly monumental" (Gropius) and dynamic. Of course, the pylons themselves make a dynamic impression, and the relationship between the exposed hinge and the rigid pillar that stands on it, the quasi-column, appears to be inconsistent.

Let us try to interpret this in the spirit of the time. Behrens introduces new elements into the architecture of factory buildings—glass surfaces of unusual size, concrete surfaces, the three-hinged girder arch. He raises these elements to the status of architecture by giving them a reference to something historical, the Greek temple. The improbable is given dignity. Let the visitor go into the hall. He will find himself surrounded by light steel framework. Neither the strong "pillars" of the side facade nor the corner pylons make an appearance. One has the feeling of having gone "behind the scenes." Behrens's "scenery" is of great significance. The Turbine Factory has been called a "seminal building," one of those buildings that mark the beginning of a new architecture. This is true. But here elements of a modern factory

German Architecture During Poelzig's Lifetime 15

24 Hans Poelzig. Chemical factory at Luban near Posen, 1911.

architecture have been forced together with Behrens's essentially Classical architecture. Incidentally, it paid off for A.E.G. in that the dignity of the architecture greatly enhanced the company's image — as Behrens had intended.

If we now look at Poelzig's chemical factory in Luban, we see that these buildings seem much less monumental, less exciting, less forceful than Behrens's building, but also less forced; they are not as daring, not on the way to a new architecture (Fig. 24). Here we are looking at a number of factory buildings. Some of them are obviously constructed from metal, since their exterior walls are of a brick construction that is not load-bearing; it only encloses space; the bricks are laid vertically in what is known as Prüss bond. Other buildings are just as obviously brick structures: the walls are built in a load-bearing bond, the windows are arched in a semicircle, they are in fact pure semicircles. Here nothing is hidden; there is no pretense. No modern elements are introduced into the architecture; rather, the building relates to the tradition of practical architecture that Poelzig always spoke of. Where the building relates *too* strongly to tradition it makes a break, something is added, and the attempt to link this to the "normal" factory building does not succeed. I am referring to the medieval-looking crow-stepped gable, a nice motif but nevertheless a motif (Fig. 25).

Another industrial building by Poelzig was

25 Hans Poelzig. Chemical factory at Luban. Stepped gable.

26 Hans Poelzig. Upper Silesia Tower at the industrial exhibition, Posen, 1911.

the "Oberschlesienturm" (Upper Silesia Tower) at the industrial fair in Posen, 1911 (Fig. 26). This time the steel structure is visible. But the main box-shaped steel-frame columns are strong, and appear on the outside in their true size; unlike Behrens's "columns" they are not given visual reinforcement. The other elements in the steel framework are so thin and close together that they look like timber framework that is slightly too thin. The reference to timber framework is reinforced by the fact that the brick infill is laid in patterns that had often been used in half-timbered houses (Fig. 27). On the restaurant level a very modern element is used, a window ribbon that goes around the whole building. Not even this looks sensational, although I am sure that nothing like it had ever been seen before. It appears so natural that one cannot get the impression of *déjà vu* out of one's mind. One does not stand in front of the tower, as one does in front of the Turbine Factory, with eyes wide open and jaw dropped in wonder. "If only our ancestors," the architect seems to be saying, "had had steel girders instead of their wooden posts, they probably would have built something very much like this."

Let us try to call to mind the attitude with which Behrens and Poelzig turned away from the Jugendstil after 1900. In Behrens it was a vehement reaction and the attempt to find a *new* form, one that could cope with the new tasks,

27 Hans Poelzig. Upper Silesia Tower. Entrance.

that would be appropriate to the new feeling of masculinity, power, the great effect of industry. The masters of the Jugendstil—van de Velde, for example—had already referred to the industrial style,[9] but they could not begin to approach it. In the case of the new form that Behrens had found, which had become manifest in the Crematorium in Hagen, it is possible to speak of a counterstyle. The encounter with industry, the commission Behrens had received from the A.E.G. in 1907 to design its products and buildings, simplifies this style, gives it a topical validity; it also gives industry dignity, and it prepares the way for the creation of a new style, since for the first time the new elements of industrial construction methods are applied to architecture, to classical architecture.

Poelzig did not need to turn his back dramatically on the Jugendstil because he had had little to do with it in the first place. He was not looking for a new form, for a "counterstyle." He seems as an architect to have placed no great value on the new elements of industrial architecture, the large window surfaces, for example. He writes about them, he no doubt spoke about them. But they do not appear in his factory in Luban. It is true that he sought an adequate form for the new needs of the day; in this much his form is new. But the way he arrived at it is analogous to the long history of practical architecture—from the aqueduct via gateways and towers of the Middle Ages to the forts of Vauban.

Chapter One: Documentation

Document 1A

I approached the writing of this book intending to clarify (mainly for myself) the question, Was Poelzig an Expressionist architect? My conclusions were summarized above in these words: "I have called Poelzig's design Expressionist. It is. But it is a different kind of Expressionism from that of Bruno Taut or Erich Mendelsohn. Here, no new world is conjured up, neither Taut's world of fellowship nor Mendelsohn's world of new forms of construction. What is new in Poelzig's work refers to architecture, which is an art, not a philosophy."

Let us see what some of Poelzig's contemporaries had to say about architecture after the First World War. Speaking at the first "Exhibition for Unknown Architects" of the Arbeitstrat für Kunst (Working Council for Art) in 1919, Walter Gropius and Bruno Taut heralded a revolutionary new beginning. First Gropius:

Doc. 1A* Walter Gropius, address to the "Exhibition for Unknown Architects," 1919

What is architecture? Why, the crystalline expression of the most noble thoughts of men, their passion, their humanity, their faith, their religion! This is what it used to be! But who living in these times cursed by utilitarianism still understands its all-embracing, soul-giving nature? How can we walk through our cities and streets and not weep with shame at these wastelands of ugliness? Let us be honest: These gray, hollow, soulless fakes among which we live and work will provide our descendants with the shameful proof of the spiritual fall of our race, proof that we have forgotten the great, the only art: architecture. Let us not imagine with our European arrogance that the impoverished buildings of our age could change the hopeless overall picture. All our works are nothing but tiny splinters. Structures inspired by utility and necessity do not quench our yearnings for a new world filled with beauty built from scratch, for the rebirth of that spiritual unity that soared to great heights in creating the miracle of the Gothic cathedral. It is no longer part of our experience. But there is one consolation for us: the idea, the development of an ardent, daring, architectural idea, way ahead of its time, an idea that could become reality in the more fortunate age that must follow. Artists, let us at last tear down the walls erected between the "arts" by the school-learning that deformed our minds and let us dedicate ourselves once more to building! Let us all join together to desire, imagine, create the new architectural philosophy. Painters and sculptors, break through the barriers to architecture and join us in the architectural process, strive with us to attain the ultimate aim of art: the creative conception of the cathedral of the future, which will once more be everything in one—architecture, sculpture, and painting.

But ideas die as soon as they become compromises. Therefore we need clearly defined watersheds between dream and reality, between starry-eyed yearning and daily work. Architects, sculptors, painters, we must all return to craftsmanship. For there is no such thing as "professional art." Artists are craftsmen in the original sense of the word, and only in rare, gracious moments of genius, which are beyond the will of the individual, can art blossom unconsciously from the work of their hands. Painters and sculptors, you too must become craftsmen once more, you must destroy the frames of salon art around your pictures, go into buildings, bless them with fairy-tales of color, take your chisels and write philosophy on the bare walls, and build in the realm of your imagination, paying no heed to technical problems. The grace of imagination is more important than all the technology in the world, which always molds itself to man's will. There are no architects at present, we are all merely preparing the way for those who will deserve the name and that means the masters of art, who will create gardens from deserts and wonder upon wonder in heaven.

---

* Walter Gropius, in leaflet published for the "Exhibition for Unknown Architects" held in Berlin in April 1919, the first exhibition organized by the Working Council for Art. Reprinted in Ulrich Conrads, ed., *Programme und Manifeste zur Architektur des 20. Jahrhunderts,* Frankfurt and Berlin, 1964, pp. 43–44; English edition, *Programs and Manifestoes on 20th-Century Architecture,* Cambridge, Mass., 1971, pp. 46–47.

Document 1B

Taut appealed to "all who believe in the future":

Doc. 1B*   Bruno Taut, address to the "Exhibition for Unknown Architects," 1919

Does architecture exist today? Do architects exist today? Erwin von Steinbach, Sinan, Aben Cencid, Diwakara, Pöppelmann — in the face of these illustrious names does anyone today dare to call himself "architect"? No, just as there is no architecture, there are no architects.

Are not we, who today are devoted to perfection, parasites in a society that does not know what architecture is, does not want it, and therefore does not need architects? Because clothing thousands of useful buildings — apartment blocks, offices, railway stations, market halls, schools, water towers, gasometers, fire stations, factories, etc. — in pleasant forms cannot be called architecture. Our "usefulness" in these things, on which we spend our days, has nothing to do with our profession, just as little as any present-day building has to do with Angkor Vat, the Alhambra, or the Zwinger in Dresden.

In our profession today we cannot create, we can only search and call. We must not cease searching for what may crystallize later, we must not cease calling for companions who will tread the difficult path with us, who know in all humility that everything today is just the very first light of dawn and that we must lose ourselves in devotion to the task of preparing for the rising of the new sun. We appeal to all who believe in the future. Any strong yearning for the future contains the seeds of architecture. One day a true *Weltanschauung* will be born and architecture, its symbol, its crystal, will also be born.

Then there will be no brooding and struggling to find art in the life of banalities, there will be one art which will light every nook and cranny. Until then the utilitarian will be bearable only if the architect has a presentiment of this sun within him. It alone is the measure of all things, differentiating strictly between the sacred and the profane, the great and the small, giving mundane things the merest glint of its radiance.

* Bruno Taut, in leaflet published for the "Exhibition for Unknown Architects," Berlin, 1919. Reprinted in Ulrich Conrads, ed., *Programme und Manifeste zur Architektur des 20. Jahrhunderts*, Frankfurt and Berlin, 1964, p. 44; English edition, *Programs and Manifestoes on 20th-Century Architecture*, Cambridge, Mass., 1971, p. 47.

Themes are touched upon here that Poelzig also talked about at this time, the relationship between the crafts and art, to mention just one. But the *tone* is different. To stay with the topic of crafts and art: The difference can be seen in Poelzig's address to the Werkbund in Stuttgart in the same year, 1919 (see Chapter 6, Doc. 6B). Here Gropius and Taut call for the return of all arts to crafts, since "there is no such thing as 'professional art,'" whereas Poelzig says that the craftsman is also an artist ("What we should understand by craftsmanship, which is in fact absolutely identical with artistic work, is the will to dedicate great love and devotion to creating forms ..."). Gropius and Taut announce a revolution in architecture, whereas Poelzig tries to gain insight into the nature of architecture.

Document 1C

Let us now hear what Erich Mendelsohn, again in 1919 (and again as part of the Arbeitstrat für Kunst [Working Council for Art]), says in the closing words of an address on the occasion of his own exhibition of sketches by the Arbeitstrat:

Doc. 1C*   Erich Mendelsohn, address to the Working Council for Art, 1919 (excerpt)

What is today a problem will one day be a challenge, what today is the view and belief of individuals will become the law for all.

* Erich Mendelsohn, "Das Problem einer neuen Baukunst," speech to the Working Council for Art, Berlin, 1919. In Erich Mendelsohn, *Das Gesamtschaffen des Architekten. Skizzen-Entwürfe-Bauten*, Berlin, 1930, p. 21.

Therefore, in order to attain the goal, that is, to solve the problem of how to find a new architecture, all movements are necessary:
the apostles of glass worlds,
the analysts of spatial elements,
those who search for form inspired by materials and structure.

Admittedly the classes of society that are under the spell of tradition will not initiate this age. Only a new will holds the future in the unconscious chaos of its inspirational force, in the originality of its all-embracing universality.

Because, just as every epoch that was decisive in the development of human civilization unified the entire known world under its spiritual will, that which we desire will also have to bring joy to all peoples, beyond our country, beyond Europe. In saying this I am not preaching internationalism. Because internationalism is nothing but the anonymous aestheticism of a world in decay. Supranationalism, however, includes national identity as a perquisite, is free humanity, which alone is capable of reestablishing an all-embracing culture.

A great will of this kind unites all who work for the same aim.

It can only come about, find sufficient divine faith, when the ultimate achievements of all peoples merge together.

We can do nothing more than make a modest contribution—our work, in good faith and willing service.

Of the three groups whose joint work would be necessary for a new architecture, Mendelsohn himself represents "those who search for form inspired by materials and structure"; by "the apostles of glass worlds" he means Bruno Taut, and by "analysts of spatial elements," the Austrians Loos and Olbrich. Here, too, it is useful to compare closely Poelzig's statement in his Werkbund speech of 1919. The fundamental difference will not escape the reader. In this revolutionary moment, Poelzig speaks of the relation to the past, to handicraft, of any future architecture.

Document 1D

Let us finally read a paragraph from Hermann Finsterlin's *Casa Nova*, written five years later; already architecture had entered a different period.

Doc. 1D*   Hermann Finsterlin, *Casa Nova,* **1924**

I beg you, cast aside the illusion that the purpose of human building is to create dwelling places, that is, a refuge for objects, plants, people, and gods. Any predetermined purpose lays a heavy inhibiting hand on the driving force of a God-given, free, and pure will. Forget yourselves, create giant divine vessels, and, in a sanctified moment when your soul is laid open, consecrate this monument, make it the eternal mother of your body and the body of your fellow men. The human realm, no longer the imprint left by a few elementary, stereographic shapes, but a refuge carved out by the interaction of souls; it will no longer be shaped by spirits of nature which feed on earthly things but by the finest human spirits, and the space will be created by intense heat and pressure in an instant—like the action of a jet in a rock. The light sources at the thinnest places between the proliferous material, the immobile vessels replacing the old alien furniture; the earth, now all that remains, is a meeting with the inevitably vertical, most delightful form concealing the newly discovered tactile organ of our soul. The first shelter of the highest animal, which is truly his own, which he has had a right to since he became man, the maternally replete, independent, now visible, and for the present still coarsely material "organ" of an unearthly giant organism, the first natural "dwelling" of the soul.

I am afraid that any rendering of Finsterlin's language into English can only be an approximation. No words are needed to show how far this "poetry" is from Poelzig's language and from his way of seeing, thinking, and feeling.

* Hermann Finsterlin, *Casa Nova*, special issue of *Wendingen*, March 1924.

CHAPTER TWO
Hans Poelzig, the Person, the Artist: Breslau 1900–1916

"I AM THE SON of Countess Poelzig and a coachman," Hans Poelzig used to say. Countess Poelzig was related by marriage to the Prince Consort Albert and thus belonged to the highest ranks of the aristocracy. Who the "coachman" was, no one knows. Countess Poelzig was living in London married to a man called Ames when she was expecting the child. Ames left her, insisting that the child should not bear his name. There is some speculation as to whose name he could have taken — that of an aristocrat, of a Jewish doctor? The countess never gave away her secret; I do not think that Poelzig knew. He had some contact with his half-brothers who helped him out financially. But they were loose contacts. The countess herself gave Hans to be cared for by Cantor Liese in Stolpe, not far from Potsdam. As a boy he was called Hans Liese. He adored old Liese. His first experiences of music were of the cantor's organ-playing in the church in Stolpe. (Poelzig is buried in the church's graveyard.) He went to grammar school in Potsdam. He was not fond of school. On leaving, he studied architecture at the Technische Hochschule in Charlottenburg (Berlin). There he found a teacher who had a profound influence on him — Karl Schäfer (1844–1908).

Karl Schäfer taught medieval architecture in Charlottenburg. Earlier he had studied architecture, worked as a freelance architect, and taught design and construction at a trade college in his hometown of Cassel. As a young man he had worked in the architect's office in Paderborn Cathedral, which is a large Gothic hall-church. During this period early in his career, Schäfer had the opportunity to become familiar with the Gothic style as actual built architecture. When he went on to teach medieval architecture in Charlottenburg, he taught not as an art historian but as an architect. He was one of those advocates of Neo-Gothic architecture who see the Gothic style as being concerned primarily with structure. He was most certainly familiar with the theories of Viollet-le-Duc (1814–1879).

Viollet saw Gothic as a style in which all forms down to the last detail are determined by the structure. A Gothic pinnacle, said Viollet, is not an ornament; it serves to give more verticality to the thrust of the vault, which is transferred by the flying buttress into the pier buttress. I am quoting this because I consider it to be one of his "more daring" theories. Pol Abraham, who refuted Viollet's theory in the thirties,[1] comments that it would have had to be a pretty hefty pinnacle to have deflected the thrust into the vertical. He took the whole theory apart and disproved it piece by piece. One of the favorite theories of Viollet and his school was that the ribs in a Gothic ribbed vault "transferred" the thrust of the vault. Pol Abraham showed that a ribbed vault works in exactly the same way as a groined vault. He undertook this work of refuting Viollet's theories with the greatest respect for the man and his theories, pursuing the matter with a bleeding heart, so to speak, because it simply had to be done. For Viollet is the head of the structuralist school to which modern architecture owes as much as it does to Louis Sullivan's functionalist school. Sullivan claimed that form follows function; Viollet said that it follows *structure* and he applied his theory of the Gothic style to other styles and in the end went so far as to say that a style that could not be shown to follow structure is not a true style but mere decoration. This was true, he said, of nonoriginal, derived styles such as the Renaissance and the styles that followed it. Auguste Choisy (1841–1909) developed these thoughts in his *Histoire de l'Architecture*. This theory can be said to be the French contribution to modern architecture, whereas functionalism was the Anglo-Saxon one. Viollet's theories had no great influence on German art history, which attached more importance to problems of form. The passionate and deeply intellectual reinterpretations of Classical space forms by artists such as Balthasar Neumann (1687–1753) aroused greater interest.

But Karl Schäfer was interested in Gothic architecture as a way of building, not as a period in art history. (He was, moreover, an almost exact contemporary of Choisy.) From him Hans Poelzig learned to respect and love history's examples of practical structures. He acknowledged Schäfer's influence right to the end and mentions him twice in his lecture "The Architect" which he gave in 1931 (see Chapter 9, Doc. 9C).

I find these considerations interesting because they indicate the aspects of Viollet's school to which Schäfer subscribed and those to which he did not. Both times Poelzig mentions him he refers to the same lecture given by Schäfer in 1896:

In 1896 old Schäfer, my unforgettable teacher, gave a lecture about architecture at the Berlin Trade Fair. He used a drawing of the terminal of the former railway station in Karlsruhe to show what architecture is not. There were large archways — forming what architects refer to as an axis, as old Schäfer said — and then all kinds of small archways in an ornamental and rhythmical arrangement. Through a small archway was the main exit, while over a huge, particularly important archway was written: For Ladies. At any rate, old Schäfer did not approve of this kind of arrangement which was common in architecture at that time.[2]

Schäfer is speaking here as a functionalist, a man of the "English" school. But one must not imagine that we are dealing with two theories of teaching that were irreconcilable. On the contrary, we are familiar with Viollet's publication *Histoire d'une maison*,[3] which is as functionalist as even Sullivan could have wished for, and we are also familiar with English structuralists. The inspiration for both theories came from the same source — the Middle Ages; Ruskin, Viollet, Morris, Norman Shaw, all were medievalists, but that also means that they were against Classicism, for example, against the sort of composition that Schäfer talks about.

Poelzig's second comment on Schäfer's lecture of 1896 was:

... in the same lecture of 1896 he said something that I have since turned over in my mind repeatedly. He said — and of course in doing so he is a child of his time — that it was impossible to use iron construction in architecture, as this technology aimed increasingly to dissolve form, to dilute it until it finally vanishes, whereas architecture, the art of building, needs mass. That was old Schäfer's opinion — we know today that iron construction has made far more delicate building forms possible, without the iron itself ever having to appear. Schäfer was quite certainly wrong about the development of contemporary architecture; he was still rooted in the arts-and-crafts way of thinking, but was he really so far off the mark in his interpretation of technological forms?[4]

Schäfer, and indeed Poelzig, are talking here about a much older controversy: Gottfried Semper (1803–79) had said that iron was not a suitable material for use in architecture, because architecture needs mass. This old controversy need not interest us here, and it evidently did not interest Poelzig either. What *is* interesting—with regard to Schäfer and Poelzig, at least—is that Schäfer deviates here from the French theory. The French—Viollet and Choisy—took the idea that architecture follows structure through to its logical conclusion and said that the architecture of the future would be a metal architecture. Viollet even experimented with iron building elements, albeit not very successfully. Here, however, Choisy's German contemporary saw certain bounds which he did not want to overstep. And, although Poelzig did overstep them in the end (in 1931) as far as steel was concerned, he did not do so gladly, as we will see. The bounds are those of craftsmanship. Along the way that led to a new architecture at the beginning of the century there were always those architects who did not like going beyond the bounds of craftsmanship. Poelzig, unless I am very much mistaken, was one of them. And here too he can be said to have been influenced by "old Schäfer."

This influence is to a large extent responsible for the fact that Poelzig dealt with new materials and constructions in a way that did not contradict tradition. He might have said, "If our fathers had known iron, steel, concrete they would have done things just as I have done." This is endorsed by Poelzig's treatment of construction in the factory in Luban and the water tower in Posen (see Figs. 24, 25, 85–90, 26, 27, 93–98). That is not merely my interpretation; he himself said so. In 1911, the year in which the factory in Luban and the tower in Posen were built, he wrote an essay entitled "The Modern Factory" in which he says:

> The French way of building in the eighteenth century never avoided problems and derived solutions to the simplest practical problems from their very basic conditions, so that the cranes, walls, gateways of this period look as if they had been formed by nature.

> Herein lies the way to the style of the future: in the renunciation of routine use of traditional symbolic forms and in the development of a variety of types that owe their form to a design process logically evolved from the new structural possibilities.[5]

This is the basis of his teaching, which as I have said, remained unchanged from start to finish. And it is based to no small degree on the teaching he had himself received from his "unforgettable teacher," Schäfer.

Let us at this point look back once more to the comparison I made with Behrens's factories. Behrens placed emphasis on progress and made recourse to a fundamental kind of classicism—which I have called "essential Neo-Classicism"—in order to legitimize this actual progress. Poelzig placed emphasis on the continuity of history and made reference to craftsmanship, which for him included the work of the engineer—seeing it as analogous, so to speak. Behrens evoked the temple, Poelzig the aqueduct. Both of them tried to bridge the schism caused by industry—or to ignore it—although this attempt is more evident in Behrens's work than in Poelzig's. In this respect the future proved them both wrong. At the time—the early days of the Werkbund—they both worked with a belief in progress based on acknowledged principles of architecture. This was still just possible then, before 1914.

I have outlined one of the principles upon which Poelzig's work as a teacher and architect in Breslau was based. How did he come to be in Breslau? Until then his career had been that of a civil servant in government building departments. After taking his degree, Poelzig began postgraduate studies and qualified as a *Regierungsbauführer* (government clerk of works); finally he was employed in the Prussian Ministry of Public Works. His only work that may possibly have attracted attention was the design in 1898 for a Town Hall, awarded a prize in the Schinkel Prize Competition which was held every year (and still is) (Fig. 28). It was a pure Gothic building, in which one can perhaps recognize the later Poelzig—*ex ungue leonem*—in

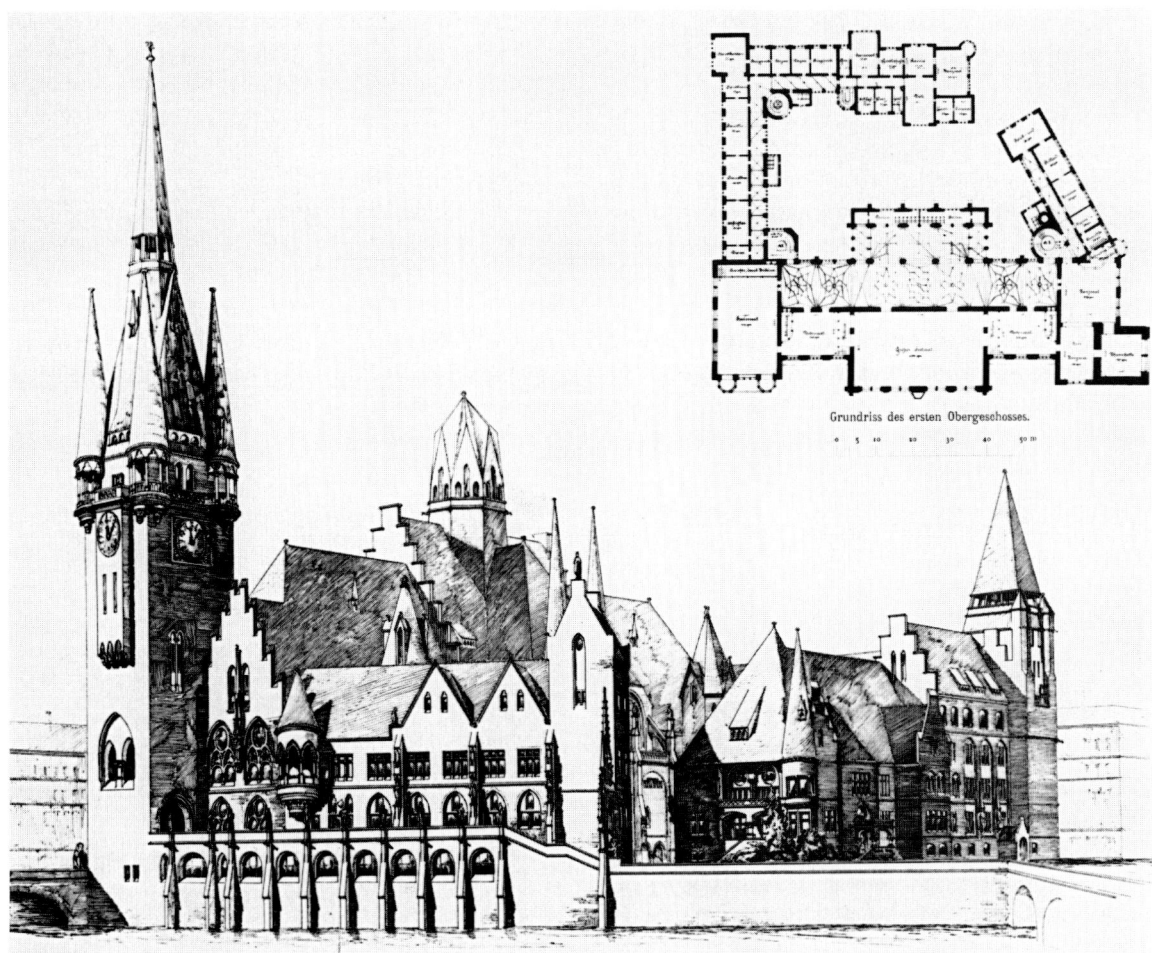

28 Hans Poelzig. "Town Hall," project for the Schinkel Prize competition, 1898.

the simplification and the plasticity of the tower on the right of the group of buildings.

This work would have attracted attention in architectural circles.* Ludwig Pallat, who was employed in the neighboring Prussian Ministry of Culture, which was responsible for the Royal School of Art and Applied Arts in Breslau, had recommended Poelzig for a teaching post, although he was unknown. (Poelzig confirmed this much later, on his sixtieth birthday in 1929, saying, "For, after all, it was you who put me on my feet in Breslau, you and no one else.") Pallat, who was an art connoisseur, must have known both the young Poelzig and the school in Breslau very well. Both were "special."

Breslau and the province of Silesia whose capital it is were particularly significant places before the war. Gerhard Hauptmann, the Naturalist dramatist, was a Silesian and lived in Agnetendorf. His brother Karl had a house in Schreiberhau and was on friendly terms with the artists' colony in Worpswede near Bremen, where Paula Modersohn and Heinrich Vogler and, for a time, Rainer Maria Rilke lived.

---

* Hartmut Frank recently published in the *Bauwelt* (No. 41, 4 November 1983) an illuminating description of Breslau at this time, the school and its development under Poelzig. I cannot improve on it so I shall follow his description and quote him directly from time to time.

Werner Sombart, the economist with social democrat leanings, also had a house built in Schreiberhau.

It was in Breslau and other parts of Silesia that the idea of setting up teaching workshops was born, so that, as Werner Sombart said later in 1908, "work could be carried out to artists' designs and tried out commercially"—an idea that was, of course, bound to meet with resistance from arts-and-crafts firms. Hartmut Frank points out that this idea has always been erroneously ascribed to the Weimar Bauhaus. But the Bauhaus was not founded until 1919 whereas this movement in Breslau dates from 1895. Frank writes:

> At a public meeting in March 1895 the Breslau Arts and Crafts Association called for "urgently needed changes to be made to the Breslau School of Fine and Applied Arts." A petition to this effect was sent to the Ministry of Culture in Berlin and met with success. The head of the school, Hermann Kühn, a textile designer, gave the go-ahead to set up teaching workshops.[6]

The first teaching workshop to be set up was an embroidery workshop.

This really was a new attitude to teaching, at least in Germany. Schools of this kind had been in existence in England as early as the mid-nineteenth century, and many people who wanted to reform the teaching (and practice) of architecture and arts and crafts had looked to England for guidance. In Germany Poelzig took up the idea, which was remarkable since he had completed his architecture studies quite conventionally and even passed civil service examinations to be a clerk of works.

In 1900 Poelzig arrived at the Königliche Kunst- und Kunstgewerbeschule (Royal School of Art and Applied Arts) at Breslau. His official job was to teach the characteristics of the different architectural styles. In actual fact, he taught design. In 1903 he became the head of the school, although he was the youngest member of the teaching staff. By this time, the school had obtained the title of "Academy."

Soon after his arrival at the school, Poelzig added a joinery shop and others for metalwork.

Let us turn again to Hartmut Frank's illuminating description of Breslau at this time and especially of the school and its development under Poelzig. As Frank writes, "Poelzig saw the workshops as being the central teaching medium in his school."

The Bauhaus in Weimar was one of the last, rather than one of the first, experiments in this direction. Furthermore, Walter Gropius, who founded the Bauhaus in 1919, had been in close contact with Poelzig and the Breslau school in 1916, when Poelzig was seriously considering proposing him as his successor. This, of course, does not mean that the Bauhaus would have been the same as the school in Breslau. It stood for ideas which were not topical until after the war.

It must be said that the teaching workshops had nothing to do with the subject that Poelzig had to concern himself with in Breslau. The subject he taught there was "History of Style." From the very beginning he did not take that too seriously. I do not even know if he ever taught history in the conventional sense. I suppose he must have. Similarly, I do not know if he attached as little importance to style then as he did a very short time later. But one thing is known: From the very beginning he held practical design classes with the students in which they had to produce sketch designs. He set great store by this teaching method and by the workshops.

He immediately provided the workshops with practical work. The decorative interiors for the extension which he added to the old town hall in Löwenberg in 1906 are well known. He did these in conjunction with the teaching workshops. What is not so well known is that as early as 1901 he designed interior furnishings for his friend and patron, Ludwig Pallat, and had them made by the joinery workshop. He wrote a series of letters on the subject to Pallat, asking him to be patient because the workshops were closed for the holidays. He also exhibited some of the furniture before giving it to Pallat. He had Pallat's wholehearted support for this, since the exhibition was a demonstration of what they were both trying to achieve.

29 Hans Poelzig. Extension of the town hall, Löwenberg (Silesia), 1903–6. The Wedding Room.

Poelzig's letters to Pallat are well worth reading. They are the most accurate documentation of a written discussion between an architect — or rather in this case an interior designer — and his client that I have ever come across.[7] They talk about a convenient way of housing Pallat's art journals; they talk about every single detail, such as the color and treatment of the wood, the kind of wood to be used, and, of course, the upholstery and the decoration of the walls. Poelzig also drew little sketches in the letters which Pallat must have been able to understand. The greatest significance was attached to functionality and craftsmanship, and even to the price.[8]

Very occasionally mention is made in the letters of aesthetics. But the topic of discussion *even then* was actually only function and craftsmanship. I remarked earlier that Hans Poelzig was one of those architects for whom it was not easy to overstep the dividing line between the work of the craftsman and that of the engineer and who did not like doing so. The letters to Pallat and, of course, to the workshops themselves, show that this was the case.

Of course, each of the Breslau workshops had their own head. They did not simply carry out Poelzig's designs — although, no doubt, they did that too. But when it was a question of decorating a ceremonial room such as the wedding room in the Löwenberg Town Hall, the head of the workshop — or possibly even the students, too—made designs which they had to harmonize with the space Poelzig had created (Fig. 29). The work was thus true cooperation between artists working independently—a Morrisian, a medieval ideal. And from the point of view of art education, it was quite certainly what every serious teacher seeks, usually in vain: this, and the contact with professional practice, with workshops, firms, deadlines, materials—and clients. (I still believe that there is no better training; my young Chinese and Malay students in Kuala Lumpur, Poelzig's "grandpupils" [and they knew it], designed wooden houses for real clients, working out every structural detail.)

In 1916 Poelzig left the Academy of Arts and Crafts and went to Dresden to take up a position as city architect. He had been teaching—and building—in Breslau for sixteen years. His work as an architect had begun at the same time as his work as a teacher. Both belong together, because Poelzig used the teaching workshops for his own practice. So it is time to look at his architecture.

So far we have looked only at two of Poelzig's industrial buildings and compared them with one by Peter Behrens built at the same time. Let us now look at one of his earliest works, a house he built in 1904 for the Exhibition of Applied Art in Breslau (Fig. 30; see Figs. 32, 33, 133). Of all kinds of buildings, the house is probably the one that underwent the most far-reaching changes as a result of the tendencies that emerged around the turn of the century. The middle classes, who were rapidly becoming affluent, had been building villas everywhere since 1860. The typical Berlin villa of the time is described by Theodor Fontane in his novel *Frau Jenny Treibel*.⁹ It had a high basement which accommodated not only rooms for storing provisions but also the kitchen and one or two servants' rooms, and possibly gardener's quarters. There was an "underground basement" for fruit and wine, since the basement itself was sunk only slightly into the ground. This meant that the reception rooms were raised above the garden, forming the *bel étage*

30 Hans Poelzig. House at Exhibition of Applied Art, Breslau, 1904. Entrance front.

with a view over the garden. Above this were the bedrooms, and in the attic there would probably be another maid's room and perhaps guest bedrooms. How the villa was decorated on the outside was left to the individual owner or architect: with pilasters and tympanum, with arcades, or with "oriels and turrets," as that kind of decoration was known which drew upon the Middle Ages for its motifs. It was also possible to decorate the house in another style. The Berliners used to tell a joke. The building contractor comes to the client: "Yer 'ouse is ready, Mr. Meier. What kind of style d'yer want putting on it?" Since about 1870 houses had been changing in England. The basement was abandoned. It had never been as popular in England as it had on the Continent. One went out of the reception rooms into the garden, which was on almost the same level.

The garden, by the way, was divided into "rooms," which corresponded to some extent to those in the house. The rooms were now lower than before. The large roof also helped to make the house fit in with the surrounding garden. Each room had its own character according to its use. Each also had its own annexes: the alcove beside the fireplace (the inglenook); the projecting, usually rectangular bay. Hermann Muthesius reported on the history of the new English house, its planning, and each of its rooms in his book *The English House*.[10] As early as the mid-nineties the English periodical *Studio*, which was widely read by the German middle classes, published extracts from it. At the same time, the American version became known — what Vincent Scully called "the stick style and the shingle style."[11] From America, in particular, came the idea of opening the stories to one another, of working with mezzanines — what the Austrian Adolf Loos later called the *Raumplan,* or "plan of volumes."

I have not yet spoken of the exterior of the English house. Increasingly, motifs taken from past styles ceased to be used for the house and there was a return to rural or small-town architecture such as that typical of the Cotswolds. Such houses are seen in the work of Voysey, Prior, and (early) Lutyens (Fig. 31). That was *one* way of building houses, and from 1900 onward it suddenly became popular in Germany. Jugendstil architects had carried out their own experiments with the house (Victor Horta in Brussels, Olbrich in Darmstadt). Adolf Loos shocked his contemporaries with his severe architecture devoid of ornament. Finally there was also a return to the time around 1800. An influential picture book of the time (1908) by Paul Mebes was even entitled *Around 1800.*

Poelzig's house at the arts-and-crafts exhibition in Breslau was one of these new houses in Germany. It belongs to the movement that wanted to adopt the local vernacular style of architecture, to describe it in the negative — no pilasters, no arcades, no "oriels and turrets." We could have expected this in view of what we have heard up till now about Poelzig. The plan is conventional despite the two-story room

31 C.F.A. Voysey. "The Pastures," house for Mrs. G. Conant, North Luffenham (Leicestershire), 1901.

marked "hall" on the drawings (in acknowledgment of the "English" movement) and its broad opening into the dining room (Fig. 32). The hall and dining room form one space that takes up the central area of the house. The house cannot be said to communicate with the garden: The living area is, after all, raised by a few steps. The house has three entrances: the main entrance (see Fig. 30), the kitchen entrance, and an entrance from the garden into a loggia next to the dining room, none of them providing the direct access to the garden that is found in Muthesius's houses from this time. The most striking thing about the house is its large roof. It looks even larger than it actually is as both gables are hung with roof tiles. On the entrance gable the tile covering even extends down to the landing of the staircase in the two-story "hall," whose volume is visible on the exterior of the building. Only on the right-hand side of the house, as seen from the entrance, is the roof "pulled" down to the ceiling of the main living area, and on this deep curved roof Poelzig set the most striking feature of the house: an oriel with a steep polygonal roof, also curved (Fig. 33). (Jokers have said: Poelzig's head. And it is true that things suggestive of his strangely shaped head can often be found in Poelzig's early works.) Behind this striking oriel on the roof is one of the smallest rooms in the house, a guest room.

If we compare the house to other modern

32 Hans Poelzig. House at Exhibition of Applied Art, Breslau, 1904. Plan.

houses of the time, to Muthesius's first house after his return from England, the house belonging to von Seefeld (Fig. 34), or to the Obenauer House by Behrens (see Figs. 3, 4), we are deeply moved by the almost violent originality of Poelzig's house. And if I call it violent I simply mean that he used a will to design and a power of design on this small building such as one would not expect. But he does not express anything alien. What is expressed and expressed emphatically is the theme of *house, roof, shelter, home*. I have intentionally used the word *express* twice: express, expression. One can begin to see why Hans Poelzig was called an Expressionist.

This house is Poelzig's contribution to what was known at the time as the "country house style," a very individual contribution. Strangely enough, the extension to the old town hall in Löwenberg (1904–6), which I have already mentioned, also belongs to the "country house style." The first thing which one notices is, once again, the very large roof (Fig. 35; see Figs. 9, 76, 78). Here it is interrupted by the terrace in front of the corridor on the first floor and continued down, a little artificially, to just above the ground-floor arcade. The old Gothic roof was very large to start with but Poelzig extends it downward in this truly forced way. It is really very funny to see how he adds a small area of roof to the innermost corner in order to facilitate the transition, and manages gently to blend the new entrance, which is pure "country house style" (one only has to look at the windows!), into this large roof. The strange capitals of the entrance arcade speak a different language; they were perhaps made in conjunction with a teaching workshop. The lower part of the staircase, with its sculptural quality, and the upper hall are certainly the work of Poelzig alone (Figs. 36, 37).

The building was received with warm applause. Gustav Wolf wrote:

Perhaps one of the most pleasing achievements is the conversion of the Löwenberg town hall by Hans Poelzig; the old has been treated with care, the new added with fresh liveliness and for all its individuality it has found a traditional manner.[12]

No one else could have done this. But let us note

33 Hans Poelzig. House at Exhibition of Applied Art, Breslau. Side elevation.

34 Hermann Muthesius. Von Seefeld house, Berlin-Zehlendorf, 1905.

here again the slightly exaggerated aspect of this powerful roof, or let us call it the joy in the emphatic.

One more work of Poelzig's from these early years deserves attention, the "Werdermühle" factory (not built) on the Oder Island in Breslau (1906), a project that also received "a good press" (Figs. 38–41a, b). Franz Geiger commented on it in an article he wrote in 1908, in which he tried to imagine how an architect would approach a brief of this kind. He could try, said Geiger, to make something of such a simple building, which was meant to serve very practical purposes, by covering it with ornaments and compositional details taken from any architectural style; that had been the nor-

35 Hans Poelzig. Extension of the town hall, Löwenberg, 1903–6.

mal practice to date. Or he could leave the building simply as it was, as a "box" that had a particular purpose to serve and was well built and solid. He continued:

If he is, however, an architect with artistic talent, he will demonstrate this clearly on the outside of the building too and in every detail. He will not put a wooden roof frame on the fireproof mill, he will not put windows in the walls that look like the windows of a house, he will *arch* the lintels of the windows if he is proud of his solid brick walls, he makes the glass bays especially glassy and the iron passageway that links the two buildings, manifestly iron ...

This way of thinking would prevent the concept of art from being alien to daily, practical work and would be the greatest gain for the beauty of man's existence.[13]

This sounds familiar; it is good Werkbund doctrine and Poelzig himself must have agreed with it. But if we take note once more of the terms "especially glassy" and "manifestly iron," and of the "solid brick walls" of which the architect is so proud, we are struck once more by the emphasis with which, as Geiger

36 Hans Poelzig. Extension of the town hall, Löwenberg. Upper part of hall.

37 (left) Hans Poelzig. Extension of the town hall, Löwenberg. Staircase.

38 (above) Hans Poelzig. "Werdermühle," factory planned for an island in the Oder River at Breslau, 1906–8, project.

34 Hans Poelzig: Reflections on His Life and Work

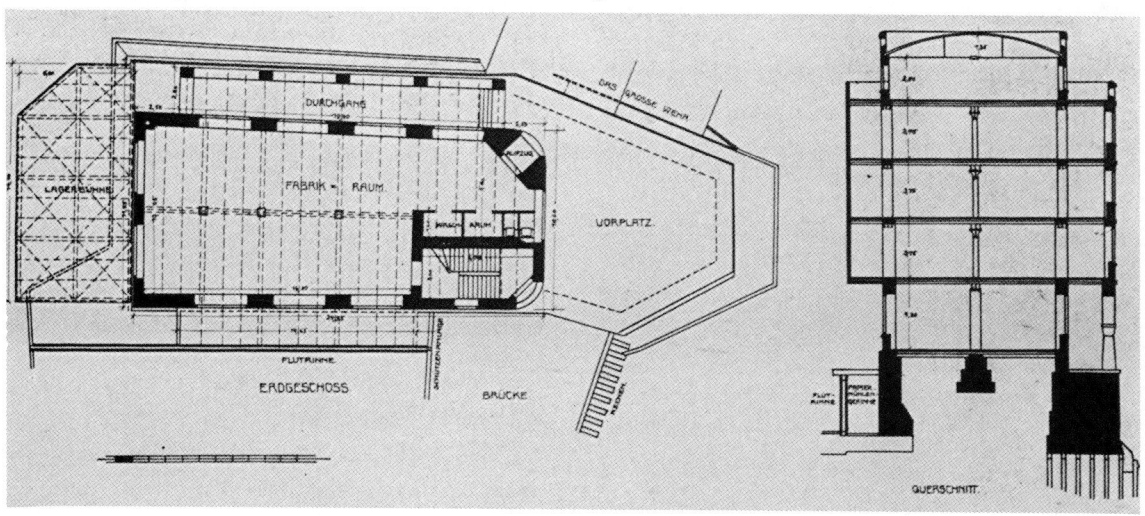

39 Hans Poelzig. "Werdermühle." Presentation drawing.

40 Hans Poelzig. "Werdermühle." Plan and section.

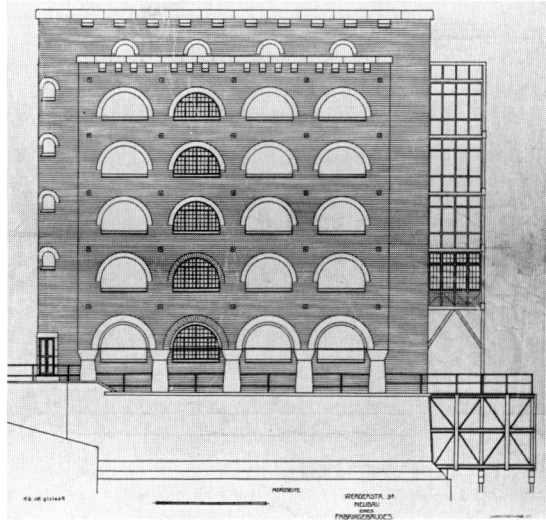
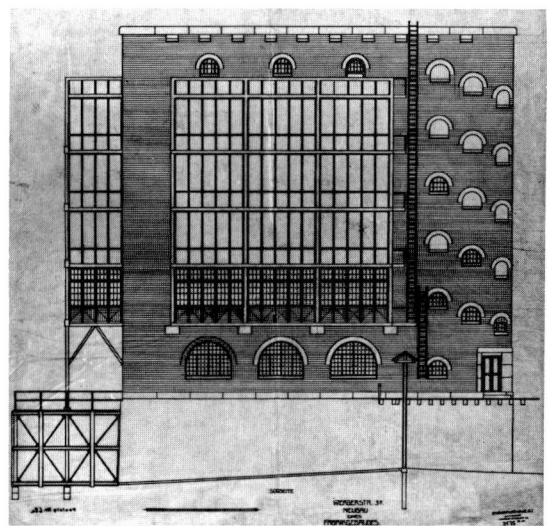

41a, b Hans Poelzig. "Werdermühle." Elevations.

quite rightly noticed, Poelzig articulated the simple facts of practical building. One could talk here of his latent expressionism. In the case of the "Werdermühle," there is also the link with old and new forms of structure, which Poelzig achieves this time by powerfully stressing both; he makes his walls visibly strong and his steel construction visibly lightweight.

As we have already seen in "The Modern Factory," he also wrote in this way about industrial architecture (see Chapter 2, Doc. 2B). Let us look at another passage from this essay:

Our factory buildings will never look as though they were meant for eternity; each building can only express the essence of its being. Whereas in old functional buildings thick walls rise up with hardly a window in them, we now need a wealth of light for the work, even our grain elevators demand more light than the old barns. We limit the strength of walls and columns to the minimum—the deep shadows cast by the reveals of the old gateways and windows cannot give expression to the buildings of our time.

And further:

In the old buildings mass dominates, and the windows, small and in deep shadow, interrupt the strong walls. Today the actual surface of the wall is often less extensive than the windows, so that emphasizing the window within the wall would tear the wall apart.[14]

Well, that will raise an eyebrow or two! That was written in 1911, the year in which Luban was built (Fig. 42; see Figs. 24, 25, 85–90). There the windows even in the steel-framed part of the building are small—rows of small nine-paned squares. In the part of the building with load-bearing masonry walls they take the form of those semicircular arches for which Poelzig had a special preference during the Breslau period. The pure semicircle is the smallest conceivable window in a bearing wall, and is entirely fitting for a bearing wall, which here is in no way "less extensive than the windows." One is tempted to ask, Did Poelzig perhaps build or design other factories that correspond better to the principles he expressed about the modern factory building? There are none that I know of. Other factories, yes, but the windows are always cut into the wall, even where the wall is of steel framework, like the Römergrube, a coal mine in Rybnik, Silesia, built in 1913 (Fig. 43). Possibly the gasworks

42 Hans Poelzig. Chemical factory at Luban near Posen, 1911.

in Reick, Dresden (1916), a pure concrete-frame construction, comes nearest to the point where opening and frame are perfectly counterbalanced, since it really is a frame here, not a wall (Fig. 44). But even in the frame structures of brick, such as the Annagrube, a coal mine in Pschow (1913–15), the frame is more dominant than the openings (Fig. 45). And in the Göritz factory in Chemnitz, which was not built until 1925–27, Poelzig returns to the arched

43 Hans Poelzig. "Römergrube," mine at Rybnik (Silesia), 1913.

44 Hans Poelzig. Gasworks at Dresden-Reick, 1916.

45 Hans Poelzig. "Annagrube," mine at Pschow (Silesia), 1913–15.

46 Hans Poelzig. Göritz factory at Chemnitz, 1925–27.

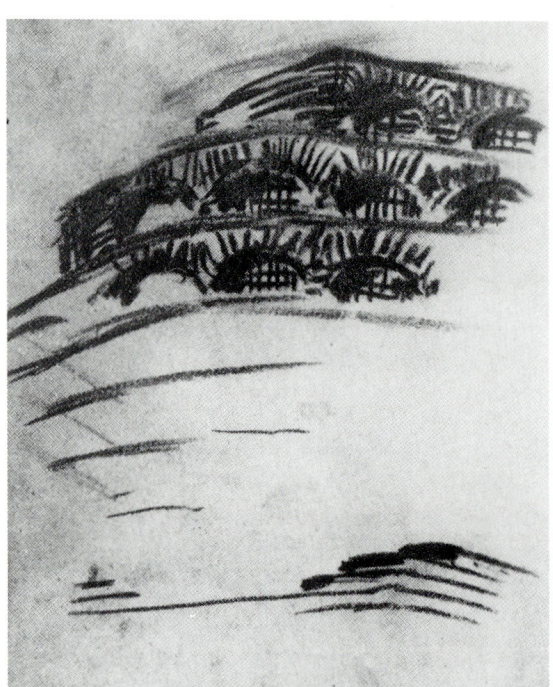

47 Hans Poelzig. Göritz factory at Chemnitz. Sketch of a detail.

48 Hans Poelzig. Göritz factory at Chemnitz. Elevation.

49 Hans Poelzig. Water tower for Hamburg, ca. 1910, project.

project for a water tower in Hamburg from 1910—that is, contemporary!—in which the Master positively revels in solid piers with deeply shadowed niches topped by throngs of semicircular arches between them (Fig. 49). Of course, here the only windows are Poelzig's semicircular windows. This, it must be said, is no longer *latent* expressionism. It is a eulogy to the mass and power of the brick building. The project must have given him great pleasure. Let us say it frankly: When Poelzig professed his belief in the lightweight in "The Modern Factory," in that which is not destined for eternity (he also says in this essay that a factory does not need to last for more than fifty years), he was simply paying lip service. He loved everything that was heavy; he loved mass, strength, "solid buildings" rather than "constructions." And to return once more to the continuity of history, which he always stressed, he said that the modern designer, the civil engineer, should work in the spirit of the architect of former times. In his own work it was not just "in the spirit": He loved to continue history into the present, it suited him to forget on occasion that he worked in this sober present of light and lightness, in it and for it. And so sometimes he hurled out hefty anachronisms from within. He obviously needed them. And they are part of his expressionism.

window—to the arched window in a decidedly rough, powerful-looking stone wall (Figs. 46–48)!

I discovered the words of Poelzig quoted above in a compilation of work and writings —by Poelzig and about Poelzig—that I myself edited in 1970. There they are printed directly opposite a picture which by no stretch of the imagination can be said to illustrate them, a

Looking at some of the early works does not just confirm the philosophy of the early Werkbund years, under whose influence they were conceived, it also brings us closer to Poelzig's latent expressionism and finally to his actual Expressionism, to a passion for the powerful that sought expression. Among the works of the Breslau period there are others that are the result of just such an "outlet." I am thinking, in particular, of the design for a Bismarck memorial at Bingerbrück-on-the-Rhine (1911; Fig. 50). Actually, *memorial* is not the right word. The figure of the Iron Chancellor appears only incidentally in the scheme; it is, in fact, a scheme for a stadium in memory of Bismarck. That is an idea "of our time" in the Werkbund sense; but the colossal substructures and no-

50 Hans Poelzig. "Bismarck Memorial" at Bingerbrück-am-Rhine, 1911, competition design. First scheme, model.

less-powerful towers of this stadium belong to the other context, the eruptive one, as it might be called. Of course, memorials were also built in those early years of the century, the most famous being Bruno Schmitz's monument near Leipzig to the Battle of the Nations (1913; Figs. 51, 52). Other memorials to Bismarck were erected, or designed, at the time, the Bismarck Tower by Wilhelm Kreis (1903), for example. This was essentially what the Berliners call "as crooked as a ten-bob bit," in other words, an outer show of strength combined with inner insecurity. Another example is Tessenow's design for the same tower, remarkable in its simplicity (Fig. 53). Kreis's monument is self-conscious, Tessenow's masterful. Poelzig's monument has inner truth. It is as though Poelzig felt that the Werkbund theory about a new decency in architecture was all very well, he took it seriously and tried to achieve it, but that was not sufficient for him. He needed something else and at an early stage he created an outlet for himself in his painting.

Many of Poelzig's paintings still exist; most of them are in the possession of his surviving children and grandchildren. I recently had the

51 Bruno Schmitz. Monument to the Battle of Leipzig, 1913. Elevation.

52 Bruno Schmitz. Monument to the Battle of Leipzig. Detail.

53 Heinrich Tessenow. "Bismarck Tower. Sketch, 1903.

opportunity to look at a picture from 1916 in the home of his daughter Ruth in Mainz: Christ on the cross between the two "thieves" (Fig. 54). It is a powerful picture and one need have no hesitation in calling it Expressionist. It is not "architects' dabbling," like the landscapes and townscapes that almost every architect painted at the time. Poelzig's paintings are to be taken seriously, at any rate as an emanation of his artistic personality. Some of these pictures were abstract, but most of them were figurative — and dramatic. He preferred large canvases. As for the style of these paintings, they remained basically unchanged from the early years right through to his last years. In his very last pictures black "shreds" appeared, which his friend Theodor Heuss interpreted as a sign of the desperation that was gaining the upper hand (see Chapter 11, Doc. 11). He may be right. The shreds too, however, had the same style, were written in the same hand. We are faced thus with a remarkable fact: Poelzig carried out three occupations at the same time and all with the same earnestness. Incidentally, let us say, *at least* three occupations, for he also worked with porcelain (with his second wife, the sculptor Marlene Moeschke) and he designed stage and film sets (see Figs. 178–180, 184–188). But let us leave these two creative experiments aside (for the time being) — they both belong to a particular phase of his life — and so the three occupations remain: teaching, painting, building. And it can certainly be said that his way of teaching did not change, nor did his way of painting. In his teaching he was, as it were, able to continue the clear "down-to-earth" Werkbund theory through to the later years; his painting was the constant "outlet" for an artist who needed more than architecture could give him, his permanent Expressionism. His architecture stood somewhere between the two. *It was subject to change—and to conflict.*

One thing becomes clear from this brief encounter with some of the works of the early years: Poelzig's work was immediately accepted, indeed admired. There are several reasons for this. For one thing, in these years before the First World War people were open to everything that was new; everything was welcomed that might lead the way out of the cul-de-sac of historicism with its exaggerated esteem of ornaments and styles and its lack of instinct for what was really important in architecture. Charles-Edouard Jeanneret (later Le Corbusier) spent some time in Germany in 1910, traveled, worked for Peter Behrens for a while (where he met Gropius, Mies, and Hannes Meyer), and wrote a glowing report about the new German architecture for his art school in La Chaux-de-Fonds.[15] And if one bears in mind that the people of the educated middle classes of the time admired not only Messel's department stores, Behrens's factories, and Muthesius's country houses, but also architecture as unusual as the Fagus factory by the young Walter Gropius and Bruno Taut's glass house, then it is no wonder that the climate was favorable to everything that was marked by the hand of the artist and was independent and daring, to everything that did not belong to one of the "schools," not even to a *new* school. There was a modern architecture at the time, possibly more than one. Messel's department stores were copied more often than he must have liked (see Fig. 73). I knew an architect of department stores at the time. He would say when asked about his department stores, "Well, I just messel them." Muthesius's country houses were imitated in every suburb. Even Behrens's A.E.G factories set a trend: for a more or less classical, generously dimensioned brick architecture. Yet no one tried to imitate Poelzig's buildings at Luban or the Posen tower. People noticed that they were not apt to become a fashion—or a style. Poelzig's works differed too much from one another for that. In 1912 one knew more or less what to expect from Behrens or even from Theodor Fischer. But each new work by Poelzig was a new emanation of his unique artistic personality; and there we have another reason that Poelzig's work was admired: the word "personality." But part of his personality was also this: He never doubted that he was Poelzig; it seemed completely natural that his works were "received." He had a consciousness of being superior that was infectious; whoever met him knew that this was Poelzig.

I would like to recall here the dialogue between King Lear and Kent: Kent, the disguised duke, asks the king if he may serve him:

> LEAR: Dost thou know me, fellow?
> KENT: No, sir; but you have that in your countenance which I would fain call master.
> LEAR: What's that?
> KENT: Authority.[16]

Poelzig had authority, that indeed "which we would fain call master." When his former students speak of him, to this day they still call him "Master." What sort of man was he?

I can only give a "frog's eye view" because that was the view I had of him, that of a student. This view told us, the students, every single time we met him that we were meeting a great man. I would like to stress that there is a difference between a great man and a famous man. I have come across a number of famous architects in my life, including Behrens, including Le Corbusier. Great men among them are few. That makes any description of Poelzig which *I* attempt so difficult: The quality that is known as greatness cannot be conveyed. What can be conveyed about Poelzig as a person from the normal viewpoint can be found in the brilliant

54 Hans Poelzig. Painting.

studies by his lifelong friend Theodor Heuss, portions of which have been incorporated into this book (see Chapter 2, Docs. 2C, 2D; Chapter 7, Doc. 7A; Chapter 11, Doc. 11). But let us return to our "frog's eye view."

If one went into Poelzig's studio in the Technische Hochschule in Charlottenburg on a Thursday or Friday, one could see a group of students huddled in a semicircle around a column of blue cigar smoke and from there one could hear someone speaking: clearly, decisively, didactically, with spirit and wit. Poelzig was holding a crit. The students' work hung on the wall. Each explained his own work, was criticized by the student whose work hung next to his, the discussion was open to everyone, and the Master summarized it and drew it to a conclusion; then he moved his stool along to the next project. It was now possible to see him. Poelzig was a heavy man: not fat, heavy. The most striking thing about his head was that the forehead rose almost vertically and the crown of the head sloped down steeply. But then the back of his head protruded again. This is known in German as a "tower skull." Poelzig had the most distinctive "tower skull" I have ever seen. He covered it up by combing his hair forward across his forehead, the "Poelzig quiff," which some of his students (of course) grew, although they had no "tower skull" to hide. His features were large, there was nothing small or weak in his face. It is known that he was a man of passions; his love for the sculptor Marlene Moeschke, who became his second wife, drove him almost to distraction during the Dresden years. For he loved his first wife and was a bourgeois character who did not lightheartedly disregard the institution of marriage. But we knew nothing of any of this, he never showed it. What helped him to hide his innermost self was his penchant for acting. Heuss says, "He also 'played' Poelzig. He was well cast."[17] As a teacher he "played Poelzig" the whole time. A certain amount of being a good teacher is acting. Auguste Perret "played Perret"—and how! I could name others. Poelzig's sense of acting was very strong; he used it consciously to achieve particular effects. For instance, he would sometimes praise a piece of work during the crit and then when he spoke to the student in private criticize it harshly. With the praise he wanted to tell the student that he did have a certain talent for the profession, but the criticism was meant to show him that he still had a lot to learn. If no criticism followed it was a strong sign of approval. One of his most successful students, Egon Eiermann, tells the story of how the Master once stood beside him and watched him drawing for ten minutes. As he went away he simply said, "Keep up the good work, my boy!"

"Then I knew," recounts Eiermann, "that I was an architect."

Let us return to the crit. Poelzig used to hold short competitions in class. If a piece of work showed promise, the student was allowed to work it up to a design study; if it was weak, the student went on to the next competition. The first part of the design study was a clay model to enable the student to *see* what he had done. Quite often a scheme would fall apart in this stage, with the Master's advice: "Spend two days going for walks and then begin again!" Very often these short competitions would be on a project that he himself happened to be occupied with, for as he said, "If I had not agonized over it myself I would not know how difficult it was."

It sometimes happened that a solution convinced him. Then he would say, "I'll use that."

And he did use it. At the end of two days' participation in one of these crits one knew something about the building type under discussion in the competition. Of course, the discussion gave Poelzig the opportunity to talk about everything under the sun. About the virtues of plagiarism, for example: Mozart "stole," he said; Handel "stole" with both hands. "And do I not do it?" Perhaps he was commenting on William Lethaby's wise words, "What you copy you have stolen. What you remember is yours."

No wonder Poelzig was a teacher of teachers. Rudolf Schwarz, Egon Eiermann, Konrad Wachsmann, and Walter Segal were students of his, to mention but a few. The exodus from Germany from 1933 onward spread his influence as far afield as Mexico City and Kuala Lumpur. I owe the fact that I became a teacher to a trick. When I was asked in the interview how I imagined teaching, I described Poelzig's method—of course, without mentioning his name.

I have already discussed the fact that there was no "Poelzig school." He tried to guide every student to his "self," even if Poelzig was not in tune with this "self." And he wanted us to approach each new work as if we had never designed anything before. He was an opponent of routine, of things that have been learned once and for all. A story from the Breslau time illustrates this. Someone brought a portfolio with beautifully drawn perspectives into the studio. Poelzig looked at each drawing carefully, pushed them back into the portfolio, held it for a moment without speaking. Then he asked, "Why have you bothered to do something you've already got the hang of?"

He himself approached each new work afresh. This is another reason why his works are so different. Theodor Heuss spoke of his Protean nature: "Hans Poelzig ... occasionally 'played' Proteus. That must have confused the cursory observer's idea of Poelzig as an artist."[18]

We shall, however, find similarities in his works, or rather in his way of working, similarities that go beyond the changes in style of which I have already spoken. Let us hear once more what Heuss has to say:

Anyone looking through his designs—and practically none of his large-scale planning schemes got beyond the design stage—will notice a couple of major motifs returning throughout the decades, recurring in another context because they were never built. They had been keeping watch in him, goading his subconscious, determining his rhythm. And so a law was alive in him, a form that forced a shape for itself, not in graphic games but closely connected with the particular brief. This alone made him fruitful.[19]

To me the inner law, the "rhythm," seems even more important than the recurrent "major motifs." It is by his "rhythm" that one can recognize him: a Proteus who, no matter what the particular transformation, always remained Poelzig.

I have said that Poelzig approached each design brief anew. He did, at any rate during his Berlin period, have preparatory work done, often to quite an advanced stage, up to the point where he appropriated it, made it his own. One of his co-workers, Dolly Drexler, recounted how he (Drexler) had in principle developed the scheme for the I.G. Farben building in Frankfurt: the circulation axis from which the office wings went off to either side. Poelzig adopted the scheme and bent the axis. Now the building "appropriated" the site on which it was to stand; now the excellent group we know so well was created (see Figs. 17, 290–302).

Poelzig had worked closely with others in Breslau; one only has to think of the teaching workshops. In Berlin, too, there was no clear division between school and office. I do not think he ever had anyone working in his office who did not come from the school. His students and co-teachers such as Erich Zimmermann accompanied his whole work. There were three stages: the large class at the Technische Hochschule; the smaller "master class" at the Academy, which was a school of fine arts; and finally the office. For Poelzig, teaching and designing were connected from the very beginning. He liked to call himself a teacher as much as he liked to call himself an artist. Up till now I have looked closely at only a few examples of his work. In the next chapter let us look at those works of his Breslau period that seem particularly informative.

Chapter Two: Documentation

Document 2A

Many witnesses could testify on Poelzig the teacher. It would not be worth doing so, for the simple reason that his students all have the same story to tell. The benefit to be gained would be this or that anecdote that hasn't been heard before. I will content myself with briefly quoting just one pupil, Heinrich Lauterbach, who was a student of Poelzig's in the Breslau days. (Lauterbach also told the story of how Poelzig mingled with a crowd of people who were complaining about an apartment house he had designed and Lauterbach's father owned [1908; see Figs. 70, 71]. Why? To join in with them.)

Doc. 2A*   Heinrich Lauterbach, reminiscence of Hans Poelzig, 1951

He set us projects to be designed in a particular material. After he had described the basic requirements, each student produced a scheme in class. After two or three hours the projects were pinned on the boards in the life drawing studio. He then had the students criticize each other's work but kept a firm hold on the discussion by asking questions or making comments. Sometimes he had the students act out their ideas. For example, during the project of furnishing a room as a music room, he cast one of the pupils as the architect, another (a girl who was just right for the part) as the client Mrs. Kommerzienrat, and a third as her husband. And then he set Mrs. Kommerzienrat onto the poor architect with hundreds of wishes and *if*'s and *but*'s. It was a very funny sketch, which taught us everything there was to know about the problem. Although it was optional, everyone attended his class. Hans Leistikow wrote: "The best thing was the class that Poelzig taught for the whole school....

* Heinrich Lauterbach, "Hans Poelzig," address at the opening of the memorial exhibition in Cassel on 24 October 1951. In a special issue of the quarterly *Schlesien*, 1963–64, pp. 205–12. Reprinted in Julius Posener, ed., *Hans Poelzig. Gesammelte Schriften und Werke*, Berlin, 1970, pp. 16–21.

These Saturdays were actually the only time I ever worked and really learned anything because I believed what Poelzig said." Poelzig continued this kind of teaching later in Dresden and Charlottenburg. To quote just a few of the numerous anecdotes: Poelzig set great store by honest effort; he couldn't bear smooth routine.... He thought it more important for a young architect to wrestle with the problems of the project—it did not matter how clumsy the results were—than to bask vainly in his own routine. He was very touchy about clichés. When someone explained why he had designed a facade in a particular way by saying "it reflected the German spirit," [Poelzig] said he would have none of that sort of talk. The German spirit had nothing to do with facades, he said, it resided deep within the human being and needed no explanation (J. Mattäei). "He taught us to approach every project as if it were the first of its kind and as if nothing had ever been resolved before" (Rudolf Schwarz). When a student once tried to excuse things that were wrong about his design by saying they only affected the rear facade of the building which no one would see, Poelzig retorted vehemently, "Who do you think you are building for? We build for the dear Lord and he sees everything!"

Document 2B

In an essay entitled "The Modern Factory," written in 1911, Poelzig treats a topic that would continue to occupy his thoughts: the relationship of the architect, the artist, to technological progress. What he says in this essay goes against what he would say later on the subject. Here he firmly supports technological progress as a liberating factor, saying, "the imagination, liberated from trivial considerations, will be all the more capable of giving these large functional buildings the strong and original expression of our time."

Not only does Poelzig support progress in this essay, he goes farther: He credits the engineer with the ability to find the valid form for his new structures by himself, even if it is sometimes necessary to give him the support of an architect, since the engineer has been badly educated in architecture.

In this essay Poelzig is speaking as a true man of the Werkbund. This will change during the First World War. Thereafter he will speak of the engineer as someone who arrives at his results —that is to say, his designs—by calculation. (This, however, cannot be done, as Poelzig ought to have known from his experience with building engineers in Breslau. Good design cannot be calculated.)

We know very well that Poelzig's own work bore little relation to the statements he makes in this essay. As I have already mentioned, the essay is "illustrated" by a water tower for Hamburg (see Fig. 102). In the book I published on Poelzig in 1970 the illustration is opposite that part of the essay where Poelzig is talking particularly emphatically about the lightness, the openness, even the short-lived nature of industrial buildings; the Hamburg water tower, however, is a *good solid building*—it was meant to glorify heaviness and the load-bearing arch.

The fact is that Poelzig, when thinking of the coming architecture (as in his 1911 article), was bound to agree with technically progressive ideas, while Poelzig, the artist, ignored them. He *did* adopt the idea concerning industrial architecture that was proclaimed by the progressive wing of the Werkbund, that in industrial architecture the technically correct construction ought to be adopted, that is to say, the most economic construction using no more material than what is strictly required to bridge the given distance between supports. He even adopted the Werkbund statement that factory buildings, at any rate, were not meant to last long. We have seen, however, that Poelzig loved the massive construction of ancient brick buildings. Even in his late office buildings for I.G. Farben in Frankfurt he did not show the steel structural skeleton, but designed in such a way that the building looks as though it had been built with solid walls (1930; see Figs. 290–302). And if you look carefully at his factory buildings, such as the one at Luban (1911; see Figs. 85–90), you will realize that he *did* mean them to last longer than a maximum of fifty years. They were built "for eternity." This, certainly, is one of the main problems of Poelzig's achievement in this century.

Doc. 2B*   Hans Poelzig, "The Modern Factory," 1911

The factory building is essentially a product of our times. In former times even the largest companies were fundamentally craft-based; they did not have what makes today's factory what it is: the machine.

Each factory building must first and foremost serve the requirements of the engineer and management, and the building will only be good if it meets the company's needs in a clear and succinct manner.

But the question remains: Can, or must, the term *architecture* be employed for a building like this? I believe that the term *architecture* must be used to eliminate what was meant by architecture in the past when it was applied to buildings of this kind:

The image of the factory has changed over the years as a result of various influences. Factories built in less affluent times were usually of red brick or white stucco and had flat roofs; they stand out hard and cold against the surrounding countryside. They are not actually beautiful, but they are in their own way honest, and after all they represent a step in the right direction, toward the evolution of something closer to perfection.

The buildings from a later period show a quite different face. If the older ones were bleak and bare, these are often positively obtrusive.

The call for an architecture that would provide a pleasant finish had on the whole come from and been answered by artistically uneducated people. They produced brick facades, interrupted by dazzling white areas of stucco, bands here, patterns there; ornaments of every kind in terra-cotta or ashlar decorated gables and walls. Above the roofs, which here too were usually flat, towered a steep gable here and there, held down by decorated anchors.

* Hans Poelzig, "Der neuzeitliche Fabrikbau," *Der Industriebau* 2 (1911) no. 5, pp. 100–106. Reprinted in Julius Posener, ed., *Hans Poelzig. Gesammelte Schriften und Werke*, Berlin, 1970, pp. 38–42.

Pseudo-art had arrived and entered a relationship with engineering that robbed the latter of its natural quality. In this field, too, a crafts method, which only remotely approached art, had had a damaging effect.

And so this too was a well-intentioned but erroneous way of avoiding the mistakes of the past. These architects tried to make the factories fit in with the landscape by covering up their hard features and giving them an expression from a bygone epoch in which other less evolved structural and building methods were common.

Their appearance, which may otherwise have been sober and cold, was robbed of all character by this well-meant compromise. Just as it is impossible to give a house that has logically and consistently adapted itself to contemporary needs the equitable countenance of a bourgeois house built a hundred years ago, it is even more out of the question to dress the factory of today in the gowns of the good old days in order to make it fit in with the face of the village or small town. The preventive medicine must be administered differently. It is the duty of the town planner, and more so of local conservationists, to allocate factories their proper place and see to it that carelessly sited plants covering huge expanses of land do not violate small towns and villages, destroying their coherence.

The factory building serves purely technical purposes, and the perfect design must exploit the possibilities of structural engineering to the full. One cannot, and must not, try to prevent the engineer/architect from working on this premise with all its extreme consequences. If his work is genuine, derived purely from the basic needs of the factory, it is bound to be convincing and will even be able to make its mark on the surroundings in a positive way.

I do believe that, for the time being, the factory engineer needs the collaboration of an architect or artist. The engineer usually has neither the capabilities nor the training to refine the drawings that were derived from technical and practical considerations and transform them into a beautiful design.

But we must realize that this is a shortcoming in the training of engineers. It would be wrong to think that this collaboration between the so-called artist and the so-called engineer could not ever be dispensed with. It may remain common in the future simply for reasons of division of labor. But one will perhaps have to try gradually to emancipate the engineer from the absolute necessity of working with an artist and make him independent.

However, the architect who is called upon to work on the aesthetic aspects of a factory or engineering structure, or who is required to design it himself without the help of engineers specialized in the field, must see the renunciation of all incidentals, all bizarre decoration, as the highest possible achievement.

And if his work is to be truly successful he must create it with true conviction, he cannot wait until the engineer puts the dish in front of him so that he may add the seasoning. He has to be involved in the work from the very beginning and has to learn to understand the inner laws, the structural dictates.

Nothing productive can emerge from an artist's dabbling in an engineering project. We have already started to regret the stone pergolas and watchtowers that have been added to slim iron bridges, although not too long ago they were considered artistic. The architect is all too fond of avoiding immersing himself in the essential meaning of the brief itself, from which the laws governing the character and the true beauty of the building must be derived. He tries his hand at a way of designing that is intended to express his ornamental interpretation of the nature of the building and in the end does not get beyond a purely "decorative" level. It is this that gives rise to the embarrassed groping around, manifest in almost all architectural projects that have no direct relation to buildings of the past.

Even if the artist tries to give the engineering structure the stamp of his personal style, he will not manage to master today's tasks. He must get to the essence of the building and even try to surpass the engineer in thinking the basic principles through to their logical conclusion....

The artist should be positively delighted to have problems to solve that have almost no constraints and for which the modern day and age is developing its own forms based on its own laws. He should not shy away from embarking upon the difficult task of immersing himself in the mathematical principles that underlie the architecture of today and the future. I would say that this is true at least for future architecture; there are no other basic principles, all others are forced and will only produce hybrid forms that seem as immature as the first attempts at giving ornamental form to machines ...

But it is indeed possible to draw a comparison between our time and the epoch of early Gothic, which, with unswerving freshness, set out to use the new, increased structural possibilities and from them gradually developed the symbolic language of this style. The French way of building in the eighteenth century never avoided problems and derived solutions to the simplest practical problems from their very basic conditions, so that the cranes, walls, gateways of this period look as if they have been formed by nature.

Herein lies the way to the style of the future: in the renunciation of routine use of traditional-symbolic forms and in the development of a variety of types that owe their form to a design process logically evolved from the new structural possibilities.

The reason that the practical buildings of our time are not stylistically mature is due partly to the relative lack of maturity of our structural possibilities, which are not capable of keeping pace with economic demands. The development of new structural methods, such as concrete construction, will increase both the freedom of the artist and the scope of design possibilities.

It will become possible to avoid many of the deplorable defects that still exist in our factories — smoke, soot, noxious smells.

Even now, due to the possibility of electric communications technology, the flexibility of distribution and organization of working groups — and with this of the building complexes — is increasing, and the factories, surrounded by charitable institutions and workers' housing, will be capable of fitting in more harmoniously with any surroundings. The large, functional buildings are the most perfect expression of our age, they are the actual monuments of today's architecture.

Without studying the past closely, without becoming conscious of the basic tectonic conditions of traditional architecture, it will not be possible to find complete freedom for new building projects or to give them the most fitting expression. But, in the case of functional buildings, all concern with the external features of past epochs that we have come to love, be it justified or purely sentimental, must be abandoned; it distracts the designing artist from the straight and narrow path toward true expression.

No whim of taste of the client can confuse the artist; the laws of logic which reign supreme do not restrict him but guide him so that he can avoid futile diversions, and the imagination, liberated from trivial considerations, will be all the more capable of giving these functional buildings the strong and original expression of our time....

A very important teacher of architecture once gave a laconic reply to an enquiry he had received in a circular about how one could make engineering structures beautiful again; he said that one should prevent an architect from being called upon....

The technology of steel construction is being constantly refined in an attempt to reduce mass so that the individual elements in the web become increasingly fine. Steel constructions do not have the solid masses that dominate in those parts of masonry buildings that have to take the greatest loads. The impartial observer will surely feel that the steel bridge goes farthest in dematerializing the individual elements, making material almost invisible; it conquers colossal spans with a grace that is virtually incorporeal.

The heavy stone watchtowers of our bridges on the Rhine, not to mention their total lack of economic justification, interrupt the sweeping line of the steel bridge....

What iron construction demands is what engineering, in general, and the factory building, in particular, demand. Economic concerns determine the building complex; the laws of present-day engineering determine the structural system, and the artist can do nothing other than give an overall form and harmony to all the contradictory demands.

The functional buildings that date from the great periods of architecture are representative of their very function, which is why they are often so overwhelming. No one who has looked at the powerful arches of Roman aqueducts with their unique rhythm will ever forget them, and the stone bridges, warehouses, cranes, all make an important contribution to the artistic expression of our medieval towns ...

... It is not my intention to try to compare our factory complexes with the functional buildings that have survived from those times, particularly not with the medieval ones. Our age, which is making technological progress at a breakneck pace, will not create buildings to last for centuries; probably every fifty years one factory building will make way for a new one.

Our factory buildings will never look as though they were meant for eternity; each building can only express the essence of its being. Whereas in old functional buildings thick walls rise up with hardly a window in them, we now need a wealth of light for the work; even our grain elevators demand more light than the old barns. We limit the strength of walls and columns to the minimum—the deep shadows cast by the reveals of the old gateways and windows cannot give expression to the buildings of our time.

The loads are usually directed to individual points, so that the walls between can be kept as thin as possible.

A brick wall just a few centimeters thick wraps itself around many buildings, simply as a skin between steel supports. It is incapable of bearing load itself and is hung on the metal frame. The very extremity of this example teaches us the direction we have to go in order to find our own expression. In the old buildings mass dominates, and the windows, small and in deep shadow, interrupt the strong walls. Today the actual surface of the wall is less extensive than the windows, so that emphasizing the window within the wall would tear the wall apart.

Let us therefore avoid any half-measures.

Let us give our buildings as calm and clear an outline as possible and arrange the windows, which should recede from the plane of the building as little as possible, in a manner which will meet the user's lighting requirements.

The difference in height of buildings, which usually occurs naturally in factory complexes, the size of the individual elements, the chimneys, the water tanks, the tower-like structures which many companies need, are perfectly adequate to give the overall complex a rhythm that can be quite powerful.

And if the artist can imbibe the basic conditions of the building, if he avoids thwarting the engineer and works with him to achieve a building that is perfect both aesthetically and technically, we too will be able to create factories which are the artistic expression of our age in the most positive sense.

Document 2C

Theodor Heuss made some remarks that shed light on Poelzig's painting and its meaning for his life and work. They are based on things Poelzig himself spoke of in October 1918 when the end of the war was approaching, but they are nevertheless valid for his painting from the beginning to the end.

Doc. 2C* Theodor Heuss, in *Hans Poelzig. Bauten und Entwürfe,* **1939**

One or two remarks in letters might show what moved him at the time when he was searching for a new way forward. From 24 October 1918: "Tomorrow I will paint. I am moving toward the abstract. Not making any abrupt changes but developing quite logically. And those stupid, narrow-minded chaps will never be able to free art.... Only architecture in its broadest sense can free us, the pure music of the stones, materials, colors, and I don't know what else!" From 28 October: "Yesterday I painted and for a change it was something that I can't put a name to. Some women, two young ones and an old one; behind them a knight with dreadful plumes, etc., is about to arrive. I have already painted several similar things. But only since yesterday have I known what I can call these works. They are ballads, nothing more—that will suffice. The two Macbeths I was the perpetrator of also fall into this category, as well as one of my earliest pictures which has more figures from antiquity. And one that is brightly colored and very

* Theodor Heuss, *Hans Poelzig. Das Lebensbild eines deutschen Baumeisters. Bauten und Entwürfe,* Berlin 1939; reprinted, Stuttgart, 1985, pp. 39, 40.

expressive with freely invented figures. In fact, all my pictures have something of the ballad about them. The difference is that the others are to an even greater extent pure music. But many souls or devils, however you like to put it, live in me. More than in any other person I know. So much so that, as far as my architecture is concerned, good old Avenarius [Ferdinand Avenarius, 1856–1923, editor of the periodical *Kunstwart*] once called me Proteus—incidentally, a term that he used only to compare me positively with others. Of course it is not true, although it is true that I have more than one side to me: All my qualities and faults spring from that. These good German artists with their so-called individual 'tone' make you sick; they are happy when they manage to produce any sound at all and then they play the same tune their whole lives long—until you can't stand it any more. There are many possibilities within me and I am not afraid of taking a leap into the unknown. But will it be possible to take any kind of leap at all after the war when the soil has been so churned up?"

These remarks do not merely bear witness to his self-confidence, which with emphatic power tries to help itself through a desperate phase, they also touch directly on that which Poelzig himself considered unspeakable for a long time. The word "ballads" is wonderfully apt, and I think it is important that the work preceded the word. It is difficult to talk about the pictures, which, at the request of their creator, were kept from the public, and it is impossible to mold them into aesthetic categories. The slightly illustrative quality of the early paintings, practically all of which he destroyed, disappeared completely. Some of the motifs remained—Apocalypse, the story of Joseph, a couple of pictures that are part of the Macbeth cycle, Don Quixote—but the motifs lose any reference to literature, form disintegrates, color begins to triumph. The formats are almost all oversized—painting by the square meter. They are quite simply devastating—full of demons, brutal, lacerated ugliness, unmasked cruelty, earthy humor, the existential fears of man and beast. And then there are other pieces that are of captivating happiness, enchanting colors, and, particularly in the later paintings, large landscapes which the eye can happily roam over, where the brush has gained a broad and commanding lightness and confidence. "The later paintings"—writing it down makes one uncertain as to whether the term can be used at all. Over a period of almost twenty years I had the opportunity to look at Poelzig's paintings four times—they were always the same paintings and yet always different. He was never satisfied—he left only a very few in a state he considered to be more or less "finished." The others he took out again, scraped paint off, threw new masses of paint onto them—the inner picture that he saw in the painting threatened him, it grew and changed. During my last encounter with his work after his death it was like looking at a tragic autobiography, seeing how the last years had pressed dark colors into his hands, how shreds of black were flung amid the happiness and harmony so that the chaos of turbulent unrest threatened to blast open the cosmic will ...

His "latent sacred quality" was denied architectural expression in stone but found semifulfillment in his painting. I say "semi-" because it was not a display of mysticism but a search for mysticism, sometimes akin to spelling in a state of trance. Just as some people can enter a different world through prayer, for him color, sensuous attraction, was the link to the supersensory. He himself did not pray but he was convinced of the existence of the supersensory. As a *homo religiosus* he had gone his own way at his own peril ...

What moved him was determined by his confrontation with the intellectual content of mysticism, and by the will of the mind to conquer the mystery of fate, predestination, freedom, divine will. His library was full of the works of mystics, the occult, astrology; references to book titles in his notebooks are often to works of this nature. During his time in Breslau he had begun to make this world his own.

Document 2D

The comments above say a great deal about Poelzig, about more than his painting. The latent sacred, mystical, even magical quality is an important element in Poelzig's feelings and art.

Again, we have to look to Heuss to learn more about it. Poelzig the architect, the man of deeds, the teacher, did not talk about these things.

Doc. 2D* Theodor Heuss, "Hans Poelzig," 1936

Hans Poelzig had a Protean nature and occasionally "played" Proteus. That must have confused the cursory observer's idea of Poelzig as an artist. Technically clean, sober and fantastic, smooth walls and proliferous roaming form motifs, here a sharp-edged cube, there an ellipse, rounded — a strange mixture. Anyone looking through his designs — and practically none of his large-scale planning schemes got beyond the design stage — will notice a couple of major motifs returning throughout the decades, recurring in another context because they were never built. They had been keeping watch in him, goading his subconscious, determining his rhythm. And so a law was alive in him, a form that forced a shape for itself, not in graphic games but closely connected with the particular brief. This alone made him fruitful.

He also "played" Poelzig. He was well cast. The role demanded drastic surprise, the seemingly effortless, harsh word in the right place, and not just one but a wealth of them, a readiness to act out the bizarre. He was a live wire, leaping around with a gleam in his eye; his behavior stopped just short of clowning, or if he was in boisterous high spirits it was pure clowning. It gave him pleasure to change people into other characters, to cause confusion in a group, one person would be given this role to play, someone else another, and then they had to get on with it. Playing the role was meant to free them and if it didn't it could only be because they were inhibited pedants. His way of speaking was very deliberate, his sentences delivered with a broad yet sweeping gesture; he would intersperse them with mime, copy someone's voice, imitate a movement — all as if on the spur of the moment and yet in actual fact he never lost sight of the basic idea behind the fun and games. Poelzig needed moments of frivolous fun like this but he did not force them. He simply created them when the occasion arose.

This Poelzig of the infectious sense of humor, the imaginative or "outrageous" idea, has been a sort of legendary figure for years. He did nothing to refute it, it was the face he put on for the outside world and it was a likable face. He had a lot of happiness to catch up on which had been missing from his childhood. He only ever spoke with horror, even bitter hostility, of his schooldays in Potsdam, when he had been put in a "pension" with a harsh, narrow-minded person. He was an orphan from the age of ten. He had been deprived of maternal love even during his early childhood — an old, good-hearted village cantor had been his foster father and Poelzig thought back to him with gratitude to the last. The village church where the old man practiced the organ and the child listened quietly in the corner was his Paradise Lost. The first inspiration the young boy had was to try to compose hymns. That sort of experience never quite goes away.

What is "not so easy," when looking at this man, is to get behind the outer surface — past his great energy and *joie de vivre,* his magnetic power to inspire people — and find the true core, his artistic work and intellectual attitude, and then having done so be faced with the task, the temptation, of talking about his soul, the unrest, the search for the transcendental, which was inspired by the occult. The will shies at the thought of trying to capture in flimsy, inadequate words, so open to misunderstanding, the secret of a unique and great man which was hidden from the public. And yet it is impossible to understand and feel his good humor and cheerfulness if one knows nothing of the tensions caused by the demons within him; impossible to appreciate the strict self-control he exercised with regard to form if one has no inkling of the chaos from which his visions emerged. The responsibility of his rational side — seen, for example, in his floor plans, the relative strictness he showed in exercising his duties as a civil servant — are quite distinct from his other side, his sheer instinctive vitality.

---

* Theodor Heuss, "Hans Poelzig," *Die Neue Rundschau* 47 (1936) no. 9, pp. 938–40.

CHAPTER THREE
Poelzig at Work: Breslau 1904–1916

EACH OF POELZIG'S WORKS covered in this chapter will be described individually. The same will be done in the other chapters of this book in which each of his works of a particular period are dealt with. The chapters concerned are Chapter 10, "Works 1924–1931," and Chapter 12, "The Late Designs 1932–1936." The works are not presented in chronological order; they are either grouped in categories, as in the case of Chapter 10, or they follow the logic of the text. Since the house for the Exhibition of Applied Art in Breslau in 1904 has already been discussed (see Chapter 2, Figs. 30, 32, 33), I shall begin this chapter with two other houses.

1906 Hans Poelzig's house in Leerbeutel near Breslau

In 1906, two years after his house for the Exhibition of Applied Art in Breslau (see Figs. 30, 32, 33) Hans Poelzig built himself a house in Leerbeutel (Figs. 55, 56). From the outside it bears no resemblance to the one at the exhibition although the plans are virtually identical. Once again the hall-dining room sequence occupies the whole of the central part of the house and once again the hall is two stories high. The similarity between the two houses even extends to the fact that the dining room and the hall are the same shape in each. In fact, on closer examination, similarities in the external form of the two houses can also be detected. In both cases the entrance to the house is behind a semicircular arch, and in Leerbeutel the tiling of the gable in front of the hall is also brought down to the level of the gallery floor. But the formal language of each house is totally different, and, to be perfectly frank, the later house, the variation on the first one, is less convincing. There is too much going on: The base is of rough stone, the ground floor is rendered with rough-cast stucco interrupted by smooth bands (a motif used to far greater effect in the village church in Maltsch, built in the same year; see Figs. 60–66). Again, as in the exhibition house, there is the same tile-covered gable, which here, however, is interrupted above the entrance, where the rough-cast stucco and the bands are continued. This is right artistically. If one imagines the tiling as a continuous covering here, the ground floor, the most important story of the house, would lose significance. The longer one looks at the elevation from an oblique angle, the more "right" this lively composition seems. Nevertheless, these two houses are compared because it shows us Poelzig at work and we discover that he was obviously not greatly concerned with the spatial organization of the house; he had already solved that problem in

55 Hans Poelzig. Own house at Leerbeutel near Breslau, 1906.

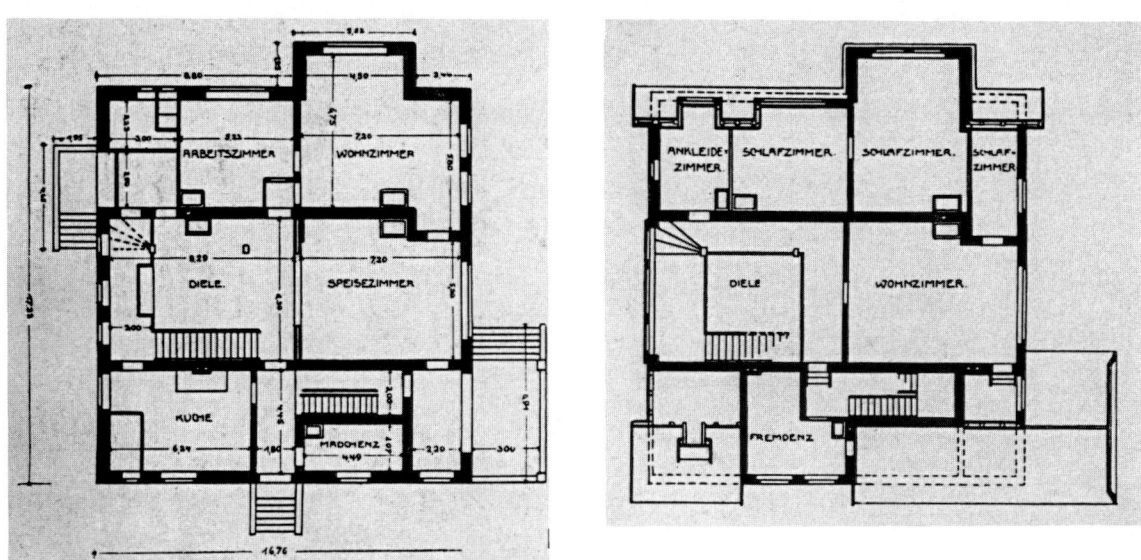

56 Hans Poelzig. Own house at Leerbeutel. Plans of ground floor and first floor.

57 Hans Poelzig. Zwirner house at Löwenberg (Silesia), 1910. View from the street.

the Breslau house. What concerned him was the new form in which this same spatial organization shows itself. Like a musician, he composed a variation on a theme, his theme here being the house.

1910 Country house and young people's home (Zwirner House) in Löwenberg (Silesia)

Theodor Heuss has the following to say on the background to this building (Figs. 57–59b):

> This magnificent building, sited in rolling hills, was built as a boys' boarding school in which teaching and living were not separated. Rooms for living, housekeeping, and sleeping, as well as classrooms, for several dozen people had to be provided. The house evolved through a true cooperation between the client and the architect, each inspiring the other to greater heights: Countless drawings were drawn, revised, rejected. The hillside site had its attractions and its drawbacks. The terrace is carried on a broad substructure (containing rooms for storing provisions). On this the ensemble rises up, imposing yet homely, in an interplay between the pitched roof, broad and pulled down and interrupted many times by the windows of the pupils' bedrooms, and the heavily stressed verticals in the form of the bays and the walls. The strong colors give the house a light-hearted note despite its heaviness.[1]

Here we find familar motifs once more: The dormer in the roof of the house at the Breslau Exhibition of Applied Art appears here twice — once in the gable facing the valley and once in the gable to the garden; the smooth bands in the rough-cast stucco are here only vertical and, as Heuss remarks, they serve to strengthen the verticality of the dormer. The curved roof covers three stories, making the building look as if it is growing out of the ground. The overall form is complete in itself; the difficulties and artificiality of earlier houses have been overcome. The house is monumental without being grand. Poelzig achieved this by not using the conventional elements that usually make a building monumental—columns, entabla-

58   Hans Poelzig. Zwirner house. View from the garden.

59a   Hans Poelzig. Zwirner house. Sketch.

tures. He uses the formal language appropriate to a dwelling.

The house is a living example of Poelzig's statement that he did not stop working on a design until nothing remained but the form. One is tempted to say he worked on the theme

59b Hans Poelzig. Zwirner house. South elevation as drawn by the architect.

"house" in the three stages we have considered, until a completely convincing form had been created.

1906 Evangelical church in Maltsch (Silesia)

This church was built at a time when it was customary to build churches in the Gothic style, even in villages (Figs. 60–66; see also Fig. 10). To do anything else was quite daring. Incidentally, it was also daring for the town council of Maltsch to commission the director of the art school in Breslau to design their church. The people of Maltsch knew of Poelzig because he had recently carried out alterations to a church in the neighboring town of Wültschkau. Poelzig's church is not Gothic, nor is it in the "local vernacular," which would have been the other alternative at the time. Perhaps the church in Maltsch is to some extent reminiscent of country churches — I am thinking of the *helm* spire, for example. But the building has certainly not been made to look like the local churches. It is highly original with its broad transept and roof whose ridge is higher in the eastern part; the broad semicircular arched windows are not Silesian but pure Poelzig, and the smooth bands in the rough-cast stucco, which articulate and decorate the elevations (we have seen them on

60 Hans Poelzig. Evangelical church at Maltsch (Silesia), 1906.

61 Hans Poelzig. Church at Maltsch. View from the north.

58 Hans Poelzig: Reflections on His Life and Work

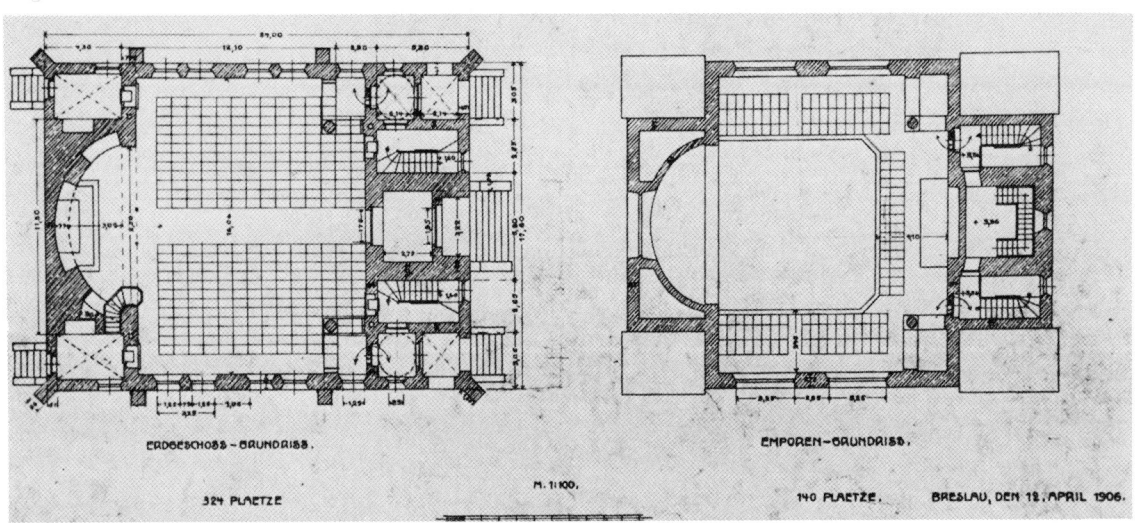

62 Hans Poelzig. Church at Maltsch. Interior.

63 Hans Poelzig. Church at Maltsch. Plans.

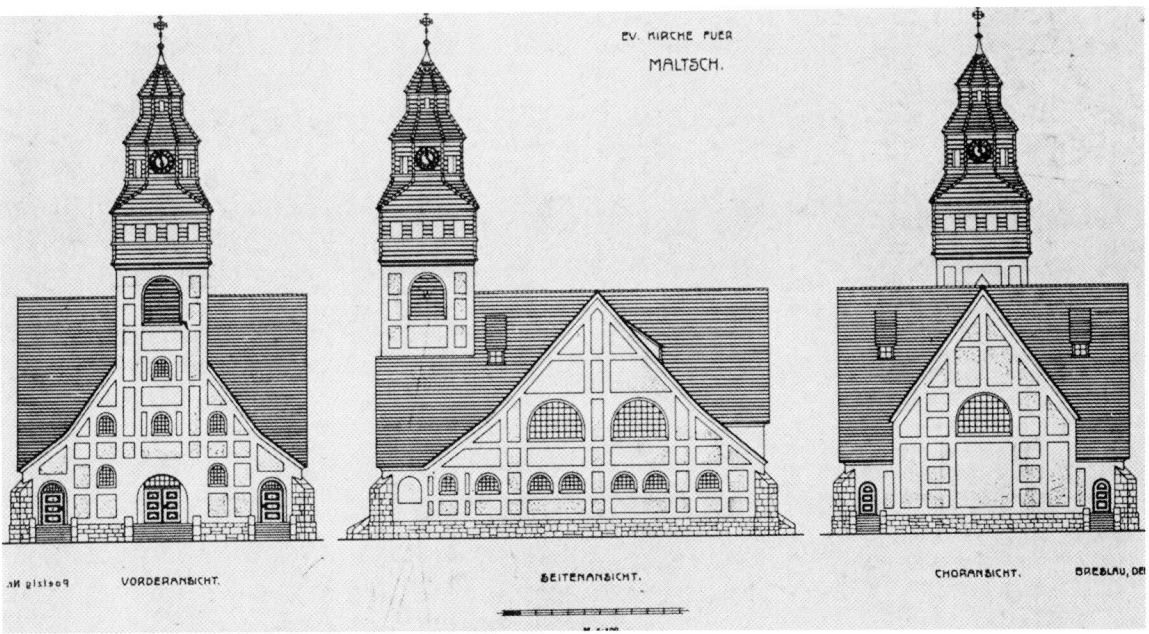

64 Hans Poelzig. Church at Maltsch. Elevations.

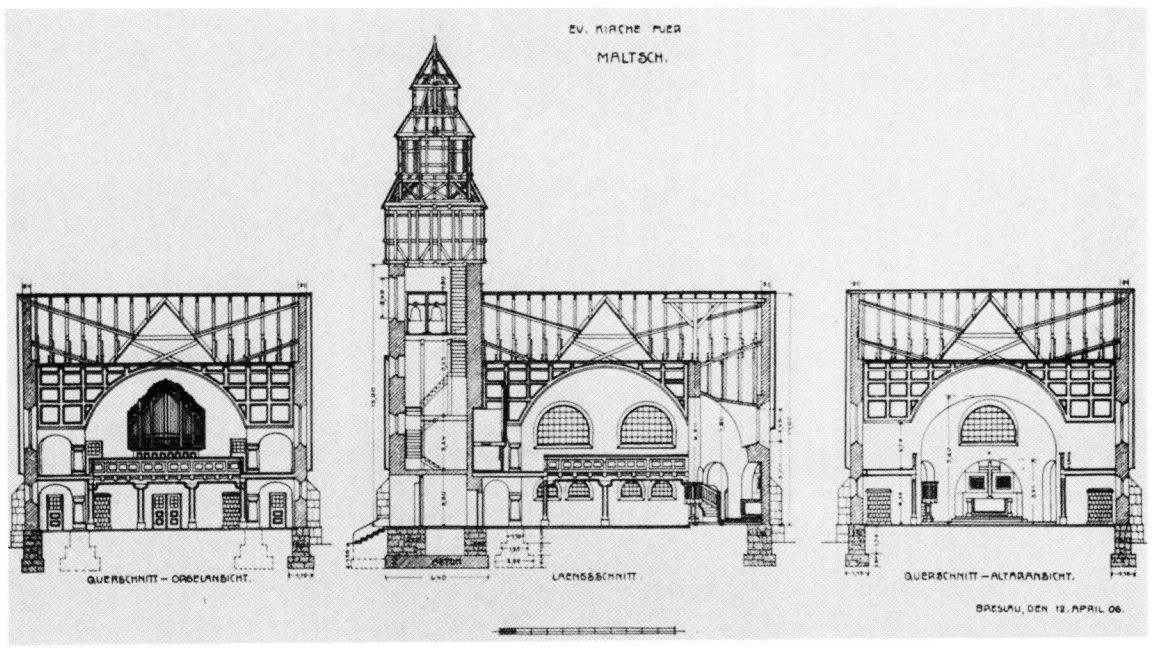

65 Hans Poelzig. Church at Maltsch. Sections.

60 Hans Poelzig: Reflections on His Life and Work

66 Hans Poelzig. Church at Maltsch. Organ loft.

the house in Leerbeutel) might from a distance be reminiscent of half-timbering, but it is quite plain that they actually have nothing to do with the half-timber style. Despite its unusual forms, the church fits into the village.

The interior is dominated by the semicircle Poelzig loved so much. It appears in the magnificent, wooden cross vault, which draws the space together, in the windows, and in the apse and its niches. The church is Evangelical, a preaching place; it is broad, open, and without false solemnity. It is one of Poelzig's most successful works. It soon became famous and has remained so to this day.

1908–12 Group of apartment buildings in Breslau

Poelzig was building for the wealthy when he designed these apartment buildings in Breslau (Figs. 67, 68a, 68b). But people complained that they looked "bare." To compensate for the lack of "architecture," it was customary at the time to treat the facade of an apartment building as if it were the facade of a house. The roof would be brought down as far as possible to give the building the character of a "country house" and the windows in each story would be different. Some architects of the time, such as Albert Gessner in Berlin, went farther and gave their apartment buildings actual "country house" facades (Fig. 69). Poelzig did not do that. There is no doubt about the fact one is looking at apartment buildings. Large horizontal windows make them modern in the sense the word was used at the time.

Incidentally, Poelzig did not make a principle of varying the windows in a building. He never made a principle of anything. There are also buildings in the group where the windows are identical on every floor. The elevation shown here even has an "architectonic" articulation. However, the relief is so shallow that it may also have looked strange.

I include the Lauterbach House with these buildings, because, although it is not an apartment building, its plans and general arrangement might be those of an apartment house

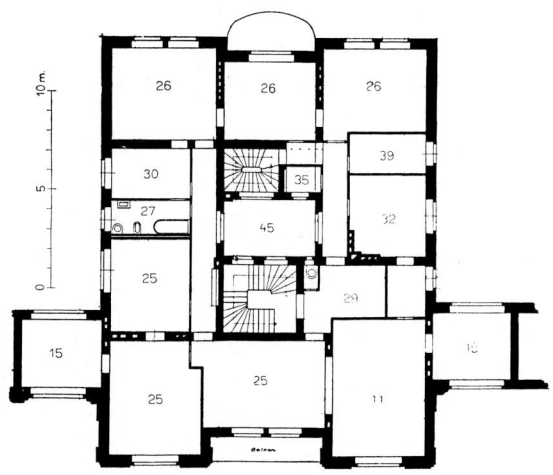

67 Hans Poelzig. Apartment house, Breslau, Menzelstrasse, 1907–8. Plan.

68a Hans Poelzig. Apartment houses in Breslau, 1908-12.

68b Hans Poelzig. Group of apartment houses in Breslau, Menzelstrasse, corner of Wölffstrasse, 1908–12.

69 Albert Gessner. Apartment house, Berlin-Charlottenberg, ca. 1905.

70 Hans Poelzig. Lauterbach house. Elevation.

71 Hans Poelzig. Lauterbach house, Breslau, 1906–8.

(Figs. 70, 71). It looks like two houses symmetrically arranged; the continuous wall in the middle also suggests this. One does, however, notice certain differences between this house and the adjacent buildings: In the central part, the windows are different in different stories. The large third-story terrace also distinguishes this particular house. Still, it does not look like any of Poelzig's one-family houses of the same period. I believe that Poelzig did not wish to interrupt, more than necessary, the unity of the group.

1911 Block of shops and offices in Junkernstrasse, Breslau

People have repeatedly compared this building with the columnar buildings of Messel and his successors, and have stressed that Poelzig showed a great degree of originality in going against the verticality fashionable at the time and making this building more horizontal, with each floor constituting a layer (Figs. 72, 73). The comparison is not quite fair, since the building in Junkernstrasse is not a department

72 Hans Poelzig. Office building in Breslau, Junkernstrasse, 1911.

73 Alfred Messel. Department store, Wertheim, Berlin, Leipzigerplatz, 1896–1906.

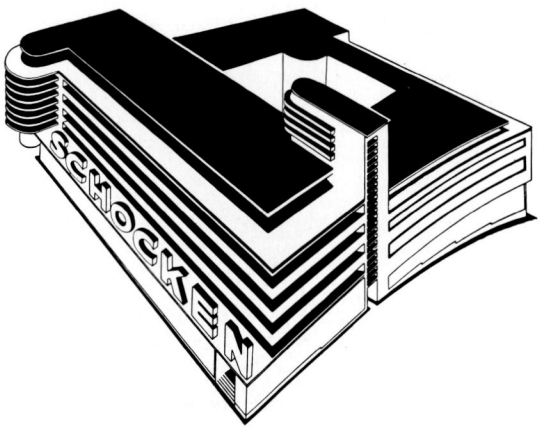

74 Erich Mendelsohn. Schocken department store, Stuttgart, 1926–28. Perspective.

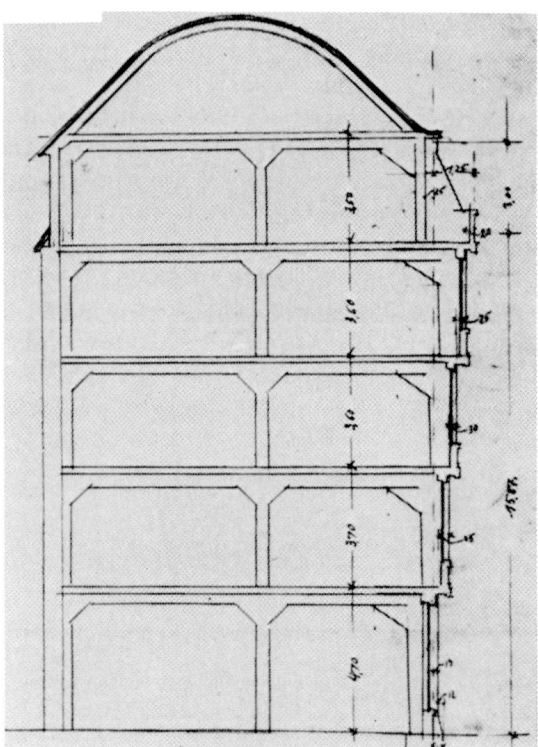

75 Hans Poelzig. Office building in Breslau, Junkernstrasse. Section.

store but an office building. It was legitimate to treat the department-store building as a whole, since goods were sold on all the floors, which were connected by spacious atriums. The office block, on the other hand, consists of independent offices on separate floors. No other building built before 1918 expresses this fact as clearly as this one. Whether the horizontality seen in Mendelsohn's work could have been inspired by this building is another topic (Fig. 74). Strictly speaking, it is not true, because Mendelsohn designed even his department stores horizontally, with strip windows in each story. In the twenties, the horizontal became a formal principle, if not to say a fashion, just as the vertical had been before the war.

The office building in Breslau is remarkable for another reason: It is made of reinforced concrete. Poelzig was trying to introduce this new method of construction into architecture. He obviously had traditional half-timbered buildings in mind, which, of course, are also framed structures. Over the ground floor, each of Poelzig's three upper stories projects slightly over the one below and the fifth floor recedes behind a shallow continuous gallery. Incidentally, the section through the building, which Heuss illustrates, and which is also shown here, is not accurate (Fig. 75). It does not show the strip window in the attic story, and on the gallery floor it shows slightly recessed columns, which Poelzig had considered using as a transition. Fortunately they were not built.

Poelzig adds consoles to the columns beneath the projecting floors. Their purpose is purely aesthetic; they have nothing to do with the concrete structure. They cannot be seen on the section. Together with the cantilevering of the stories, they are intended to bring the new structural system into the historical order. They mark this building as being pre–First World War. Its logical consistency, and the modesty of the aesthetic means used to link it to tradition, mark it as a Poelzig building. It is the only building of its kind built at the time.

1903–6 Extension to the town hall in Löwenberg (Silesia)

In the preceding chapter, I pointed out that the design of Poelzig's extension to the old town hall in Löwenberg was closely related to his houses and particularly to the one built at the same time (1904) for the Exhibition of Applied Art in Breslau (Figs. 76–78; see Figs. 9, 35, 30, 32, 33). Poelzig blends this new building in with the old by continuing the arcades of the old corner building, with its Renaissance gable, along to his new entrance building. The way it actually was built may make it seem a little artificial, since the area beneath the terrace is empty. On the plan he has marked "market hall" but that does not seem very convincing. There is an older version of the ground-floor plan that has three shops beneath the terrace. The arcades are even continued around the new entrance building, although there the simple masonry pillars are replaced by columns with very strangely shaped capitals, which were, perhaps, created in collaboration with the head

76 Hans Poelzig. Extension of town hall, Löwenberg (Silesia), 1903–6.

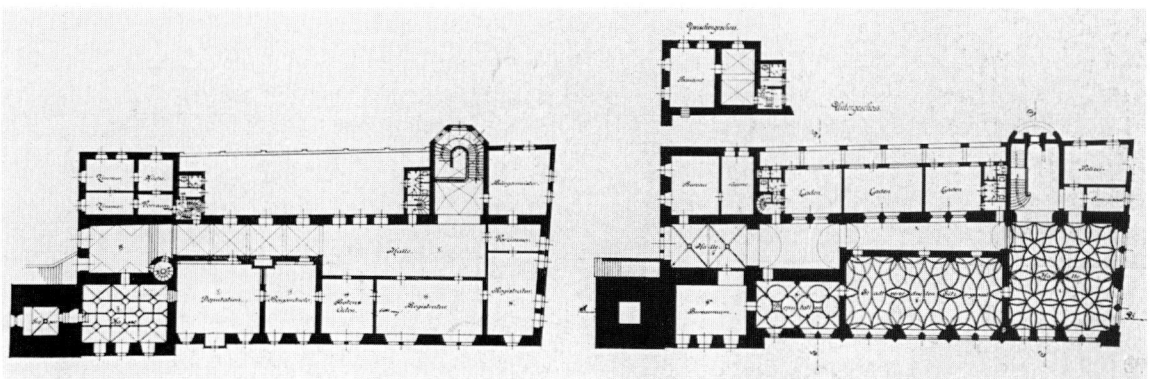

77 (left) Hans Poelzig. Extension of town hall, Löwenberg. Entrance.

78 (above) Hans Poelzig. Extension of town hall, Löwenberg. Plans of ground floor and first floor.

of one of the workshops. The extension to the town hall is the best example — and I fear one of the few examples — of the close cooperation between the architect and the head of one of the teaching workshops (and the students) that Poelzig, both as an architect and as director of the school, believed so important.

1915 Franciscan monastery near Glatz (Silesia), project

This design for a monastery actually looks more like a public building than does the Löwenberg town hall, or at least Poelzig gave it a much more impressive appearance with columns, pilasters, a tower, a striking semicircular entrance building (compare this with the modest semirotunda in Löwenberg — yet in this design there may be an element reminiscent of Löwenberg), and as a culmination the grandiose chapel at the end of the building (Figs. 79 – 81;

79 Hans Poelzig. Franciscan monastery at Glatz (Silesia), 1915, project. Perspective view.

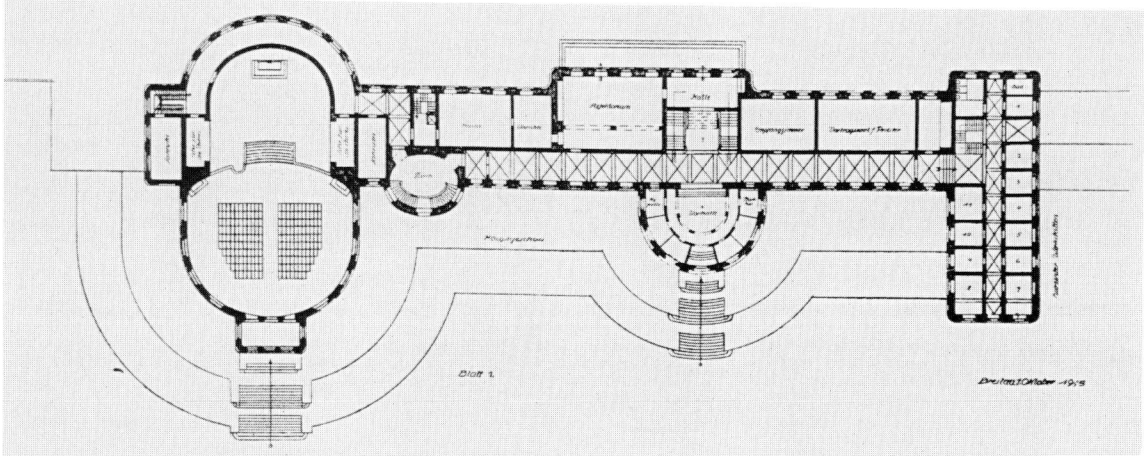

80 Hans Poelzig. Franciscan monastery at Glatz. Plan.

81 Hans Poelzig. Franciscan monastery at Glatz. Perspective sketch.

82 Hans Poelzig. "Werdermühle," factory planned for an island in the Oder River at Breslau, 1906–8, project.

see Figs. 9, 35, 76–78). It is surprising that the Franciscans would have wanted an impressive building. (Or could it be that they did not want it?)

Let us be frank; it is an unsuccessful scheme. It bears the stamp of the time, a style that even Poelzig had occasionally adopted following his work for the festival of the centenary of the Wars of Liberation (1813–1913) in Breslau, when he had used a kind of Doric column (see Figs. 121, 122, 124–129). By "the stamp of the time" I mean a new classicism—it has mockingly been called Neo-Biedermeier—to which many architects, most architects one could say, fell prey shortly before the outbreak of the war. This is true even of Hermann Muthesius, the English country house architect. There was a theory about this Neo-Classicism, both in Germany and in England, the birthplace of the country house. In Germany, Friedrich Ostendorf wrote in his *Sechs Bücher vom Bauen* (Six

Books about Architecture) that there had been no good residential buildings since the French *dixhuitième,* and that he saw no reason not to make reference to this good tradition.[2] In England, Geoffrey Scott wrote *The Architecture of Humanism,* in which he classified Renaissance and Baroque as the apogee of European architecture and the theories and practices of the nineteenth century as "fallacies."[3] Both made a firm stand against the modern architecture of the time—country house architecture—and both were successful. Even the protagonists of the country house movement, Voysey and Muthesius, were influenced. Voysey showed it by subscribing to a sort of Gothic, an architecture influenced by style, that had never until then been seen in his simple country houses. Muthesius showed it by starting to design in a Neo-Baroque style(!). It is evident in the design for the Franciscan monastery that even Poelzig could not quite escape the pervading atmosphere of the time. As if in an attempt to find his true self again, he designed the interior of the chapel as a sombre vault and succumbed to his obsession with semicircular niches and windows—a true orgy of semicircles. Incidentally, I can find absolutely no connection between the interior and exterior in the sketches of this building. Just one thing: A second look makes clear that the outside of the building is typically Poelzig (the second roof on the long building, the stepped design in the chapel composition).

Even so, it cannot be said that the parts of the building belong together. It is indeed a bad scheme, that reveals a crisis in Poelzig's work at this time. Here, as elsewhere, he has tried to achieve more than was asked for in the program.

1906–8 Werdermühle (factory) on Oder Island in Breslau, project

Theodor Heuss points out that the Werdermühle was the very first modern factory ever designed (Fig. 82; see Figs. 38–41). Behrens did not build his first factory for A.E.G., the Turbine Factory, until 1909 (see Figs. 19, 20, 22,

83 Peter Behrens. Montagehalle, A.E.G. factory building, Berlin, Hussitenstrasse, 1911–12.

84 Peter Behrens. A.E.G. small-motors factory, Berlin, Voltastrasse, 1911.

23), and his other buildings for A.E.G. were not completed before 1912 (Figs. 83, 84). Heuss writes:

The engineer had in fact asked Poelzig to provide the customary decorative exterior for the building complex, for which the inner planning was already completed. Nevertheless, he obviously was impressed by the energy of the design and continued to support it when Poelzig placed the two massive cubes, in dark brick with a granite base, next to each other. Their main characteristics were their rounded corners, the narrow rim used to give simple emphasis to the upper edge of the building, and two, slightly cantilevered, large bays in steel frame construction....And yet, as Poelzig later recounts, with a certain amount of bitterness, the design finally met with opposition from the mayor of Breslau. The eye and the imagination were not yet prepared for something of this sort. Evidently a private experiment, of the kind the A.E.G. would undertake in the years to come with Peter Behrens, was needed before something new could be ventured.[4]

Had it been built, the Werdermühle would have represented the beginning of a new approach to industrial buildings which was later to be put into practice in Luban.

Poelzig himself described what attracted architects to building factories:

Those very artists who, because they had rejected the use of historic architectural styles for official buildings, were barred from working on so-called prestige buildings, turned to industrial architecture....

We ... were all positively craving for a field as yet untilled, where there were no preconceived ideas. People had become accustomed at the time to seeing churches in the Gothic style, synagogues looking Oriental, post offices in the German Renaissance style, and museums and civil service buildings in a kind of Italian Renaissance style. For court buildings the Baroque normally used in monasteries was mostly adopted.

Every attempt to make a stand against this had failed and industrial architecture alone represented the line of least resistance, a field that was all the more readily left to us as it seemed to be of no importance for official architecture.[5]

85   Hans Poelzig. Chemical factory at Luban near Posen, 1911.

86   Hans Poelzig. Chemical factory at Luban.

1911–12 Chemical factory in Luban (Posen)

First, a personal remark. It was a long time before I recognized Poelzig's factory in Luban as architecture. And this was in the 1920s when I was a student of architecture. I found Behrens's factories both daunting and fascinating. This impression was formed by the way highly modern elements of factory architecture — large windows and equally large unbroken surfaces of brick — were lent an air of overwhelming authority by references to antiquity: the "tem-

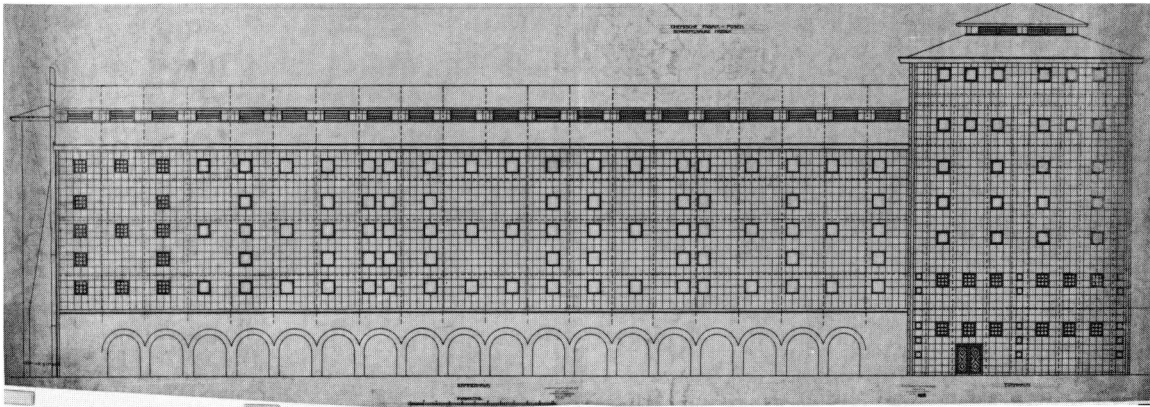

87 Hans Poelzig. Chemical factory at Luban. Elevation of the building shown in Figure 86. The ground-floor arcade is vaulted. The stories above are of "Prüss" construction, that is, the wall is not load-bearing.

88 Hans Poelzig. Chemical factory at Luban. The stepped-up building shows "Prüss" construction (non-load-bearing). The three-story building in front shows a load-bearing brick wall; the semicircular window arches are vaulted.

89　Hans Poelzig. Chemical factory at Luban. Again, one can distinguish both "Prüss" walls and solid brick walls. The small building in the foreground is covered with slate.

90　Hans Poelzig. Chemical factory at Luban. The smaller of the two stepped gables.

ple" of the Turbine Factory (see Figs. 19, 20, 22, 23), the colossal portico of the small-motors factory in Voltastrasse (see Fig. 84). It was impossible to ignore these factories. It was, however, possible for the eye trained only on these buildings to ignore the factory in Luban (Figs. 85–90; see Figs. 24, 25, 42).

That is why I find it all the more remarkable that some critics in the prewar years did recognize the significance of this factory. The yearbook of the Deutsche Werkbund for 1913, entitled *Art in Industry and Commerce,* published nine illustrations of Luban.[6] And the other remarkable thing is that the client placed his full confidence in the architect and gave him a free hand to act as he liked. Walter Curt Behrendt, a well-known critic, wrote in 1913:

The major commission for the chemicals factory in Posen gave [Poelzig's] talent the opportunity to find its full expression and set free latent power....If one compares this work with similar achievements by Peter Behrens, one notices in the certainty of his feeling for structures and in his highly developed sense of the sculptural quality of the architectural form the superiority of the academic [that is, the architect who has studied his subject at university—Au.] over the self-taught painter-architect who thinks only in two dimensions.[7]

Compared to the Werdermühle project (see Figs. 38–41, 82), where arcades with columns and capitals with Romanesque overtones are still found, Luban has very few references to traditional architecture. Here only a few "quotations" remain: simple arcades and crow-stepped gables. But, as I pointed out in Chapter 2, even these gables seem a little forced; they do not fit in with the formal language of the factory and warehouse.

As I said, it took some time before I understood that this was industrial architecture and in fact *better* than that of Behrens, simply *because* it is less stunning. The Luban factory is one of Poelzig's major works and some critics consider it to be his best.

1913 Römergrube coal mine in Rybnik (Upper Silesia), project

This project bears comparison with the Upper Silesia Tower in Posen (Fig. 91; see Figs. 26, 27, 93–98). Both projects have narrow steel frame-

91 Hans Poelzig. "Römergrube," mine at Rybnik (Silesia), 1913.

92 Hans Poelzig. "Annagrube," mine at Pschow (Silesia), 1913–15.

work; at Rybnik the members are even closer together than in Posen, and the diagonal crosses are used decoratively, particularly in the tower. In both projects the overall form of the buildings is very striking. These three works—Luban (Figs. 24, 25, 42, 85–90), the Posen tower, and Rybnik—show no trace of the mannerism that was becoming evident at the time, even in factory architecture. This, incidentally, was not just a result of Behrens's influence. The captains of industry wanted their factories to be impressive; Behrens himself speaks of the advertising effect of factory buildings of this kind. To achieve this, antique elements were employed or the vertical emphasis that dominated department store design was adopted. It cannot be said that Poelzig was totally immune to all this; we will look next at a building (the Annagrube at Pschow) that, compared with the three described above, can be called fashionable. These three, however, are *essentially* Poelzig.

1913–15 Annagrube coal mine in Pschow (Upper Silesia)

The Annagrube is without doubt an excellent industrial building: powerful, unequivocal, corporeal, and absolutely exemplary in its use of brick (Fig. 92; see Fig. 45). But here the striving for "architecture" is discernible; the admirable independence of Poelzig's designs for industrial buildings is certainly not as evident in this building.

1911 Upper Silesia Tower at the Industrial Exhibition in Posen

Although it was first used exclusively as an exhibition building (even when the restaurant was later replaced by the water tank that originally had been planned, the lower rooms were still used for exhibitions), this tower can be called an industrial building. It is famous as the Posen Water Tower (Figs. 93–98; see Figs. 26, 27). The exhibition rooms are dominated by the tower structure, which is clearly displayed. It is a steel-frame structure through and through; the main columns are also part of a steel frame.

74 Hans Poelzig: Reflections on His Life and Work

93 (top) Hans Poelzig. Upper Silesia Tower at the industrial exhibition, Posen, 1911.

94 (above) Hans Poelzig. Upper Silesia Tower. Distant view.

95 (right) Hans Poelzig. Upper Silesia Tower. Restaurant at the top of the tower.

96 Hans Poelzig. Upper Silesia Tower. The staircase.

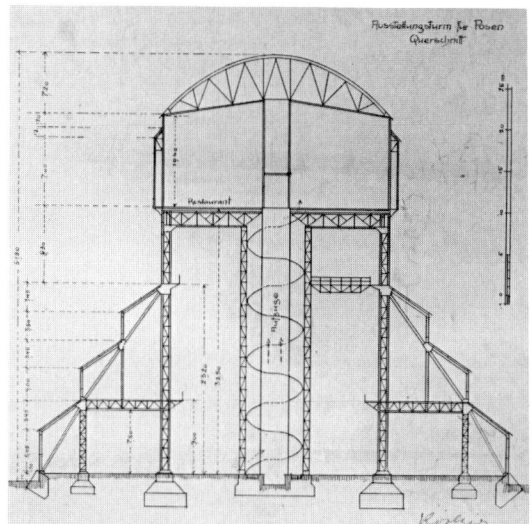

97 Hans Poelzig. Upper Silesia Tower. Section.

98 Hans Poelzig. Upper Silesia Tower. Exhibition space. The steel construction is clearly shown.

One gets the impression that the structure is explaining itself everywhere in splendid detail: Everything is "said." Only once is there any exaggeration—in the design of the staircase. The brackets certainly did not need to be so massive, nor did the core of the newel, which is in fact a waterpipe. The staircase is Baroque in character, and its very contrast to the small-scale structure of the building makes it impressive.

1908 Klingenberg (Saxony) dam

The project was a challenge to Poelzig's expressive imagination, inspiring him to depict the resistance of the wall to the pressure of the water (Fig. 99). He does this in the central section, which grows out of the sloping wall, straightens up, and continues over the top edge of the wall. This emphasizing of the central section has no technical justification, and in the dam as built it is weaker than Poelzig envisaged in his original drawings.

It is no surprise to find the beloved rounded arch in this project. The niches indicate the thickness of the wall. Here everything really is representation—symbol, one could say—so it is legitimate to say that the scheme for Klingenberg is a step toward Poelzig's most expressive designs of the Breslau period, the water tower project for Hamburg and the Bismarck Memorial in Bingerbrück. Poelzig never denied himself expression; it was his passion. It is possible to differentiate, however, between those works of his Breslau period that exaggerated this and those that moderated it. Klingenberg belongs to the first category, Luban to the second. Today I am inclined to prefer Luban.

Ca. 1910 Water tower in Hamburg, project

The water tower is the apotheosis of two earlier projects (Figs. 100–102). It can be seen how the niches are getting deeper, and the impression that the upper part with the water tank is *being supported* becomes increasingly strong. The

99 Hans Poelzig. Klingenberg Dam (Saxony), 1906. Perspective presentation.

emotional force of the design is undeniable as is the obsession with powerful walls, which could be interpreted as the yearning for a time when the architect was still allowed to build such wonderfully strong walls. Poelzig was not the only architect who had problems with the fact that technology was increasingly dematerializing buildings. Gottfried Semper had already pointed out that the beauty of Egyptian granite statues was somehow connected with the difficulty of forming and smoothing this hard stone with primitive tools. The effort that went into the work process is evident in the finished work. But what happens, asks Semper, now that we are able to cut granite like "bread and cheese"?[8] Around the turn of the century van de Velde was also concerned with this question. He too was of the opinion that each step forward taken by technology made it possible to dematerialize the building further. He was in favor of this development. But iron architecture was for him the limit; he called it a travesty of architecture.[9] Since Semper, who was strictly against showing the structural iron, various theoreticians, including John Ruskin, Cornelius Gurlitt, and Hermann Muthesius, had been waging an "iron dispute." Walter Gropius was still involved in it and wrote in the

78 Hans Poelzig: Reflections on His Life and Work

100 Hans Poelzig. Water tower for Hamburg, ca. 1910, project.

101 Hans Poelzig. Water tower for Hamburg. Second version.

1912 yearbook of the Deutsche Werkbund:

A broad wooden beam carried on two thin steel supports is actually structurally sufficient but the aesthetically sensitive eye is offended by the lack of balance between the element supported and those that are supporting it, because the strength of steel is invisible and to the eye these steel supports appear to be inadequate.[10]

The structural form, Gropius says, is different from the art form. Poelzig wanted to make the structural form into art form. He said so and he practiced what he preached in buildings such as the Posen tower. That does not change the fact that dematerialization went against his instinct, and he often simply could not resist designing strong walls. He even made walls strong that had to take only small loads.

But even at this time there were already architects who drew the opposite conclusion. In 1913 Max Taut submitted a competition design for a water tower in Nauen (Figs. 103, 104). It was a reinforced concrete construction. Although in the first scheme the concrete frame is visible, it has a wall around it. The wall is abandoned in the final scheme.

Poelzig at Work: Breslau 1904–1916   79

102 (above) Hans Poelzig. Water tower for Hamburg. Third version.

103 (top right) Max Taut. Water tower at Nauen, 1913, competition design. First version.

104 (bottom right) Max Taut. Water tower at Nauen, competition design. Second version.

1910 Bismarck Memorial in Bingerbrück, project

Poelzig's competition design for a memorial to mark Bismarck's one hundredth birthday was not a simple monument (Figs. 105–107; see Fig. 50). That was in the spirit of the competition brief, which had called for a symbolic building, not a freestanding statue of Bismarck. Poelzig combined the monument with a stadium, which was however not as large as modern sports complexes. His memorial was conceived spatially. The stadium was in the lower part, leaning against the hill; a broad staircase in three flights led up to a courtyard —entered between broad towers—in the center of which was a statue of Bismarck. The courtyard was to be used for ceremonial occasions. The architecture, especially the colossal stepped pillars and round-arched niches in the walls, recalls the project for a water tower in Hamburg that dates from approximately the same time (see Figs. 100–102). It even surpasses it in the dramatic force of its deep walls. This was the first version.

The project occupied Poelzig greatly; it suited his sense of drama, which found expression in the strong walls articulated by rounded niches. There is, however, a second version that draws together the two parts of the first one (see Fig. 107). They are now of the same height, and the stadium occupies the whole building. The wall to the valley is one story higher and is flanked by two towers. The whole complex is most striking when seen from the Rhine Valley below (see Fig. 105). But the most remarkable thing about this second version is its formal language: The niches and round arches have disappeared, the wall and even the towers are treated like a sculpture with rounded abutments close together, tapering toward the top. They are closest together on the towers, where they in fact touch. These forms are unprecedented; it is as if Poelzig, having tried out so many variations on the deep arched niche, a historic Roman architectural form, had found his own appropriate expression for the overwhelmingly powerful wall.

We will see that he adopts it again in 1921 in a design for a bank in Dresden, which is a less

105 Hans Poelzig. "Bismarck Memorial" at Bingerbrück-am-Rhine, 1911, competition design. First scheme.

106 Hans Poelzig. "Bismarck Memorial." First scheme, model.

107 Hans Poelzig. "Bismarck Memorial." Second scheme.

108 Hans Poelzig. Bank building, Dresden, 1921, project.

appropriate building for it (Fig. 108). This design dates from that period of his work which is termed Expressionist. The Bismarck Memorial was also felt to be Expressionist. Poelzig's project had less chance of success than that of Wilhelm Kreis. In any case, nothing came of the intention to build a memorial at Bingerbrück. Nevertheless, the project occupies an important place in Poelzig's *oeuvre*. Reference to historical forms is abandoned, the unheard of is ventured.

1909 Bridge Schlossbrücke in Königsberg (Kaliningrad), project

The bridge is a structural form that always interested Poelzig, but incidentally not just him: The bridge became a focus of interest at the time because in the late nineteenth century architects had been denied any influence on the design of bridges. The bridge was the engineer's domain. The architect was simply commissioned to fit the pylons out with some kind of stylistic form. The architect, said Poelzig, was asked "simply to put a decorative finish on any basic form, not to think through a project artistically from first principles."[11]

What Poelzig wanted the architect to be allowed to do often exceeded his capabilities, and

109 Hans Poelzig. Bridge proposed for castle at Königsberg (Kaliningrad), 1909, project.

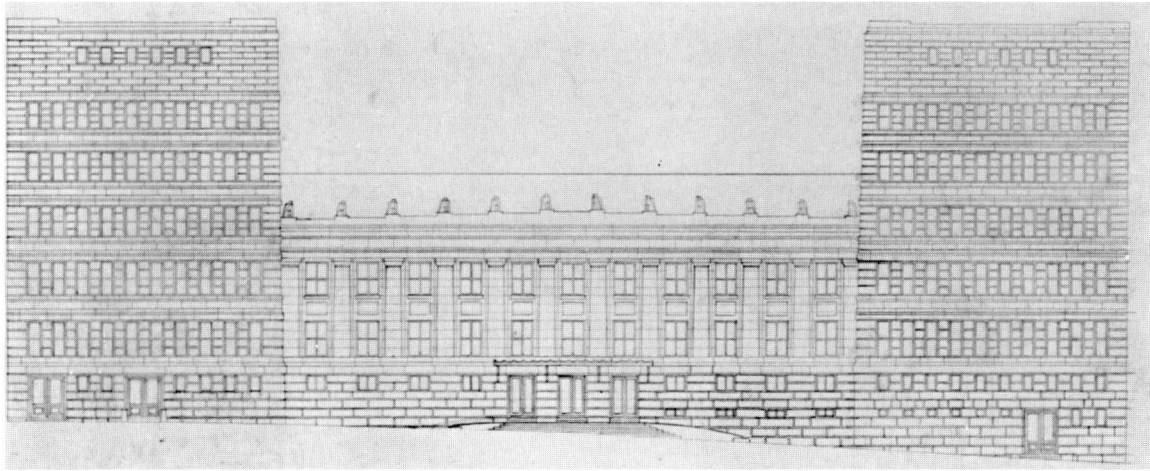

110 Hans Poelzig. German Embassy in Washington, 1910, project.

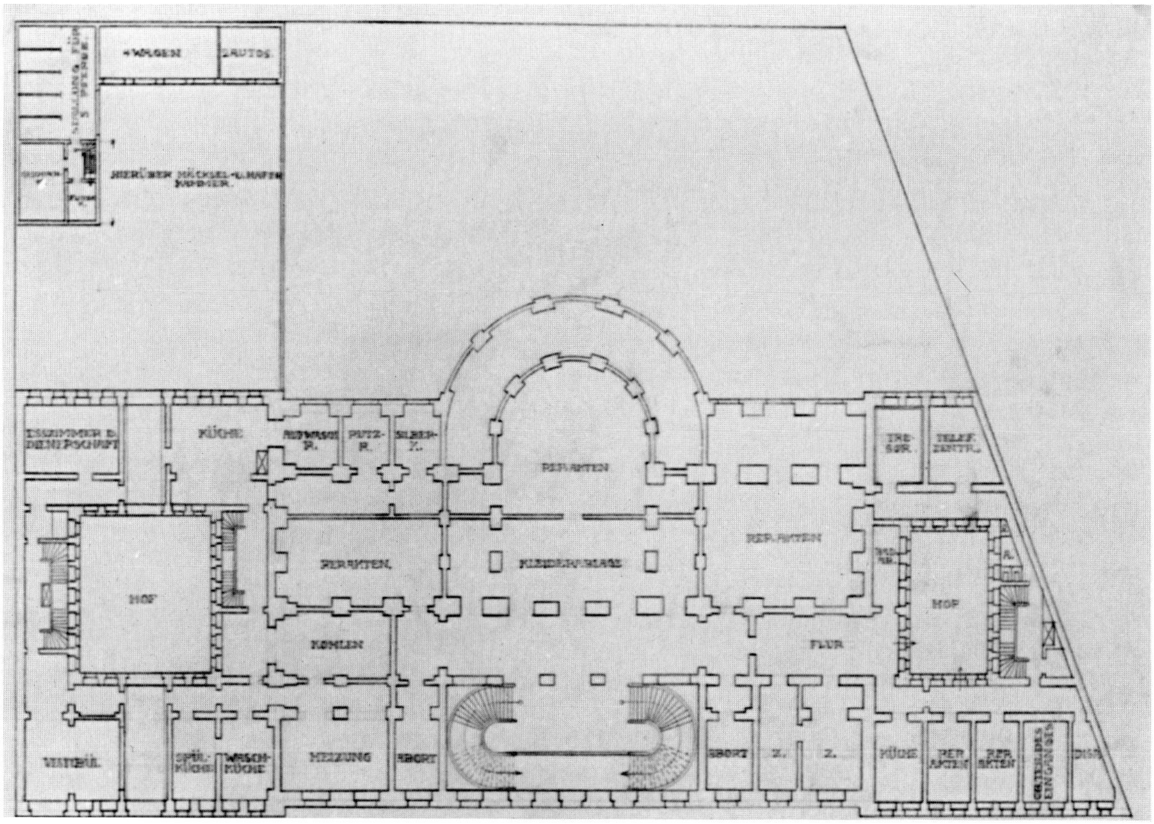

111 Hans Poelzig. German Embassy in Washington. Plan.

Poelzig himself got things quite wrong in some of his bridge designs. This was the case with some of his steel bridges over the Rhine, designed in 1928 and 1929 in conjunction with the firm of Gollnow & Sons. Poelzig saw the Königsberg Palace Bridge as a technical sculpture, with the stress on the word *sculpture* (Fig. 109). The form of the pylons is not technical. I find the bridge an unqualified success as a sculpture—note the gentle transition between the flight of steps for pedestrians and the pylon to the bank.

1910 Embassy in Washington, competition design

The competition design for the German embassy in Washington is an outsider in Poelzig's *oeuvre* (Figs. 110, 111). It was done at a time of distinguished embassy designs and buildings. Compare Peter Behrens's embassy in St. Petersburg (1911–12; Fig. 112), and it can be said in Poelzig's favor that his design is more modest. The colonnade does not oppress the building; both side wings, with their low stories with office and living accommodations, hold their own. By far the greatest part of the facade is the rustic wall with small windows, more "Florentine" than ancient, with the side "towers" that protrude only slightly in front of the rusticated base of the official part of the building forming virtually a single plane with it. I see this coherently uniform quality as the greatest virtue of the project; this, and not the Doric semicolumns, which are not even semicolumns for they too recede into the plane, was intended to make the greatest impression. A building type which is not exactly congenial has been treated in Poelzig's own special way.

1912 Royal Opera House in Berlin, competition design

The Royal Opera House competition had a complicated history and then came to nothing. In 1909 the site was chosen, on Königsplatz, opposite the Reichstag building where the victory

112 Peter Behrens. German Embassy in St. Petersburg, 1911–12.

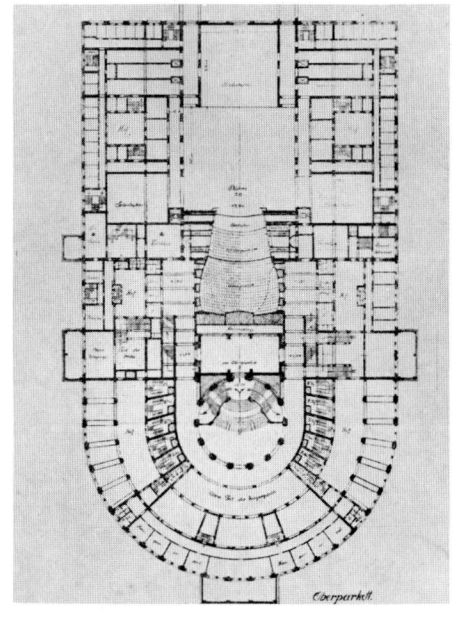

113 Hans Poelzig. Opera house in Berlin. Plan.

114 Hans Poelzig. Opera house in Berlin, 1912, competition design. Presentation drawing.

115 Hans Poelzig. Opera house in Berlin. Page from his sketchbook.

column commemorating Bismarck's three wars then stood. That was a very official site in the city of Berlin, capital of the German Reich. In the 1920s a much more modest opera house known as the Krolloper was actually opened on this site.[12] In 1910 a competition was held with only eight participants. In 1912 a second invited competition was held, but then finally it was opened up to all German architects.

The opera house designs were published by Hans Schliepmann, and his book is a document of its time.[13] Like the designs for the Bismarck Memorial and the Washington embassy, all the schemes submitted were ostentatious. This was due partly to the building itself, partly to the highly official nature of the site, partly to the brief, and partly just to the period. The Prussian king, Friedrich Wilhelm IV, a man of culture, had made fun of Schinkel's theater, the Schauspielhaus, saying, "An excellent building! It even has a small theater in it." What would he have said about Poelzig's opera project of 1912 (Figs. 113–115)? It is pure Wilhelminism. The auditorium is quite small compared with the huge foyer spaces. Even Poelzig, who following Semper's example of making the stage and auditorium visible in the outer form of the building, only manages to make it *seem* visible. The middle of the large semicircle is not the auditorium but the pure circle of the stairwell. The "little theater" disappears behind it, lost in the mass of the building with its large foyer and fly tower. Poelzig did at least use Semper's first opera house in Dresden as a model (1835; Figs. 116, 117). All the other architects designed monumental facades. The better ones at least followed good examples. Bruno Möhring's opera house facade (Fig. 118) was inspired by Schinkel's museum (1823–26; Fig. 119); the only thing is that Schinkel's museum was not what was asked for here. (Incidentally, a slight hint of Schinkel's museum can be detected in the design of Poelzig's fly tower.) One of Poelzig's sketches shows clearly his idea of the exterior of the building, which is not a large, curved wall with half-columns but a wall folded or sculpted into segments (see Fig. 115).

116 Gottfried Semper. Dresden Opera House, 1835.

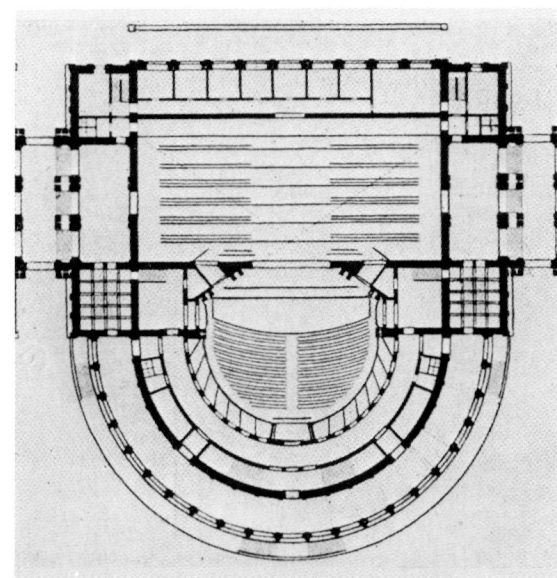

117 Gottfried Semper. Dresden Opera House. Plan.

118 Bruno Möhring. Opera house in Berlin, 1912, competition design. Presentation drawing.

119 Karl Friedrich Schinkel. "Old Museum," Berlin, 1823–26.

Moeller van den Bruck writes of Poelzig's scheme in his book published in 1916, *Der Preussische Stil* (The Prussian Style):

But not only the Classical consciousness has been reinstated [in the prewar years—Au.], Baroque elements also force their way onto the scene, the feeling not only for surface but also for the plastic quality of a building returns, and when Poelzig created his sumptuous design for the new Berlin Opera House, for this building which has both to serve the Muse and be prestigious, it seemed as if a link between Rococo and early Classicism, between Knobelsdorf and Schinkel, between Gluck and Mozart, had been forged; it was playful and dignified, joyful and quite wonderful, exactly the link that was needed here.[14]

That is a rather bombastic way of putting it. But we shall soon have the opportunity to see that the reference to the Baroque, and, indeed, maybe also the thought that Poelzig was trying to create a synthesis between the classical/Prussian and the Baroque consciousness, are not so farfetched after all.

1913 Buildings at the Centennial Exhibition in Breslau

The buildings for the exhibition held in Breslau in 1913 to commemorate the Wars of Liberation of 1813 were the last major commission that Poelzig accepted in Breslau; in fact, it was the largest of all his commissions there. He may not have been accustomed to work of this kind, because here he was not in charge but was playing second fiddle to Max Berg, the city architect of Breslau, who in his Jahrhunderthalle, or Centennial Hall (1913), built not only the largest concrete ribbed dome of the time—it had a diameter of 65 meters—but also the most beautiful concrete structure built before the First World War (Figs. 120, 121). Poelzig's exhibition buildings—particularly his garden with its pergola which is parabolic in plan, and the entrance gateway to the exhibition with its broad access avenue and the buildings that line it—all relate to the Centennial Hall (Figs. 122–129) and provide a wonderful setting for it.

A further difficulty was that Poelzig used reinforced concrete for the Historical Exhibition building (see Figs. 125–128). Unlike Berg, he felt obliged to have something in this concrete building as a reminder of the early nineteenth century, the time of the Wars of Liberation. Poelzig himself said about this:

This was because the exhibition building served to commemorate 1813 and was thus full of elements of antiquity *à la Empire* or *à la Schinkel*. But, as the building with its columns and piers was meant to be in tamped concrete, I tried to adapt the forms to this new method of construction.[15]

Whether that explains the particular form of his

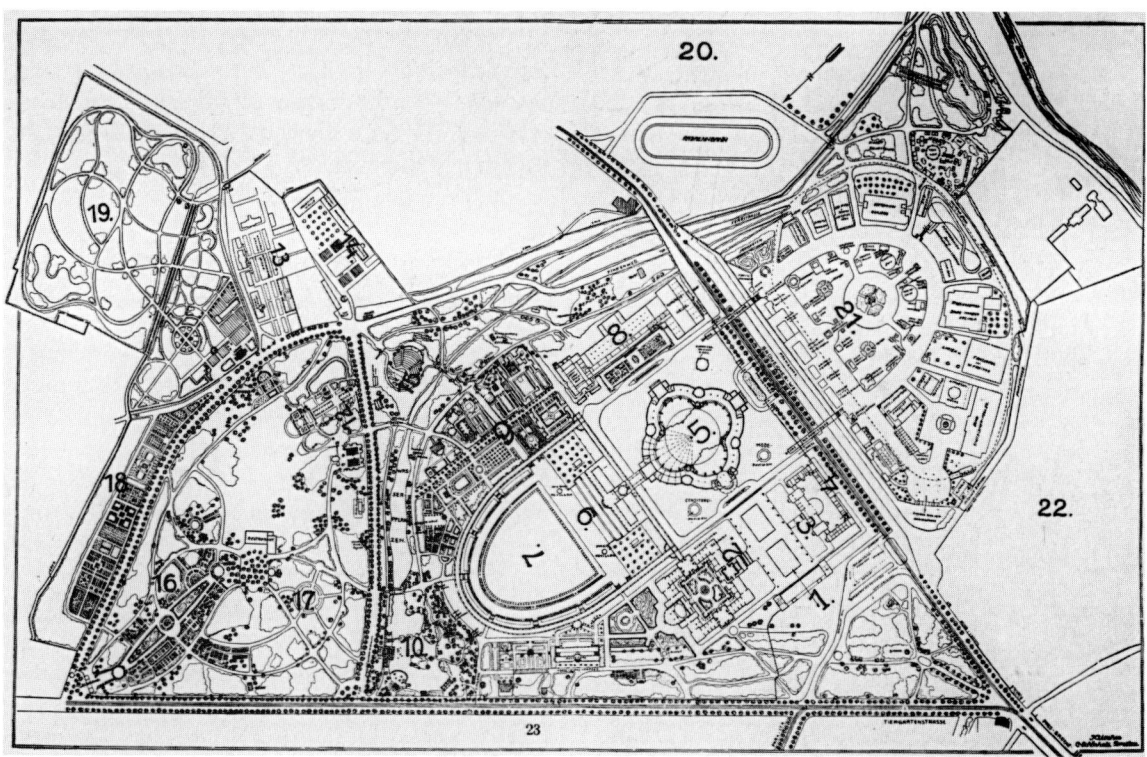

120 Max Berg. Centennial Exhibition, Breslau, 1913. Plan.

121 Max Berg. Jahrhunderthalle, Centennial Exhibition, Breslau, 1912–13. Interior before alterations.

122 Hans Poelzig. Pergola at Centennial Exhibition, Breslau, 1913. Presentation drawing. In background, Max Berg's Jahrhunderthalle.

Poelzig at Work: Breslau 1904–1916   89

123   Hans Poelzig. Entrance area, Centennial Exhibition, Breslau, 1913.

124   Hans Poelzig. Pergola at Centennial Exhibition, Breslau, 1913. In background, Poelzig's Historical Exhibition Building.

Poelzig at Work: Breslau 1904–1916   91

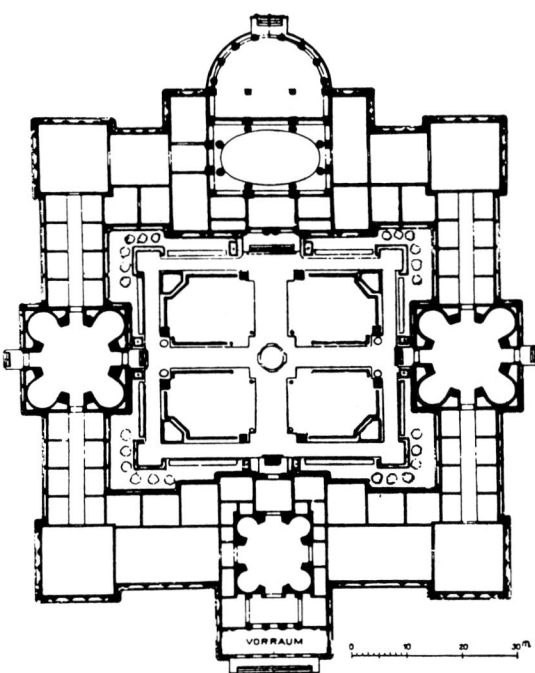

125   Hans Poelzig. Historical Exhibition Building, Centennial Exhibition, Breslau, 1913. Plan.

127   Hans Poelzig. Historical Exhibition Building. Courtyard. The columns are cast in concrete.

Doric columns, whether "Poelzig capitals" are easier to tamp than Greek Doric capitals would have been, I cannot say. I must confess that the idea of pouring concrete into decorative molds does not conform to the principle of concrete construction. Be that as it may, Poelzig succeeded in making his concrete columns very beautiful and very precise. The pergola with its paired columns is powerful enough (see Figs. 122, 124) and the room with the oval dome on eight columns must have been a pure delight (see Fig. 126).

As I went through Poelzig's other works in the Breslau period I found that he was actually quite indifferent to style-specific forms. Particularly before 1913 he avoided using any forms in his buildings, even the Löwenberg town hall addition, that were too directly connected with any particular styles. Did the classical "atmosphere" of the time, which I mentioned in passing when discussing the design for a Franciscan monastery in Glatz, also leave its traces in Poelzig's work? It is possible. At any rate the Doric columns he used in 1913 in Breslau were never again found in his work.

People like to overlook the fact that Poelzig built quite a number of other buildings at the Breslau exhibition, which was a many-sided undertaking and by no means had the sole purpose of commemorating 1813. Quite a few of the buildings have astonishingly modern overtones; at first sight they look like buildings from the twenties.

A comparison is irresistible: The Breslau Centennial Exhibition was more modern than the Werkbund Exhibition that took place the following year in Cologne and at which there were a small number of buildings, such as Bruno Taut's Glass Pavilion (see Fig. 12) and

126   (left) Hans Poelzig. Historical Exhibition Building. Interior.

92 Hans Poelzig: Reflections on His Life and Work

128 Hans Poelzig. Historical Exhibition Building. Exhibition room.

129 Hans Poelzig. "Rheingold" wine restaurant, Centennial Exhibition, Breslau, 1913.

Walter Gropius's office building and factory, which used a very new formal language; but the large majority of exhibition buildings in Cologne return to a more uncompromising classicism than Poelzig's, with his experiment with Doric columns in concrete. And the Cologne buildings were designed by the top names in architecture before the war: Peter Behrens, Theodor Fischer, Richard Riemerschmid, Bruno Paul, Hermann Muthesius. We will see Poelzig competing with a number of these architects in 1916 for the "House of Friendship" commission in Constantinople, and we will see that while *they* kept to their Neo-Classicism, Poelzig did not.

1913 Redesign of the central civic buildings of the town of Rüstringen near Oldenburg, urban design competition

This competition design occupies a special position in Poelzig's *oeuvre*. No similar project can be encountered for another fifteen years, until the scheme for the city center of an industrial

130 Hans Poelzig. Town hall square at Rüstringen (Wilhelmshafen), 1913, competition project. Left to right: girls' school, auditorium, covered market.

131 Hans Poelzig. Rüstringen project. Left to right: boys' school, town hall, girls' school.

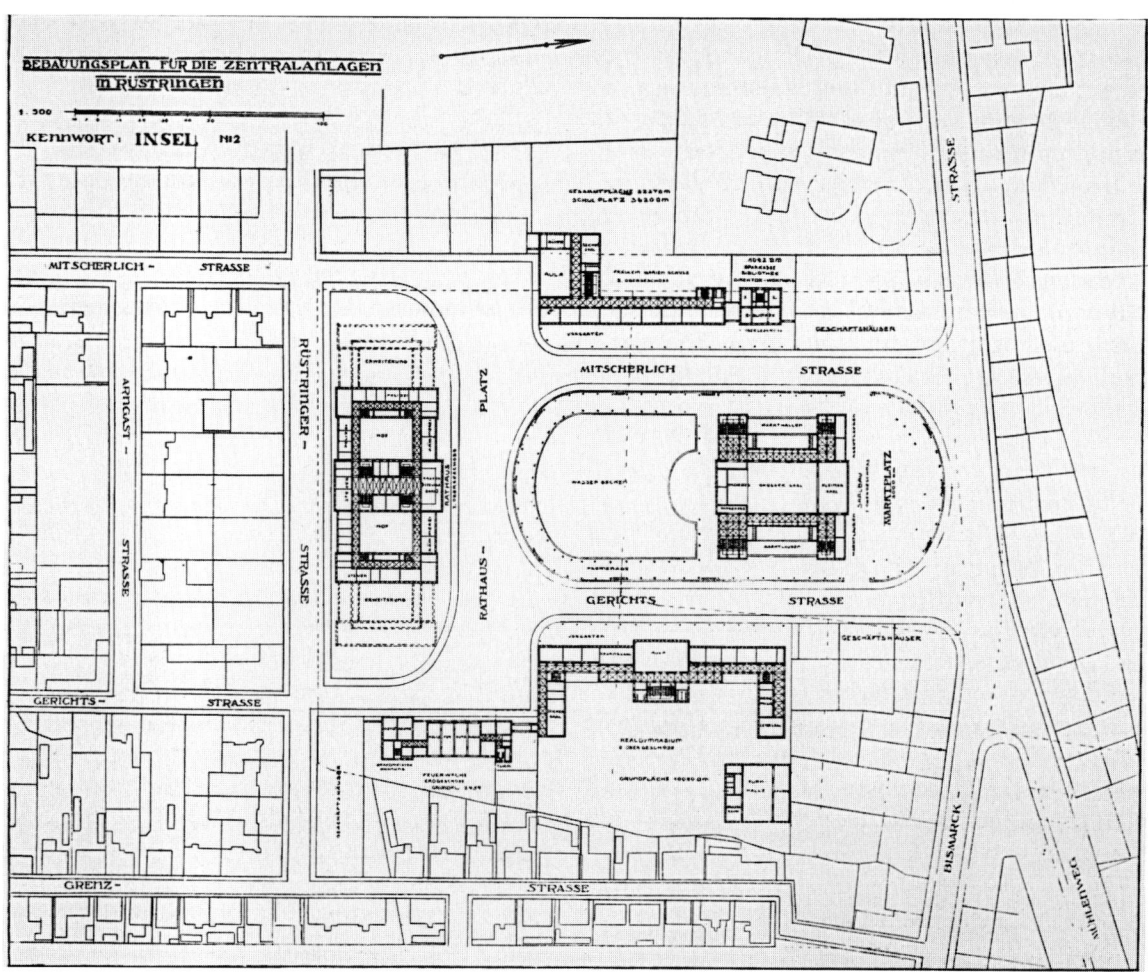

132 Hans Poelzig. Rüstringen project. General plan.

town, Hindenburg, in Upper Silesia (see Chapter 10, Fig. 275). There, too, the problem was to create artificially a city center for a rapidly expanding industrial and residential area. In Hindenburg, the industry in question was mining; in Rüstringen it was connected with the wartime fleet, whose port was Wilhelmshaven. Rüstringen was meant to be the center of the "united municipalities that surrounded in a wide radius the military and factory town of Wilhelmshaven," as described by Willy Hahn, the architect who wrote a comprehensive report about the competition.[16] In Hindenburg the town hall was to be surrounded by housing, but a theater also was to be built in the town center. The program for Rüstringen was more ambitious: In the new center a market hall was to be built next to the town hall; in addition, there were to be a large girls' school and a boys' school, a fire station, a savings bank, and a municipal hall for 1,000 to 1,200 people "with plenty of ancillary rooms" (Willy Hahn). An impossible program, but at the time, just before the outbreak of the war, it was obviously considered realistic, although the critical reporter Hahn does point out a difficulty: The spatial arrangements that the participating architects proposed would create the desired effect only if all these buildings were built immediately (which Hahn did not think seemed likely). For this reason a number of architects put some of the buildings called for in the brief in the side streets. It was a limited competition and some of the best-known architects of the time were invited: Among them, besides Poelzig, there was Martin Wagner, who, like the architects Sell and Hans Bernoulli from Basle, worked at the time in the Rüstringen town planning office. Some of the schemes were picturesque, following Sitte's famous book on urban design "according to its artistic fundamentals." These included a delightful scheme by the architects Lübbers and Dieter of Rüstringen, which had little squares, sight lines, and urban oases cut off from the traffic streets. Poelzig never had any time for this kind of urban design. He called it "designing with a camera." He, and Martin Wagner too, grouped all the municipal buildings that were stipulated in the competition brief around a large square in front of the town hall (Figs. 130–132). Poelzig placed the municipal hall opposite the town hall and behind the town hall he had a much smaller marketplace with the schools on either side of it. The plan is monumental in the classical sense. This is contradicted by the nonclassical character of the buildings: They have gables that give them a lively articulation, and in each building there is an alternation of very large main gables with a series of smaller ones. In order to further stress the unity of the architecture around the square, Poelzig gave all the buildings the same vertical emphasis, that is, the windows are all close together and the same distance apart. He returned to this vertical articulation in 1929 in the facade for Broadcasting House in Berlin (see Figs. 288, 289). But there it is only the main facade that has this kind of articulation, whereas in the Rüstringen scheme one encounters the same close-spaced vertical articulation in whichever direction one looks. That gives the whole scheme a certain stiffness, despite the large gables of the town hall, the boys' school, and the municipal hall. It may be part of the reason why this design by Poelzig has been forgotten. I did not know about it until Dieter Radicke drew my attention to it quite recently, and even he, the head of the Poelzig archive in the drawings collection of the Technische Hochschule, "only came across it the other day" (November 1987).

I remarked in connection with the design for a Franciscan monastery in Glatz (Silesia) of 1915 that around the outbreak of the war Poelzig's architecture was in a crisis that did not come to an end until 1916 with the Expressionist designs from his Dresden period. A glance at the Rüstringen scheme reaffirms this.

CHAPTER FOUR
A Final Word on Breslau

A FINAL WORD on Poelzig's time in Breslau. First of all this was the time just before the First World War, which, although I experienced it as a child, is not easy for me to recall now. It has slipped away from us.

The most important influence of this time on German architecture was the founding of the Werkbund. The Werkbund was protesting against a situation that is even more difficult for us to recall. Its members wanted this protest to bring about a brave new world and they were convinced that this was possible; after all, they thought, they were not asking for anything absolute or unheard of. What they were actually protesting against was the fact that there was no longer any connection between architecture and daily life. They wanted to reestablish this connection. In 1908, at the first meeting of the Werkbund after its foundation, the architect Theodor Fischer set a deadline for the completion of this task—eight years, very little time indeed.[1] The members of the Werkbund must have been very confident that it was possible for them to complete their chosen task in such a short time. It was not possible: The Werkbund still exists. It must be said, however, that at least one reason that they were prevented from reaping the full benefit of their efforts was the catastrophe that occurred in 1914, the catastrophe the founders of the Werkbund had not expected, or had not wanted to expect. As I have said elsewhere about the feeling of the time, "They were waiting for a catastrophe they did not really believe in."[2]

What I do remember very clearly, however, is the alienation of architecture from life, which the Werkbund was protesting against. As a child, all buildings seemed alien and hostile to me; they were clearly the work of specialists, architects as I later found out. These were people who devoted their time to mysterious things such as proportion, style, and ornament, and also to what was known as the quality of space. All these were things one had to approach slowly by study, contemplation, and gradual understanding. The house we lived in in Berlin during the first years of my life, a suburban villa with medieval overtones, left me with an impression of darkness and malaise. I found my parents' furniture, in the heavy style of the German Renaissance popular before 1900, even more sinister. The grandfather clock, which I regarded with a childlike horror and called the "stove clock," haunted me in nightmares so that I did not like going near it even in broad daylight. But, then, the light of day hardly managed to penetrate into the dark rooms where people at the time liked to sit, evidently finding them pleasant. I am recounting these memories to show what the Werkbund was

133 Hans Poelzig. House at Exhibition of Applied Art, Breslau, 1904. Kitchen, showing built-in furniture.

fighting against. A distaste for this kind of building can be found in all the writings of Hans Poelzig that date from this period. And it had a lot to do with the Werkbund.

The Werkbund was in fact extraordinarily successful. It was as if people had simply been waiting for something like it. That this was so is shown by the decision of the large Berlin company Allgemeine Elektrizitäts-Gesellschaft (A.E.G.) to appoint Peter Behrens as its general designer. This was in 1907, a few months before the Werkbund was founded in Munich. Quite independently A.E.G. arrived at conclusions similar to those of the Werkbund, and, what is more, the company was soon to recognize that good design pays off. This had become increasingly evident since the turn of the century. Factories, department stores, and businesses of every kind began to take an active interest in every aspect of design—display techniques, for example: how to present goods so that the customer would want to enter the shop. Trade and industry both discovered the commercial value of good design, which had to be straightforward, simple, and convincing— in a word, an advertisement for the company. The Werkbund adopted this point of view, either because it wanted to be accepted by the great powers of the time, trade and industry, or because its founders were truly convinced of its importance. Both suppositions are probably true. The Werkbund had such rapid success in

134 Hans Poelzig. Furniture suite, ca. 1910. At present in the possession of Fritz Stern, New York.

135 Hans Poelzig. Cabinet. In the possession of Fritz Stern, New York.

this respect that some of its members felt uncomfortable about it. This feeling came to a head in the Werkbund itself at the historic moment in July 1914 when Hermann Muthesius called upon the members at the Werkbund meeting to devote themselves to the development of "type-forms" rather than beautiful, artistically conceived individual articles. This was not surprising; it was completely consistent with the philosophy of the Werkbund, which would not have developed beyond William Morris, would not have taken the machine seriously in its ability to produce well-designed articles for everyday use, if it had not been serious about "type-forms." But when Muthesius went too far, applying his ideas about development of types to German exports, those members of the Werkbund who thought of themselves primarily as artists protested. One of the younger members, Bruno Taut, went so far as to propose the need for an "art dictator." He even named his choices: van de Velde and Poelzig.

And why Poelzig? Because he had not become involved in this side of the Werkbund work, the advertising side, as it were. Poelzig just paid attention to the one job at hand. Even if the job was furnishing a family kitchen, like the one at the Exhibition of Applied Art at Breslau, or designing furniture for more formal rooms, he would devote his attention to each individual piece (Figs. 133–136). It was truly custom-made work. It perfectly embodied the new simplicity, was as such Werkbund work, and yet it was tailored to the comfort and particular taste of the client, as can be seen in Poelzig's letters to Ludwig Pallat (discussed in Chapter 2).

Poelzig was known, furthermore, as one who never had ready-made solutions, derived from past experience. He always treated each job he undertook as something quite special. This may be seen in my general reflections on Poelzig and in the sections where I discuss his works. Heuss called upon Ferdinand Avenarius as an important witness, who had remarked on Poelzig's "astonishing versatility":

In an article in his *Kunstwart,* Avenarius wrote a very appropriate remark about Poelzig: "He saturates himself in each job," he said, to illustrate that no

136 Hans Poelzig. Furniture suite. In the possession of Fritz Stern, New York.

schema, no particular canon, no individual "Poelzig mark" forced uniformity on his work, but that its extremely rich variety grew and continues to grow out of his imagination and understanding, and from the wealth of forms he freely drew upon. Can this really be called an "astonishing versatility"?[3]

This "versatility," this ability to approach each job with completely new ideas, would seem to contradict Poelzig's preference for particular forms. We have seen how the arched window appears again and again in its elementary form as a semicircular window. The semicircle *is* a basic motif in Poelzig's feeling for form, or at least it was at that time. It has something to do with his sense of the weight of material and of the "building" in the archaic meaning of the word; after all, at a time when construction in steel had reached maturity and concrete construction was already in its early stages of development, with achievements such as Berg's Jahrhunderthalle (see Fig. 121), the heavy masonry wall and semicircular arch resisting its weight was a building form of the past. But, no matter what he might have *said*, Poelzig kept to this form. There arose grotesque contradictions between what he said and what he designed.

At the beginning of the war Poelzig's work had reached a limit, though on a few occasions he transcended it. He also grappled with the tendency toward Classicism that had emerged during the last years before the war (Centennial Exhibition at Breslau; see Figs. 122–129). He very nearly reached an impasse, as can be seen for example in his scheme for the monastery at Glatz (see Figs. 79–81). He managed, however, to get out of the impasse at least once, in the second project for the Bismarck Monument on the Rhine River, where for the first time entirely new forms appear (see Figs. 50, 105–107). He had a wealth of achievements behind him, buildings and projects whose culmination was probably the factory in Luban (see Figs. 24, 25, 42, 85–90). He enjoyed a great reputation. In 1916, when he turned his back on his beloved Breslau, to which he owed a great deal, he was ready for a new beginning.

Chapter Four: Documentation

Document 4

The essay "The Process of Fermentation in Architecture," which is one of the earliest known writings by Poelzig, was written for a particular occasion, the Exhibition of Applied Art in Dresden in 1906, which has been called the first Werkbund exhibition because this was when the subsequent founders of the Werkbund first met and considered forming an association of this kind. Poelzig's essay reflects the situation that led to the founding of the Werkbund: The eclecticism of the nineteenth century had been replaced, or at least interrupted, by the Jugendstil (Art Nouveau), which in turn had also proved to be a dead end. In Dresden the Jugendstil was still very present—van de Velde had exhibited one of his most unequivocal Jugendstil interiors. Poelzig praised these exhibits and, in particular, the "decorative skill of their creators." "Although," he continued, "it becomes equally obvious from both the good and the bad solutions that truthful architecture cannot be achieved with the resources of decoration alone."

Doc. 4*   Hans Poelzig, "Fermentation in Architecture," 1906 (abridged)

The buildings at the Dresden exhibition of arts and crafts in 1906 reflect the essence of the fermentation process which our architecture must still go through, the end of which is not yet in sight and whose products can at present hardly be discerned. The importance of architecture no longer lies in the church sector, nor do monumental buildings of a secular character have any decisive influence anymore. Economic issues dominate life in this

* Hans Poelzig, "Gärung in der Architektur. Das deutsche Kunstgewerbe," Munich, 1906. Reprinted in Ulrich Conrads, ed., *Programme und Manifeste zur Architektur des 20. Jahrhunderts,* Frankfurt and Berlin, 1964, pp. 10–13; English edition, *Programs and Manifestoes on 20th-Century Architecture,* Cambridge, Mass., 1971, pp. 14–17.

modern age. The people's and artist's involvement therefore is focused on architectural problems of an economic nature, be it the individual dwelling or the design of the city as a whole ...

For several decades the principle of external interpretation determined the attempts to design forms in quite different materials using a play of lines forced into a particular system—without paying any attention to scale and importance. Apart from the fact that it greatly restricts inventiveness, this schematized approach may not be harmful on a small scale, but applied to large objects, truly tectonic works, it produces monstrosities. A total absence of tectonic solutions followed ...

... It is a widespread and fundamental error of this time of fermentation that it often tries to force things to happen suddenly that in fact need whole epochs to develop and that external features are used to impart to individual pieces of work a touch of excellence. The artist is being distracted from what ought to be his main concern: to deal strictly and consistently with the task in hand in keeping with his temperament and abilities....

There now follows a very clear statement of Poelzig's own point of view—that the structural solutions of the past are indispensable and that the new structural systems should be treated analogously, so to speak. Poelzig expresses principles here to which he remained attached all his life.

We cannot reject the past when trying to solve the building problems of our time, or, rather, we can reject external features but not the work that went into solving tectonic problems in the past.

In spite of all the achievements and changes in structural engineering, most of the building materials are still the same and many of the structural systems of the past remain unsurpassed. We are bound to stand on the shoulders of our predecessors and if we start to experiment without this foundation, trying to develop everything from scratch, we deprive ourselves of our firmest footing.

And when tackling those tasks that the use of new building materials implies, only a detailed study of what is possible and good with traditional materials and tasks can enable us to see things clearly and give us the right kind of freedom....

The work of the architect is primarily the same as that of the engineer, and particularly today's architecture should never be illogical. However, we are all too often sentimental and operate romantically.... We are still seeking to a large extent only to rescue the mood of bygone epochs without considering of what avail they are to us....

Each truly tectonic form of building is essentially determined. It may be made attractive by ornament,... but first of all the essence of the building has to be found....

And the artist who approaches the design of elements of architectural composition only with considerations of external and decorative "features" is distracted from finding this pure core.

Housing is the first sector that is beginning to free itself, to articulate demands truly from within, demands that will give it authenticity and must on no account be ignored....

The new movement is carrying the banner of objectivity in the battle against traditional forms that have lost their meaning.... Objectivity in architecture is only possible on the basis of sound construction and a formal language derived from it.

Important buildings of a new kind can only be created in this way.

There is still confusion in the composition of our architectural language, which fails to recognize the essential. We are still pursuing fashionable affectations that after a very short time, having been vulgarized by imitations, are treated with contempt, while true architecture, which is the product of intensive intellectual effort on the part of the artist, offers the imitator little opportunity for plagiarism.

... It is high time to stop trying to create a style,... to demand instead nothing more than that the architect be remorselessly objective and, when he has clearly recognized the problem, that he think it through to the end with taste and care.

CHAPTER FIVE
Departure into the Unknown: Dresden 1916–1920

ON 12 FEBRUARY 1916 Poelzig wrote to Karl Schmidt, the founder and head of the Deutsche Werkstätten für Handwerkskunst (German Arts and Crafts Workshops), in Hellerau near Dresden, that he had "already started to gather moss in Breslau and would like to shake it off again." Schmidt drew the attention of the Dresden city council to Poelzig when they were looking for someone to fill the post of city architect.

Just a few words about Karl Schmidt: He had not only founded the furniture workshops—or, let's be honest, the furniture factory, with its name full of promise—and very soon made it into one of the most renowned factories for manufacturing the new German utility furniture, but he had also built accommodations around the factory for his master craftsmen, journeymen, and some of the workers. He had entrusted some of the best architects in the Werkbund with the planning of this village: Richard Riemerschmid of Munich did the master plan and designed most of the houses (Fig. 137); Heinrich Tessenow built some groups of workers' houses and a "School for Rhythmic Gymnastics" for Dalcroze which also had a few houses around it; Hermann Muthesius built houses—small villas—for the higher-ranking staff of the "Workshops." One of the special features of the planning was that in many cases the architects knew who was going to move into the houses and asked them to express their wishes, indeed, in very precise terms: whether, for example, they would like a kitchen that was just for cooking or one that could be used as a living room as well. The architects based their planning on these individual wishes, which often took the form of sketches. Karl Schmidt wanted to give the factory and the housing estate the appearance of a cooperative, as far as this was possible in a firm run on capitalist lines. It is difficult to estimate how successful he was. There is one extant document, the autobiography of a worker from Sudetenland called Wenzel Holek,[1] in which it becomes clear that the houses were too expensive for unskilled workers and that community spirit—which, says Holek, could be a wonderful thing—was something of a lost cause in Hellerau. There is also a document that comments on the high-sounding name of the factory: Hermann Muthesius, who held the Hellerau furniture in high esteem, kept his slides of it in a box marked "Dresden machine-made furniture" [*sic!*]. Karl Schmidt was one of the most important members of the Werkbund, and the misconceptions he clung to are not just endearing, they are worth taking note of, since for one thing they brought about actual changes in the world, and, secondly, it was these misconceptions that were

137 Richard Riemerschmid. Deutsche Werkstätten (German Arts and Crafts Workshops), Hellerau near Dresden, 1908.

the main characteristic of the Werkbund movement of the time and the whole reform movement with all its different facets. It was a time in which one could still have illusions—creative illusions.

So Karl Schmidt was in touch with Poelzig (which is not surprising) and suggested him as the new city architect in Dresden. Poelzig was not averse to the idea: New surroundings, new and, he hoped, greater possibilities for work were exactly what he needed. During the negotiations he set great store by being able to teach at the same time. But that was a difficult second job for a city architect. Poelzig held a course in design in Dresden but he did not have tenure. He found it difficult to live without teaching; it had always been part of his work and his life. But just how much he wanted the post in Dresden can also be deduced from the fact that he refused a much better financial offer from the Technische Hochschule in Berlin-Charlottenburg.

He was simply in a phase of high, if not to say feverish, productivity. Plans were drawn up for cemeteries, a hospital, a power station, development of the banks of the Elbe. There are sketches showing a planning scheme for a new district of the city of Dresden.

A museum complex was also planned. It was Baroque in layout—the influence of the Baroque city of Dresden—but nevertheless, looking at the main group, it was unmistakably Poelzig.

Poelzig went to Dresden with high hopes. He was to be disappointed. From a large number of projects the only thing that remains is one industrial building, or rather the extension to an existing building, the gasworks in Dresden-Reick (Figs. 138, 139). This represents the architect's confrontation with reinforced concrete construction. The collaboration with the engineer must have been good. These structures are wonderfully formed; the hand of the architect is clearly visible. It is like a response to the Doric columns of reinforced concrete from the Centennial Exhibition in Breslau in 1913 (see Figs. 124, 126, 127). Everything else remained in the design stage.

In Dresden Poelzig found himself in an unaccustomed situation. What disturbed him most was the official side of the work of a city architect, the never-ending meetings, which caused him to let out a great sigh, saying that he had rented his head to the people of Dresden, not his arse. In 1931 in a speech before the Bund Deutscher Architekten entitled "The Architect" (see Chapter 9, Doc. 9C), he still spoke of the difficulties of the architect in civil service. And from his work as an architect for the city of Dresden emerged, as I said, almost exclusively unbuilt projects. But these projects have entered the annals of architectural history. They mark the beginning of the phase in his work that has been called Expressionist and the beginning of Expressionist architecture in Germany. Before the Grosses Schauspielhaus there had been only one Expressionist building—Bruno Taut's Glass Pavilion at the Werkbund Exhibition in Cologne in 1914 (see Fig. 12). Everything else that emerged during this time of war consisted mostly of Utopian sketches, "star domes," Alpine monuments (see Figs. 13, 140). Of course, it was due to the war that Poelzig could get hardly anything built. But the war itself affected him very strongly indeed. Heuss says he viewed the war and its outcome with great pessimism which he tried to block out of

138 Hans Poelzig. Gasworks at Dresden-Reick, 1916.

139 Hans Poelzig. Gasworks at Dresden-Reick. Detail showing concrete construction.

his mind with an almost violent productivity. This may be, but it was not the only war-related reason for his productivity.

In 1916, the year of Verdun and the Battle of the Somme, it was clear that this war was no bright and breezy campaign, as Bismarck's wars seemed in retrospect. It was also clear that it had engendered forms of destruction that were terrifying, and that it affected *everyone*. People knew that after the war, no matter what its outcome might be, nothing would be the same as before and many welcomed this fact. The time when a group such as the Werkbund could speak of art as a factor influencing the economy, which was called in this context "the most important force of all,"[2] would never come again. And thus, in an artist like Poelzig, both the horrors and the hopes of the war brought about an increase in productivity. The war set free his own formal language, something that the emotionally dramatic theme of the Bismarck Memorial had done once before (see Figs. 50, 105–107). Now, during the war, a theme with as little emotional potential as a fire station provides the opportunity for a breakthrough into his own highly active imagination.

Poelzig did three schemes for the fire station, each one with a rough model—a "massing model" (Fig. 141). This was how he always worked; the model was the stage immediately after the preliminary design. In the first version of the fire station the different parts are very distinctly separate from one another and treated as was customary in modern architecture before the war, that is, verticality dominates. In this, something about the scheme does not seem right. Or perhaps we should say that from the outset there was something in this first

Departure into the Unknown: Dresden 1916–1920   105

140 Bruno Taut. "Domstern" ("Star dome"), Utopian sketch from the series "Alpine Architektur," Berlin, 1917–19.

scheme, with its disjointed character, that was superior, namely, its plan, a lovely oval for which a single overall form would have been the obvious choice (Fig. 142). The plan form was like an anticipation of the single form, and in his second scheme Poelzig took up his own inspiration and indeed took it up in an extreme way (Fig. 143). The whole mass of the building starts to flow. The lower parts of the building gradually rise to link up to higher ones; the signal tower, which previously had been stepped, now has a Rococo-like silhouette; close-together steep niches rise up on all sides of the building. They contain windows that are quite evidently office windows. The whole thing has a projecting base running around it containing doorways, or rather they are doorway-like niches, as doors are actually needed only at certain places in the building. The most striking thing about this scheme is that the question as to how the details of a building like this could actually be carried out was never really posed, nor was the question as to how this single, overall form would relate to the different groups of rooms marked on the plan. A single coherent form was forced upon the building

141 Hans Poelzig. Fire station for Dresden, 1916–17, project. First version, model.

and the details were only roughly sketched in; it is as if the architect put off dealing with such practical considerations, thinking that they would sort themselves out later.

And then a third scheme was produced, which was meant to be built and was buildable if one ignores the fact that even this scheme would have been rather too grand for the simple theme of a fire station (Fig. 144). Poelzig had used the "Roman" pillar-and-arch motif, with which he was, of course, familiar (and which would reappear in the work he did during the last phase of his life). Here the windows of the offices and other rooms appear very clearly in the niches; all the windows are identical. The upper part of the niches is left empty. The very strong "frame"—pillars and niches that run around the entire building—ensures that the building retains its quality of being a coherent whole; even the flowing transition between parts of the building of different heights is hinted at by a slight rise in the upper edge. The projecting base with the "doorways" has been abandoned. The places where doorways are needed are now evident. The scheme has become buildable, although it must be said that it still seems forced: The fire station is forced into a megaform. However, if we compare the *extreme* version, that is, the second scheme, with the most extreme work from the Breslau period, the second version of the Bismarck Memorial (see Figs. 143, 107), we see that the Memorial is at least buildable, whereas the second version of the fire station is not, and the third is *in practical terms* not buildable because the costs would have been unacceptable. Nevertheless, it must be said that something of this nature did in fact happen in our century: The tremendous "arcade" of the Palace of Justice in Chandigarh (India), by Le Corbusier, outweighs the "useful" part of the building to a far greater extent than is the case with Poelzig's pillars and arches in the fire station (Fig. 145). And yet it must be said that Poelzig is entering the realm of fantasy here, a realm he would inhabit for several years to come. And if I just

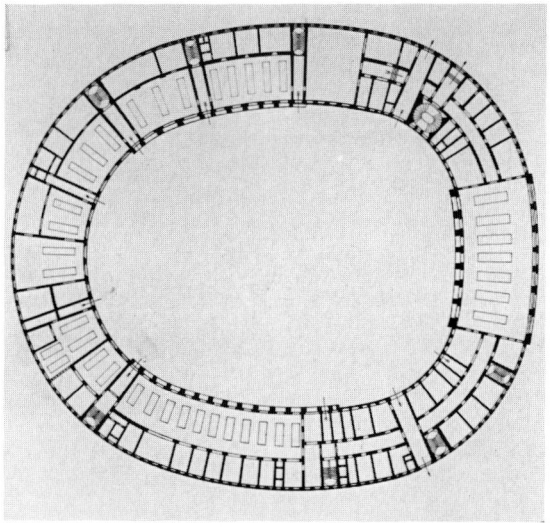

142 Hans Poelzig. Fire station for Dresden. Plan. The plan is the same in Poelzig's three versions of the project. Here again, one may refer to a "theme and variations."

said that the designs done in this phase could nevertheless be termed buildable, I meant relatively speaking, in comparison to "the star domes" and "Alpine monuments" of younger architects such as Taut. Having said that, the extreme, second version of the fire station must be classified as *scarcely* more buildable than these.

If one looks through Poelzig's sketches dating from this period one finds studies in which he tries to make details buildable that had first been dashed off in a cursory fashion (Fig. 146).

143 (top) Fire station for Dresden. Second (extreme) version, model.

144 (center) Hans Poelzig. Fire station for Dresden. Third version, elevation.

145 (bottom left) Le Corbusier. Palais de Justice, Chandigarh, capital of Punjab, India, 1956.

146 (bottom right) Hans Poelzig. Sketch for an elevation, early 1920s.

Departure into the Unknown: Dresden 1916–1920

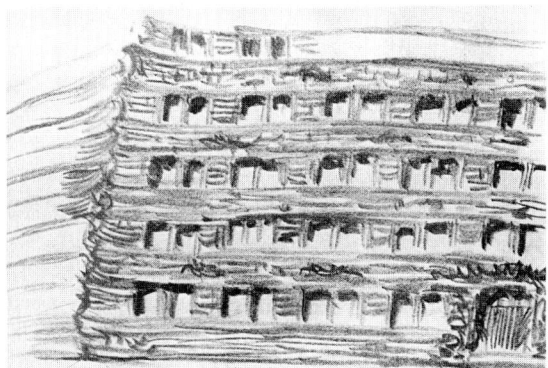

147 Otto Bartning. "Sternkirche" ("Star Church"), 1921–22. Project.

Maybe he would have succeeded in doing this with the second version of the fire station if he had been allowed to continue the project. When he arrived in Dresden he was forty-seven years old and an accomplished architect. It may well be that he could have carried out the schemes from the Dresden period and the early years in Berlin, although one may doubt it, considering the sketches he produced for a concert hall in Dresden (1918) and the famous first sketches for the Salzburg Festival Theater (1921) (see Figs. 189–192). It does look as if Poelzig surrendered totally to visionary work at the time, without, at least in the first instance, ever thinking about the question of whether his vision could actually become a building. I once heard Erich Mendelsohn say of a totally unbuildable project sketch, "The engineers simply *must* be able to construct it."

At the time of the First World War, Poelzig probably thought along very similar lines: The craftsmen simply *must* be able to do it. It is, however, difficult to imagine which craftsmen in our century could have done something like that. The Zwinger in Dresden, which Poelzig had before his eyes, was no doubt misleading. In Poelzig's extreme designs, vision and buildable reality are now asunder. In the final analysis, the fact that they did not get beyond the design stage is not unfortunate. As designs, however, they demonstrate the possibilities of architecture, even today. When Poelzig did build he was perfectly able to assess what was feasible. The designs remained *famous* designs,

Departure into the Unknown: Dresden 1916–1920

148 Georg Bähr. Frauenkirche (Our Lady's Church), Dresden, 1726–38; destroyed 1945.

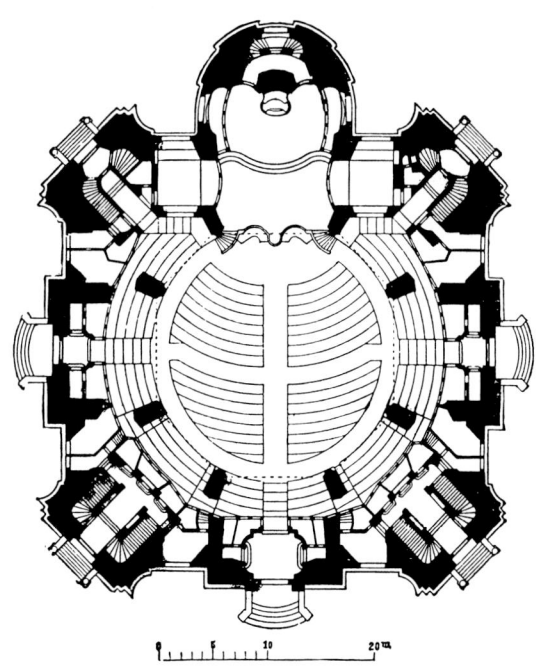

149 Georg Bähr. Frauenkirche. Plan.

150 Hans Poelzig. Town hall for Dresden, 1917, project. Model.

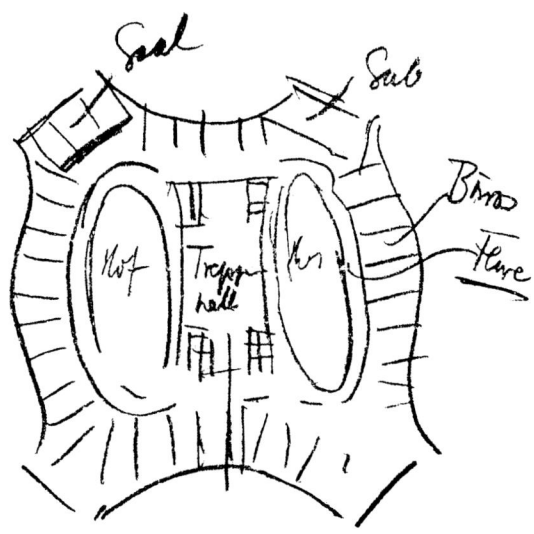

151 Hans Poelzig. Town hall for Dresden. Sketch of a plan.

152 Erich Mendelsohn. "Dünenarchitektur," sketch, 1920.

153 Peter Behrens. "House of Friendship" ("Haus der Freundschaft"), Constantinople, 1916, competition design.

154 Bruno Taut. "House of Friendship," 1916, competition design.

historically important designs, and there are some that show Poelzig's true significance. He was someone who went further in the architecture of the feasible than almost any architect of the time with the possible exception of Peter Behrens, who managed to create an Expressionist space that actually was built—the entrance hall in Höchst—and of Otto Bartning, whose "Star Church" is of the same quality as Poelzig's spatial visions (Fig. 147).

I have mentioned the Rococo and Baroque. The Baroque influence becomes far more perceptible in the Salzburg project, but there is no doubt that this influence of—or, to be more precise, this profound preoccupation with—Baroque architecture stems from what the city of Dresden had to show Poelzig. Dresden is *the* Baroque city, with Gaetano Chiaveri's Hofkirche, Matthäus Daniel Pöppelmann's Zwinger, and Georg Bähr's Frauenkirche (Figs. 148, 149). It was one of the most beautiful cities in Germany before it was wiped out in the air raid of February 1945 and Poelzig enjoyed Dresden and let it inspire him. Dresden was just what he needed when he was trying to set free his own architectural language. This becomes clear in another major project that was never built: the town hall (Figs. 150, 151). The town hall is both Baroque and Poelzig.

Incidentally, the projects and buildings by Bartning and Behrens that I mentioned alongside those of Poelzig also have historical influences, which is remarkable since Bartning belonged to a younger generation of architects; he was a contemporary of Gropius. His "Star Church" is of Gothic inspiration, an Expressionist-Gothic vision (see Fig. 147). The same is true of Peter Behrens's buildings in Höchst. To my knowledge the only visions of an architecture that breaks with history, breaks with it more than Taut's visions (in whose "star dome" the Gothic inspiration is *visible;* even its details are Gothic), are those of Erich Mendelsohn (Fig. 152). I feel it is necessary to point this out in this context. Mendelsohn's sketches are all too easily forgotten today.

In speaking of the Dresden period, we must bear in mind one project that does not fit into the scheme of things; it does *not* take its inspiration from the Baroque and it is buildable. I am referring to the design for the "House of Friendship" in Constantinople (1916). Poelzig designed this at the beginning of his time in Dresden. We know that he was altogether skep-

155 Hans Poelzig. "House of Friendship," 1916, competition design. Sketch showing the building in the ancient city.

156 Hans Poelzig. "House of Friendship." Perspective presentation.

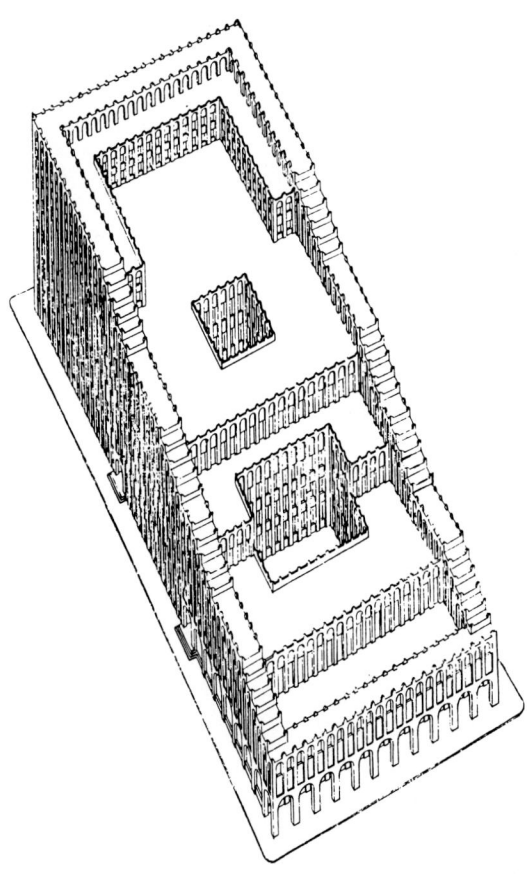

157 Hans Poelzig. "House of Friendship." Axonometry.

tical about the idea. He aired his opinions about it in quite a drastic way in letters. But when it became a serious proposition, when the Werkbund, the promoter of the project, nominated him as one of the twelve architects to take part in a Werkbund competition, Poelzig was suddenly very taken with the idea.

The Werkbund had made a good choice: Among the architects taking part in the competition were Peter Behrens, Richard Riemerschmid, Theodor Fischer, Bruno Paul, and the young Bruno Taut. The participants acted as a jury, assessing each other's — or rather their own — work, a procedure that has obvious drawbacks. As was to be expected, the result was that the first prize was awarded to the most

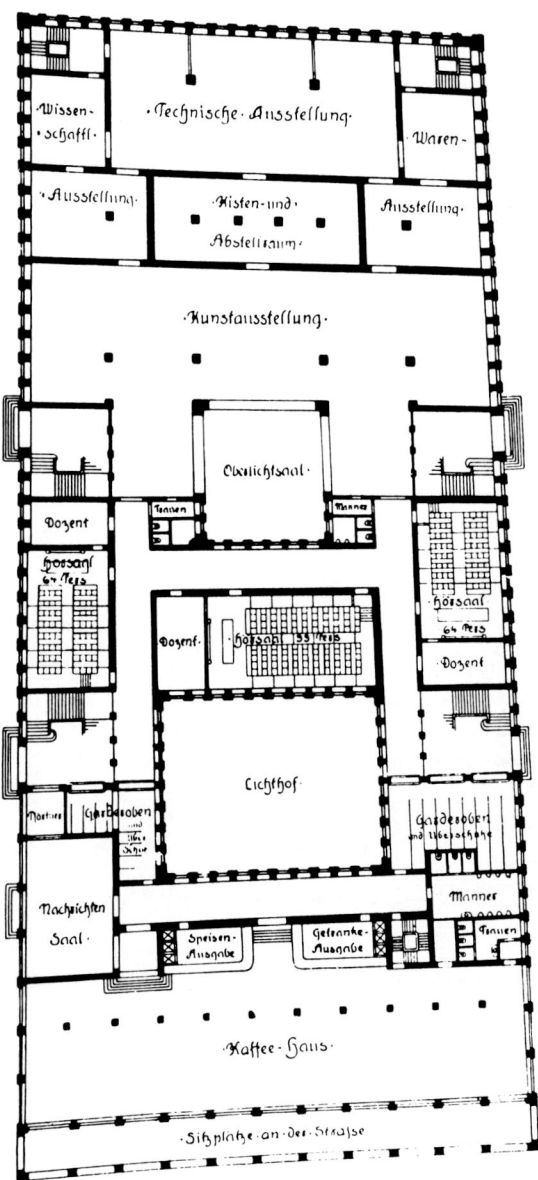

158 Hans Poelzig. "House of Friendship." Ground-floor plan with café and exhibition rooms.

traditional, classicist scheme, which was by German Bestelmeyer. Theodor Heuss, then secretary of the Werkbund, published and discussed the results in a Werkbund book (see Chapter 5, Doc. 5). Looking through the book

Departure into the Unknown: Dresden 1916–1920   113

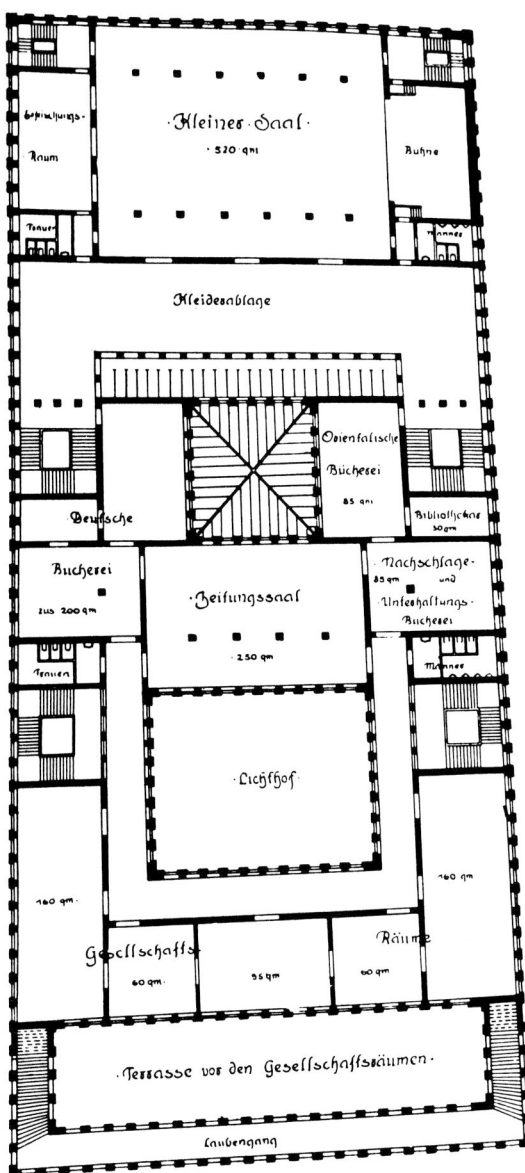

159   Hans Poelzig. "House of Friendship." First-floor plan. At the top, the small assembly hall.

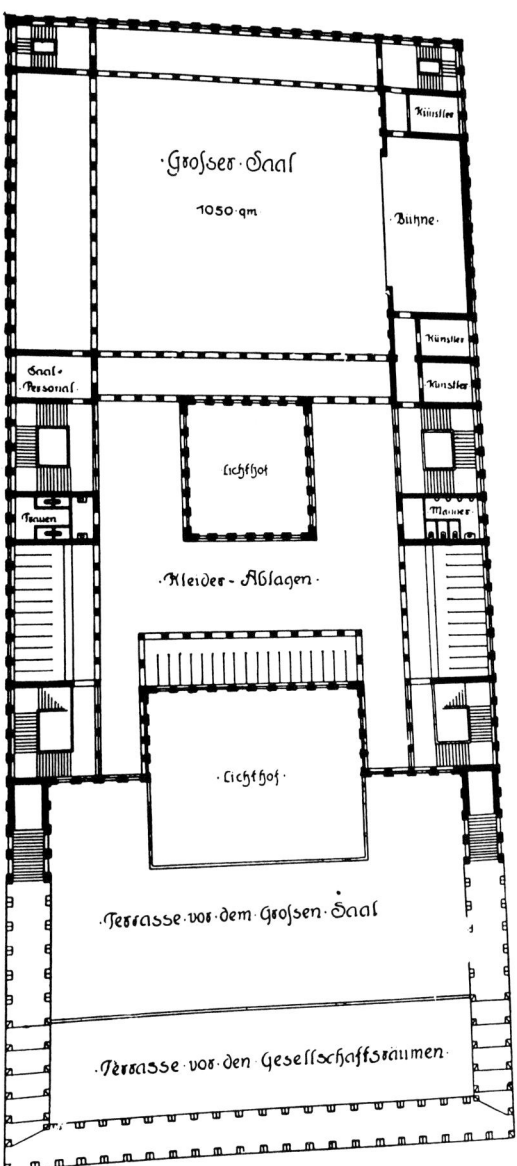

160   Hans Poelzig. "House of Friendship." Second-floor plan. At the top, the large assembly hall.

one notices that here again Poelzig's project is not like the others. The farce presented by the Werkbund Exhibition of July 1914 in Cologne — a classicism that even Muthesius, who had built two buildings of this nature, said seemed lifeless — was repeated in the competition for the "House of Friendship." The most famous names submitted the most conventional designs. Even Bruno Taut fell prey to the magic of the name Constantinople and produced a

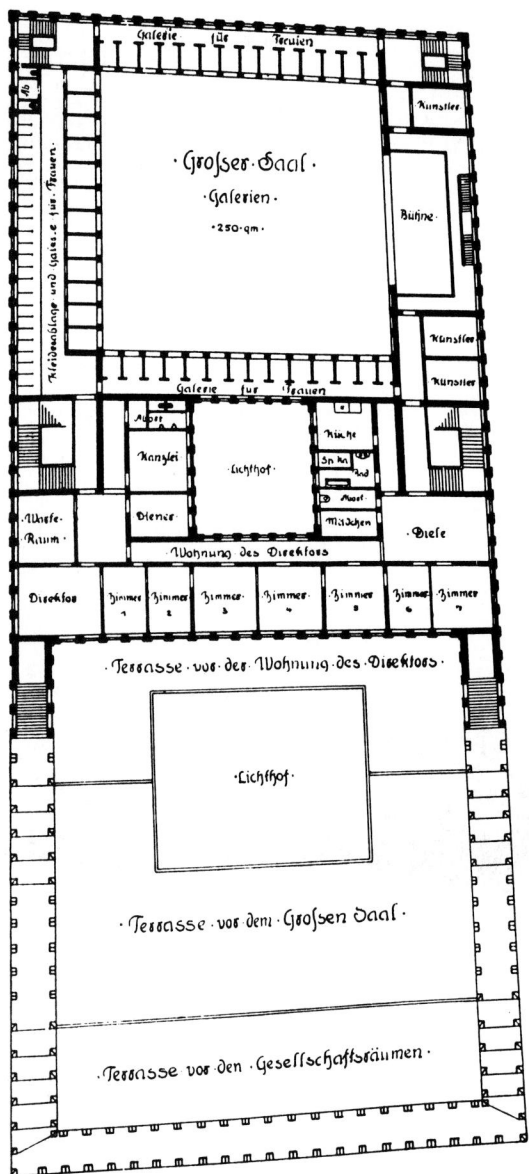

161 Hans Poelzig. "House of Friendship." Third-floor plan.

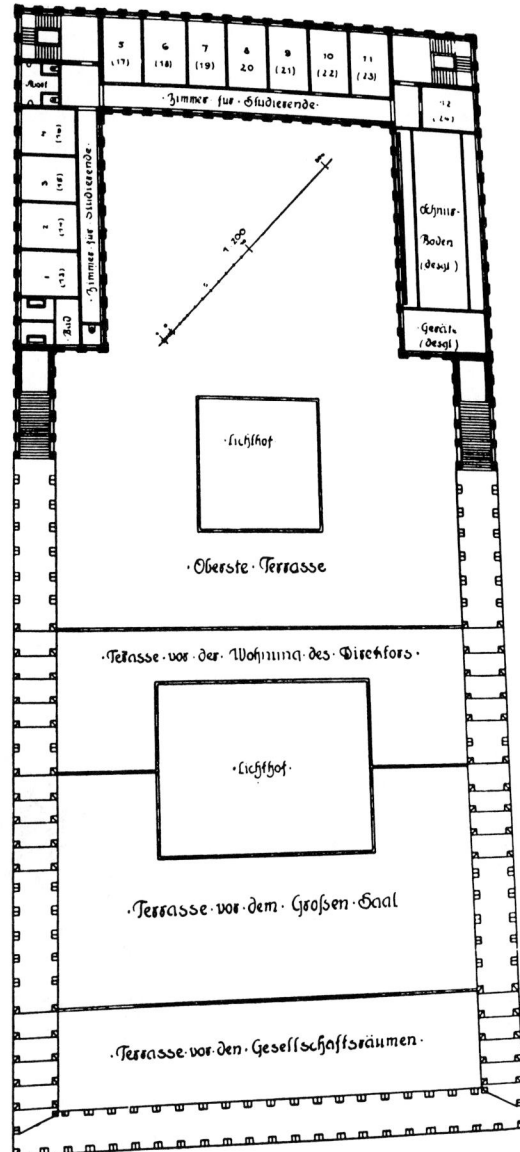

162 Hans Poelzig. "House of Friendship." Fourth-floor plan. At the top, students' rooms.

project for a domed building (Figs. 153, 154).

Poelzig placed a terraced cube in the middle of the historic part of the city (Figs. 155, 156). From the confusion of small houses surrounding the building, its highest wall, the rear wall, suddenly rises up and steps down in five terraces, "Gardens of Semiramis," while the side walls have only three steps with battered walls to provide the transition (Fig. 157). It was evidently too original for his Werkbund colleagues. It was said that a "victory memorial" like that would have been appropriate if the

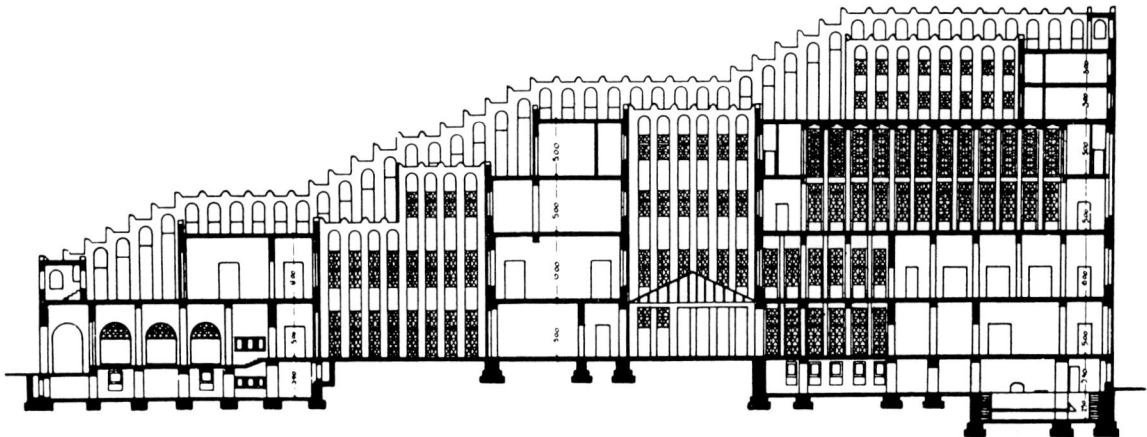

163 Hans Poelzig. "House of Friendship." Long section.

164 Hans Poelzig. "House of Friendship." Elevation.

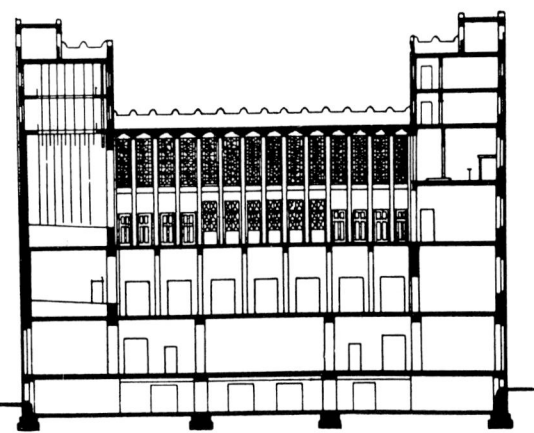

165 Hans Poelzig. "House of Friendship." Cross section.

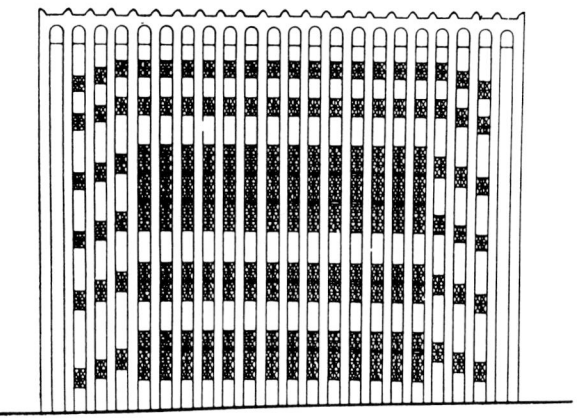

166 Hans Poelzig. "House of Friendship." Rear elevation.

Germans had conquered Constantinople, but that Poelzig's design was not a "house of friendship." Theodor Heuss wrote about these reservations, finding that in the end they could not really be dismissed. But *he* recognized that Poelzig had come up with the best arrangement of the different groups of rooms (Figs. 158–166). The house really was carefully and precisely thought out, truly architectural; the terraces, too, which had a view over the Bosporus, served a practical purpose. The fact that Heuss recognized this was the beginning of his friendship with Poelzig: The "House of Friendship" became the house of *their* friendship.

The conclusion to be drawn from Heuss's publication of the competition is that the most famous of German architects in 1916 had remained at the stage they had reached before the war: Only Poelzig had progressed beyond it. I said earlier that in the final analysis it was not unfortunate that some of his projects never got off the drawing board: They would not have withstood the test of reality. The "House of Friendship," however, was buildable. It would have enhanced the silhouette of Constantinople and would have been a great work of German architecture, which at the time was trying to move on to "pastures new." But no "House of Friendship" was ever built. The course of the war did not allow it. And Poelzig's project would not have been built in any case, because it was not officially entered in the competition.

Chapter Five: Documentation

Document 5

In his introduction to a special publication on the design competition for a proposed "House of Friendship" in Istanbul, Theodor Heuss wrote as follows:

Doc. 5*   Theodor Heuss, Introduction, *The House of Friendship in Constantinople*, 1917

Poelzig's design is without a doubt the most inventive and daring of all the designs. It strikes a completely new and original chord and its genuine strength dispels even the skeptical misgiving that such a powerful gesture might be too unconventional, self-confident, and grandiose for the occasion of Germany offering friendship and asking for hospitality in a foreign country. However, Poelzig treated with absolute logical consistency every "practical requirement," which was the rather too vague wording used in the program. His solution would have meant exceeding the budget somewhat to avoid savagely reducing the size of the ancillary rooms. These are questions of opportunism, which, although important, are not significant from our point of view.

One could perhaps suspect that the scheme was created around a monumental basic idea, the motif of rising terraces, and that it was a form of "drawing board architecture" that labored one idea to death at the expense of structural possibilities and considerations of practical use. But, in fact, it is nothing of the sort. For the exterior shape, where the stark power of a steep, precipitous cliff encounters the almost homely charm of the falling horizontal layers, is as surprising as the plan is convincing, clear, and simple. If one looks at the work starting not with perspectives or sections but with the plans, one finds a pleasant and logical scheme that, in the dimensioning of the spaces and the way they are grouped, dispenses so utterly with anything forced or unnatural that the harmony between the exterior and interior reveals the criteria of careful order and imaginative design.

This much must be said: The building has been carefully integrated into the composition of the city, but as an organism it can barely be understood from the street. The rising rhythms of its terraces can be discerned in the silhouette, but the eye cannot take in their actual physical presence and it is therefore difficult to really feel them. How will the surface of the rear wall, which is divided into narrow vertical strips and reflects the inner organism in the fenestration and the variation of heights of the staircase windows, appear on the street itself, what effect will it have there? The eye searches on this gigantic wall for a point of orientation, for a clear articulation to provide stability and calm. One could imagine that the "gradient" of the building, the shortened sides, could, from a sufficient distance, be very pleasant, for in the variation of dimensions, which takes its tempo from the different sizes of the terraces (and thus from practical objectives), there is an absolutely fixed rhythm. In the case of the rear wall, however, the imagination fails and one almost believes that the "romantic quality" of this highly inventive work is based on the terse rationalism of a silo-like industrial building. In the Divan Jolu itself, to which the relatively low facade reaches out, the power of the entire complex will scarcely be perceived; there the system of vertically rising arches will convey an impression of calm, harmony, and relative simplicity.

I have spoken in more detail of Poelzig's design than of the others; that is in the nature of the work. Although its form is linked to practical functions, it does express an abstract architectural idea, which positively challenges the imagination. The almost gracious system of drawings, whose meagre, slender, fragile lines seem to envelop a volume that exists virtually only in the imagination, holds the temptation to translate all this into color and material, walls, glass, shadows, into brick or limestone, to throw sun and rain on it and surround it with a prosaic everyday life with all its noise and dirt. One could dare, admittedly it is

---

* Theodor Heuss, Introduction, in *Das Haus der Freundschaft in Konstantinopel, ein Wettbewerb deutscher Architekten*, special publication on the competition by the Deutsche Werkbund, Munich, 1917, pp. 35–37.

tempting, to imagine the ceremonial aspect as being more reticent and the festive, gay quality as being more blithe, lighthearted, colorful than would be appropriate for everyday life, even on the Bosphorus ...

Without doubt, a great concept, a coherent whole. The first inclination is to see only the brilliant idea, whose uncompromising boldness is disturbing. But the clear accuracy of the plan is in a certain respect more convincing than the pomp of the perspective — for the imaginativeness of the Oriental fairy tale is closely related to simple, clear objectivity.

Heuss's remarks are important for us because he makes no secret of his reluctance to accept the "uncompromising boldness" that "disturbs" him. Glimpses of it can be seen repeatedly. He positively clings to the "clear accuracy of the plan." Of those designs by Poelzig that can be called Expressionist, the "House of Friendship" is in formal terms the least extreme. And yet the extent to which it has a startling effect on the eye of an open-minded contemporary witness is very clear from Heuss's description.

CHAPTER SIX
Transition from Dresden to Berlin: The Grosses Schauspielhaus

ALTHOUGH POELZIG HAD BEGUN to "gather moss" in Breslau, as he said in a letter to Karl Schmidt, dated 12 February 1916, it must have been quite difficult for him to leave the Breslau Academy, which he had done so much to build up (see Chapter 2). He took great interest in the question of who his successor would be and made a number of suggestions. He thought of Heinrich Tessenow, of Walter Gropius, and of the person who did, in fact, become his successor—August Endell. He carried on an exchange of letters with Walter Gropius in which he tried to correct Gropius's somewhat Utopian ideas about the introduction of industry into architects' training. He described what he himself had built up in Breslau: a school in which the teaching workshops occupied a position of central importance. Gropius was thus very familiar with this school when he opened his first Bauhaus in 1919 in Weimar —with teaching workshops.

The fact that Poelzig wanted to teach again "full-time" certainly played a part in his decision to leave Dresden, although he could not hope to be able to build up a second school with teaching workshops.

He was well able to combine teaching with architecture. I have already described how he introduced his students to his own work as an architect and finally employed them in his office (see Chapter 2). This was the link between teaching and design that he sought and was able to realize. The post of city architect, whose demands he had never shirked in Dresden, actually stood in the way of this ideal. Moreover, by the end of the First World War, at the very latest, all possibilities of building in Dresden had been exhausted.

Nevertheless when Poelzig did leave Dresden for good in 1920 it was not without bidding it a fond farewell. He had gained many friends there, including the mayor, Blüher, and he loved the city. He essentially owed what can be called the Baroque element in his work to the city of Dresden. At the time when he was planning the most Baroque of his buildings, the Festival Theater for Salzburg, he perhaps felt like the younger brother of the German Baroque architects. He certainly had something of this about him and he cultivated it.

In Berlin, even before he had moved there definitively, he had presented a building, "The theatre of the five thousand," as the client, the great stage director Max Reinhardt, originally wanted to call it, or the "Grosses Schauspielhaus," as it came to be called (Figs. 167–169). (It seated 3,500.) The Grosses Schauspielhaus is the only one of Poelzig's truly Expressionist projects of the period during and after the First World War that was actually built, the only one

167 Hans Poelzig. Grosses Schauspielhaus, Berlin, 1919. Auditorium. The cupola is suspended, and looks suspended. The "supports" do not look convincing.

of his buildings in which he was able to *realize* his own formal language. That would justify calling it his most authentic building. But the Grosses Schauspielhaus, completed in 1919, was only a conversion. The iron skeleton supporting it was originally part of a market hall that had been converted into a circus. Max Reinhardt had staged a classic Greek play in the circus, Sophocles' *Oedipus Rex*. The idea of permanently being able to stage such productions, of having a theater that could be used to bring the audience closer to the action on stage, was one of the factors that most influenced Reinhardt's decision to convert the Schumann Circus into the Grosses Schauspielhaus. The theater was designed with a wide proscenium stage that could be made narrower for conventional productions, three aprons, and stalls that could be used as part of the stage—the "orchestra" of antiquity. Reinhardt wanted to use a dome to emphasize the importance of this part of the auditorium. From the "orchestra" the seating rises up in the form of an amphitheater. The small number of boxes form part of the amphitheater. (Strictly speaking, there should not have been any boxes in a theater of this kind.) The iron columns caused the architect

168 (opposite) Hans Poelzig. Grosses Schauspielhaus. Plan and section.

+30,33
+31,0
Schnurboden +28,13
Rauchabzugsoffn für d. Bühne
Kuppelhorizont
Lichtgraben
Bühnen-Hochstellung +8,76
Mittel-Stellg. +6,71
Tiefstellg +4,66
Hauptbühne
1. Vorb.
2. Vorbühne bezw. Orchester
3 Vorbühne
Tiefbühne
Bewegl. Treppe
Vorr. f. Darsteller bezw. Parkettbesucher
Umgang II. Rg
Umgang I. Rg
Wandel-
Halle
Haupteingangsh. u. Wind
0 5 10 20 30m

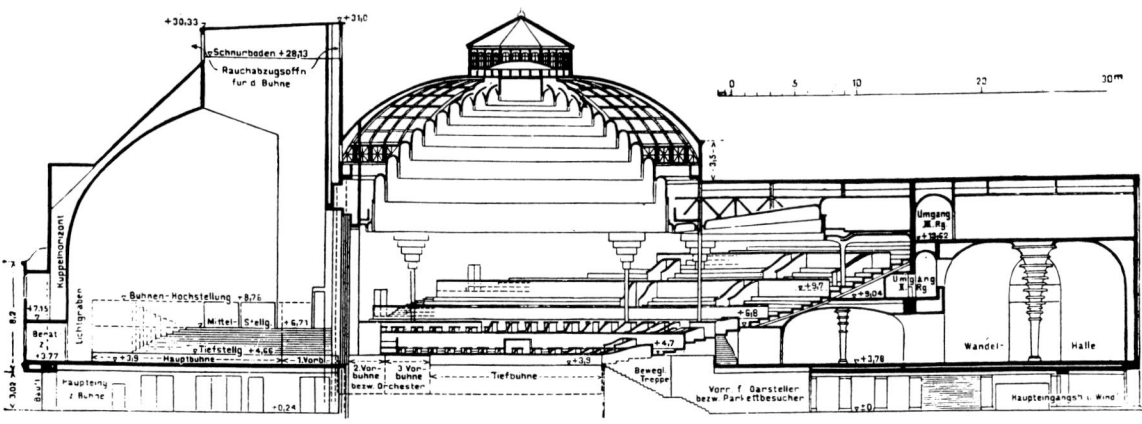

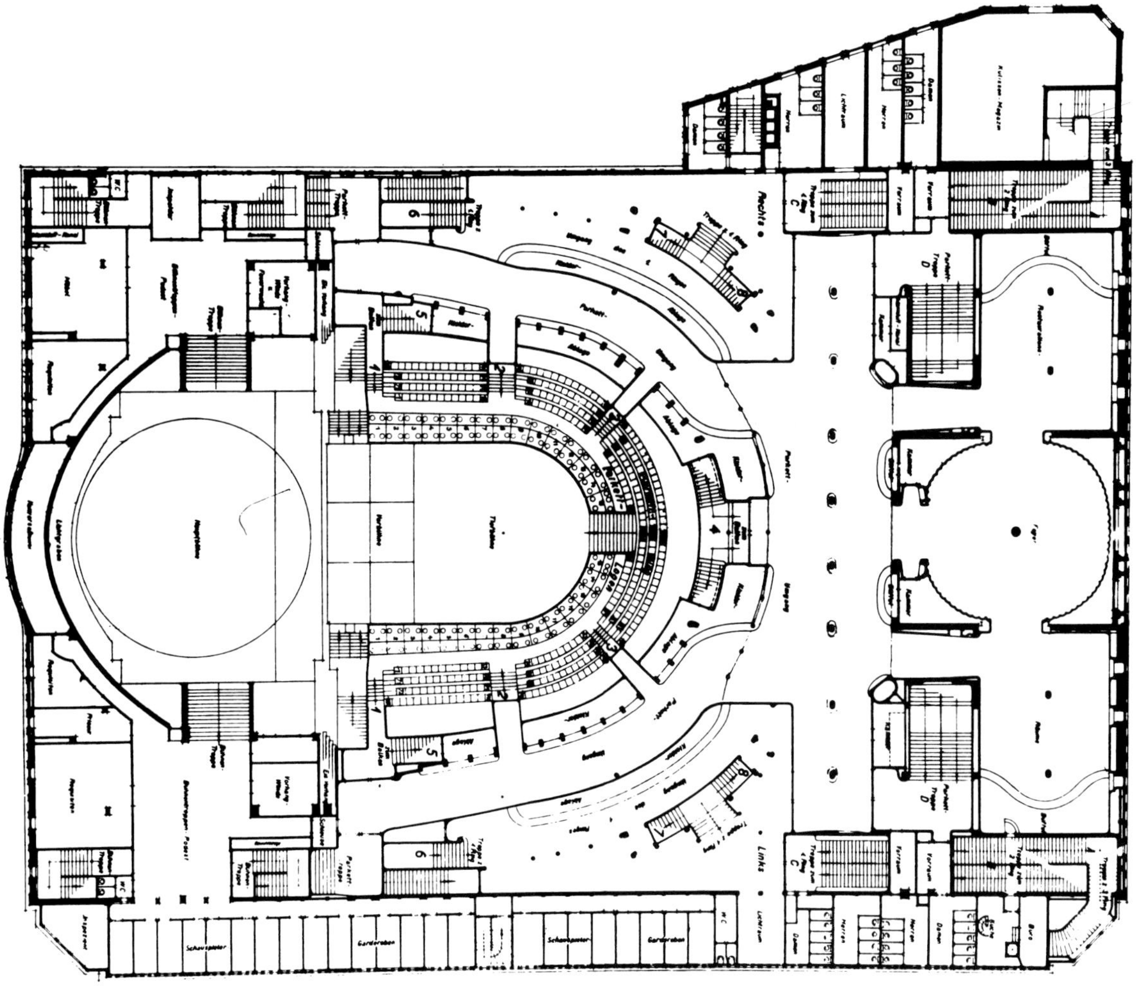

169 Hans Poelzig. Grosses Schauspielhaus. Perspective presentation of the building.

particular problems. In some places they had to be removed—for example, within the proscenium, which was 36 meters wide. Everywhere else they were clad. The lighting was indirect throughout—in the auditorium, foyer, and aisles. Poelzig covered the dome that Reinhardt had asked for with pendants whose purpose was to mitigate the acoustic disadvantages of a dome by roughening the smooth surface. Poelzig took this invention so seriously that he tried to patent it. But Berliners saw things differently and called the theater, where the pendants reappeared in the cladding of the columns in the auditorium, the "Stalactite Grotto" (Fig. 170; see Fig. 167). That became the theater's second "official" name.

There was no other theater at this time with an auditorium like the one in the Grosses Schauspielhaus; in fact, there is still no other theater like it. The question is very much whether it was the popular theater Reinhardt had intended. It had little time to prove itself, since it was declared unprofitable after only one season. Allow me to quote from a review I wrote much later (in 1979) about the space:

From the very beginning it was not what it was meant to be: a space to create a link between the people and what was happening in their midst. It is possible that Reinhardt came closer to achieving this aim in the *Oedipus* production he staged when the building was still a circus. If this is true then it can only be *because* the circus had not yet been decorated as a "stalactite grotto." The very improvised quality, which directed people's whole attention to the stylized crowd effects taking place in the circus ring and on stage, proved to be appropriate.[1]

That is a purist criticism and I hesitate to use it about this theater. For no one ever denied that it was magnificent and indeed theater in the best sense of the word. This was true also of the aisles and the foyers (Fig. 171). It was especially true of the foyer with a tree-like column in the center from which the ceiling of the round space seems to grow—a room, incidentally, that is based on an idea of Marlene Moeschke's (Figs. 172–175). The Grosses Schauspielhaus

170   Hans Poelzig. Grosses Schauspielhaus. Auditorium. The lighting is indirect, partly from behind the "stalactites."

was popular from the start and remained so and probably contributed to Poelzig's popularity more than any other of his buildings.

And let us not forget something else: Poelzig loved color and here at last he had the unique opportunity to follow his inclinations. This was also the fulfillment of a wish for color in architecture that was topical at the time, an integral part of what Expressionist architecture had been striving for. Bruno Taut was not the only architect who demanded that color finally be accorded its rightful place.

It was possible in the Grosses Schauspielhaus. Here color in conjunction with the new indirect lighting could enhance the new form. The building was burgundy red on the exterior, and the amphitheater was painted pale yellow. Such use of color would have happened again in Salzburg if Poelzig's Festival Theater had been built, but in fact it happened only here, just this once. The fact *that* it happened — that ideas of Expressionist architecture about color, form, and light were put into practice — increases the significance of the Grosses Schauspielhaus.

The interiors were so striking that the exterior of the building has largely been forgotten, although at the time that unerring critic, Erich Mendelsohn, considered it to be an important step toward a new kind of architecture. (Mendelsohn had criticized Poelzig's project for the town hall in Dresden [see Figs. 150, 151]):

171　Hans Poelzig. Grosses Schauspielhaus. Foyer.

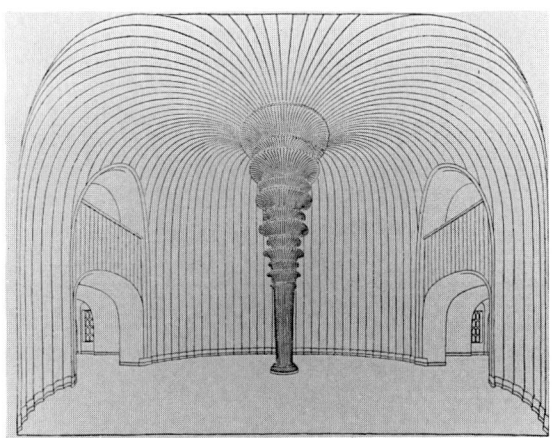

172　Hans Poelzig. Grosses Schauspielhaus. The circular foyer, drawing.

173　Hans Poelzig. Grosses Schauspielhaus. The circular foyer, sketch.

Nevertheless the excitement that the project really did arouse seemed to emanate from the luxuriance of its pagoda-like tiers, the richness of its light reflections, but not from any dynamics in the tyrannically emphasized mass. A dynamic effect of this kind was attained to a far greater extent in the last work by the same artist. The photograph taken from an oblique angle shows this very clearly. Here we do not see stories piled up on top of one another in the form of steps but individual massive elements thrown up toward one another and against one another to the height of a skyscraper [see Fig. 169]. Here for the first time the new life of architecture seems finally to have been achieved.[2]

The Grosses Schauspielhaus was not demolished until quite recently; I did not hear of anyone protesting against it (Fig. 176).[3] The interiors and particularly the auditorium had been altered beyond recognition a long time ago. Anyone who had known the interiors could see fragments here and there, like memories, fragments that incidentally seemed to con-

174 Hans Poelzig. Grosses Schauspielhaus. The circular foyer, photograph.

176 Hans Poelzig. Grosses Schauspielhaus. Main entrance.

175 Hans Poelzig. Grosses Schauspielhaus. Sketch of columns.

firm the transience, the theatrical quality of these spaces.

Returning to my criticism of 1979, I said that even the production in the circus was not "popular theater" because that simply was not possible during the reign of Wilhelm II. One might think that the Grosses Schauspielhaus, built after the shock of 1918, would have had a better chance of becoming popular theater. The art critic Karl Scheffler, who had recommended Poelzig to Max Reinhardt, made the following comment:

The theater of the three thousand looks like a structure of the revolution, a symbol of democracy; it is popular theater to a greater extent than any other popular theater to date has ever been, when every last seat is taken it is like a social institution; and the idea of drawing the stage into the auditorium and making the spectators become actors, as it were, has something very topical about it, something political.

But unfortunately everything was deceptive, Scheffler continued,

... for here everything from the first to the last is sham. This colossal, solid looking ... building is a glittering stage set, a complicated, artistic, architectural mask of plasterboard. All the elements that seem to be growing, to carry, to support and vault, are actually being carried, supported, vaulted. The entire mass of the building is suspended on the old iron frame. The whole thing is a web of wire with plaster thrown on it. The plaster has been modeled and then painted with bold colors. Here even the architecture is playacting. This kind of architecture, thrown up like this, has nothing to do with craftsmanship in the good old-fashioned sense of the word.[4]

There is something convincing about this criticism. But let us be fair.[5] Under the circumstances, Poelzig had no other choice than to "hang his interiors on the old iron frame"; and he was well aware of the "sham." He himself wrote:

What seemed very difficult was the problem of linking the existing iron columns and arches with the dome and of taking away from the dome, which does not have any strutting on the stage side, the impression that it is not being supported adequately. By the arrangement of the hanging pendants the dome has in fact been represented, aesthetically too, as a suspended dome. But we had to try to create a transition between the lower edge of the dome and the flat ceiling of the auditorium.[6]

Here Poelzig himself puts his finger on the weak spot: the "transition," which does in fact give the impression—if one does not look too closely—of carrying something, and which in any case looks not quite right, unauthentic, at best decorative. I do not know how the problem could have been solved. Poelzig did not solve it.

I would like to emphasize something here: that the only building (conversion) that Poelzig in fact carried out in his phase of liberated architecture, begun in Dresden, in his own style of architecture, his Expressionist phase, was in fact as Scheffler says playacting; made of plasterboard, not a solid building but an installation in an existing building, poured into a mold, painted, and lit; and that it had absolutely "nothing to do with craftsmanship in the good old-fashioned sense of the word."

And that is tragic, or sad, or at least tragicomic, when one recalls that Poelzig had a passion for *built mass*, as we have seen in a whole series of projects, starting with the Werdermühle (see Fig. 82), and when one learns that Poelzig, at the very time he was working on the Grosses Schauspielhaus (1919), made a speech as president of the Deutsche Werkbund that was devoted to craftsmanship (see Chapter 6, Doc. 6B).

We are familiar with Poelzig's closeness to craftsmanship: He is the advocate of teaching workshops as a "central part" of training, including architects' training, the advocate of close collaboration of the architect with artists and craftsmen, something he put into practice during the conversion of the town hall in Löwenberg. After the war, Poelzig had taken up the cause of the Werkbund, which had suffered such a severe blow in the dispute about whether the type-object or the object as work of art was more important that it seemed for a while as if it would not be able to recover.

When I say Poelzig took up the cause of the Werkbund it sounds as if he did so in a rather condescending manner. That is indeed how it was. He had no affinity for associations and soon afterward, during the inevitable argument with the Werkbund, he said with a deep sigh that when he got to heaven he did not want "to sit on the same cloud as those chaps."[7] But now in 1919 he put his hopes in the Werkbund, on condition that it come out clearly on the side of those who had spoken out against Muthesius's proposal in the dispute in Cologne about "the type." Those were the people with whom Poelzig had most in common, particularly the young architects Gropius and Bruno Taut. It was Taut, Karl Ernst Osthaus (the industrialist from Hagen in Westphalia, who took an active interest in the emergence of a new architecture), and Poelzig's friend Karl Schmidt who pressed him to accept the presidency of the Werkbund. The relationship with the manufacturing and marketing sectors of the economy, by which the Werkbund, and Hermann Muthesius in particular, had set such great store prior to 1914, was now to be refuted outright. The general opinion at the time (after 1918) was that it had, in fact, become pointless. Abroad, too, Poelzig said (although he did not consider "abroad" to be so important), Germany would gain recognition only through the outstanding quality of its workmanship: the workmanship of *craftsmen*. That is a clear response to Muthesius's theory of 1914. Poelzig wanted the Werkbund to endorse wholeheartedly the theory of high-quality individual work and there were excellent chances of this happening. The catastrophe of 1918 had put the seal on the fall not only of Wilhelm II's Reich but of the whole era with its materialist philosophy, its belief in ever-increasing comfort, in the unimpeded progress of the impersonal even to the detriment of the personal. In this respect even some patriots like Poelzig welcomed the catastrophe of 1918. Poelzig found therefore that a substantial number of Werkbund members were willing to lend an ear to his appeal for craftsmanship. Even men such as Walter Gropius — Gropius, who as late as 1911 had been working in the office of Peter Behrens, a factory architect and industrial designer, and himself had been a successful industrial designer — now spoke out in favor of craftsmanship. Both had always existed in the Werkbund — craftsmanship *and* industrial design. The difference was that in times of prosperity the emphasis had been on industrial design and now in 1919 it was on craftsmanship, although even then the industrialists who belonged to the Werkbund lodged a protest against Poelzig's "craftsmanship speech" which he had to respond to. Of course, Poelzig also recognized at the time that mass-produced utility articles had to have "type-related" forms. The forms of such mass-produced articles had to be typical if only because repetition would otherwise make them unbearable. But he says quite clearly that this was not actually a matter for the Werkbund. But what did Poelzig understand by the word *craftsmanship*?

By craftsmanship [he said], I mean something absolutely spiritual, a basic attitude of the mind, not technical perfection in some sector or other. What we should understand by craftsmanship, which is in fact absolutely identical with artistic work, is the will to dedicate great love and devotion to creating forms, a task during which no thought at all is given to the economic exploitation of the work, or perhaps in the very last instance only. That is the basic difference between this kind of work and all purely industrial activities.

Industry in the broadest sense of the term is concerned only with technical things and is guided primarily by economic considerations.[8]

Now, in the Middle Ages, the great age of craftsmanship, there was a saying: "Craftsmanship has a base of gold" *("Handwerk hat goldenen Boden")*. A craftsman who does not also think about the personal gain obtained by his work is not a craftsman. Nor is someone who wants to create *forms* and nothing but forms a craftsman. A craftsman makes chairs and cupboards, spoons and coffee pots, which admittedly have a form, but he does not create forms. That is what an abstract artist does. Poelzig's idea of the craftsman contrasts sharply with that of someone like Tessenow, who used to speak of the hard life of craftsmen and of the rigid social order they were subjected to, and insisted upon the fact that craftsmen do not create "as the spirit moves them." They are, Tessenow said, subject to that which is useful or deemed to be useful. To me, this idea of crafts and craftsmen appears, I am bound to admit, closer to reality than the one Poelzig expresses in his Stuttgart speech. *Forms?* At the same time Poelzig said of his own work that he worked on a project until nothing remained but form. This word also makes me feel a little uneasy. For, after all, people live in houses, not in forms, a fact that Poelzig the teacher always acknowledged, even stressed. Architecture is not the art of pure forms, which certain kinds of painting and sculpting can be. Architecture has something to do with the purpose of the house, the church, the school, and I believe it is art on the condition that it bears this in mind.

And here a strange link is seen between the contrasts we began with: the stage set which was the Grosses Schauspielhaus and which, as Karl Scheffler said, had "nothing to do with craftsmanship in the good old-fashioned sense of the word," and the craftsmanship Poelzig referred to in his Stuttgart speech, which had equally little to do with good old-fashioned craftsmanship. The sweat of the brow was missing, the material offering resistance, asking to be forced into shape, was missing, the simple daily use for the object, be it a spoon or a house, was missing. What Poelzig presented in his Stuttgart speech was an idealized picture of the craftsman.

Let us look back at the work he did during his time in Breslau. I have stressed to what extent his projects then were concerned with form, but I also tried to show that they were never *exclusively* form; they bore the mark of everyday life. The projects he did during the phase that began in Dresden, and the one that was built, the Grosses Schauspielhaus, no longer bear this mark. In examining the extreme design for a fire station I spoke of a rift having opened up between the vision and the possible ways of making it reality (see Figs. 141–144). This continues to be the case; it is characteristic of the whole phase of Poelzig's *oeuvre* that has been termed Expressionist. The unity of form and purpose has been questioned.

I am not denying that as early as Breslau form was the most important thing for Poelzig. One only has to look at the way the house in Breslau (1904) and his own house at Leerbeutel (1906) looked different although they were almost identical in plan (see Figs. 32, 56). The Zwirner house in Löwenberg became pure form the way almost no other building at the time did (see Figs. 57–59b). At the risk of being accused of splitting hairs, I must insist that it nevertheless remained a house, and that is exactly what I mean by "bearing the mark of everyday life."

Chapter Six: Documentation

Document 6A

The idea that the auditorium of the Grosses Schauspielhaus was meant to promote a close relationship between the play and the public was strongly welcomed by the writer Arnold Zweig. This was evident in his eulogistic article inspired by and written for the Grosses Schauspielhaus.

Doc. 6A* Arnold Zweig, "Theater, Mass, Individual," 1920 (excerpt)

Yes, the work begets the masses, the community, it draws upon its own strength to coax the sparks, the flame from the boards. Does it not with its opening scenes, which create atmosphere, set the stage, dictate the conditions, the very laws, mold the thousands of individual preconceived ideas that each member of the audience has come with into one universal idea? One objective: the event; one attitude: ever more avid participation; one wish: the denouement; one frame of mind: abandon? With each action, each movement, does not the diversity of a thousand different interests give way to a unity, to one spirit, the spirit of the work? Do all these souls really have a choice when Sophocles' Antigone stands before them in all the purity of her radical humanity, when in this hate-filled, totally destroyed German world, from the very depths of her soul she says, "I live not for hate but for love" and unshakeably seals her words with death? Then or never the flame of the spirit sweeps through the audience and rouses a shared feeling in their hearts; the emotion with which she graces the work, the catharsis that transforms thousands, the unity finally attained through awe, the edifying, ennobling, consecrating power of such an evening performs the miracle of retransforming petrified, isolated individuals into a deeply moved, purified community. If this does not happen there is no point in ever building another theater, they can all be closed. For with utmost purity this spirit overcomes the solitary one at night as he reads, for him the orchestra and stage of his imagination suffice; he, the reader, is ordained by the geniuses of the poetry and the poet and a feeling of community with the spirits of all those throughout the ages, whose souls were enthralled and enchanted by the winds of such poetic magic. The purpose of theater is the edification of an audience, symbol of a whole people, symbol of mankind, and in this it achieves fulfillment. In the liberation of the feelings of brother and sister it finds its fulfillment. The feelings of each individual are heightened as they come into contact with each other, the edification becomes more authentic, more fruitful. And indeed only when a crowd is edified and melts into one does it become authentic. The day when true poetry can make a whole legion of people weep without shame, as they can laugh without shame, when the tears of a whole people can flow for one victim, will be the day that will be the salvation of us all.

Document 6B

Quoted here are important parts of the speech Poelzig gave in 1919 to a meeting of the Werkbund in Stuttgart.

Doc. 6B* Hans Poelzig, address to the Werkbund, 1919 (excerpts)

It is important to me to explain where we stand and in what spirit the Werkbund should tackle the tasks that I believe present themselves. Moreover, I will quite generally try to show the line we should adopt if our work is to be justified and successful.

I will try to do justice to everything that I believe holds promise for the future. But I am not inter-

---

* Arnold Zweig, "Theater, Menge, Mensch," in *Schriften des deutschen Theaters*, ed. Max Reinhardt, Berlin, 1920, pp. 25–36. Reprinted in Julius Posener, ed., *Hans Poelzig. Gesammelte Schriften und Werke*, Berlin, 1970, pp. 125–30.

* Hans Poelzig, speech to the Werkbund, *Mitteilungen des Deutschen Werkbundes*, 1919, no. 4, pp. 109–24. Reprinted in Julius Posener, ed., *Hans Poelzig. Gesammelte Schriften und Werke*, Berlin, 1970, pp. 111–21.

ested in justice that is indiscriminate and therefore condemned to uncreativity....

Ultimately we artists heed only hesitantly and reluctantly the call that drives us out of our workshops and into the public arena where we have to deal with that which ought to happen. And yet we are the ones who, untainted by practical considerations, recognize the signs of the present time and the future, and are most apt to comment on what affects us. We feel the ground shaking under our feet and we want to help prepare new ground, which may serve future generations. We want to restore the Werkbund to its original position, where it was rooted in idealism and not in compromise and resignation. The Werkbund was founded by a group of artists who wanted to tread virgin territory in terms of style and who strove for a profound link between fine art and crafts. They wanted to wrench fine art and craftsmanship out of their isolation and allow their interaction....

Even in the introduction to his 1919 Werkbund speech, Poelzig sees the Werkbund of 1907 as he *wants* to see it. In the founding speech, given on 7 October 1907 in Munich, Fritz Schumacher had called economic power the most important of all forces. Poelzig continues:

The Werkbund must bear in mind that it was engendered by a spiritual not an economic movement. This spiritual aspect has been buried under the diverse political and economic activities of the Werkbund and it is time to reinstate it in all its purity. Fine art and crafts are the foundations on which the work of the Werkbund must be built. They are in effect one and the same thing....

By craftsmanship I mean something absolutely spiritual, a basic attitude of the mind, not technical perfection in some sector or other. What we should understand by craftsmanship, which is in fact absolutely identical with artistic work, is the will to dedicate great love and devotion to creating forms, a task during which no thought at all is given to the economic exploitation of the work, or perhaps in the very last instance only. That is the basic difference between this kind of work and all purely industrial activities.

Industry in the broadest sense of the term is concerned only with technical things and is guided primarily by economic considerations. Fine art and crafts, on the other hand, flourish only when economic considerations merely indicate how far the creative processes, in which form plays the decisive role, can go.

[For a comment on these views of Poelzig's, see above, pages 127–28.]

It goes without saying that transitional stages do exist, that certain craftsmen might as well be called entrepreneurs and that some factory owners put their whole heart and soul into the goods they manufacture. So when we talk of craftsmanship we mean a spiritual, an ethical concept. We mean the practice of a craft—or an art—for its own sake, industrialism of any kind being something basically different.

Nor should thoughts of export possibilities guide our work in any way. This kind of consideration implies compromise and adaptation to demand, to the wishes of interested parties. We must work free from any consideration of this kind, following nothing but our artistic and craftsman's conscience, and leaving all other considerations to industry.

The meeting in Stuttgart in 1919 was the first major gathering of the Werkbund after the Cologne meeting in 1914, which had taken place just as the war was beginning. Poelzig makes reference to the proposals Muthesius made in Cologne and rejects them. Later in the speech he mentions the dispute in the Werkbund in Cologne. The whole speech is a rejection of the Werkbund's prewar philosophy, particularly as expressed by Muthesius. In retrospect, this kind of comment seems justified, essential even. At the beginning of the war there was disagreement within the Werkbund and a total lack of clarity about its objectives. The situation after the war was entirely different: What was called for now was a fundamentally different Werkbund—or no Werkbund at all.

Fine art and crafts create things which when perfected have eternal validity and cannot be destroyed without causing severe damage. Any artist or craftsman who does not want to create things of eternal value is neither a true artist nor a craftsman. In those areas that border on industry, works are produced in which taste plays a primary role. But taste follows laws that can only be established by artistic achievement on a higher level. It follows formulae that are recognized as being comfortable and easily applicable. Anything that is made by an artist or craftsman and has a strong expression successfully defends itself against any attempt at calling it tasteful.

Exclamation mark! This *is* Expressionism! It is the rejection of just the kind of antiseptic taste, as it was later called, that the Werkbund had tried to follow before 1914.

Therefore, if the Werkbund does not want its role in those fields that are subject to fashion and change to be simply that of mediator or provider of inspiration, it must turn its attention to the true meaning of art and of craftsmanship.

On the whole, trade and industry have done nothing but make a prostitute of art. Their interest is all too often in the attraction of what is fashionable, always new, by which I do not mean original creation but the emphasizing of some kind of striking gimmick that will charm the masses and entice them to buy. Trade has no interest in the production of something of eternal value, not even in craftsmanship that will last for a long time. Trade is often not interested in supply and demand but in finding ways to stimulate an artificial demand. Industrial considerations have already played too great a role in the Werkbund. We must return to the original roots of our creativity....

Years ago the dispute about types raged in Cologne; in my opinion it stemmed from this very lack of clarity. Typical forms are good for mass-produced industrial articles, in fact, they are indispensable. These products only gain character when anything requiring artistic work or craftsmanship is dispensed with. Even a well-thought-out form that does not confine itself to the most simple, most typical, is bound to become unbearable with repetition. The form must be typical and must not try to be particularly original, since it is difficult to combine originality with typical forms.

But at the same time everything must be avoided that would lead to these forms being created too easily, simply through the omission of certain things. Omission from the very beginning simply causes impoverishment of ideas, and forms and good types can only be created after long, painstaking work, during which experience gradually casts off anything that is inadequate and finally—not by an *a priori* selection but through the variety, the richness of the design—produces a result that admits the validity of only the most concise form.

But the so-called art industry, that is to say the industry that tries merely with cheap mannerisms to give itself an artistic veneer, should be abandoned; half measures are worse than none at all and it is better for the inadequacy to be clearly revealed than be hidden under a decorative cloak.

I feel that again and again we are dogged by an error of logic, which wants to place products manufactured by purely industrial methods on the same level as those made by arts-and-crafts methods. The technological product requires technological and practical considerations and loses its value as soon as a technically more perfect, more practical, and cheaper product is made. It is thrown on the scrap heap and is viewed quite rightly as having little value, as its value was based on purely technical and economic factors.

Arts-and-crafts products have eternal value. The value of a wonderfully formed Baroque cupboard is not detracted from by the fact that a newer cupboard is more practical, lighter, and cheaper. Furniture produced on the basis of economic and technical aspects, such as American office furniture, does lose in value if one tries to improve it by applying artistic originality.

These errors of logic are at the root of the fatal concept of "applied arts." ...

Industrial methods can be used only for things that have no ambition to be anything but practical. They create their own forms by gradually shedding anything superfluous and impractical, finally attaining a valid form, which has nevertheless evolved in a totally different way from that of arts-and-crafts articles.... A primitively carved medieval oak door is beautiful despite the fact that technically speaking it is not perfect, and it does not lose its value when a technically better door is created, since its qualities are of a purely arts-and-crafts nature. On the contrary, a primitive work of art can have a more profound effect than one that is technically more advanced, while the automobile built in the year 1900, which perhaps once aroused our admiration, now seems ludicrous next to one of later design. It is a simple fact that arts-and-crafts creations owe their existence to different functions of the soul.

But of course I do not want to be misunderstood; I do not want people to think that I do not esteem the work produced by our technical firms. On the contrary, here people have been working in a way that was considerably less egoistic, more concerned with the task in hand, and without interest in satisfying vanities than in the sector of artistic work, or at least semiartistic work, of today....

There are certain points of contact between building ... and pure technology; and building adopts the achievements of technology, which came about through the application of technical and scientific methods and also economic factors. Any attempt by architecture to get involved in purely technological fields—the production of automobiles and other vehicles, in fact of anything mechanical—is, I feel, a mistake. To try to build in such a way that technical considerations determine the appearance is also a mistake. Such buildings will look cold and mechanical.

In this respect most water towers, silos, skyscrapers cannot be said to be true works of architecture when compared with the aqueducts, fortifications surrounding towns and castles, and warehouses of the past. In addition, the ethos of the artist and craftsman is needed, which, while drawing upon technical possibilities, remains the only thing capable of giving form to the building.

While the average engineer builds a bad water tower, a bad factory, judged in terms of its appearance, it has to be admitted that the average architect who tries to solve the problem from a purely superficial, formal point of view, usually produces something even worse....

The technical possibilities available to our building craft are superior to those of the Middle Ages, but it is equally possible to give appropriate architectural form to construction in concrete or steel structures as it was in the Middle Ages to the construction of a wooden barn. The fact that compromises here lead to anything from deterioration to stylistic unclarity can be seen in the technical buildings that try to fit in with established laws of rhythm, taken from antiquity for example, or try to hide behind an architecturally rhythmic mask, which contradicts the logic of the method of construction used.

This is Poelzig's favorite theme, to which he remained faithful to the end, both in his work and in what he said: that essentially the architect can, and should, treat the new technical possibilities no differently than the architect of former ages treated the possibilities available to his craft. The last criticism is aimed expressly at Behrens's A.E.G. factories and in particular at the "temple" of the turbine factory.

Similarly, the design of our houses cannot logically be based on technical and hygienic principles, cannot be treated in the same way as mechanical, practical articles, which are thrown away after use. The form of a human being's home needs emotional and spiritual values, which something created using purely practical criteria cannot provide, no matter how good it is. Let us even be impractical if in doing so a ray of our creativity will shine into the human soul.

Poelzig continues with a short survey of the previous twenty-five years—Art Nouveau, Neo-Classicism, and vernacular art and their rejection by the younger generation. It is a very brief summary: He does not mention the attempts at reform by architects of his generation, nor his own attempts.

To anyone who sees things at all logically it is clear that the spirit of our contemporary construction methods energetically opposes the formal language of antique architecture. Our method of construction cries out for forces to be broken down, dispersed, for clear articulation; it is much closer to the medieval way of doing things than to the antique. I say medieval, not Gothic, since a reference to the complicated formal language of the mature Gothic would only cause confusion....

Spread out before us are the art treasures of thousands of years. We cannot close our eyes to them even if we try, yet we must learn from them only what stylistic coherence actually consists of without clinging to formal rules of past epochs.

I believe that the imminent time of impoverishment offers the right basis for a stylistic purge in architecture. The means are sparse and force restriction....

Many of the young architects want to accord color in architecture, even for exteriors, the role of a pioneering element that can give stylistic coherence. They are right. The clear move toward color, toward "truly using color again in architecture," would be the most thorough and simple way of dispensing with the confusion and overabundance of forms.... There seems to me to be no doubt about the fact that our towns and villages, and above all our housing estates, which for economic reasons alone are forced to use recurrent types, would gain a great new attractiveness from the articulation of the rows with rhythm and color, and that this would be the best and most natural way of counteracting the uniformity of rows of identical houses.

True understanding of architecture is so unspeakably important because it determines the appearance of our homeland which has been so disfigured by the half-hearted architecture of recent decades....

But it is not possible to instate architecture as a major art overnight. This will be possible only when a coherent major revolution of souls has taken place, when the conviction that we must create things for eternity has gained general recognition.

We have to understand once more that great art, if it is not to lose its validity as art, needs content that can inspire enthusiasm and is in close contact with the soul of the people. We must be indifferent to the commercial values that have been forced upon works of art, we must once more serve art with awe, as the few great artists of our time did in a selfless struggle, while the majority of artists became trapped in the quagmire of business interests. We must try to re-create the link to our native culture, condemn art for art's sake and be willing to join forces in the service of the work itself. These are the high objectives we must set ourselves and in order to attain them we need the cooperation of all those who are sincere about art....

The speech contains other theories of a nationalistic nature. Poelzig *was* a man of nationalist convictions; this has already been pointed out. And a nationalistic element can also be found in German Expressionism. It was part of the reflection on fundamental values: They were meant to be German values. It was also part of the rejection of the economic way of thinking in the time before the First World War. According to artists like Poelzig, the Werkbund was cured of it by the war and the end of the war.

In the following section of the 1919 Werkbund speech, Poelzig deals with the education of artists and architects, referring to his own practice as a teacher in Breslau but without referring to Breslau.

The young artists in the academies and schools of arts and crafts who recognize the fruitlessness of their education to date are now themselves passionately demanding that their schools be transformed into teaching workshops in which they can participate, if possible from the very first day, in the actual creative process and the building itself....

Hitherto arts and crafts have resisted this fundamental change. The apprenticeship system wanted to be recognized as the only valid method; art saw its salvation in the academies....

What is required is a solution that incorporates both aspects: Crafts must be built up anew in workshops that correspond as completely as possible to a good master apprenticeship, including its economic aspects, and the study of art should also have this crafts training as a foundation....

It may seem impossible immediately to create conditions similar to those in the Middle Ages, and yet we must strive with all our strength to ensure that arts-and-crafts training is carried out on a practical basis, on the building itself, and that the apprentice is confronted with economic restrictions and inhibitions from the outset, for it was the absence of these that posed a problem in the teaching workshops of the schools.

And, as it will not be possible to dispense with the schools, we must transform them from superfluous institutions into essential institutions that everyone who wants to work in the fields of arts and crafts will have to pass through....

The very freedom of art is a two-edged gift. The greatest and most sincere works were created in a seeming lack of freedom....

In conclusion, Poelzig turns again to the Werkbund:

The work of the Werkbund must therefore be firmly rooted in craftsmanship and art, not in industry and technology. We can force the world to recognize the quality of our work only if we now place our work on the ethical foundation of crafts and art....

I do not know if it will soon become possible to export our products successfully. Even if this were the case, the thought of this possibility must never shape our work.... From a purely economic point of view this may have brought temporary benefits but in principle it was a total failure....

We Germans are not a people who reject *a priori* inspiration from abroad, and now too we will accept it from any quarter. But we must translate it into terms appropriate to our kind of work, to whose purification we intend to dedicate ourselves with all our might....

But if the Werkbund wants to engage in the battle it needs the support of the young people....

We must not shy away from the turbulent wild appearance of young art. The froth will fly away and only the form will remain which will be of eternal value....

The Werkbund must become the conscience of the nation....

The war has impoverished us to a greater extent even than we realize at present. The soil we will have to sow will be meager. If we do not lose our courage this meager soil can have a healing effect, shedding everything that is sick and too luxuriant and which was threatening to smother our creative work. And if the war and our enemies have made us almost into beggars we intend to retain our pride as the Gueux did and manage through our work to transform the shameful name given to us by our enemies into an honorable name.

I have already mentioned in the main text that the industrialists present protested against the rejection of industry and that Poelzig had to respond somehow. His answers do not sound very convincing. The thrust of the speech is so much against the old Werkbund that it was in fact difficult to see what industry's role could be in a new Werkbund as envisaged by Poelzig. Evidently the industrialists assumed that it would not be practically possible for the Werkbund to separate from industry. They must have assumed that industry's strong position as an influencing factor in the whole production process would enable it to assert itself later. They were right: As early as 1922 the issue of art, crafts, *and* industry was topical again in the Weimar Bauhaus *and in the Werkbund.*

CHAPTER SEVEN
The Festival Theater for Salzburg

POELZIG'S STUTTGART SPEECH of 1919 is also a statement of the Werkbund's attitude after the war (see Chapter 6, Doc. 6B). Now the Werkbund rejected the rather commercial outlook it held during those prosperous years preceding the war. It is important to remember, Poelzig said, that the Werkbund was a spiritual movement, not an economic one. This appeal, this attempt to mobilize the artist who looked neither to the left nor the right, being wrapped up in his work and indifferent to worldly things, for a short time met with a positive reaction. But the Werkbund was in constant turbulence — as was Poelzig himself. The political revolution had already failed in January 1919, when its leaders, Karl Liebknecht and Rosa Luxemburg, were murdered in Berlin. But the movement that had sparked off the decline of the old order in 1918 did not end there but lived on in the intellectual and artistic world in a wealth of contradictory ideas, in new ideas and experiments about education, in attempts to live differently, in the theater.

In the preceding chapter we followed Poelzig's transition from Dresden to Berlin. For Poelzig the transition began even before the end of the war and did not come to a provisional end until 1920. A *transition:* Poelzig felt that something new was beginning in which he would have an important part to play. For this reason he found his role in the Werkbund very congenial. He had the confidence to exert influence, including political influence, in the broadest sense of the word. But the Werkbund was and remained the only forum he used.

Since politics have been mentioned, we must examine briefly this side of Poelzig's character. Let us first of all state what he was not: a social revolutionary. He did not support left-wing politics and he abhorred the Spartacist movement. In 1921 he wrote that he wanted to join a nationalist secret society, or found one if none existed.[1] But a secret society is not reactionary — its aim is to take action. At this time the term *conservative revolution* was coined, an idea that met with a good deal of support among young people from a bourgeois background. As far as I know, Poelzig never seriously analyzed these ideas, but "conservative revolutionary" describes quite well what he was, or let us say what he always was latently. He might have been just this, and maybe in the twenties that feeling grew stronger and became more common. The term *latent* has already been used in connection with Poelzig: Latent ideas could be seen both in his work and in what he said during his time in Breslau — in his rejection of the bad practice of the time and in his historical consciousness.

The time before the First World War — which

was quite dynamic and open to new ideas, and yet without haste, without any desire to realize the unheard of—seemed in retrospect, after the catastrophe that ensued, to be materialistic and inert because *now* artists felt the urge to explore new avenues, to *do* the unheard of. Poelzig felt it too. But, as has already been pointed out, he did not, like some younger architects, want to forge ahead "into virgin territory."[2] He had belonged to some of the new revolutionary groups such as the "November Group" but only briefly. He never felt at home in them. He *was* a conservative revolutionary, to whom the new was the old, and the old the new. We have seen that in his work in Breslau. At that time, the old, which in his hands could become new, was the aqueduct, the town walls, the portals of Romanesque churches, stepped back and drawing the eye deep into the interior of the building. But it was the old reinterpreted in practical terms. In Breslau, Poelzig was perhaps more involved in practical building than in what could be called architecture. He did at the time see a new way forward inherent in the new practical developments that were emerging in the building sector.

A change took place during his Dresden years. Now it was the Baroque, the Romanesque, the German Late Gothic that attracted him and that he had in his mind's eye as distant models. This was particularly true of the Baroque—to be more precise, the German Baroque. If one wanted to try and summarize the difference, one could say that before the war Poelzig strove for continuity in architecture using new forms of construction, and now he is concerned with *culture*, which he seeks to renew by linking it to historic cultures. I do not want to state the case any more strongly than that, for if forms that clearly evoke the Rococo period, such as those that appear in the sketches for the Festival Theater in Salzburg (see Fig. 183), could lead one to believe that Poelzig wanted to revive the German eighteenth century, the structure of the buildings in this project will disprove this belief. Both Festival Theaters and the open-air amphitheater are terraced, an architectural form that Poelzig had used before Salzburg (Fig. 177). I need only recall the "House of Friendship," which is not Baroque (see Figs. 155–166). My point is that Poelzig once again uses the old to create something new, just like the good conservative revolutionary that he was. But now he is no longer translating old building forms into new construction forms but is taking an old culture and hoping to create a new culture.

This is in keeping with the general atmosphere, if it can be called that, of the years from the early to the mid-twenties, when a different kind of architecture, "modern" architecture, started to emerge. It has been called a flight into the spiritual, which was an obvious way out in those years when there was little material wealth and prospects for improvement seemed limited. The contempt for materialism during the years before the war, mentioned above, was now combined with a true hunger for meaning, for guidance, for a culture appropriate to a people that was in a hard situation. The insistence upon the German character of this culture was a kind of revenge of the spirit on those who had gained the upper hand in material terms. At the time, book after book was published on the subject of German culture, which, it went without saying, was superior to the "superficial" culture of the victors. I need only mention *one* book title to make clear what I mean: *Esprit und Geist* by an author named Alfred Wechsler. *Esprit* and *Geist*—the meaning is clear. The French possess at the very most *esprit*, the gift of conversation, the elegant but quite superficial quality, the fireworks display of syllogisms! *Geist*—or true spirit—on the other hand, is something quite different, something German, *exclusively* German. Hans Poelzig was not absolutely free from this intellectual arrogance. It can be detected in an extract from a speech he gave in Salzburg about his project for the Festival Theater:

... we are dealing with Salzburg ..., a German city, which has slipped down a long way south, is influenced by the south and yet is still German, since it is Baroque, not in the purely stylistic sense of the word, but in its attitude, in its art. All German art is

The Festival Theater for Salzburg

177 Hans Poelzig. Salzburg Festival Theater, 1920–22, project. Early scheme for a group of theaters on a hill in Hellbrunn Park.

more or less Baroque, eccentric, peculiar, unacademic, from the Romanesque period to German Gothic and up to Rococo.³

"Intellectual arrogance" — harsh words. One could also speak here of a reflection on the eternal values of national culture, which is something quite understandable at one of the lowest points in the history of a nation. Many members of the German educated middle classes joined in this movement (and incidentally not only since 1918). The German youth movement *Wandervogel* was full of people who thought that way. They used to stress that the quality that is specifically "German" was not easy to grasp; they spoke and wrote a good deal about the way the French form was much more easily accessible than the German, of how someone like Johann Sebastian Bach or the sculptor of the figures on the cathedral of Naumburg or the Baroque master Balthasar Neumann were in the first instance inaccessible, showing contempt toward beautiful form, destroying it even, but having a profundity that the German character was particularly capable of. Poelzig's attitude was quite close to this, although at the same time he placed great importance on being a European, having also inherited European culture.

Certain elements of European culture were favored at the time. The leading figure was Shakespeare. Poelzig's cultural horizon corresponded to that of his contemporaries, although he had his own personal preferences and dislikes. For instance, he never shared in the general enthusiasm for El Greco, nor for the German painter Matthias Grünewald, whose qualities as a painter he seriously doubted. But, like so many others in Germany in 1918, he did seek comfort, stability, and hope in culture, in a culture that found its expression in strong, characteristic forms, not in moderate and classical ones. This was, of course, natural in an Expressionist period. And he saw his own architecture as part of this culture, or let us say as a stepping-stone to it, for he was well aware of the fact that the Germans did not yet have a culture and would have to fight to recover it.

His material situation was also unstable and uncertain. Negotiations were going on for work in both Berlin and Cologne. He had no great love for Berlin. He wrote:

Berlin isn't the right place—that is becoming clearer and clearer. It is possible to do some kind of work here but not to build. Form doesn't stand up in this rare atmosphere, or at least not unless it is made of paper. Potsdam would be better.[4]

And he did in fact settle in Potsdam, in one of the "Communs," the small outbuildings behind the "New Palace" that Friedrich II had built in the park of his palace Sans Souci near Potsdam after the Seven Years' War, mainly, it is said, in order to show the world that he still had money even after the war. Poelzig planned to set up a sort of community there with workshops of different kinds—a "Breslau-type" idea, one might say. Nothing came of it; instead he had to share the *Commun* with the Isadora Duncan School of Dance, which he was less enthusiastic about. He had come to Berlin hoping for more commissions after the Grosses Schauspielhaus. In this, Berlin disappointed him: For several years, in fact until 1924, he built nothing there. He did, however, begin to teach immediately, although not at the architecture school of the Technische Hochschule in Charlottenburg until 1924. He held a master class at the art school—the Academy, as it was called. He continued this, incidentally, even when he became a professor at the Technische Hochschule. The class at the Hochschule was large—thirty to forty students—whereas the one at the Academy was more intimate. It can be seen as the transition to his own studio.

He began in Berlin in a very modest way. Since he had no building commissions, he turned his attention to ceramics, working with porcelain, in collaboration with Marlene Moeschke who became his second wife (Fig.

178 Hans Poelzig. Ornament in porcelain. This study is visibly influenced by the eighteenth-century Rococo style. It is equally unmistakably the work of Poelzig.

The Festival Theater for Salzburg 139

179 Hans Poelzig. Sketch dating from the early 1920s, probably a preliminary study for a set design for Mozart's *Don Giovanni*.

178). He also designed sets for several major stage productions (Figs. 179, 180; see Figs. 184, 185). He did not turn to designing for the stage simply because he had no commissions to build. One only has to look at them to realize

181 Hans Poelzig. Sketch of wooded hills, probably inspired by Hellbrunn Park, proposed site of the Salzburg Festival Theater.

180 Hans Poelzig. Colored sketch dating from the early 1920s. Set design for *Don Giovanni*.

140   Hans Poelzig: Reflections on His Life and Work

that they must have been the central focus of his creative work at the time. We have talked about his painting, which throughout his life went hand in hand with his work as an architect (see Chapter 2). We have at least mentioned in passing his architectural sketches. They accompanied his work as an architect and became particularly important after 1916, when Poelzig was no longer an adherent of the Werkbund as it had been before the war but had become an artist who was breaking new ground. The sketches were his comments on this new ground (Figs. 181–183). Some of his sketches are intended to show that it was possible to

182   Hans Poelzig. Architectural sketch in Rococo style.

183   Hans Poelzig. Sketch relating to the Salzburg Festival Theater project.

184 Hans Poelzig. Sketch of set design for *King Lear*.

build these designs. They did not get very far and in fact most of them are not very convincing. But nevertheless Poelzig had to make this attempt and the sketches are worth looking at from this point of view. One series of architectural sketches has nothing to do with his built work: the skyscraper sketches, for instance, or the well-known sketch showing bridges and airplanes (see Figs. 200, 201, 199).

The stage sets are interpretations (Figs. 184, 185; see Fig. 180). Looking at the *Don Giovanni* sketches is like hearing the music, and the sketch for *King Lear* is quite astonishing. Lear is descending a staircase that is far too steep. It makes one aware of the impossible nature of this character and indeed of his tragedy. Poelzig finally also designed film sets, and in one case built a whole film town for *The Golem*, the sinister story of the Prague miracle-working rabbi Loeb (Figs. 186–188). The rabbi was played by

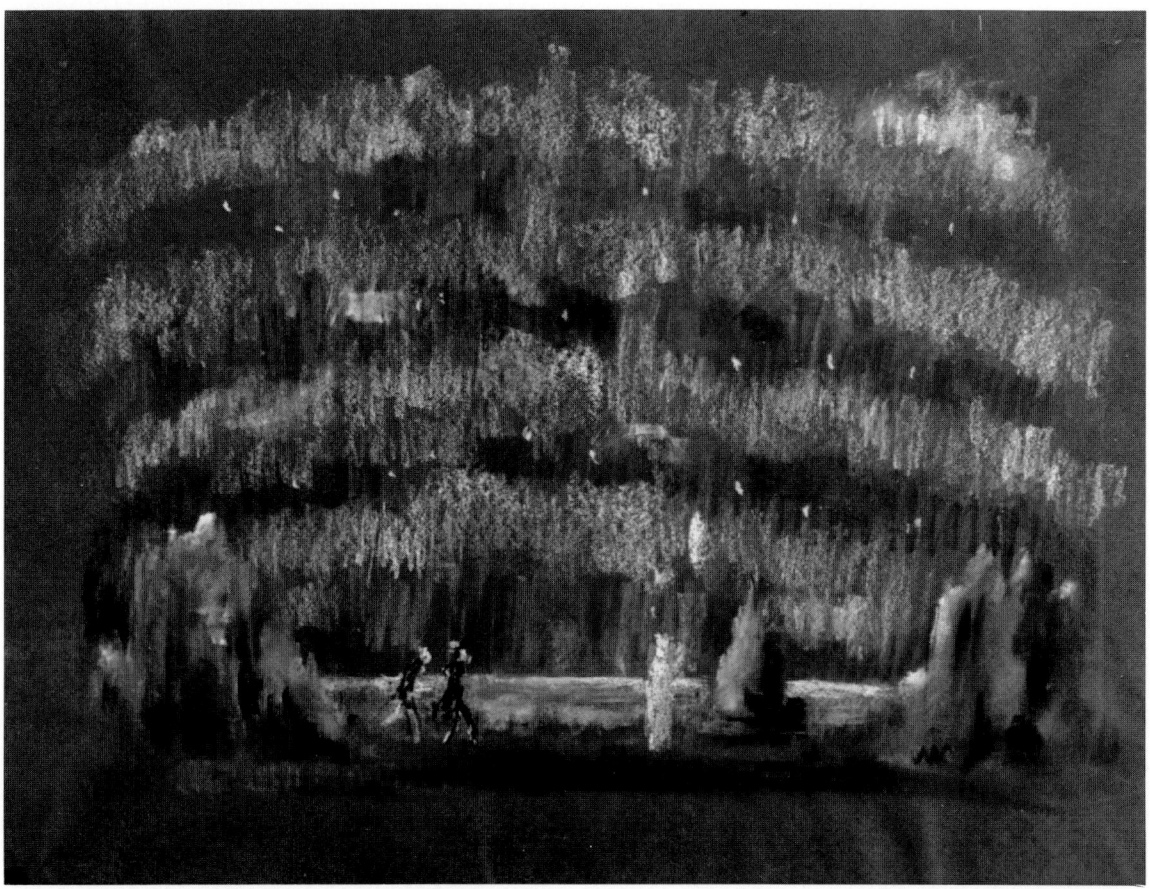

185 Hans Poelzig. Sketch of stage set for *Hamlet*.

Paul Wegener who also directed the film (see Chapter 7, Doc. 7A). The two artists remained friends. The main project of this time, however, in which Poelzig was deeply involved and for which he produced three schemes (as he had for the fire station in Dresden), was for a Festival Theater in Hellbrunn Park, outside Salzburg.

The Viennese professor Alfred Roller, a painter and applied artist who had great influence on art in Vienna, contacted Poelzig in the summer of 1919, and suggested that he take part in a competition for a Festival Theater in Salzburg. "Competition" is not quite the right description as only *one* other architect had been invited, Josef Hoffmann of Vienna. Hoffmann did not turn down the invitation, but he did not submit a scheme. He thought Poelzig's design was wonderful and said he hoped it would be carried out. Roller spoke on behalf of the Festival Theater Association, which had been founded in Vienna in 1916. Now that the war was over, the Association took up the idea of the project seriously. This in itself sounds fantastic in view of the poverty of the postwar years in Austria. Roller worked out an accommodation schedule, which he kept quite imprecise, no doubt intentionally, in order to leave the architect as much freedom as possible. Poelzig looked at Hellbrunn Park in which the buildings were to be situated and was full of enthusiasm. In the speech he held when

186 Hans Poelzig. Sketch for a poster for the film *The Golem*.

187 Hans Poelzig. *The Golem*, street scene. "Golem City" was built especially for the film following Poelzig's designs.

188 Hans Poelzig. *The Golem*, interior.

presenting his scheme he said:

He [the architect] will quite naturally be caught up in the atmosphere of fantasy surrounding the whole area and the works of art that are there. And when he sees Mirabell and Hellbrunn, when he has that natural theater of stone before his very eyes, he will be driven into a kind of frenzy, which will prevent him from thinking of anything but how he can create something comparable to, or even greater than, this riot of forms. And this frenzy will get the better of him and he may throw Professor Roller's brief into a corner in an attempt to tackle the problem from a totally different angle.[5]

He, Poelzig, tackled it by grouping three

144   Hans Poelzig: Reflections on His Life and Work

189   Hans Poelzig. Salzburg Festival Theater, 1920–22, project. Later version with group of theaters including an amphitheater.

190   Hans Poelzig. Salzburg Festival Theater. The opera house, entrance from the park. Sketch by Erich Zimmermann.

The Festival Theater for Salzburg   145

191   Hans Poelzig. Salzburg Festival Theater. The opera house, interior.

auditoriums around a "natural theater"—the large opera house, the smaller house, and the open-air amphitheater beneath the main house to which they were linked by a visual axis and also by a number of open-air corridors (Figs. 189, 190). He sunk terraced spaces into the terrain, which he emphasized by the two circular-terraced theater buildings, and made them all into a single composition—or sculpture. All this was designed using forms derived from the Late Baroque or Rococo. This was engendered by the aura of Dresden and by the magic spell of Mozart, which hung over everything—Mozart was born in Salzburg. But the architecture of the terraces is not Rococo, it is pure Poelzig. No one else could have created it.

The interior of the main house—Poelzig did not draw that of the small house—is even more closely linked to the architecture of the eighteenth century than is the exterior of the building (Fig. 191). It is an auditorium of boxes, the greatest imaginable contrast to the amphitheater Poelzig had just built in Berlin (see Figs. 167–176). Even Scheffler, who viewed the Grosses Schauspielhaus critically, saw its potential as a popular theater, a "democratic institution." The models for the interiors of the Festival Theater are of a more courtly nature: There are seven circles of boxes, and the box form seems to be continued upward, the recesses are continued; the ceiling is not set back from the sides; the room is a single hollow form, a dome rising up from the ground that does not come to rest until the very top, partially for reasons of acoustics. But the main reason was Poelzig's desire to build it as one coherent form. The design for a concert hall for Dresden, which dates from more or less the same time (1918) as the auditorium in Salzburg, is without doubt a preliminary study for the latter, including its coherent form (Fig. 192). The fact that the "orchestra," the space in front of the stage, is free of seating recalls the Grosses Schauspielhaus. A curved staircase rises from the "orchestra" to the stage and above the stage there are two tiers of organ pipes. The room has its own inherent sound. I am tempted to apply to it the apt comment on Scharoun's Philharmonic made by one of my Malaysian students: "The music is already in the room."

As Poelzig said himself, the terracing of the building has a purpose, namely, to provide the different tiers of boxes with exits from the building. They were not, however, emergency exits. The idea was that the audience would be able to stroll around all the terraces in the intervals.

This seems to me to be the right moment to let Poelzig speak for himself. In the address he gave when he presented his scheme to the Festival Theater Association in Salzburg he said the following:

I felt I had to contradict the publications that were bent on advocating the amphitheater and nothing else. Is it so terribly undemocratic and antisocial to make tiers, or to be more precise boxes? Is there no performance, particularly no musical performance, that one does not enjoy more when not part of the masses?

I realize very well, that contemporary theater of the kind Professor Reinhardt was striving for needs the great unity of the mass audience, needs the suggestive power that emanates from a mass of this kind, and therefore demands primarily an amphitheater.

But when I wanted to build an architectural sky over an amphitheater, when I tried to further de-

192 Hans Poelzig. Concert hall for Dresden, 1918, project. Sketch for an interior.

193 Oskar Kaufmann. Komödie Theater, Berlin, 1924.

194 Hans Poelzig. Salzburg Festival Theater. The opera house, second version.

195 Hans Poelzig. Salzburg Festival Theater. The opera house, third version.

velop the dome of the Grosses Schauspielhaus in Berlin into a ceiling that would be acoustically better while not detracting from its power, I cut lines of boxes into that ceiling. And I placed the staircases to these boxes in such a way that the outer shell of the building stepped down in rhythmically alternating terraces. So what I had achieved in other projects through a great deal of additional design, and what had come about in the opera house in Berlin in a very makeshift way, by the creation of fire exits, happened here of its own accord, by virtue of the fact that the whole building on the side that faces the mountains is articulated into terraces or steps.[6]

The speech can be found in the documentation appended to this chapter (Doc. 7B). It is the most unequivocal statement made during Poelzig's Expressionist period and it clearly shows

196 Hans Poelzig. The Salzburg Festival Theater. The opera house, third version. Interior.

the epochs in German art and architectural history which he felt it was his calling to continue.

I have said that the concert hall for Dresden could probably not have been built. The very idea of details of this kind being carried out in our century is quite fantastic. This is true also of the interior and, in fact, of the whole building in Salzburg.

Should this be seen as a weakness of the project? How else could a building have looked that has overtones of the eighteenth century and yet is not eighteenth century but is Poelzig? There is no doubt about the fact that Poelzig was determined to build it, that it was not a vague fantasy. He *would have* built it if he had been given the opportunity—a horrific thought. Because although the building is true Poelzig it does not belong in this century. People in the twenties were not afraid to actually build buildings that recalled the eighteenth century. There are several theaters in Berlin by the architect Oskar Kaufmann whose auditoriums have Rococo overtones. They are richly decorated with stucco but the individual ornaments are Expressionist Rococo—a little too jagged for the eighteenth century (Fig. 193). Would Poelzig too have used this kind of ornamentation? His detailing would no doubt have been more original *and* more discreet than that of Kaufmann. And yet ...

Poelzig was not given the chance to carry out the project. The program was changed: Only *one* theater was required. There are two schemes for this program; he designed the interiors for the third version only. The exterior of the building retains its terracing but not the corridor links since the small house and the amphitheater no longer existed (Fig. 194). The second scheme still has the staircases leading from the terraces into the park. They are no longer there in the third scheme which has an almost chilly severity (Fig. 195). It would have been perfectly pos-

The Festival Theater for Salzburg 149

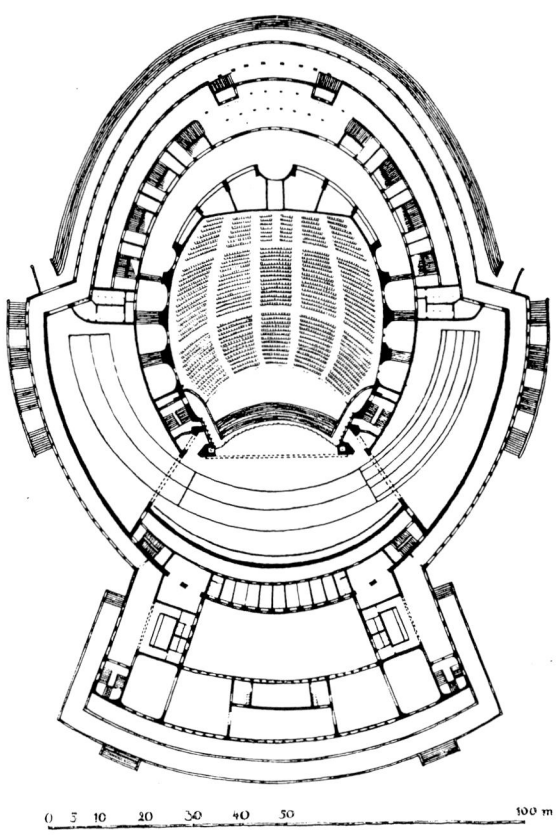

197 Hans Poelzig. Salzburg Festival Theater. The opera house, third version. Plan.

sible to build it. That is also true for the interior, which was an auditorium of circles rather than boxes and had a dome with closely spaced ornamental ribs (Fig. 196).[7] Even the organ pipes above the proscenium arch, which now has several tiers, are integrated into the ornamental ribs and remain only just visible. In 1924 Poelzig went on to build an interior with similar decoration — the Capitol Cinema in Berlin (see Figs. 211–218). The third version of the Salzburg project, as I said, could have been built (Figs. 197, 198). In it Poelzig returned from his voyage into the eighteenth century.

This should not be interpreted as a qualitative judgment. I personally prefer the first version. But Poelzig must in the end have realized that it was not possible to build this space or the exterior in the form it took in the first sketch. The three schemes for the Festival Theater are almost like the three schemes for the Dresden fire station (see Figs. 141–144), the difference being that then Poelzig was on his way into the realm of fantasy whereas now he is on his way back again. We shall not encounter another sketch in his work resembling those for the first version of the Festival Theater. Salzburg is a watershed. A new phase begins here — his confrontation with the realities of the 1920s, which I shall now go on to examine.

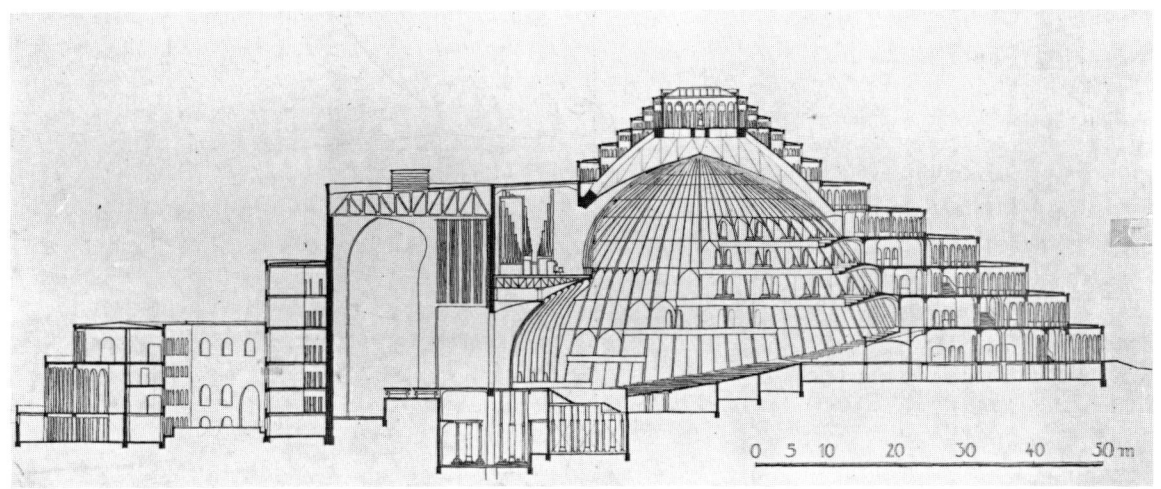

198 Hans Poelzig. Salzburg Festival Theater. The opera house, third version. Section.

Chapter Seven: Documentation

Document 7A

Theodor Heuss's remarks on Poelzig's city set for the film *The Golem* sound, as is so often the case with his remarks, utterly authentic:

Doc. 7A*   Theodor Heuss, in *Hans Poelzig. Bauten und Entwürfe*, 1939

There were also a number of film manuscripts in his estate, some of them written directly by him, some other people's work which he had commented on and made more concise. It was thanks to Paul Wegener that he came to work on the film. There was a bond between their natures on a very elemental level: their powerful vitality, earthy sense of humor, and a meeting of mind and soul. In their intellectual and spiritual attitudes they were linked by a leaning toward the old Eastern world with its secrets, mysticism, its fantasy, rather than to the rational certainties of the Western world which made the impression of being so confident.

... The most positive result of their work together was the commission to build a whole set, a medieval ghetto, for *The Golem*. The result was very strange. Poelzig's main concern was not to design an historically accurate milieu but to find the right form to correspond to the strangeness of the subject matter. One can note the skill with which he creates three-dimensional depth in the nooks and crannies of the streets and squares, something that was still unusual in films of that time (1920). With a plastic freedom that disregards simple structural considerations, he lends an intense eloquence to the facades, doors, turrets, windows, oriels. In an interior he takes the vaulting beyond the limits of the structurally possible, places mysterious staircases and corridors in such a way that light and shadow become ghoulish decorations. At the time, the era of silent films, he said himself with dry sarcasm that at least the houses should "speak Yiddish" — a joyous spirit of invention fills the sinister and gloomy world.

Later Poelzig saw this work as a practice run. For a long time he toyed with the idea of a fantastic film version of *Gulliver's Travels*, a romantic ballad of black knights and white knights accompanied him through the years. There is an almost finished script that he wrote about the "Fall of Vineta." The notes in the margin, full of architectural remarks, show the extent to which the visual design was to be even more developed than that for *The Golem*.

Document 7B

In 1921 Poelzig addressed the Festival Theater Association in Salzburg, describing his approach to the design of a Festspielhaus, which the city planned for a site in Hellbrunn Park.

Doc. 7B†   Hans Poelzig, "Festival Theater in Salzburg," 1921

The artist is concerned solely with form, and what captivates him in every problem is the question of how to develop a form from a given subject. And as artistic creation stems from intuition, and is merely controlled by reason, there are sometimes abrupt transitions that may seem quite illogical and do not necessarily develop in a linear way, certainly not in the case of a problem such as this one, which is influenced to a great extent by the surrounding countryside.

The problem of the Festival Theater for Salzburg is unique and it certainly does not make a sensitive architect immediately think of technical and practical considerations. He will quite naturally first be caught up in the atmosphere of fantasy surrounding the whole area and the works of art that are there. So when he sees Mirabell and Hellbrunn, when he has that natural theater of stone before

---

* Theodor Heuss. *Hans Poelzig. Bauten und Entwürfe. Das Lebensbild eines deutschen Baumeisters*, Berlin, 1939; reprint, Stuttgart, 1985.

† Hans Poelzig, "Festspielhaus in Salzburg," speech given at a meeting of the Salzburg Festival Theater Association in 1921. In Julius Posener, ed., *Hans Poelzig. Gesammelte Schriften und Werke*, Berlin, 1970, pp. 142–51.

his very eyes, he will be driven into a kind of frenzy, which will prevent him from thinking of anything but how he can create something comparable to, or even greater than, this riot of forms. And this frenzy will get the better of him and he may throw Professor Roller's brief into a corner in an attempt to tackle the problem from a totally different angle.

To the artist all purely technical considerations are from the very outset quite disgusting. Though he knows that these purely technical considerations cannot be avoided and must be dealt with, he also knows and feels instinctively that they play far too great a role in life today, so that again and again he will take up arms against the supremacy of technology. Technical and artistic ways of looking at things are, and always will be, stark opposites, and the artist knows only too well that German art in particular gains its magic from being many-sided, eccentric, circuitous, thoroughly irrational.

The purely technical will never be able to shed its cold appearance, and the obvious poverty of feeling our buildings today have compared with those from the past is largely because they are so terribly practical.

And now a Festival Theater for Salzburg! Not on *any* site in town, but out in open country, among the mountains, with a view of the Alps, and, what is more, in competition with the many-shaped creations of people who had time and leisure, who allowed their imagination to run free and create art.

Of course, the first reaction of the artist is vehement protest against everything that imposes practical constraints on a Festival Theater of this kind. He thinks only of the chance to plant creations of his own imagination—in so far as he is free to do so—in this site and only then does he try to reduce his designs to the level required by present-day life. And grudgingly he relinquishes one adventurous feature of the design after the other, one leap of his imagination after the other, until perhaps he finally does manage to put something definitive there, in which as much as possible of his imagination remains but which has become usable (what a dreadful epithet for a work of art) for the purpose required.

And if, ladies and gentlemen, I join with conviction in the eulogy to the virtually impractical, to the technically imperfect, crooked, even sprawling, I do so because the artist in me is protesting more and more loudly against the demand to be practical, and because Salzburg and the problems to be solved there have fanned the flames of this protest even more strongly. One only has to look at an old plan of a house, palace, or church, be it from the Middle Ages or the German Baroque period: It will be weird and crooked. A truly straight line can hardly be found, the whole thing sings a song based on the interplay of the shapes. And if you wander through one of these houses or castles right up to the attic you are enveloped by a feeling of secrecy and joy, perhaps even horror, and when you walk into a church you are enveloped by a feeling of mysticism. And in today's school, in today's church? Everything is terribly correct. The axes are correct, the water closets are in the right place, the widths of the doors and corridors have been carefully calculated. In the church one even has a good view from every seat. But even the too-precisely-calculated lighting of the classrooms in a school, perfect in terms of hygiene and technology, is monotonous, the ornamentation, designed with horrifying consciousness, actually hurts to look at, and in the church rationalism sits in state on an altar and permits no mystical feelings to arise.

Now I am sure you will believe me when I say that I am not trying to advocate conscious naivety, imitation, or the superficial creation of atmosphere; the new Catholic churches with their medieval trimmings truly equal the lack of imagination of the Protestant churches, totally lacking in atmosphere; they are built for the correct number of parishioners but never to the glory of God.

No, I would like us to create art in the only spirit in which art can flourish and has flourished so far—in all cultures. Art has nothing to do with purpose; it is without purpose. It is better to neglect purpose and create a true work of art than to allow purpose—that is, cold rationality—to triumph. Art similarly has nothing to do with time limits, or at least not with the tyranny of time limits, which we tend to subject ourselves to today. Anyone who wants to further art or create art must be able to take his time. It is better to take years to plan and build than to force a work of art to be planned and built hastily simply for the sake of a momentary advantage. This would appear nowadays to be a heretical statement but I feel I have a right to make it since on more than one occasion I have myself been forced by circumstances to plan and build a project in an incredibly short time and have managed to do so.

But, ladies and gentlemen, we are dealing here with Salzburg, a city which is a gem, and with a site for the building which is unrivaled. It is a German city that has slipped down a long way south, is influenced by the south and yet is still German, since it is Baroque, not in the purely stylistic sense of the word, but in its attitude, in its art. All German art is more or less Baroque, eccentric, peculiar, unacademic, from the Romanesque period to German Gothic and up to Rococo.

And if, as the brief says, you do not want your building to be an imitation of an historic form, which would seem to me to go without saying, I am nevertheless designing for Salzburg and, whether I like it or not, if I want the new building to be in harmony with the past, I must confront myself with the magic of the past. In any case, I don't know how an artist can work without the past, without searching for and finding an emotional attitude to it, without devouring it completely in order to then overcome it and create something that can stand alongside it in its own right. Everyone has done this, even the artists from the past, they in particular. How else would it be possible for the creations even of Italian Baroque architects working on German soil, consciously or unconsciously influenced by their Gothic surroundings, to have finally turned their work into what is known as German Baroque, which increasingly assumed the characteristics of the Gothic, thus becoming increasingly like it? Here again it is merely a question of how. I too hate history when it tries to restrict me and love it when it arouses my artistic instincts. And it seems to me that the artistic heritage of the Germans particularly today, as we have been annihilated by destiny and are now slowly recovering, will appear more significant than ever. Once more the philologically and historically trained preachers are there saying we have to repeat what happened one hundred years ago, that is to say, seek refuge in Neo-Classicism, while others are advocating a poor people's style, since we are now poor. No, no, and again no, I say! Let us in spite of everything look forward cheerfully to the future and create a style for the future that is appropriate for a strong nation. And let us at the same time pick up the tradition of our culture in a spiritual sense, not as slaves to form. The Germans adopted Gothic and after the school-like period of the masons' lodges heightened it in the style of St. Stefan in Vienna, the Lorenzkirche in Nuremberg, and the Albrechtsburg in Meissen. The Germans heightened the classical Baroque of the Italians in the works of Prandtauer and Hildebrandt, the Asam brothers and Pöppelmann, to such an extent that any rationalist western European elements disappeared. Where is the nation in Europe that could produce something to match the Zwinger in Dresden, the South German or Austrian Baroque? The many-faceted, profoundly mystical, grotesque, and charming soul of the Germans comes to life again in these buildings. This German Baroque manner, this rural Rococo, without sophistication, playful, sometimes harsh, severe, even clumsy, this strong and yet weird manner has always been present—in Dürer's *Melancholy,* in the work of Altdorfer, in the attitude of Romanesque cathedrals, particularly those of the transitional style, once the foreign manner that had been adopted had been overcome, and also in the architecture of the German Late Renaissance. The thread of continuity was broken again and again by alien invasions from the west and the south and it was not until the late phase of all styles that the Germans found their own manner again, which the French and Italians considered barbaric.

It is a fact that German art—which up to the end of the eighteenth century made all towns and cities, particularly in South Germany and Austria, so eternally rich—was not truly annihilated until art theory gained dominance. Throughout the ages the justification of this or that movement in art has been the subject of philosophizing, and at all times of strong artistic tension the pros and cons of stylistic attitudes have been vehemently discussed. But an academic way of looking at things, which gradually became more and more dictatorial, descended like a dark fog over the blossoms of a naive and joyous way of creating art. A style that had been developed with the highest degree of artistic sensitivity and was highly refined but devoted to only one kind of building—the ancient Greek temple—was taken as the ultimate truth, so that our buildings were forced to conform to the rules of this style. Certainly recognizing a need for purification, not only the Germans but also the French tried to tread the path of antiquity. But the Germans assumed the right to create a made-to-measure straitjacket for art by requiring that architecture meticulously incorporate the results of constantly new scientific research. After the endless research on the different "styles" carried out in the nineteenth century, we are still in this straitjacket. Schooling smothered the natural instincts of the German people, so that today they are only capable of thinking in intellectual concepts and have completely forgotten how to use their eyes.

And this scientific, intellectualized training, along with the dominance of technical thinking, has banished the architect to a life at the drawing board. In the nineteenth century infinitely more architectural drawings were produced than in all the thousands of years since the world began, and yet in no other period were such bad buildings built. Today if we want to progress and extricate ourselves from these erroneous ways, we must recognize this contradiction. An architect who thought about how to improve architects' training and wrote a very thorough book on the subject coined a very fitting sentence: The first drawing that was produced essentially for its own sake marked the beginning of architecture's downfall. In the nineteenth century an infinite number of drawings were produced solely for their own sake. Already in the Renaissance and Baroque periods sins of this kind were committed, but not until the nineteenth century did this over-fervent drawing on the part of architects become a plague that totally annihilated their ability to think and work in three dimensions.

Architects lost their sense of space, they drew and redrew, forgetting that, as architecture is the art of space and therefore three-dimensional, a drawing very imperfectly depicts a building, so that a drawing can only be an aid to building.

The buildings of the Chinese, the Indians, the ancient Greeks and Romans, those of the Romanesque period, the Gothic period, much of the Renaissance, and most of the Baroque period have an intense plastic quality. The majority of those of the nineteenth century, and of our time too, were created without that quality and consist merely of a series of individual surfaces loosely connected with one another without forming a whole.

And if we ask once more how we can progress we must realize that tradition can only help us mentally but not in a directly formal way; it can only help us to realize where our unique qualities and strengths lie. And this cannot be as difficult for any other people in Europe as it is for the Germans. The watershed between East and West runs through Germany. We are the country that is the center of Europe. We understand both worlds, but we were always stronger and more original when we turned away from the West and gravitated toward the mystical ways of the East.

I have deviated quite considerably from the subject of the Festival Theater; I have spoken *pro domo* for that which I believe and represent as an artist. And that is certainly what you ask of me.

I must say something else. Professor Roller has very commendably drawn up a brief which he says himself is not intended to be completely binding. But it is nevertheless the only brief that has been drawn up to date and Professor Roller will have to grant me absolution for the fact that, although I have based my work on it, I shall also present views that are contrary to it in order to make my position clear. This brief, which is the basis of my work to date, expresses the desire for a building that is "extremely simple, almost without ornamentation," with an interior that is without ornamentation and in dark tones. This in effect means, according to how you want to interpret it, that restraint is being recommended or ordered. This desired restraint must be based on a carefully considered intention, which is to ensure that there are no distractions so that the audience can concentrate on the play. Also, in certain cases it should be possible to rearrange the auditorium to suit any particular production.... The brief states that the auditorium is to be dark and without ornamentation —in other words, without any social significance....

Is this the right way? I feel that the stage, where the unheard-of will often take place, often something very colorful and lively, should form a much greater unity with the auditorium than is usual. Is this possible, given the concept underlying the brief? Here the artist in me rebels, the artist who wants his rights as the artists in the past had their rights. It is my firm conviction that any restraint, any denial, is wrong because it contradicts the essence of a work of art.

This raises again the whole problem of architecture, which has been so pushed into the background in our time. And once more I look to the past, to a time when there was no doubt about what architecture meant. How was it in the Baroque period, how did the stage relate to the auditorium? One thing is quite clear: Both spaces storm and rage to the same rhythm, and, whether a proscenium stage is used or not, there is a unity between the stage and the auditorium. The proscenium stage does not cut the audience off from the action on stage, its architecture sings and is in tune with the auditorium; only its great depth contradicts today's ideas. This is where I believe the problem lies. It does not really matter whether the stage opening is larger or smaller, it is the harmony of the artistic treatment of the stage and the auditorium that is important. And the auditorium must not fade into insignificance, because this would condemn the stage to the same fate. With all due respect and admiration for the achievements of our stage designers, I must say that their work is not yet accurate enough. The stage set, whether representing the sky or the earth, a banqueting hall or a hut, must have architectural qualities and be in harmony with the style of the auditorium. This is what we must strive for; otherwise we will once more reach an impasse. And it is no use quoting the Classical Greek theater as evidence for the opposite case. It had a stage that was architecturally articulated and, what is more, it was an open-air theater; above the spectators hovered the sky and the clouds and around them were mountains and trees. Here all these things have to be built. Above the people in the auditorium a sky has to be built, a sky with an architectural form continuing over the stage which also has an architectural form. I keep mentioning architecture not because I am an architect—I do not believe that I am exclusively an architect—but because I believe that architecture holds the key to solving all of today's artistic problems and because the Festival Theater in Salzburg has a cultural problem to solve. What we must do is gather the arts together. This will not be achieved by theoretical explanations or resolutions, however much they may seem to be in keeping with our times. Architecture alone can weld the fine arts together—the right kind of architecture. No Neo-Classicism, no puritanism, however well meant, can help here, but only an architecture that gives space to every kind of art and lets this grow out of the building itself.

In Gothic, Baroque, and Rococo architecture no figure ever exists in isolation, it grows out of the building in the form of an ornamental pinnacle. It is of secondary importance whether the ornamental curve necessary for the overall harmony depicts something figurative; something like a figure is only appropriate if it reinforces the architecture and makes it ring true.

I do not wish to go too much into detail here. I am, however, certain that a new art form of this kind can only emerge from craftsmanship. It is up to the architect as one of the leading craftsmen to develop an architecture that by its whole nature forces every craftsman to be a part of the orchestration of the building from the very beginning— each according to his skill and the possibilities offered by the project.

And that is why I preach richness, abundance of the spirit and of form, a richness that captures in form each action of the craftsman. We may restrict ourselves in our choice of materials and choose the less valuable, more obvious, more easily available, and therefore least expensive. The cheapest coat of paint, when it strays into the rich realm of interpretation, can conjure up great beauty, and the stone quarried and worked locally will give the most authentic basic color for the building in its setting.

I have deviated again from the problem in the strictest sense, but I felt obliged to say all this. And to return to the building project: To date, the really precise belief, which architects need in order to develop a scheme, has not been available. Professor Roller has leaped into the breach with his brief and will have to forgive me for having been forced to call upon it several times to explain contrary opinions—I did this only for purposes of clarification. But the fact that the people responsible for the artistic aspects of the project have not yet drawn up a specific brief was, of course, a little unfortunate for the technical part of the project and has forced me to use my imagination. It is not up to the architect to draw up a brief for a building, nor can he assume part of the client's role. He would then, of course, begin to bend the brief to fit in with the way he would like the form to be and could easily invent conditions that bear no relation to reality.

In view of the extreme brevity of the time available to me, it drove me to despair to have to throw myself into the controversies about the theater itself and become involved in the pros and cons of each side, in the arguments that have raged throughout the last decades and have still not been brought to a successful conclusion. And as far as I can gather, the German sin of standing on principle plays a major role in this. Aggressive articles by established theater architects, or by young architects allowing themselves to put forward theories in order to gain their doctorates, usually attack theaters that have several circles and postulate the purity of the amphitheater. Some are irritated by the fact that circles are undemocratic, others by the fire hazard, and still others base their ideas on the work of their colleague Schinkel and see their work as a continuation of his. All this reminds us of the attempts of Semper and Wagner. Semper often created a bad impression because he allowed his clients and their consideration of the audiences to drive him farther and farther away from the new forms he had originally designed.

I am always extremely suspicious when a true artist is obliged to accept a demand dictated to him by someone else. Please do not misunderstand me, I have great respect for amateurs who, with great love and devotion, throw themselves into a problem that is outside their profession. They are the innocent, whose intuition, combined with often admirable tenacity, enables them to find the root of an idea that experts have dismissed with a shrug of the shoulders. But I am not an expert on theaters and therefore do not have to concern myself with the problem, and if a brilliant theater expert asked me to create a theater with ten circles because this would fit in with his artistic intentions I would grapple with the problem and try to develop an appropriate artistic form. Form and form alone is what is important to me. Once again I have tried to commit an act of heresy that does not accord with Professor Roller's belief.

I felt I had to contradict the publications that were bent on advocating the amphitheater and nothing else. Is it so terribly undemocratic and antisocial to make tiers, or to be more precise boxes? Is there no performance, particularly no musical performance, that one does not enjoy more when not part of the masses?

I realize very well that contemporary theater of the kind Professor Reinhardt is striving for needs the great unity of the mass audience, needs the suggestive power that emanates from a mass of this kind, and therefore demands primarily an amphitheater.

But when I wanted to create an architectural sky over an amphitheater, when I tried to further develop the dome of the Grosses Schauspielhaus in Berlin into a ceiling that would be acoustically better while not detracting from its power, I cut lines of boxes into that ceiling. And I placed the staircases to these boxes in such a way that the outer shell of the building stepped down in rhythmically alternating terraces. So what I achieved in other projects through a great deal of additional design, and what had come about in the opera house in Berlin in a very makeshift way, by the creation of fire exits, has happened here [in the Festival Theater] of its own accord, by virtue of the fact that the whole building on the side that faces the mountains is articulated into terraces or steps.

It is not the purpose of this speech to describe in more detail the scheme I have brought with me. That is best done using the drawings and model. And these relate mainly to the overall complex. It is true, however, that the formal structure and silhouette are strongly determined by the individual parts, so that the architect has no choice but to go into some detail, albeit sketchily, about the individual entities that make up the whole complex.

And having fulfilled the needs of the project, having paid attention to what the visitors to a Festival Theater can expect and in this case must expect, one thing is certain in my opinion: The practical and technical aspects should not be paramount here, the quickest and most convenient must not triumph over the artistic intentions of the architect. Anyone visiting this festival complex must have time, must forget all thoughts of haste, and the design of the complex must make him forget himself and become immersed in the processes of watching and listening.

The drama already contained in the architecture of the space ought to captivate him and lull him into forgetting our world which has been made the slave of technology.

Without exaggeration, the site which Professor Roller, with his unerring artistic instinct, has chosen is wonderful. But it makes enormous demands on the artist when he has to design the form of the building down to the last detail. Salzburg and Hellbrunn demand an extraordinary effort from the artist if he wants his design to stand the test of time. For this is what everyone must wish and hope, that the building that will be built here will not serve a temporary theatrical or musical need for a few decades only. It must be a building which, even if the ideas about theater change, can still assert its form; and apart from perfectly fulfilling its purpose, it must be a seminal building that will herald the dawn of a new age in the arts in German countries.

I have refrained from interrupting this speech to comment on it, and, since it is of intrinsic importance to this text, I have included the passage toward the end in which Poelzig talks of how he designed the interior, although the reader is already familiar with it. I have even left in the repetitions, the parts where Poelzig rails again and again against technology and emphasizes that form and form alone is the only thing that moves him—although, in fact, this text is more about content than anything else, about the theater and the theater in Salzburg. For Poelzig, Salzburg is not only a city and countryside that send the architect into "a kind of frenzy," it also represents a culture and a history. He talks also about the relationship the present wants to establish with this history; although to a great extent this was Poelzig's personal obsession, he was not alone in wanting this. I have left all this untouched because I believe it is the finest thing Poelzig ever said. He concludes his address by stating his intention to build a seminal building that will herald the dawn of a new age in the arts in German countries. And if that may sound immodest to the reader, I can only say Poelzig had the right to speak in this way.

The reader will see for himself what became of it. In concrete terms, nothing became of it. The Festival Theater was never built, nor did it become the spiritual point of departure for a new epoch in the arts. It was—let us be honest—an illusion. And the next period of his work will show that Poelzig was forced to adopt a different attitude toward the new powers he hated so much: technology and science.

CHAPTER EIGHT
A New Beginning: Berlin

The Lessons of Salzburg

A FESTIVAL THEATER was built in Salzburg, and it is still to this day, as everyone knows, an unparalleled international success. It was built —but not by Poelzig, and not in Hellbrunn. It was erected in the so-called Felsen Reitschule, in the very center of the city, and I can describe from personal experience what it means for Salzburg. Every summer Salzburg has more crowds of tourists than any other city I have ever visited. It is quite literally impossible to move in the streets. The cliffs, at the foot of which this wonderful city was built, have endless garages tunneled into them. At the close of the festival there is a very lively social life. (No one would have been more surprised than Wolfgang Amadeus Mozart, whose name is somehow associated with this cultural tourism —the house where he was born swarms with tourists. He would certainly not have wished this success upon his hometown—he *hated* Salzburg.) So much on the Festival Theater *in* Salzburg.

But what about Hellbrunn? Of course, every visitor feels the "kind of frenzy" that captivated Poelzig when he saw this site. Hellbrunn is a Baroque pleasure palace to the south of Salzburg. It lies between the city with its unforgettable silhouette and the Alps whose foothills come right down to the edge of the city and surround it. Hellbrunn's park is in the plain but within it is a wooded hill with a natural ravine, which was called the "stone theater." From this theater there is a view of the Alps and to the north a view of the green domes of the city beneath the castle, the "Veste Salzburg." There is no doubt that it is one of the most beautiful places in the world. "But," my companion asked in reference to the Festival Theater project, "where did they want to put the ancillary buildings—the hotels, restaurants, garages?" Where indeed? Maybe it was healthy realism that prevented the Viennese architect Josef Hoffmann from submitting a scheme without exactly saying that he did not want to. Poelzig, and those who pursued this impossible undertaking with him for a while, obviously did not possess this realism. Poelzig's design for the Festival Theater in Hellbrunn was the work of enthusiasts (see Figs. 189–191, 194–198). I have used the plural since Poelzig was not the only person who clung with his heart and soul to the idea of a festival theater on the hill at Hellbrunn. And although it was never built, it still had an effect in that it increased even further Poelzig's already considerable prestige. He now became *the phenomenon* in German architecture.

The years immediately after the war were

characterized by a paucity of buildings and a wealth of imagination. Organizations were founded, such as the Working Council for Art whose revolutionary intentions are obvious from its name; the "November Group," called after the November revolution, which people hoped would have further consequences; and finally Bruno Taut's "Glass Chain," a circle of friends who met in the name of Utopia. They produced sketches of things to come. Taut said "Let us be Utopian!" and spoke of the "watershed" between Utopia and built architecture. Occasionally something *was* built. Taut became city architect of Magdeburg, and during his period of office he was responsible for brightly colored architecture and for one very beautiful large hall, one of the few large buildings that were realized at that time. The Chilehaus in Hamburg by Fritz Höger (see Fig. 16) and Peter Behrens's office building for the dyeworks at Höchst near Frankfurt are two others. What was mostly built were housing projects where new — and cheap — construction methods were tried out. But a lot of fantasizing went on: Scharoun, the Luckhardt brothers, Finsterlin, Max Taut, even Gropius, belonged to the "Glass Chain" and wanted to carry on the cause of the failed revolution in sketches and manifestoes. Just how popular imagination remained, even at a time when it no longer was the one and only quality to be aimed at, can be deduced from Adolf Behne's strange definition of objectivity: "Objectivity *[Sachlichkeit]* is imagination that works with precise things."[1] These architects did not quite want to abandon imagination. It was prosperity — more than "objectivity" — that in 1924 ensured that imagination lost importance. The water flowed from Taut's "watershed" toward the feasible.

I have wanted to give some indication here of the architectural scene from which Poelzig's Salzburg scheme arose. I said "scheme" in the singular, since the first scheme, which was the most visionary, was the one that caused the greatest stir — and still does (see Figs. 189, 190). It was the result of the "kind of frenzy," stimulated by the project and its setting, that set free Poelzig's creative powers. The first scheme for Salzburg was his most uncompromising venture into the realm of the imaginary (uncompromising in that it was more sustained, better defined than his extreme design for the Dresden fire station had been [see Fig. 143]). Let me repeat that against the background of the prevalent Expressionist architecture, the Festival Theater was both Baroque and yet still Poelzig. Of an earlier design, I said it was "Poelzig and yet Baroque." I am here putting the stress on the word *Baroque,* on the will to forge a link to those aspects of German culture that were most German: a sense of space and an ability to transform space that amounted to musicality. It is no coincidence that *musical* was one of Poelzig's favorite words. Even the few masterpieces of Expressionism that actually were built take their reference from history — as, incidentally, do some of the designs that are the farthest removed from reality. Bruno Taut's *"Domstern"* ("Star Dome"), for example, is Gothic (see Fig. 140); Gothic is the predominant influence. The very fact that Poelzig turned to the Baroque puts his visionary work in a different class from that of his contemporaries. He alone achieved a synthesis that raised people's hopes at the time, because it looked as if it would be a step forward spatially. Clearly expressed in form, his work had a "built" quality, even if the individual designs were not always feasible; this work was the attempt, so typically "Poelzig," to create a quintessence of past and future: musical space.

The third scheme for the Festival Theater represents the end of this attempt in its most "historic," visibly Baroque, form (see Figs. 195 – 198). Poelzig is now moving toward a style that was gaining popularity. The forms are becoming calmer. *These* forms can be built; some of those used in the first attempt could possibly have been built. This is true of the interior details. How the individual forms on the outside of the building could actually have been hewn from stone is not easy to imagine.

From now on there is a division between his architectural work and his work with ceramics

199 Hans Poelzig. Sketch with bridges.

and as a designer for stage and film sets. The latter remain in the realms of history and of the imagination but the approach to architecture had changed. A design like Poelzig's highly imaginative scheme for Salzburg had become a thing of the past. A divergence between designs intended to be built and pure play with forms can be observed in Poelzig's work, as in that of other architects. Erich Mendelsohn is a good example: He had tried to build one of his sketches of "fluid" concrete architecture, the Einstein Tower, and having found it impossible to build it in concrete, was obliged to use brick, a tedious process. Thereafter his designs for buildings became more realistic and his sketches even more fantastic. For the artist, the art of the architect is an act of resignation. Those, like Heinrich Tessenow, who affirmed this act, were lucky. Poelzig had to abandon something and to look elsewhere for the kind of satisfaction he could not find in architecture.

I will therefore refrain from saying a great deal about his designs for the theater and film and his work with porcelain. I am concerned with the architect. I see his other work—his painting, too—as a vent, which his permanently active imagination needed. He did produce works of art in these fields but they did not, at least in my view, have any effect on his architecture. Or is it possible to point to a line that could be said to lead from the city he built for *The Golem* to his own architecture? It is a different matter with the sketches, which he produced continually. They are architectural sketches, often spatial sketches. The sketches he did in connection with the Grosses Schauspielhaus give a glimpse of a space that Poelzig quite certainly wanted to create—a continuum of space. Other sketches do the same thing, the one with the bridges, for example (Fig. 199). The bridge motif is repeated *ad infinitum.* Strange that Poelzig has airplanes flying over this ravine that he "built." The spatial continuum places Poelzig near Piranesi, whom he certainly admired. Other sketches show the improbable rising out of the familiar, the painterly Italian town (Fig. 200). "I would like to build something like this," the sketch seems to be saying. Of course, he added to the extreme Salzburg design even more extreme sketches. One finds skyscraper sketches, which are reminiscent of New York City (Fig. 201). Poelzig never went to America, incidentally. In fact, if I am not mistaken, he had little desire to go there. But he was fascinated by the fact that things hitherto unheard of actually existed. His sketches for stage sets are of a quite different nature, for example a design for *Don Giovanni,* done in his Salzburg period (see Fig. 181). If one tries to talk about the sketches being of a particular style, one could say that a lot of them are Gothic, or Baroque, or Gothic-Baroque. As he said in his Salzburg speech, those are the two kinds of German architecture that fascinated him (see Chapter 7, Doc. 7B). It is striking that his old structures—the Poelzig semicircle in a strong wall—hardly occur after the war, not until they are called back for the "Schauburg" in 1932 (see Figs. 320–325).

His *architectural* designs continue the path that began with the third design for Salzburg. It should be pointed out immediately that despite Poelzig's prestige, none of his designs was built. This, too, one is tempted to say, is a reason, perhaps *the* reason, for his strong activity in other areas of art. I have already described how he was disappointed by what Berlin had to offer him as an architect after he had set up an

200 Hans Poelzig. Sketch of a city. In the foreground, houses in Mediterranean style.

201 Hans Poelzig. Sketch of buildings with towers at the four corners.

office there. By 1924 he still had not built anything. If one looks at the years in Dresden and the years in Berlin in the list of his works one discovers nothing but unbuilt projects in the years between 1916 and 1923–24, with the exception of the Grosses Schauspielhaus (and some very minor buildings). For a man who had built a great deal in Breslau and was at the height of his fame and productivity, this must have been almost unbearable. I have spoken already about some of the Dresden projects. Let us continue down the list of works:

A New Beginning: Berlin 161

202 Hans Poelzig. Gas storage tower for Dresden, 1917, project. Model.

1917	Dresden	Gasometer (Fig. 202)	Unrealized
	Dresden	Town hall	Unrealized
	Dresden	Group of museums	Unrealized
	Dresden	City plan	Unrealized
	Dresden	Bridge over the Elbe (Fig. 203)	Unrealized
	Dresden	Concert hall	Unrealized
1919	Berlin	Grosses Schauspielhaus	
1920	Dresden	Porcelain Pavilion (exhibition building)	
	Dresden	Film set for *Der Golem*	
1920-22	Salzburg	Festival Theater	Unrealized
1921	Dresden	Hotel	Unrealized
	Dresden	Bank	Unrealized
	Dresden	Hotel	Unrealized
	Hellerau	Wooden houses	Unrealized
	Dresden	Majolica chapel (Fig. 204)	Unrealized
1922	Berlin	High-rise at Friedrichstrasse station	Unrealized
	Cologne	Commericial center	Unrealized
	Dresden	Majolica fountain	
1923-24	Hannover	Office building for the Mayer brothers (Fig. 205)	

The total of projects realized between 1917 and 1922: two pieces of ceramics work—a Porcelain Pavilion and a majolica fountain. Apart from the Grosses Schauspielhaus, that is all. The office building in Hannover that marks the renewal of Poelzig's work as an architect in 1923–24 is one of his weakest buildings: This time it really is "zigzag style" that he uses to decorate a simple brick building (see Fig. 205). There is no other way of describing it. One can positively hear him saying to himself: "How can I make this thing into something?"

Of greater interest than the realized works of this period are several projects that were never built. Let us look now at some of these and finally at Poelzig's Capitol Cinema in Berlin (1925).

High-rise building at Friedrichstrasse station, Berlin, 1922, project

A number of famous architects took part in the competition for this building, including Hans Scharoun and Ludwig Mies van der Rohe,

203 Hans Poelzig. Bridge across the Elbe River in Dresden, 1918, project.

204 Hans Poelzig. Chapel for Dresden, 1921, project. Model carried out in Majolica.

205 Hans Poelzig. Mayer Brothers administration building, Hannover, 1924.

A New Beginning: Berlin 163

206 (above) Hans Poelzig. High-rise office building near Friedrichstrasse station. Berlin, 1921–22, competition design.

207 (top right) Louis Sullivan. Guaranty Building, Buffalo, 1895.

208 (bottom right) Ludwig Mies van der Rohe. High-rise office building near Friedrichstrasse station, Berlin 1921–22, competition design.

architects of the younger generation. The triangular form with concave sides in Poelzig's design would reappear later in his project for a library beside the Reichstag building (Fig. 206; see Fig. 270). The ground floor and mezzanine with large windows, accommodating shops

209 Hans Poelzig. Hotel for Dresden, 1921, project.

210 Hans Poelzig. Merchants' Building, Cologne, 1922, project.

and a restaurant, along with the verticality of the floors above where the offices were to be, recall Louis Sullivan's Guaranty Building in Buffalo and other skyscrapers by him (Fig. 207). The strong upper rim of these buildings is missing from Poelzig's building. It is a good, or let's say an excellent, modern building of its time, but beside Scharoun's imaginative and innovative design and Mies van der Rohe's simple, coherent glass form (Fig. 208), it has not proved to be a memorable design.

Hotel in Dresden, 1921, project

Poelzig's hotel project was dominated by the terrace motif (Fig. 209). One can see how intensively he worked on the theme of a terraced building at this time. The terracing is appropriate for a hotel, particularly the central section housing the restaurants. The way the stories also step back slightly on the rear facade of the hotel draws the building together magnificently. The horizontality of the stories dominates. The corners are rounded. All the roof terraces are surrounded by arcades. They provide a finish to the top of the building. It is regrettable that this excellent project never got farther than the drawing board.

Earlier I mentioned the project for a bank in Dresden in connection with the second version of the Bismarck Memorial (see Figs. 108, 107). There is, as I said, a similarity between the two in the solid walls, reinforced by rounded pillars, elements more appropriate for the memorial than the bank.

Merchants' Building, Cologne, 1922, project

The commercial center in Cologne, which finally was to be sited behind the choir of the cathedral and was planned in this context, brings to mind familiar motifs: The terracing, the rows of arched windows in the terraces, recall the third version of the theater project for Salzburg (Fig. 210; see Figs. 195–198). The terraced building surrounds the exchange hall, whose eastern facade, without windows and

211 Hans Poelzig. Shop and office building containing the Capitol Cinema, near the Zoological Garden, Berlin, 1925. First version, sketch.

slightly convex, occupies the central section of the back of the building. The commercial center is one of the most beautiful volumes Poelzig ever designed. I believe that the scheme also shows tactful respect for the cathedral. But this important piece of work, too, was never to get beyond the project stage. Designs like this, however, like the hotel in Dresden (see Fig. 209) and the commercial center for Cologne, show how Poelzig was trying to find a modern urban architecture. It was an architecture in layers, in terraces—modeled, one could say.

Capitol Cinema, Berlin, 1925

The projects developed during these years embody a particular attitude, or should I say a feeling, for form. They are terraced, rounded, molded. They are still related to Salzburg. The first major building in Berlin, the Capitol Cinema, and the complex of shops it was part of, in the center of the western part of Berlin, was a step into the unknown. One of the preliminary sketches shows that Poelzig took this step hesitantly (Fig. 211). This sketch already contains

212 Hans Poelzig. Shop and office building containing the Capitol Cinema, 1925. Entrance to the cinema.

what was to be a characteristic feature of the shops: broad openings between pillars. Here, however, they are part of a terraced building. In the complex as actually built, the terraces are no longer there. What remains is a two-story columned building with an attic, on top of which sits the octagonal auditorium, slightly set back (Fig. 212). There were earlier versions to this building, shops without a cinema, planned for a nearby plot. There, too, there was originally a terraced section, and there, too, it was abandoned. On this building the system was developed, as was the shape of the pillars and the profiles of the beams hinted at above them. It was perhaps very useful that Poelzig hit upon the theme of shops at exactly this time — the mid-twenties. Shops could only be in a framed structure; walls with arches above the doors and windows would have been useless. Poelzig therefore had to start afresh and naturally moved in the direction of the new architecture that was taking shape at this time. This architecture was, as I stressed at the beginning of this study, the work of the younger generation, and a certain reticence is noticeable in Poelzig's version. I have already mentioned the elements Poelzig worked with: pillars that are not flush with the facade but slope on both sides and have only one narrow vertical fillet in the center, that is, pillars that evoke, however re-

A New Beginning: Berlin   167

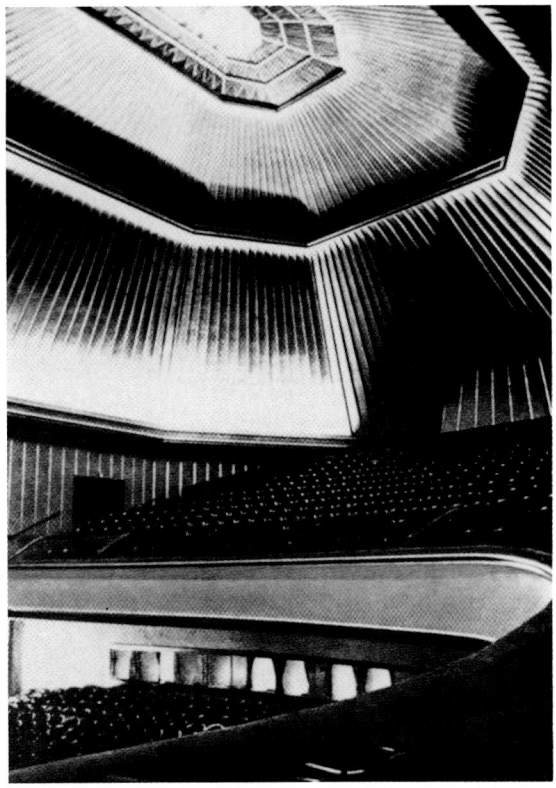

213 Hans Poelzig. Capitol Cinema. Auditorium.

214 Hans Poelzig. Capitol Cinema. Stage framing.

motely, the Classical column, and on top of them is something that can be interpreted as a very shallow entablature. The fact that the upper pillars are considerably shorter and seem slimmer than those on the ground floor corresponds to the Doric temple. *One* contemporary critic, Erich Mendelsohn, found this Neo-Classical pretence so irritating that he spoke of a "vague feeling that hovers in space."[2] However one likes to describe it, it is the attempt of an historically educated architect to relate the framed building to historical forms. Classical architecture, to which Poelzig actually had no genuine relationship, was the only obvious choice here. It is almost touching to see how Poelzig tries to prove the old saying that an architect is a bricklayer who has learned Latin. There was also the added difficulty that the

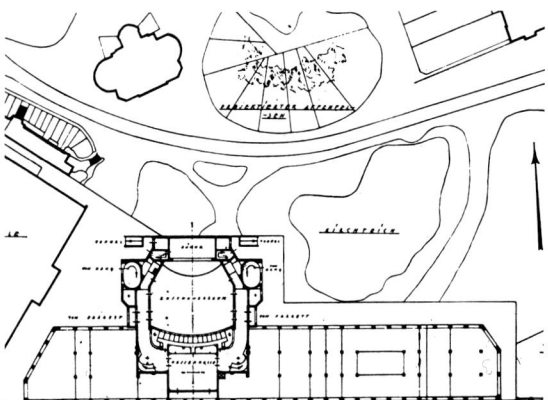

215 Hans Poelzig. Shop and office building containing the Capitol Cinema. Layout plan. The building stood between the Emperor Wilhelm Memorial Church and the Zoo. It was destroyed in the Second World War.

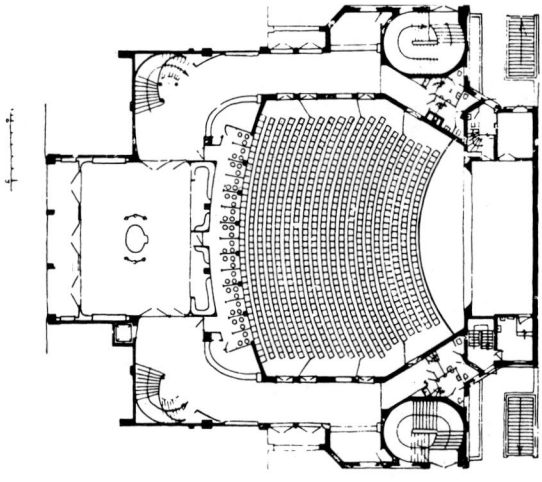
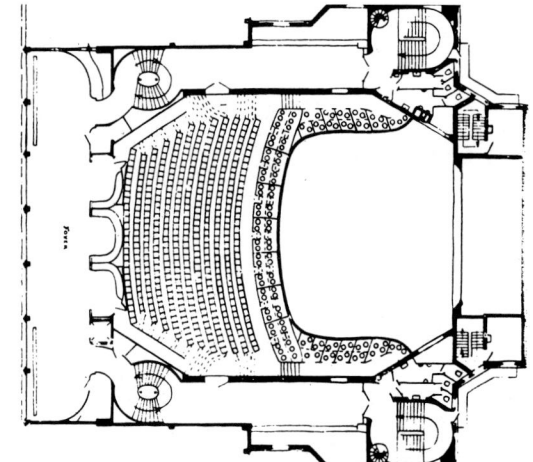
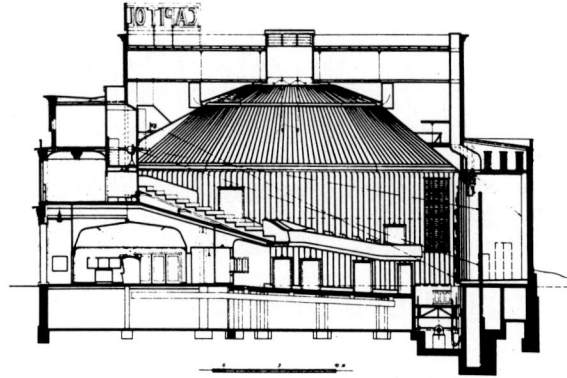

216 (above) Hans Poelzig. Capitol Cinema. Plans and section.

217 (right) Hans Poelzig. Capitol Cinema. Bar and staircase.

218 (opposite) Hans Poelzig. Capitol Cinema. Staircase.

general public in 1925 neither understood Latin nor did they expect an architect to speak it, so that to understand *this* Latin one had to be an architect and look very closely.

Entering the cinema one finds oneself in a different world—Poelzig's world (Figs. 213–218). Rarely is the space inside a building so different from its outward appearance. This is seen in the auditorium, an elongated octagon, whose walls and dome are decorated with

closely spaced ribs, not unlike the decorative ribs in the theater in the third version of the Salzburg project (see Fig. 196). The contrast to the exterior is even stronger in the corridors and staircases, particularly the latter. It is as if the architect had been waiting for the chance finally to be himself. The lighting is indirect almost throughout—as in the Grosses Schauspielhaus. I feel it is a pity that Poelzig used any direct lighting at all. The light fixtures, particularly those next to the proscenium arch, do not fit well in this very fine room.

The Capitol was the first postwar cinema of architectural quality. It makes a correspondingly strong statement. Before the war there had been a small cinema by Bruno Taut on Kottbusserdamm and Oskar Kaufmann's Cines cinema at Nollendorfplatz, which I shall come back to in connection with Poelzig's Deli cinema in Breslau (see Chapter 10 and Figs. 235–239).

The Capitol Cinema was, moreover, the beginning of Poelzig's work as an architect in Berlin, after a break of almost five years since the Grosses Schauspielhaus. It can be classed as a difficult beginning. The framed building with Neo-Classical overtones was one thing, the interiors something quite different. The use of framed construction represents the first move toward an architecture that was just emerging at this very moment. Its most important advocate at the time was probably Max Taut. The interiors contain a positive profusion of possibilities—or are they memories? In the Capitol Cinema, Poelzig takes an important step beyond the Salzburg phase, and if we recall that the Salzburg phase had actually begun in Dresden, one can say he took a decisive step beyond the whole middle phase of his work, the phase that is known as his Expressionist phase. From now on he will try not to avoid new things and yet remain himself.

CHAPTER NINE
Success

ALLOW ME TO RECALL HERE BRIEFLY the developments taking place in German architecture in the 1920s. The years between 1926 and the early thirties became known as the "Bauhaus years." They were and were not the Bauhaus years. The avant-garde was, like every avant-garde, a minority. But since they were a very conspicuous minority whose activities had far-reaching and lasting consequences, their reputation has eclipsed that of the mainstream architects who shaped architecture in Germany at the time. These architects all had to confront the avant-garde. One way of doing this was to attack them. Paul Schmitthenner, and the Stuttgart School he inspired, did this (Fig. 219). These were the architects who took the next step—beyond the avant-garde to the Third Reich. Most of the architects of that time, however, following Emil Fahrenkamp's example, designed "modern" buildings (Fig. 220). Peter Behrens had commissions—and designed modern buildings. Poelzig finally had commissions again and was forced to come to terms with the new architecture that developed around the mid-twenties. (See Chapter 9, Docs. 9A and 9C.)

Even the avant-garde proper was not identical with the Bauhaus. The Trade Unions Building in Berlin, which Max Taut (Bruno Taut's brother) designed in 1922–24, was pure reinforced concrete construction. In 1924 Max Taut continued to use this method of construction with great energy for the rear part of the building for the Book Printers' Trade Union in Berlin (Figs. 221, 222).

From 1925 onward Bruno Taut, in collaboration with Martin Wagner, Berlin's new city architect, built large housing projects on the edge of the city (see Fig. 18). At the same time, Ernst May and Ferdinand Kramer were building housing estates in and around Frankfurt. Le Corbusier's *Vers Une Architecture*, published in 1923, was widely read. In Holland J.J.P. Oud's modern housing estates replaced the Expressionism of architects such as Piet Kramer (Fig. 223). Rotterdam, it was said, had displaced Amsterdam. In 1927 the Werkbund's "Weissenhof" housing estate was built near Stuttgart (see Figs. 305–307, 309). In Berlin in the late twenties other large housing estates were built, such as the "Siemensstadt" and "Weisse Stadt" (Fig. 224), as well as the estate built by the Construction Research Company of the Reich (Reichsforschungsgesellschaft für Wirtschaftlichkeit im Bau- und Wohnungswesen) in Haselhorst near Spandau, which was intended to test the system of row housing, both in theory and in practice. Other individual works of great

219 Paul Schmitthenner. House in Im Fischtal estate, Berlin-Zehlendorf, 1927.

220 Emil Fahrenkamp. Shell Building, Berlin, 1931.

importance, such as Mies van der Rohe's Barcelona Pavilion and his Tugendhat House in Brno, were also built at this time.

For a while it looked as if the avant-garde had gained the upper hand, in spite of ever stronger opposition. In 1927, however, a housing estate called "Im Fischtal" was built as a counterdemonstration next to the "Onkel Tom" estate in Zehlendorf, designed by Taut, Salvisberg, and Häring: pitched roofs versus flat roofs (see Figs. 18, 219, 308, 310). Tessenow, Schmitthenner, Schopohl—and Poelzig—built houses at Im Fischtal. Some of the most conservative of these architects came together under the name "The Block" for the purpose of opposing the group of modernists known as "The Ring." (Poelzig belonged to neither group. Tessenow belonged to The Ring.) The Block accused the avant-garde of wanting to invent an architecture *ab ovo*, based purely on rational considerations that did not draw upon the past in any way: Form follows function (as Louis Sullivan had proclaimed much earlier). Hugo Häring's idea was that form is dictated by circumstance, that it is the inevitable result of the requirements of housing (or whatever the project in question) and of the technology available to solve the problem, and that it is

221 Max Taut. Book Printers' Building, Berlin, 1924–26. Rear wing.

therefore something to be discovered, not invented. The architect had to recognize these requirements, he said, and not worry about form — it would simply "emerge."

One point in the theory—and practice—of the avant-garde seems to me to be particularly worthy of mention. The living requirements, which the architect had to recognize in order to be able to design housing, were not derived from the habits, preferences, or ideas of the people who were to live in the buildings. In-

222 Max Taut. Book Printers' Building. Street elevation.

224 Otto Rudolf Salvisberg. Apartment block in the Weisse Stadt estate in Reinickendorf, Berlin, 1929–30. Apartments open onto galleries.

223 J.J.P. Oud. Row houses, Hook of Holland, 1925–29.

quiry into these things had been the point of departure of the work of Karl Schmidt and his architects when they planned a village in connection with the German Arts and Crafts Workshops in Hellerau (see Chapter 5); they had asked questions. But the avant-garde of 1925 asked no questions; they simply built answers. Since social housing had to be cheap, if things were organized in the smallest possible space and designed in such a way that every household job could be carried out as comfortably as possible, and if moreover this small space was treated in such a way that it gave the impression of being larger, if care was taken to provide sufficient light, air, heat, and hygiene, this was in principle all that was left for the designer to do. And if the inhabitants, who were used to something different (worse), did not like it at first, that did not matter — they would soon get used to it. It would not be long before they realized that they were much better off in the new apartment than in the dark, musty, old one they had lived in before. The architects of the avant-garde were convinced that they had to make people happy against their will. The people had been so badly educated through years of living in brutal, totally inadequate buildings that they did not know any more what was good for them. I have been talking about housing, but whether it was a question of housing or of schools, offices, factories, civil service buildings, or theaters, the principle was the same: The requirements were, one might say, constructed by the architects. The results did look reasonable, but even the architects, mostly of the generation active before 1914, did recognize that the up-and-coming modern architecture was not so close to reality as it pretended to be. Old Muthesius called the Weissenhof Estate — and all new architecture — "an artistic movement" and compared it with Art

Nouveau!¹ He was actually not so far wrong: The avant-garde architects paid more attention to form than they liked to admit. Poelzig once said about Mies van der Rohe's architecture, "What is the point of getting rid of ornament if one transforms the whole building into a single ornament?" He probably had the Barcelona Pavilion in mind, which is like a Mondrian painting in three dimensions. Poelzig was perceptive and sensitive enough to recognize that beneath the layer of false pretensions *form* was the most important thing here. He couldn't resist being sarcastic. But even if the modern architects had followed their own theories and actually designed housing on the basis of living requirements—and schools on the basis of teaching and learning requirements—and had used the most appropriate methods of construction, Poelzig would still have turned away from the avant-garde with no less vehemence.

He had acknowledged that household appliances and furniture for the majority of those who needed them would have to be mass-produced. He had even admitted this in 1919 in his speech to the Werkbund in Stuttgart, the subject of which had been craftsmanship—and art (see Chapter 6, Doc. 6B).

But the needs of the masses had never interested him very much, and in Stuttgart he said that they should not interest the Werkbund either. Poelzig had never had an affinity for social housing. He had planned a number of housing estates, although I don't believe any of them was ever built, and he had built some apartment blocks on Bülowplatz (now Rosa-Luxemburg-Platz) in Berlin. They are not among his best works. Poelzig was and consciously remained an artist, he never wavered on this point. He was an artist and a craftsman as he understood the term, a craftsman, as he said in Stuttgart, being so close to the artist that the two could essentially not be distinguished. Poelzig must have been thinking of the Middle Ages here, before there was a rift between the two, as he also said in Stuttgart: "A primitively carved medieval oak door is beauti-

225 Maffai locomotive. From *Transport*, Deutscher Werkbund Yearbook, 1914.

226 Rumplertaube airplane. From *Transport*, D.W.B. Yearbook, 1914.

ful despite the fact that technically speaking it is not perfect, and it does not lose its value when a technically better door is created ... while the automobile built in the year 1900, which perhaps once aroused our admiration, now seems ludicrous next to one of later design."² Therefore, Poelzig argued, technical form was not possible. As technical form was the result of technological progress, it would not survive when technology advanced farther; each improvement would invalidate not only the technical product itself but also its form.

Poelzig never relinquished this point of

Success 175

227 Ocean liner *George Washington*. From *Transport*, D.W.B. Yearbook, 1914.

229 Automobile designed by Ernst Neumann, Berlin. From *Transport*, D.W.B. Yearbook, 1914.

228 Motorboat designed by M. H. Bauer, Berlin. From *Transport*, D.W.B. Yearbook, 1914.

view. In the address he gave to the Bund Deutscher Architekten in 1931, entitled "The Architect" (see Chapter 9, Doc. 9C), he said on the same subject: "As it advances, technology is obviously striving more and more to get rid of material and consequently of form.... There is therefore no point in trying to attach artistic significance to technical forms."[3]

Even in 1931 he still refused to acknowledge the possibility that technical form could have meaning, be significant. In 1922, Walter Riezler, editor of the Werkbund journal *Die Form*, commented on an essay Poelzig had published in the journal, again on his favorite topic: the fact that progress causes any technical form to become out of date.[4] Riezler wrote: "As soon as a form has been found for a technical problem that is appropriate and reveals the inner life, it is no longer possible to talk of forms becoming 'out of date.'"[5] (See Doc. 9B.)

This was good old prewar Werkbund doctrine. How else could the 1914 Werkbund yearbook devoted to "Transport" have contained illustrations of a series of modern means of transport: locomotives, ocean liners, cars, even airplanes (Figs. 225–229). Motorboats were also included in order to show that modern technology (the motor) did not necessarily change the shape of the appliance (the boat).

Modern technology was not, in every instance, something new. It might be seen as part of an ongoing development, an idea for which Poelzig must have felt some sympathy. The forms of these technical objects were—and remain—remarkable. The most remarkable, incidentally, are those that were not the product of "designers": The locomotives produced by the Maffei company in Munich seem less dated than the motor cars designed by Ernst Neumann (see Figs. 225, 229).

I said that Poelzig must have had some sympathy for this idea. I do not know what he said about the photographs illustrating it in the yearbook. I would think he liked them. And yet, he had no affinity for technical form—nor for technology itself; both made him uneasy. He could have quoted Goethe's words and said that technology "represses quiet growth."[6] One would, however, have to ask whether he himself was a wholehearted advocate of "quiet growth." Scheffler saw in Poelzig's nature a touch of "Americanism." Although he repeatedly sought a link with craftsmanship, Poelzig was certainly not himself a craftsman to the extent that Tessenow was (Fig. 230). He knew that he needed modern technology to build larger projects. (Incidentally, Tessenow knew that as well.) Poelzig had known this even in his Breslau days. But his relationship to technology became increasingly less objective the more the avant-garde praised technology and tried to discover artistic qualities in it. In Breslau his attitude to technology had been impartial: Technology existed, it could be used when necessary and that was a good thing. Poelzig showed it for what it was, without fear and without pathos. The Upper Silesia Tower in Posen is a good example of his treatment of technology (see Figs. 26, 27, 93–98). During the war he lost this objectivity. If one compares the Posen tower with the Göritz factory in Chemnitz, which was not built until 1925–27, one is surprised at the exaggerated roughness of the joints in the factory, the excessively strong arch stones over the windows (see Figs. 46–48). It is as if Poelzig wanted to have a rest by

230 Heinrich Tessenow. Entrance door, ca. 1913.

using what was familiar to him once more—masonry walls and arches.

Poelzig's unemotional interpretation of technology in those early years of the Werkbund was probably an illusion. These years abounded in creative illusions; I already mentioned them in connection with Karl Schmidt in Hellerau (see Chapter 5). Few people at the time could see any farther. Hermann Muthesius was one of the people who did: His demand to the Werkbund in 1914 that they should turn their attention to types, that is, to the mass-produced article and its form, fell on deaf ears among the Werkbund members. In a lecture given during the war in 1917 entitled "Handmade and Mass-produced Articles," Muthesius expresses his view even more emphatically:

... for it is not the hand-made article, but the machine-made article, which we find wherever we look.[7]

He speaks of developing type-forms

> whose significance for our future development is so great, even if individualist tendencies in art today fight against it so passionately [a reference to the Cologne dispute—Au.].[8]

In conclusion he talks about a change having taken place in forms and the sense of form:

> It [a sense of form] dominates our movements, expresses itself in our language, even in the way we walk.... This unconscious aesthetic sense has brought about that balance between function and form in the everyday work of man, which is the conscious aim of any artist pursuing tectonic design. It has filed down wild, shapeless things, rounded off their silhouettes, refined their details. They are the reflection of the sensibility of an entire age, which is unaffected by the whims and changes in architecture and applied arts.[9]

To the extent this was still the philosophy of the Werkbund, at least before 1914, in its general preference for simplicity and concise form, Poelzig might have endorsed it. But it was more than that: It implied that this conscious feeling for concise form relates primarily to the mass-produced article, which, as Muthesius puts it, "we see wherever we look." Poelzig rejected this implication—after the war even more than before it. After the war there had initially been a move away from industry, a reluctance to acknowledge it as a major force in life which was constantly increasing in influence. People tried to convince themselves that industry had lost significance, in Germany at least, and that it would remain insignificant.

After the end of the years of poverty things looked different again and it was those very same young architects who had rejected type-forms in 1914 and had appealed for craftsmanship in 1918—I am thinking of Gropius—who now thought completely differently. They fully acknowledged industry as a major force in life and with it technology. They also recognized the importance of technology as *an integral part of form,* of industrial design and any kind of technical form. Poelzig did not go along with this, or rather he went as far as he was obliged to as an architect. He acknowledged the importance of modern *construction methods* and occasionally even said that technology helped to achieve more delicate forms of construction and that this potential should be made use of, although he hastened to add that it was not necessary to actually *show* the construction system.[10] To this extent he did acknowledge the new building technology. Whether he liked it or not is another question. He rejected the whole theory of the influence of manufacturing methods—mass production, I mean—on the *form* of the everyday articles we have around us, the things Gropius called "Haus und Hausrat." Poelzig wanted to have nothing to do with this, arguing as ever that technology had no part to play in design, so that a "technological form" was not possible. He once said on this, "Art is; technology becomes—no one would dare to speak of art developing."[11]

He did not recognize any development in art because he thought that the value, the existence of art, was independent of any kind of development and that that was why *all* genuine art is always valid. The consequence of this for the architect who wants to be a true artist is that the time he is living in is one in which too high a value is placed on technology and its forms, even by architects (!), and that culture is therefore heading for a depression. It is up to artists, he said, men like himself, to create the foundations for a culture that is worthy of the name, even if it is highly unlikely that those who take this work upon themselves would ever *experience* this culture themselves. Nevertheless they must lay the foundations by remaining *architects.*

This is the task Poelzig saw himself confronted with. He probably felt less optimistic than he had in Breslau when the tasks had seemed more limited, but he was nonetheless firm in his resolve to remain an architect, even under the new conditions, and *to remain himself* by serving art and using technology. This could

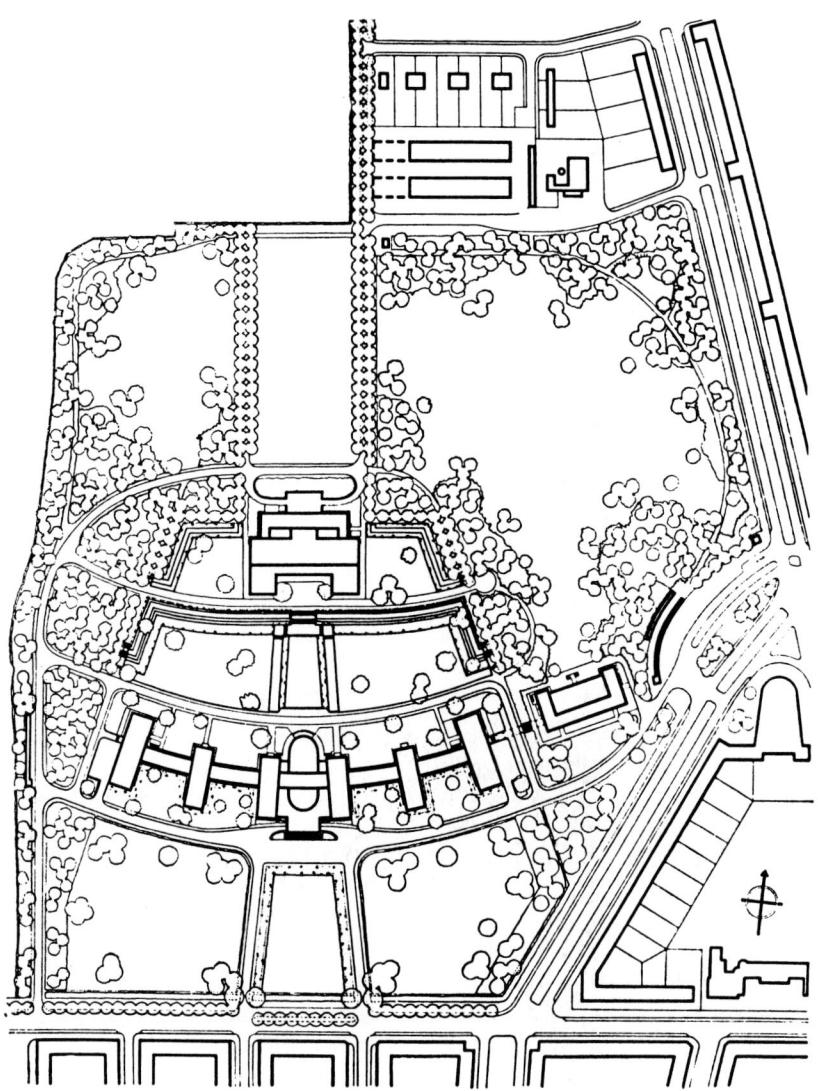

231 Hans Poelzig. I. G. Farben administration building, Frankfurt-am-Main, 1928-30. Site plan.

happen only through his increasing acceptance of the general technological atmosphere of his time and by use of its techniques. To have resisted this would have been pointless (although he did occasionally allow himself to seek refuge in older technology, as in the factory in Chemnitz), but he remained himself in his *treatment of space* — both in the overall form of groups of buildings and in their interiors. I have de-

scribed how with the shop complex that contained the Capitol Cinema he tried initially to put offices above the shops and by combining these different functions to create a more lively formal effect — a lively terracing (see Chapter 8). The attempt was not successful; the contrast between the interior and the exterior of the Capitol Cinema building is very striking. On closer examination of his other work from the period, which roughly begins with the Capitol, it will become evident that he tried repeatedly to give form to the *overall* complex. It must be said that sometimes the impression is created that he was trying to enforce a form. In Chapter 2 I described briefly how Poelzig worked. He had the preliminary work done for him up to a certain point where he made it his own. In the building for the I.G. Farben dyeworks in Frankfurt, for example, this was the point where he "shaped" Dolly Drexler's rectangular scheme, taking the volumes with their straight lines and curving them (Fig. 231). Here he really did make the building his own; this was the decisive point about the buildings. The result of this process of "making a building his own" was not always so successful. There are buildings and projects where one can positively see Poelzig's frustration with their form. His speeches appended to the end of this chapter reveal this frustration (see Docs. 9A, 9C).

I have called this chapter "Success." This was not intended to indicate that the spell was broken, that his work ceased to consist for the main part of unrealized projects. His drawing boards were still full of these projects. Yet in these years he received commissions for the largest building projects of his life — and many of them were built, commissions such as the building for I.G. Farben in Frankfurt and Broadcasting House and the exhibition pavilions in Berlin (see Figs. 17, 231, 276–302). In Berlin, too, a number of projects were cut: Most of his plans for the exhibition grounds were abandoned but the pavilions at least were built.

It was also during these years perhaps that his achievements as a teacher were greatest. They were so great because, unlike so many of his colleagues, he avoided taking sides as a teacher in the battle between technology and architecture, between rationalism and architecture. He let us embrace technology if we wanted to or rationalism if we wanted to. He never tried to stop us. He showed us the meaning of architecture more through his personality than through his work. And so the years in Berlin between the Capitol Cinema and the I.G. Farben building are the years of his greatest influence. The climax was just before 1930. Whether the works he produced at this time bear comparison with those from his Breslau period remains for me an open question. I think they should not be compared at all since the conditions had changed.

Just a word, finally, on the change in his working conditions. Toward the end of 1924 he was appointed to the Technische Hochschule in Berlin-Charlottenburg. He had been teaching a master class at the art school, the Academy as it was known, since 1922. Incidentally, the art school and the Technische Hochschule were next to each other, which was an advantage. His appointment to the Technische Hochschule made it impossible for him to keep an office in Potsdam only, or rather on the other side of Potsdam, in one of the "Communs" of the "New Palace." He was given an office in the Academy. The large class at the Technische Hochschule, the master class at the Academy, and the office were now all close together, which allowed his students entry into his inner, and finally his innermost, circle. Poelzig was not an academic teacher; he was "the Master," and his students in Berlin used this term affectionately. He was the Master who made no distinction between teaching and his own work.

Chapter Nine: Documentation

Document 9A

The document that shows most clearly Poelzig's new attitude after the First World War is an essay he published in 1922 in the Werkbund journal, *Die Form,* entitled "On Architecture in Our Time." It is reprinted here with only minor deletions.

Doc. 9A* Hans Poelzig, "On Architecture in Our Time," 1922

People today, particularly the Germans, find nothing more difficult than learning to look at a work of art with an impartial eye. The Germans, one could say, look with their ears.

Their theoretical training has accustomed them to read about many things and then form an opinion. And the more the soul thirsts for knowledge about the arts the more it is at the mercy of what is written, occasionally written quite clearly but more often in a very confused way, so that the reader is delighted when he finds a catchword he then can use. If this happens to be an architectural term— "vernacular style," "arts-and-crafts style," "utilitarian style," or any other "style"—if Germans believe it will nourish their souls, they usually fall for it. A naive way of looking at things is almost totally lacking....

... Until now, people have had very little time for architecture as an art form....

There follows a description of the movements in architecture throughout the nineteenth century and up to the time when Poelzig was writing. There were references of this kind in the Werkbund speech (see Chapter 6, Doc. 6B). One difference, which I believe is important, is that Poelzig here talks about the effect of the technological age on architecture; we are,

*Hans Poelzig, "Vom Bauen unserer Zeit," *Die Form,* 1922, no. 1, pp. 16–29. Reprinted in Julius Posener, ed., *Hans Poelzig. Gesammelte Schriften und Werke,* Berlin, 1970, pp. 170–86.

"despite the world war and all its consequences, in the very midst of it." For this reason, he says, the present cannot be compared with any period in the recent past; it is more like Rome around the time of the birth of Christ. This idea would not have been expressed in this way if Spengler had not then published his book, *The Decline of the Western World* (1918–22).

At that time, too, different artistic traditions from all over the world converged.... But our present perception of Roman architecture is based on aqueducts, bridges, and thermal baths, that is to say, on a kind of building that did not lend itself to formalist treatment....

Our age too has, or rather had, a technical, materialist orientation, although now, just as in ancient Rome, a new religious feeling does seem to be imminent. Yet so far it is the technical buildings that are characteristic and will in future seem even more so—railway stations, bridges, commercial buildings of all kinds—since these buildings are the only ones that exist in their own right, far removed from any formalism, and because of this they reveal something of the real spirit of our times, which has been—at least until now— superficial, material, technological.

They are the only buildings that can bear witness to the spirit of the recent past and our own time —no church or palace tells us about the actual spirit of architecture at this time....

The only successful buildings are those that are truly rooted in the life of our time. Commerce and transport define the character, and a large railway station or a department store makes the ordinary man on the street feel more alive, while he pays no attention whatsoever to a church, his soul not being in harmony with it....

Compare this last statement with the Salzburg speech (see Chapter 7, Doc. 7B)! Something has happened: The hope "of creating a seminal building that will herald the dawn of a new age in the arts in German countries" has been abandoned. A new epoch of a different kind has begun, one of confrontation with the technological age, even one of inevitable compromises.

The basis upon which these buildings were created is the same as that of all other things produced in our time that are purely technical. And if one starts by looking at these other things — bicycles, motorcars, ships, and so on — it becomes easier to compare them with works of art. All these things were created to serve the purely practical needs of human beings. They achieve a clear, perfectly satisfactory, even organic form. But they disappear without trace from the visible world when they no longer satisfy man's constantly developing practical needs and are replaced by other, more appropriate forms....

The fate of technical buildings is similar. Steel-framed factory buildings disappear when they no longer serve their purpose, when they have become too small and no longer fulfill the practical needs. The life of a factory is very short and depends on nothing but its economic usefulness. At best they look attractive; they may have a silhouette that is powerful or impressive in some other way. They were born not of love but of necessity, and when that necessity disappears they, too, are doomed....

The point is that none of these buildings was intended to exist for ever. The people who created them thought in terms of transience, they thought of a use for them that was transitory. They are the ephemeral Mayflies in the life of the world. The impression that an ironworks makes, or large docks, can be demonic, but it is never artistic in the true sense of the word, that is, *divine*.

The creations of mankind reflect their thinking. Something that was created with eternity in mind will give the impression of being eternal. The fact that Roman aqueducts, or many old bridges and fortresses, have an air of the eternal is due to the attitude of the people who when creating them believed they had to create eternal values. Something of the nonutilitarian, which is the prerogative of true art, went into these buildings. Moreover, the castles of the Middle Ages are not purely technical buildings in today's sense of the word but were also intended to express resistance and strength and thus had not only practical qualities but an artistic, symbolic value....

Everything that is technical, and thus every purely technical form, is transitory; man relentlessly destroys it when it no longer serves its purpose. The art form, however, is of eternal value and cannot be destroyed without creating a loss. With its destruction a part of the beauty of our world disappears because it is born of love and not of pure rationality; its roots reach into the spiritual world, while the technologist, as he himself proudly admits, has to consider worldly needs and purposes. This is not meant to be a comment on the ethics of the technologist and the engineer, but simply to describe the limits of their realm. On the contrary, their ethics are higher than those of most artists, because they stand by their work and create values anonymously, forced to do so by the spirit of the time.

We cannot eliminate this spirit of the time; even children, who are almost exclusively interested in technical things, in machines and airplanes, have succumbed to it. It is not negative in itself, it only becomes malignant when we let ourselves be ruled by it and do not put it in its only rightful place, which is the practical side of life. Every positive aspect of a particular time produces an equally strong negative aspect, so that what we have gained in practical knowledge we have lost in terms of spiritual growth and thus we have lost the very ground in which art flourishes....

Two factors appear to determine our activities: the achievements of technology, and the overpowerful formal tradition, which, since photography — the most convenient and seemingly so objective means of duplication — entered the service of art research and dissemination, has at repeated intervals inundated mankind with books, brochures, and magazines....

Steel dominates all the characteristic large buildings of our time, be they steel proper or reinforced concrete structures. The structural economy of reinforced concrete is also due to the fact that concrete is used in combination with steel. The technical possibilities that remained the same for thousands of years,...have changed to such an extent that the thoughtless use of steel structures on an old building — for example, to install shops —

produces a stylistic discrepancy that cannot be resolved because it is not possible to overcome the technical contrast between the construction methods.

While spanning a wide opening in stone can only be done with an arch, which reassures the eye that the load is being supported, the eye that is accustomed only to stone or wooden buildings sees steel as ripping open an unnatural hole in a wall, where the load and the support seem to clash, with nothing to relate them.

The musicality of an old town square, which is created by the characteristics of stone and wooden buildings, is, of course, destroyed the moment the steel structure of the shops relentlessly tears apart the ground floor. The buildings have their legs amputated and are given stilts to stand on. And anyone who has ever seen the stylistic attempts of the architects to assure that the shops have the advantages of broad openings covered with iron girders while preserving the musicality of the stone building in the upper stories, no matter what style they are, knows that they usually failed and will always be doomed to fail....

Stone and metal in structure are sharply opposed to each other: Stone needs mass, steel needs dispersal of mass. Gothic architecture went farthest in dispersing the mass of a stone building and yet this method of stone architecture, which went to the utmost limits in its dispersal of mass, in its articulation of walls into columns and panels, is separated from steel structures by a deep, unbridgeable gulf....

Gothic vaults cross each other and merge together in the half light of the space, the towers with their delicate open tracery melt into the mists, the rich choir of a cathedral with several aisles also creates its effect through the multitude of crisscrossing ribs and the resulting dissolution of solid form. This is precisely the same as the effect—of course, not in formal terms—of the iron and steel structures of the railway stations, or the great bridges with their crossing iron ribs. Through the total dissolution of surface and the reduction in material, the overcoming of weight, they seem to be flying, to be set free.

If steel ever appears in a building on its own, or possibly combined with lightweight thin stone panels, the basic principles of the style will be clear. The mathematical and structural principles will determine the strengths, the distribution, the sections, all calculated to be the minimum possible; only slight instinctive adjustments can be made to the design of the columns, joists, arches, which have also been mathematically calculated. Nothing can be added, no reinforcing elements or counterbalances that are not part of the same creative process, part of the same design. Anything that is added solely for emotional or decorative reasons spoils the purity of the form, the natural appearance.

But the stone building in its pure form provides man with housing, and lighter coverings of softer material are actually sufficient to make the interior, too, seem appropriate as a place for all expression of human life. Steel can only stand naked, without covering, in buildings that serve directly the technical and economic life of man; because of its material, a steel post in a living room appears unbearable....

In the same way that a single iron girder in a stone building can cause stylistic confusion, a building that for practical reasons is constructed with stone columns and steel stanchions and girders begins to lose its musicality, since harmony between the material and the basic circumstances must be a prerequisite for all stylistic work, unless the architect succeeds in creating a clear rhythm between the parts of the building of different materials, or in finding a satisfactory synthesis between the different building materials. For instance, in a department store that has main columns of granite with steel and glass infill panels, it is possible to give each of the materials its own appropriate dimensions and form and thus successfully avoid stylistic confusion.

Poelzig expresses the hope for appropriate treatment of the different materials and methods of construction, both old and new, where the steel is not necessarily revealed, to retain the music of architecture.

Music is the least, architecture the most, earth-bound art form. But since architecture is the most abstract of all the fine arts, it can produce the purest and at the same time most mystical sounds so that it can transfigure material into the purest form....

Comparing contemporary architecture with music can explain most clearly the relationship it has, or rather *should have*, to tradition. And this is shown most convincingly in the most modern buildings—modern in the true sense of the word, that is, those whose use and structure have the closest relationship to the present day and the fewest parallels with the past.

Before I return to steel structures, which I talked of earlier for the purposes of comparison, I would like to make a general remark on the role of tradition. For anyone involved in building it would be absurd voluntarily to ignore technical progress, and on the other hand an outright demand is often made that tradition be abandoned totally in order to make a building look modern....

Methods formerly unknown are now available to give access to all the traditions that exist. They are thus accorded the same esteem by the Zeitgeist for their artistic validity and can be viewed with an objectivity hitherto impossible....

In contrast to the situation at the beginning of the Gothic period, new methods of construction exist today that produce a completely new effect. The Gothic style was on the same technical ground as that of the preceding period, and yet it arrived at new, more daring designs—in structural terms, too—without needing to grapple with totally new kinds of structural problems.

What has been put forward here today—and by today I mean the last twenty to thirty years—as the new style has not advanced beyond superficialities; it was often the subject of highly intellectual literature, but it remained on paper, was never truly born. Art Nouveau, in its attempt to transfer the form of machines, which captivate the eye with their wonderful precision, to buildings, had to fail, since a tool, no matter how powerful, can never impose its design on a building. This was the effect of the errors of logic made by the literature of our time: The Greeks would never have let the lines of their ships or chariots, no matter how beautiful, have an influence on the design of their buildings.

Reviewing all the works of recent years, we find that many large buildings that incorporate the latest structural methods have entered into a forced marriage with the Classical canon, in order to produce an image that is rhythmically satisfying and familiar to the contemporary eye. Steel structures not only had to endure being covered up for purely technical reasons as well as for durability, but also because architects wanted to pretend they did not exist and were happy to deprive them of any independent form of expression. Tradition here played only a destructive role, and to some extent earlier steel buildings make a purer and more innocent impression than the hybrid creations of our time. And so it is not surprising if young people today deny tradition and sing the praises of glass and steel architecture, thinking that it can provide the vehicle for the purest expression of today's style....

This marks approximately the point where Poelzig began to turn his attention to the younger generation. This too is a sign that he was moving out of the phase in his work that began in Dresden and culminated in Salzburg. In the Salzburg speech there was not yet any mention of the next generation.

Here Poelzig also turns against the architects and applied artists who practiced "the Expressionist style" as seen in Fritz Höger's Chilehaus in Hamburg (see Fig. 16). I shall not quote it here. But, incidentally, it should not be forgotten that although Poelzig's own architectural style between 1916 and 1921 can be called Expressionist, it had no connection whatsoever to the "zigzag style" exemplified by the Chilehaus.

There is no question that they are right with all buildings that require exclusive or primary use of these materials; however, it is equally unquestionable that only a limited number of buildings fall into this category and that, for example, even for a clearly modern project, a large municipal building with its variety of related rooms, it is not sufficient to use glass, steel, or reinforced concrete. It is no good making a principle of using these methods of construction and these materials, which in many cases would not prove adequate.

The root of this logical error can be found in an attitude that is virtually universal and still thinks of architecture purely in terms of decoration. On the one hand tradition is interpreted in a purely formalist, decorative way, and on the other hand architects let themselves be dazzled by the decorative potential of the new construction methods. The younger generation is too "educated," too theoretical in its thinking, to be able to treat tradition and technology with the naivety required.

Poelzig goes on to speak of tradition and traditionalism and how they dominated teaching at the universities.

Anyone who tries to steal only the formal aspects of tradition will be dazzled and dominated by it. On the other hand, anyone who admires tradition but approaches it critically and takes from it only those elements that are in organic harmony with our times will be richly rewarded by tradition; it will help him to lend his design something of eternal value.

Michelangelo wanted to put the Pantheon on St. Peter's cathedral and in doing so created a completely new and original shape for the dome of St. Peter's. Like Michelangelo, the artist must admire tradition, accepting the aspects of it that he feels have the same architectural musicality, but he must then go on to create something original. In most cases, today's steel or concrete building needs clothing. This clothing must, however, allow the structure of the material that is actually carrying the load of the building to shine through....

The present-day architect must integrate construction into design. His planning will not be organic unless he considers from the very beginning the method of construction and the section of the building....

He must understand enough about modern methods of construction to give his building a form fit for its purpose and not deviate from this for the sake of any decorative whims be they traditional or fashionable. For example, anyone building a dome today that is not supported but hanging will have to try to express this function in formal terms, if he wants the building to look authentic.

And after the architect has taken care of the structural character of today's building he will have to turn his attention to the rhythmical musicality of the overall form. He needs training in order to understand this kind of musicality, even to be able to recognize its harmonies. Only this training will enable him to recognize and be inspired by the melodies of the architecture of the past.

This is the only true value for an architect with an interest in tradition. He must not force a harmony adopted from earlier epochs onto a modern building nor force the structure of a building into the straitjacket of traditional melody. But when composing his harmony he must work on the basis of the whole, the overall form, and proceed gradually from the rhythmical arrangement of the piers and openings down to the details....

It is true, however, that a certain dryness that is full of character is better than a false wealth of imagination, reveling in absurdities. And equally horrifying is the absurd habit of using arbitrarily chosen traditional forms to dress up buildings. There is no architectural rhythm from the past, certainly none of those that have their roots in ancient Classical architecture, that could readily be applied to a building that uses truly modern systems of construction throughout. It is not possible to bring Classicism back from the grave. Its methods are in stark contrast to the vertical emphasis of modern architecture. And yet it is the modern architects themselves whose treatment of this verticality is far too schematized. Also, the steel or concrete pier is by necessity thicker at the bottom than at the top, and a very tall pier that is the same thickness throughout contradicts the normal feeling for load and structure. If one wanted to express the fact that a wall in front of columns is hung, it would have to appear to be thinner at the bottom than at the top. If, on the other hand, one wanted to use aesthetic means to make the wall appear static and structurally correct, the columns would have to taper upward rhythmically.

In any case, this will be obvious to any engineer who follows his natural intuition or works everything out logically. Columns that are the same thickness throughout, without cap or base, can only be the result of an attitude that is concerned with nothing but superficial decoration.

All the forms that man creates are abstractions derived from man and are somehow related to the way the human body stands and moves. At any rate, buildings that do not express a sense of top and bottom are without head and foot; those in which it is not clearly visible that the architectural melody of the building is intact and cannot arbitrarily be added to are outrageous, fashionable monstrosities.

I believe it is totally wrong and untenable to make architecture students begin their studies with Classical antiquity. What is important in the study of architectural laws of rhythm are the most simple values. One must not put the cart before the horse here but be glad if the beginner achieves a fairly simple building form with an uncomplicated melody. And in doing this, Classical antiquity, which took one building type, the temple, and refined it to the utmost, is of absolutely no use; nor is any other formal style that is used out of context, be it Classical, Neo-Classical, or Baroque.

Imitating the old music can be a useful exercise if one ignores ornament as much as possible, because ornament brings in detail that may be valuable but it is only of secondary importance and distracts from capturing the essential form of the building and its fundamental articulation. One would have achieved all that is normally possible if one succeeds in teaching the architect with natural musical talent to create buildings that do not appear to be drawings or in the usual sense designed because they are based on a strong sense of the plastic and a healthy sense of structure. It is only natural that rustic buildings, for example, harmonize with old buildings of the same materials and similar composition. A building will be most sound if this harmony is undefined, difficult or impossible to identify historically, and if it steers clear of formalism.

Poelzig also talks once more of the use of color in architecture, something he had already mentioned in the Werkbund speech of 1919 (see Chapter 6, Doc. 6B).

Unquestionably, no artist should do anything dictated by a movement in art; he is answerable only to his own conscience.... Anyone who remains objective and develops form on the basis of a strict analysis of the basic practical and technical circumstances, using his very own artistic creativity, cannot go far wrong. Objectivity and artistic passion are sisters; both are born out of love for purpose, material, and form. And anyone who has understood tradition, or rather that which speaks to his innermost nature, which stirs up the depths of his soul and causes new harmonies to be heard, is armed against any kind of superficial influences that use the word *modern* only for effect. And he will also recognize the true value of recent movements and know, for example, that van de Velde's furniture is still excellent today, while those artists who copied only its superficial aspects were doomed to founder and their works are now long forgotten. New works of art that have been created organically will last and can stand alongside the old, despite the disadvantage that they were created rather too quickly. All good things need time, and, given the enormous improvements in technological equipment, its complexity, and the haste with which we produce our buildings, which is too fast for them to mature properly, it is not surprising that no new *Generalbass* has been found for architecture, that the harmonies are not yet pure.

And yet only in architecture can the salvation of our art, of art itself, be found....

Praiseworthy though any attempt to bring forces together might be, all artificially constructed attempts to bring about this only too desirable state cannot succeed. The spark must come from people's lives, from mankind. It must demand commanding works, which are necessary to enhance man's feeling for life, to restore spirituality to his soul, and it must help to create the link to the supersensory which is, and always will be, the source of all art.

This last paragraph could be part of the Werkbund speech or the Salzburg speech. Poelzig refuses to relinquish his convictions, and it is legitimate to say that he never relinquished them. Previously, however, he had not talked about external circumstances as he does here.

Document 9B

In response to the theory of the transitory nature of technical form, which Poelzig propounded very emphatically in the preceding article (Doc. 9A), Walter Riezler, editor of the Werkbund journal *Die Form*, in which it had appeared, wrote a comment on it, which also appeared in *Die Form*.

Doc. 9B*   Walter Riezler, "Do Technical Forms Become Outdated?" 1922

In our first issue Hans Poelzig points out that, unlike works of art, the purely technical building only has the life span of a Mayfly. The very moment that its technical purpose has been fulfilled, he says, it disappears from the world, and it does not occur to anyone to preserve it for the sake of its beauty. The question is, Does this external fate reflect the inward meaning; does technical form lose its vitality the moment it becomes technically "out-of-date," or does it somehow have its own justification, just as artistic form remains valid, although it is bound to an "old-fashioned" object?

When one thinks how out-of-date technical forms—locomotives, motorcars, and the like—look almost absurd, one is tempted to answer no to this last question. It would seem that the power of "progress"—which, amid the wealth of spiritual developments, no one believes in anymore—has supremacy in this domain over everything else, so that the vitality really does depend on the technical purpose being fulfilled in the manner possible at the time. On closer examination, however, it turns out that the absurd effect of many technical forms is not due to out-of-date construction but to the inability to find the appropriate, lively form needed for that particular stage of technical development. It has often been stressed that in times when new technical possibilities are developed, the forms at first remain as they always were, and only gradually follow the new construction methods and functions. Good examples for this are the transitions from the stone bridge to the iron bridge, from the sailing ship to the steamship, from the carriage to the motorcar. We have all more or less experienced this kind of development or at least seen evidence of it.

The picture changes, however, the minute the fear that makes people cling to earlier forms that have lost their meaning is overcome. As soon as a form has been found for a technical problem that is appropriate and reveals the inner life, it is no longer possible to talk of forms becoming "out-of-date." Then older forms can still be replaced by newer ones, when technical progress produces new, more daring possibilities, whose form is all the more important to us for this very reason. But the older form stays alive alongside it, and if we cease directly comparing the two forms we will be able to see the older form as the expression of a very particular function. In some areas of technical form—for instance, steel-frame construction—we are already at a stage today where we find older forms, which are technically out-of-date, attractive and lively for the very reason that an authentic form corresponding to that particular stage of development was found. So much for steel-frame construction. The same very probably applies to all other kinds of technical development.

Admittedly these works will have the same fate in the future. They will be discarded as soon as they have performed their technical purpose. But in that, they merely share the fate that awaited most works of art in former days: They, too, were not as a rule created for eternity. Their fate, too, was sealed at the moment when the present demanded its rights and wanted to replace the old works with its own new ones.

I therefore believe that the difference between artistic and technical forms does not lie in their re-

* "Über das Veralten technischer Formen," *Die Form*, 1922, no. 2, p. 31. Reprinted in Julius Posener, ed., *Hans Poelzig. Gesammelte Schriften und Werke*, Berlin, 1970, p. 188

lationship to time and eternity but in something else: in their relationship to the human soul, to the oneness of the world, to the Godhead.

Document 9C

To conclude the period in Poelzig's life that I have called "Success," it seems right to quote his speech "The Architect," although the speech actually was given at a later date. "The Architect," delivered to the Bund Deutscher Architekten (Federation of German Architects) in Berlin on 4 June 1931, is Poelzig's last word on a subject that had preoccupied him since his Werkbund speech in 1919—the conflict between technology and art in architecture. By the end of this period, during which he had repeatedly been forced to come to terms with the conflict in his own work, his attitude to technology had become more relaxed, although his feelings on the subject remained essentially unchanged.

This is not the only topic dealt with in the speech, "The Architect." It was given at a meeting of the association of independent architects, the B.D.A., and tries to provide a definition of the role of the architect as a protection against the influences he had been confronted with since the end of the war. One of the main factors was the change in the relationship between architect and client. Alongside the threat of technology, Poelzig viewed the fact that for many projects there would be no client in the traditional sense as the most serious threat to the profession as it had been defined until then. He is certainly right in pointing out the importance of the other person responsible for the building. He shows that in former days the client was more important than the architect. That was perhaps still the case before the war for clients having a house built for themselves, for example, when Poelzig was building a house for Zwirner in Löwenberg. Poelzig must have observed this personal influence—or collaboration—decreasing constantly. The modern architects of the next generation—Le Corbusier, for example, though he was not alone in this—wanted to build for "tomorrow's man" (*l'homme de demain*), and the client of the time became, so to speak, the representative of this *homme de demain*, who in fact did not exist, could not exist, and never would exist. Poelzig did not talk about this in his speech "The Architect" but he did talk about the *architecture* of the next generation, which now, in 1931, had not been "Expressionist" for a long time. Rather, it was the modern architecture of Le Corbusier, Mies, Gropius. Poelzig liked to think that this architecture too was simply a passing fashion. But he does not argue this idea through to its logical conclusion either.

Poelzig also addresses the topic of government building authorities. He himself had held the position of city architect in Dresden, and the fact that he built virtually nothing during this period was due to the events of the time—mainly the war. He did, however, have firsthand experience of the profession of a civil service architect and rejected it not simply because he was giving this speech to an assembly of independent architects but out of conviction. Since he had established his practice in Berlin, one particular figure, the city architect Ludwig Hoffmann, had irritated him more than anyone. This might not have been the case, or at least not to the same extent, if Poelzig had worked in Berlin before the war. Hoffmann had held the post of city architect since 1896; his architecture and his general philosophy were rooted in the prewar era. In his final years of office—until 1924—he probably *did* stand in the way of new movements in architecture. Hoffmann is, without being named, present in this section of the speech. This topic is given strong emphasis in the speech, and I did not want to omit it although it really is an issue specific to the time. Building authorities today have other things to do than get involved directly with architectural design.

Similarly, the job of the architect as Poelzig outlines it in his speech is not entirely valid anymore. What seems to me more important is the fact that it was no longer entirely valid at that time either. He sees the dangers threatening the profession very clearly and tries to come to terms with them. In 1931, a time when he had a strong sense of his own power, success, and prestige, he launches an attempt to assert his own view of the architect's profession as the only valid one, as being definitive. It is only in retrospect that the position of the architect he describes seems invalid. I must admit that to this day no one has managed to replace it with as powerful a description of what the architect is trying to do, striving for, achieving. This is why the speech is still impressive today.

Doc. 9C* Hans Poelzig, "The Architect," 1931

It is, of course, impossible to reflect on the role of the architect without investigating his relationship to his environment, to parallel or contrary human developments and endeavors. And if in the process I happen to criticize certain institutions—even those that seem to be virtually sanctioned by tradition—I would beg for absolution in advance. What I am about to say is not intended to cause a dispute, to show antipathy toward any particular institution, but it does amount to a battle, a battle as it should be, for or against a cause, in order to make things clear and help bring about an improvement.

And if one seeks to gain a reasonable degree of clarity about the architect, a profession that has been interpreted in so many different ways recently, it is necessary to look at his sphere of work, to first of all think about the very nature of architecture....

Poelzig next recalls a speech given in 1896 by his revered teacher, Karl Schäfer, in which

* Hans Poelzig, "Der Architekt," speech given at the 28th Federal Assembly of the Bund Deutscher Architekten (Federation of German Architects) in Berlin on 4 June 1931. Published with a foreword by Theodor Heuss, ed. Eugen Fabricius, Tübingen, 1954. Also reprinted by Julius Posener, ed., *Hans Poelzig. Gesammelte Schriften und Werke*, Berlin, 1970, pp. 229–46.

Schäfer described "what architecture is not" (discussed earlier in Chapter 3). Poelzig continues:

At around the same time [1896] another architect gave an ecstatic speech about contemporary architecture. He said he was very much in agreement with it, explained how glad he was that the difficult style issue had been solved, and proclaimed, "Mix the styles merrily!"

Today it is almost as if the "merry mixture" is thought to have been achieved when ... the basic technical aspects of a building have been solved satisfactorily. For the time being we have dropped the style question and are trying to align the technical fundamentals of architecture with the new developments in technology today.

We have learned from technology to rethink the concept of architecture.

Liebermann said: "Painting means leaving things out." We have now also reached this point in modern architecture following a long period in which architecture was usually thought to be about adding something....

Does this definitively capture the essence of architecture? The path that led to present-day architecture began with the reform of industrial architecture. We older architects, when we threw ourselves into industrial architecture an age ago, were all positively craving for a field as yet untilled, where there were no preconceived ideas. People had become accustomed at the time to seeing churches in the Gothic style, synagogues looking Oriental, post offices in the German Renaissance style, and museums and civil service buildings in a kind of Italian Renaissance style. For court buildings the Baroque normally used in monasteries was adopted.

Every attempt to make a stand against this had failed and industrial architecture alone represented the line of least resistance, a field that was all the more readily left to us as it seemed to be of no importance for official architecture.

There is no doubt that the first buildings designed in this spirit were very soon a great success, when people recognized that industrial buildings could have a beauty of their own, a beauty that was related in essence to the design of old warehouses, bridges, and the like.

In his own works—bridges, railway sheds—the engineer had, on the basis of his calculations, produced a form whose beauty had until then been overlooked, was considered mechanical, and quite often was made artistically respectable by the addition of some architectural trimmings. Then not only the mathematical and structural justification of this form was acknowledged but also the fact that it has, in its own way, artistic justification, at least for technical buildings.

This is the stage we are still at today, we have covered a large portion of our journey in an incredibly short time. The formal bonds to traditional architecture have been broken. Where will developments lead us now? Modernism has been acknowledged, though only a few years ago a so-called modern building, which refused to be subjected to an historically dictated canon, would have met with great obstacles from the authorities in Berlin.

"New objectivity" *[Neue Sachlichkeit]* has now been acknowledged, all that remains is to build it, "cost what it may," as the joke goes.

The game with ornament, with surface variation, with decoration in the customary sense of the word, has now been forbidden, so to speak. But has the game really stopped? Ornaments previously made by craftsmen or even by machines are now often replaced by costly materials: paint, glass, metals, stone. The interplay of their surfaces is meant to replace the interplay of ornamental rhythms, and there is no doubt that they fit in more easily with the naked, gaunt form of modern buildings, that gloss and color do enhance the shapes of the building without endangering its unity. I see no danger here, but there is a real danger when the architect who has had the game with ornaments taken out of his hands by the current developments in architecture begins instead to play with construction. This game is expensive, and the rapture, the thrill that ornamentation can bring, was hardly more intoxicating than the rapture an architect can fall prey to if he is given a free rein with today's structural possibilities—structural possibilities that seem to know no bounds.

Poelzig is referring here to *Neue Sachlichkeit* (New Objectivity). Originally the name of the art movement that had replaced Expressionism beginning about 1923, the term was adopted by modern architects in Germany to describe the new architecture.

This kind of new objectivity has concealed just as much false romanticism and, in the final analysis, lack of objectivity as has every other period that allowed itself to be intoxicated by a catchy name. Spanning great distances with expensive girders where there is no need is totally lacking in objectivity, as is omitting columns that would make the construction cheaper and lighter. And the craze for enormous glass surfaces for which there is no good reason is actually no less erroneous than the previous attitude of the architect who believed that proper architecture needed heavy massing and great expanses of masonry.

The game will and must appear again and again. Building is a basic instinct to play that even children feel. Architecture is the highest form of play, just as the world is one of God's games. *Dum ludere videmur,* while we seem to be playing we are reaching our greatest achievements. Wrinkled foreheads, intellectual probing, will never produce art. Admittedly the architect is constantly torn from his dreams and needs the greatest degree of discipline to be able to make the adjustment from his inner world to the requirements of the outside world.

But was not architecture in the past a craft? Is it not today technology? Is it not the aim of New Objectivity to deny architecture anything that is not objective and practical? It is possible to propound a theory like this, but to induce people to follow it is absolutely impossible. It is true, the situation today is such that, with the possible exception of the Palace of the League of Nations in Geneva, we do not have buildings to erect that, like the churches in the Middle Ages or the palaces of the eighteenth century, serve to crystallize a symbol in artistic form. (It seems, incidentally, that this Geneva project could only be achieved by five architects who in three years have not managed to produce a single scheme.)

The rest of us know that our buildings call for a purely economic and technical approach, that the minimum amount of space, material, and time possible must be used in solving the problem. Over and above this constraint we are free and we must not reach a stage where a romantic idealization of the machine makes everything that is technological as sacred to us as, say, the Renaissance canon was to the nineteenth-century architect; it is not that technology is not valuable and necessary, but one ought not to glorify technical form. And it would be too easy to take pleasure in every single gas pipe and radiator, every concrete structure, to try and show every technical contraption in the belief that this was the proof of Modernity. The fact that all technical forms have only a relative significance, whereas art has absolute significance, is forgotten in this process, as is the fact that new construction techniques call for new forms, indeed that the most perfect technical system is one that is formally as unobtrusive as possible. The technical ideal is achieved with a minimum of material and forms....

As it advances, technology is obviously striving more and more to get rid of material and consequently of form. Today's dynamos are tiny in comparison to the gigantic machines of yesterday, and all technical forms, which we architects today are still in vain trying to cope with (radiators, all manner of pipes, et cetera), will, I am firmly convinced, disappear or become so small that they will no longer have any significance as forms. There is therefore no point in trying to attach artistic significance to technical forms, as this would repeat the error committed by the Art Nouveau movement, which tried to make the forms of technology, which all too rapidly became out-of-date, an ornamental expression with general validity for architecture.

What is important in architecture? Form, of course, and to be more precise symbolic form. Are technical forms symbolic, can they ever be symbolic? Are the forms of art transitory? They themselves can be destroyed, admittedly, but is their influence transitory?...

Technology follows the laws of nature, it is nature taken a step farther. It is almost as if the demonic powers are trying to take on a shape once more, and, as can be seen in airships and airplanes, a fantastic resemblance to prehistoric natural forms is becoming evident. Thus, a second nature of demonic grandeur is emerging, but it is not art.

The logic of art is not based on calculations, it contradicts any arithmetical system, it is, so to speak, a form of higher mathematics. The logic of art goes against nature—against the laws of nature. The Greek temple has nothing to do with a structure in the arithmetical sense: None of its lines corresponds to a determinable mathematical form; the curves follow an order higher than the mathematical one. Even the Gothic cathedral is in the technical sense not a practical structure; in its vaulting, in particular, it is a perfectly forced stone structure that is painstakingly held up by brackets and connectors. Gothic architecture was, and still is, a magnificent game, a spatial theater.

The engineer goes his way unerringly, but what he creates is natural, his works do not become symbolic, they do not become part of a style. Their validity comes from the technology and only the technology. They can, and must, influence the current style, as in former days natural forms influenced styles, so that the nature of Nordic countries engendered an architecture different from that which developed in Greece.

And since technology and technical forms are now to be found throughout the world, since no one is capable of constructing a building today without technical knowledge, it is only logical that the new architectural style is showing, and will continue to show, an international face, that for the first time in the history of the world architectural forms will be the same the world over. But today's architecture is naturalistic, in musical terms it is, indeed, atonal. We have to progress beyond this atonality and must not accept too hastily a modern construction method whose harmony is cheap, relying on coarse contrasts and striking rhythms....

And some people will soon yearn to be able to sleep peacefully again in the bed of an historical style. It is not a new Classical art that will soon be ours in the near future; we are threatened once more by Neo-Classicism, which closes its eyes in the face of the difficult problems that we still have to deal with. If a naturalistic, atonal architecture that has not yet found its symbolism does not serve our purpose, then a symbolism based on spent forms, developed in a different culture, will not be able to do so, nor will a resuscitated mummy that has no truly vital forms to offer but at most aesthetic ones. One would have to turn the clock back on technical progress, close one's eyes, ignore these new natural forms of technology....

In art man places himself outside nature, in technology he continues nature. Admittedly, the architect as an artist cannot ignore technology, or craftsmanship, as the material vector for his creativity. Art used to be the highest pinnacle of the craftsman's design activity, it added to the utilitarian-present dimension a purposeless-eternal dimension....

Today, technology is pursuing its own course with its own achievements, using, for example, radio or wireless telegraphy to lose itself in the formless and elevate itself to technological magic.

Art, and with it architecture, cannot follow this course. Architecture is concerned with spatial design, with form for its own sake. Its laws are not on the technical plane, although this can serve architecture, and indeed must influence its forms.

No one dares refute the demonic grandeur of technical forms—but they are worlds away from the sphere of art and architecture, which in the past reached their greatest heights, produced their best achievements, in the religious sphere. Technology is rooted in natural sciences, architecture in the arts, in religion, and in philosophy.

Does anyone dare to judge even a country house today purely on its technical quality? Were only technical considerations decisive in the design and composition of the rooms, the design of the overall form of the house? And if they alone were decisive, would that produce a house? At the very most a "machine for living" would be produced. Those who coined this expression surely only meant by it that one should think about the organism with the relentlessly logical thoroughness of an engineer.

After all, the natural materials, stone or wood, are only complemented by technical materials, iron or concrete; the earlier, simple methods of heating, lighting, et cetera are only replaced by more complicated, more highly developed technical methods, and the architect only has to make use of all these possibilities in order to create the best possible housing for people.

Man today is fleeing from the rarified nature of technology, looking for refuge in more elemental forms of nature—he is trying to reestablish a link to the soil; the small houses in allotment gardens are the greatest contrast to the "machine for living" of the past, that is, mass housing, the tenements that were erected for purely economic reasons with no regard for human needs.

We must not allow technology and economics to race ahead uncontrolled; calculations that are based solely on economics and do not include human aspects will never be successful. The technician can afford to be a specialist in his field and nothing more; if an architect does this he will never understand his profession....

If medicine tends to lose its natural powers, the outsiders, the clever quacks, will find a new way....

And if architecture loses its natural power the amateurs, the quacks, will take over. The members of the guilds in the Late Gothic period defended themselves against the arrival of the Renaissance dilettantes—to no avail but nevertheless with great energy—and the arrival of the dilettantes around the turn of the century no doubt brought about the emergence—this time not a reemergence—of our present architectural philosophy. Art Nouveau, in its attempt to find a natural cure, went too far, but it did manage at least to soften the blow.

But the stream has dug out a new channel for itself and flooded the whole area around it, particularly German architecture, and its direction was affirmed ten years later by Holland, which had not been affected by the war....

And what dominates today's architecture? Practical considerations? Are the large windows practical, is the flat roof given preference for practical reasons? Form dominates, design, the new symbol of a new life that satisfies today's hunger for light and air. The sensitive amateur is quite likely to let himself be persuaded by a talented artist to have a totally impractical house, one that has the form he likes so much, rather than a practical home that has no apparent form. He is seeking enrichment of his spiritual life.

Woe betide the architect who forgets that it is from here that the world of architecture has to be changed, it is here that the lever must be inserted—if he stoops to technical and economic works, to barracks-like type-forms, to the ant hill, the beehive. Animals build naturally, technically—even man's technical discoveries cannot excel the honeycomb in terms of utmost concision. Man must give spirit and life to material, not mechanize life. The amateur, the well-balanced human being, with all his sensitivity and musicality, builds better things than any architect who is inhibited by purely specialist considerations. Building is a human activity, it does not support aesthetic and specialist quibbling.

And furthermore: The history of architecture throughout the ages is just as much the history of those who commissioned buildings, the clients, as of those who built them, the architects. There are a number of periods in which we know only the names of the clients, not the artists. The reverse side of this is that in other periods the artist was almost overestimated. It is necessary to find the right balance again. No artist can create anything worthwhile without resonance from his client; indeed it is only through harmonious collaboration between both parties that an authentic building can be created.

For this to happen a spark must pass from the client to the architect. No architect can work for long without conditions and constraints, without a commission. His creativity will wither; there is nothing worse than to tell an architect he can do what he likes....

And the sorry state of painting and sculpture today—not just in the economic sense—results largely from the fact that artists are not receiving commissions. Artistic values are not called for, no one is eager for them; at the most, an artist might be eager for someone to be eager for his work. Art exhibitions, where only a generation ago unpopular works were slashed with knives, are now deeply tranquil except on the day of their opening. What can a poor artist create in this atmosphere? Where can he find his courage, his inspiration, when there is a total absence of stimuli and opposition, especially opposition? He can paint or sculpt whatever he likes, his works of art will no longer be attacked. And that is the worst possible thing. Fanatic opposition begets life and gives strength just as much as enthusiastic praise. Indifference is deadly....

Today, now that New Objectivity is equated with poverty, decoration is extremely simple. I do not mean that the basic idea behind the building is simple. On the contrary, in this respect the building may be called complicated, eccentric, properly speaking, incomprehensible. Buildings are smooth and sober on the surface so as to correspond to contemporary taste....

Here, a new part of the speech begins.

True ornament is symbolic, the Classical column is pure music, it is totally unnatural, has no relation to nature; even the acanthus on the Corinthian column was not a result of conscious stylization of natural forms; it was a new creation on a different plane. It must be obvious that this kind of ornament cannot develop as part of, or as a result of, today's atonal architecture, and it does not in fact matter whether a distribution of surfaces according to color or plastic form is aimed at as a contrast to the smoothness normally found today. It will and must happen when the aversion to the monotony of color and plastic form has increased. After all, modern designers of women's fashion never totally abandoned purely decorative elements despite modern lines. *Que la femme veut*—and if what woman wants is richer variety, she will get it very soon, first of all in the home, and architects and art teachers can protest as much as they like....

But once bitten twice shy; I am still skeptical. I have seen too many failed attempts, the worst ones being those that use an overpowering ornamental symbolism....

Next, Poelzig returns to the importance of the individual client, who is being replaced by the bureaucracy.

And if there is no impassioned client, no one to plant the creative seed or help it to germinate, all is lost. No art form, least of all architecture, can survive without this opposite pole; the past has taught us that this pole was for a long time seen as the only important factor....

The bureaucracy of the republic has taken on enormous proportions. It was always impossible for anyone to die and be buried without permission from the authorities, but now the dominance of the bureaucrats makes life itself virtually impossible.

The visits to authorities to seek planning permission have, in view of the number of different organs involved, become like pilgrimages. For example, a client of mine for whom I recently designed a filling station, had to make seventy-seven, I repeat seventy-seven, visits to the authorities only to be refused planning permission in the end....

The client is not the architect's only opposite number. Alongside him the planning authorities raise their heads threateningly. This battle must be fought by the client and the architect together. It is obvious that the civil servants themselves do not take pleasure in this system....

It is true that we, private architects, must take up arms on our own behalf and also on behalf of the civil servants, who really cannot be expected to tolerate planning applications being tossed to and fro like a ball, from one authority to the other, wasting time and killing the brain. No one in any of the authorities can make a decision, they have to ask each other for permission, and the central authorities, which are run by very able people, are faced with the Sisyphean task of trying to unravel the confusion. We would be ungrateful if we did not accord these people the highest recognition for their help; we are in fact positively dependent on their help. A civil servant is after all human and should not be plagued with any more unnecessary tasks than he can bear.

We will make no progress at all if we see everything only from our own point of view, from a one-sided perspective; we must be able to put ourselves in the other person's position. And if I do that, as I can since I have personal experience of this job, then I must energetically advocate the abolition of the building authorities, or at least of their direct involvement in design....

... The whole principle of a government authority that practices architecture is wrong. No one is really happy with the idea, they all groan more or less under the weight of the organization, or at least they do if they are creative people, not automatons. They either break under the strain, or their senses become deadened and they come to terms with the situation and even think it is good.

The city architect, in the meantime, rushes from one meeting to the next; especially since he has become a political figure he is forced to sit and sit, anywhere but in his own studio. At best he runs through his studio and manages with great effort to scrape together a few hours a week for his own architectural work. Do you know a single city architect who does not complain about this?... Is there a city architect anywhere, no matter how able, who, worn out by the grindstone of the system, does not do as much harm in his second period of office as he did good in his first term when he was still relatively fresh? And it must be said that the highest official in the building administration of a city borough is relatively well off; he can at least stand his ground as a public figure. Admittedly he is prone to getting above himself.... In his government department the city architect has no artistic opposition; what he says and does must of necessity be good....

And is it really possible, in the long term I mean —a short-term experiment would not be convincing, and decrees and ordinances are no substitute for lively creation—to bring about an artistic view of things, by government order, as it were? After all, a brilliant and very strong personality can put new life into a worn-out organism but he would be in danger of sacrificing his own life in the process. Schinkel, whose area of responsibility covered only a fraction of present-day Prussia, to keep himself fresh worked very early in the morning on artistic, usually painting, problems; he was intensely absorbed in the attempt to solve them and exhausted himself long before his time.

It is a number of years since the then-head of the church-building division of the finance ministry told me that, thank God, he had plenty to do; due to destruction caused by the war he had thirty-four churches to build in East Prussia alone. Imagine—not motorcars but churches off the production line! It is horrific to expect a man, no matter how talented, to perform such a task. One can accept, if need be, a schematic treatment for all sorts of buildings, barns and farmyard sheds can be standardized, but just imagine churches!

One only has to imagine what would have happened if the papal authorities in Rome had had a centralized building authority to provide Christian countries with monasteries and churches since the year one thousand. What actually happened? The abbots and their architect lay brothers, who went to northern Germany for example, took the local material and adapted it to what they had learned in the south. This is how brick Gothic buildings came into being, which were not only as good as the buildings of the older cultures in terms of importance and purity of form, but were actually better.

Strict centralization of creative architectural work is bound to destroy its spontaneity. Anyone who is forced to build a large number of the same kind of building over a period of decades becomes a specialist, and a specialist no longer builds but manufactures. And while manufacture might be suitable for smaller, simpler, transportable units, such as homes in America, it is totally inappropriate for any kind of more complex unit. I would think that anyone who has, for example, produced variations on a standard house for decades can hardly stand the sight of his own work anymore, because it is bound to become lifeless and other people will certainly not be able to stand the sight of it. When I myself worked for the building authorities—a terrible time for me as I was so unsuited to the work—I often spoke to one of my highest superiors about changing the system.

Struggle is the life force of all things, struggle is missing from our lives. There is no opposite pole from which the intellectual sparks fly. The struggle between the client and the architect cannot be replaced by rules and regulations.... I am referring to the honorable, intellectual struggle between the client as an independent thinker and the architect. Who, if he is honest, wants to say who played a greater part in the planning at any particular time, the client or the architect? This struggle can be very painful for the architect. Sometimes he will lose unjustly. He will sometimes have to suffer a good deal, even if his client, as in the days of Frederick the Great, can no longer have him thrown in jail. And this struggle, this interaction that is so necessary, does not exist in government building departments. I would like to ask the school and church authorities, the health departments and universities, to put their hands on their hearts and say if they would not like to choose the architects for their buildings themselves?...

The struggle with the client keeps the architect on his toes; in the free market, whether rightly or wrongly, the question will constantly be asked as to whether an architect is still suitable for a particular project; free choice implies selection each time and the independent architect must be constantly involved if he is to assert himself. This struggle can, as I said, be very cruel; it can cause weak characters to compromise and give up their convictions, but it keeps us alive, whereas the battle with the bureaucracy is simply exhausting.

After all, what is important is achievement!...

I freely admit that in the past too, particularly until the middle of the last century, or even later, the buildings constructed under the Prussian building authorities were extremely good. They were buildings that were sometimes concise, objective in the best sense of the word, barracks, foresters' or workers' houses in the country, in short, mainly buildings for which type-forms are appropriate. And even if the objection that these buildings were in the same style no matter where they stood is valid, this is still better than the subsequent situation, where a conscious decision was taken centrally to build them all in the local vernacular style.

But do we still need state building departments to develop type-forms? Is everything not already a type-form anyway—and are we not in danger of overrating types? I do not believe that we still need civil service departments to design the best types and preserve technical experience. Whatever can successfully become a type-form is obvious from architectural literature and models. And as far as gathering experience is concerned ...? For goodness sake, not too much. Technical developments override experience constantly and too many regulations only inhibit healthy progress....

Isn't it time anyway that we considered whether this course toward increased bureaucracy can still be pursued, or whether the trend should not be reversed, wound back to a point at which there is some sort of balance between the professions and the state?...

I do not want to go into more depth on this point as it would mean moving into the realm of politics....

The one aspect of Count Coudenhove's program ["Pan-Europa," a programmatic study published in 1923 by Nicolas, Count Coudenhove-Calergi (1894–1972) — Au.] I like is the one that urges us to think European and not American or Russian and emphasizes the value of the intellectual personality in contrast to the masses, and this and this alone is the true objective and value of European culture. And the true value of democracy must be not to put chains on the individual and force him to be part of the masses but to free him....

It would, of course, be folly to try and abolish an institution without having something better to take its place, something that would be as close to a feasible ideal as possible....

Poelzig suggests creating the position of "architectural directors" in government departments:

They are directors of architecture in the theatrical sense — *director* was a term coined by Martin Wagner when he was a city architect. They may assume the intellectual role of the client, the opposite pole to the architect who takes part in the creative process. And if you were to ask me whether these architectural directors, if they are architects, should also to a certain extent actively participate in the artistic process, I would quote the Bible and say, My God, yes, one should not tie up the mouth of the ox that is threshing. Of course, they too can produce their own buildings as long as they do not work in a way that will create a new bureaucracy.

Poelzig turns to the situation of architecture in recent times. We must not forget that he is talking about the 1920s, a time during which major changes occurred in the profession of the architect and his relationship to the public. Finally he returns to the architect himself. What makes an architect? How should one teach architecture? — And the ultimate question, What is the architect?

It is true. That which fifteen years ago no one would have dared hope for or fear has now happened: Architecture has become popular. The public are interested in it....

But who is the born architect? Someone who can draw? No, if he has no other talents than this he is perhaps a commercial artist. Someone who has imagination? No, unless he can discipline himself he is just a dreamer. Count Keyserling once said something that is very true: "The greatest enemy of a genius is his talent," by which he meant that skill that comes too easily prevents someone from looking at a problem in depth. And it is above all in the struggle against one's own nature or against its weaknesses that the individual can reach his highest achievements. Demosthenes became the Greeks' greatest orator because he stammered.... And it is therefore no wonder that some of our greatest architects were bad at drawing....

Only someone who works in the profession can teach that to students. I can teach only what I can do myself, what I have experienced, not what I know. My teaching would otherwise be lifeless....

Only the master can teach the students this, and the vehicle for knowledge is not calculating reason but Eros.

Art is a game, a serious game, and the rules of the game are what we call style. Who makes these rules today, who teaches them? Who teaches them to the students in a way they can understand? The poor things! No one will lead them astray today more than someone who offers them a readily understandable cliché, a cutout pattern they can use at any time to make a form that can be put onto a building so that it can stand its ground, so they think, as a form. These are short-lived laurels that quickly wilt.

We are still in the grips of naturalism, atonal architecture; we still think we must wrestle with each problem as if for the first time in order to force it to take on form. And if we succeed in freeing the form of a building from its time, and give it the touch of timelessness that every true artistic form has, we have done enough....

And nothing but the cultural development of mankind decides the new form, the future architecture we all long for....

The architect has a great responsibility; the whole appearance of a town can be created or destroyed for centuries to come. People are beginning to realize this once more....

What then is architecture? In Paul Valéry's "Eupalinos, or On architecture," a dialogue between Socrates and Phaedrus in Hades (translated into German by Rilke), Phaedrus makes the following observations: "Have you noticed as you walk through this town, that of all the buildings some are silent, others speak, and others, and these are the most rare, even sing? This liveliness is in no way connected with their purpose or their general design, just as the cause of their silence is not connected with these things either. It depends on the talent of the architect, or rather on the favor of the Muses.

"It is true that those buildings that neither speak nor sing deserve nothing but disdain: They are dead objects, lower in rank than those piles of stones that the carts of entrepreneurs spit out and which, at least in the way they happen to fall, can sometimes amuse the interested eye....

"As for monuments that content themselves with speaking, I have every respect for them if what they say is clear. They say, for example: This is where traders meet. This is where judges hold their deliberations. This is where prisoners sigh. This is where those who love excess can ... (at this point I said to Eupalinos that I had seen quite admirable places of this latter kind, but he didn't hear me). These market halls, these courts, these jails speak the most precise language, if those who built them understand enough about the subject. Some of them draw an excited, ever-changing crowd, they offer them entrance halls and doorways. They invite them to enter through doors and through easily accessible staircases, to come into the spacious, well-lit halls, form groups and abandon themselves to what is happening around them.... The homes of justice, however, must present the severity and justice of our laws to the eye."

In this profound and beautiful dialogue there is not a mention of technology, not even in the ancient sense of craftsmanship, no mention of economics. "Render to Caesar the things that are Caesar's and to God the things that are God's!" ...

We want to capture for our work something that will not astonish for just a short time, not something that tries to capture attention by screaming loudly, but something that speaks or even sings in a way that will be understood in the future, a future that knows nothing of all the surprises we experienced from the new technical inventions and possibilities, but will understand only the eternal melody that we have, perhaps, managed to capture in our works.

CHAPTER TEN
Works 1924–1931

THEATERS AND CINEMAS

WE HAVE JUST BEEN LOOKING at Poelzig's Capitol Cinema and his designs for the theater in Salzburg. It would seem logical to begin this chapter, which reviews the individual works, with theaters and cinemas. They are also a good example of Poelzig's attempt to start afresh each time and to try to raise the theater space from the banality of the familiar. This is immediately noticeable in the first project I shall deal with.

1924 Municipal theater in Rheydt (Lower Rhine), project

This is an ordinary-sized theater with some 700 seats that gains its special character from the way the stalls rise up like an amphitheater to the level of the first circle (Figs. 232, 233). There are rows of seats down the sides of the circle itself. The majority of seats are, however, in the stalls, which slope evenly in the relatively high, oval-shaped auditorium. The brick exterior of the building has a vertical articulation with a slightly curved facade between two round stair towers of equal height (Fig. 234). I think it would have looked more inviting in reality than the slightly severe perspective would suggest. The theater makes a strangely cold impression in this drawing. The interior space was the special feature of this building. The auditorium and foyers are large in comparison to the stage, which has only a modest backstage area and wings and a small number of dressing rooms.

1925 Capitol Cinema, Berlin

I have already spoken of the Capitol Cinema, which marks an important turning point in Poelzig's work but here I would like to look at its interiors again (see Chapter 8 and Figs. 213, 214, 216–218). The Capitol is one of the few high-quality cinema buildings of its time. Some critics thought it was of too high quality for a cinema and too much like a theater. These are indeed types of buildings that need to be designed quite differently. In a cinema all the seats must face the screen, whereas in a theater the stage can occupy a freer space, which allows more freedom in the seating arrangement. In the Capitol the auditorium was meant to fulfill the social expectations of a theater, and as a concession to this the short side sections of the circle have a number of boxes with seats that do not directly face the screen. The shape of the auditorium, an elongated octagon, brings these two expectations together very skillfully. The raised ceiling above this octagon draws the

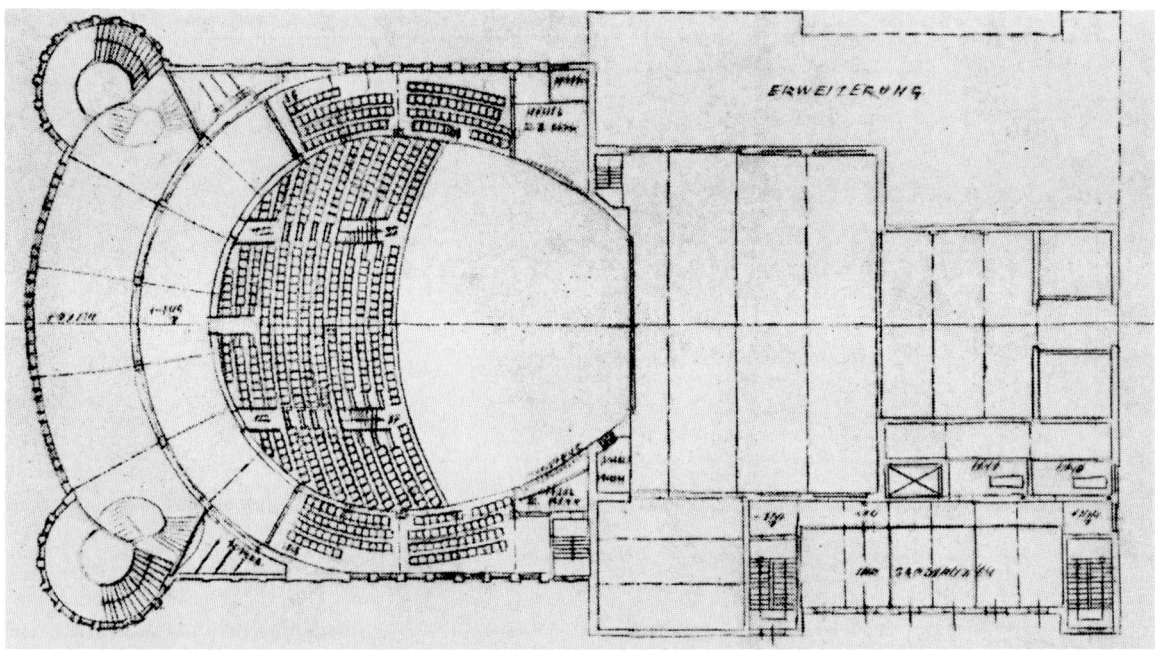

232 Hans Poelzig. Theater for Rheydt, 1924, project. Plan.

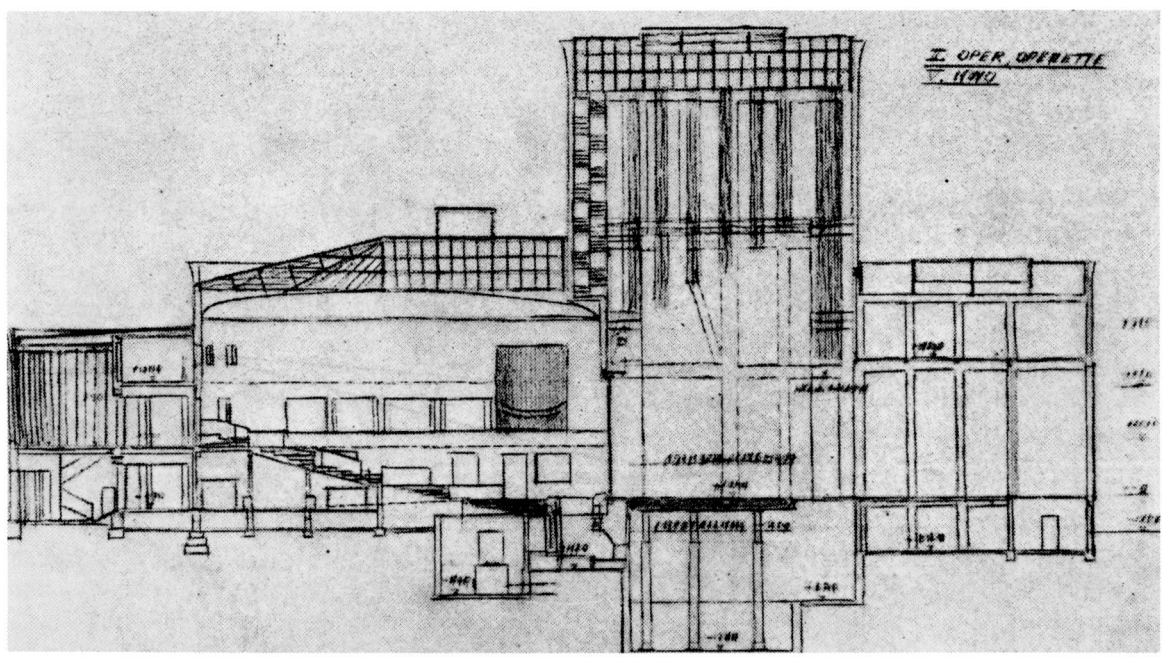

233 Hans Poelzig. Theater for Rheydt. Section.

234 Hans Poelzig. Theater for Rheydt. Perspective presentation.

space together. The projection box is in a recess in the octagon.

One enters the cinema through a ticket hall which, together with the open entrance porch in front of it, is square in plan. The ticket booth is in the center, at the back are two small niches with seats, and between them there is a door leading to the boxes beneath the circle. The boxes are separated from the auditorium by a wall and their doors look like windows. The positioning of the boxes makes the overhang of the circle, which is minimal anyway, seem even shorter. Usually any theater auditorium with only a single, deep, amphitheater-like circle has the problem that its circle projects a long way over the stalls. Here it hardly projects at all.

Poelzig had complained that there was very little space for staircases, corridors, and service rooms. The plan shows clearly the tricks he had to use to accommodate the toilets (see Fig. 215). Of the stairs he said, "the interesting, spiral shape and structure of the stairs enabled me to express this problem sculpturally thus making a virtue of necessity."

1926 Deli Cinema, Breslau

In the Deli Cinema, too, the circle with its amphitheater-like rake has side sections (Figs. 235–237). But here they are stairs that lead down to the front part of the stalls. There was a model for this solution that Poelzig was famil-

235 Hans Poelzig. Deli Cinema, Breslau, 1925. Auditorium toward the screen.

iar with—the Cines film theater on Nollendorfplatz in Berlin by Oskar Kaufmann (1912[!]; Figs. 238, 239). In Kaufmann's building the stairs serve a practical purpose—the entrance to the cinema is at the front. One has to admit that in Poelzig's building they are purely decorative. It is doubtful whether people ever really used them. The spatial effect created by the positioning of the staircases is very attractive and contributes to the "harmony" of the whole space.

1928–29 Babylon Cinema, Berlin

The Babylon Cinema is in one of the few buildings planned as part of a housing scheme surrounding the Volksbühne theater by Oskar Kaufmann on Bülowplatz (now Rosa-Luxemburg-Platz) in Berlin that were actually built. I shall return to the whole project later.

The cinema is not very large; it now seats 600, although originally, before alterations were made to the circle, it seated some 750 (Figs. 240, 241). It fulfills the requirement that all cinema seats should face the screen and therefore once more has a deep amphitheatrical circle. Even this circle has short side sections but only for access.

This cinema, like the Deli, has direct lighting. However, while the ceiling in the Deli is covered with a pattern of lamps that look like stars, here there is only a rosette in the center and

Works 1924–1931   201

236 Hans Poelzig. Deli Cinema. Staircase leading to the gallery.

238 Oskar Kaufmann. Cines Cinema, Berlin, Nollendorfplatz, 1912–13. Staircase leading to the gallery.

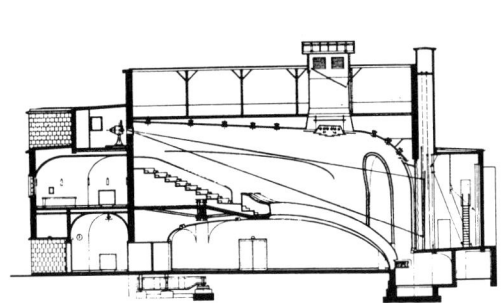

237 Hans Poelzig. Deli Cinema. Section.

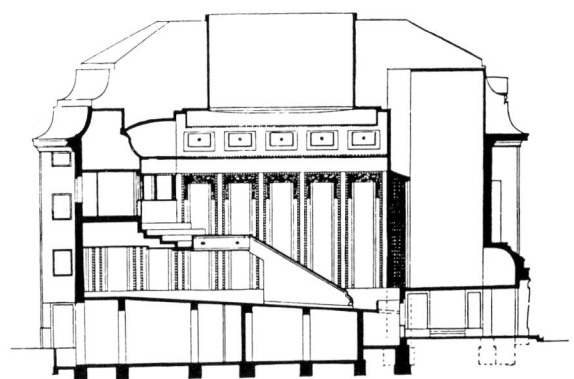

239 Cines Cinema. Section.

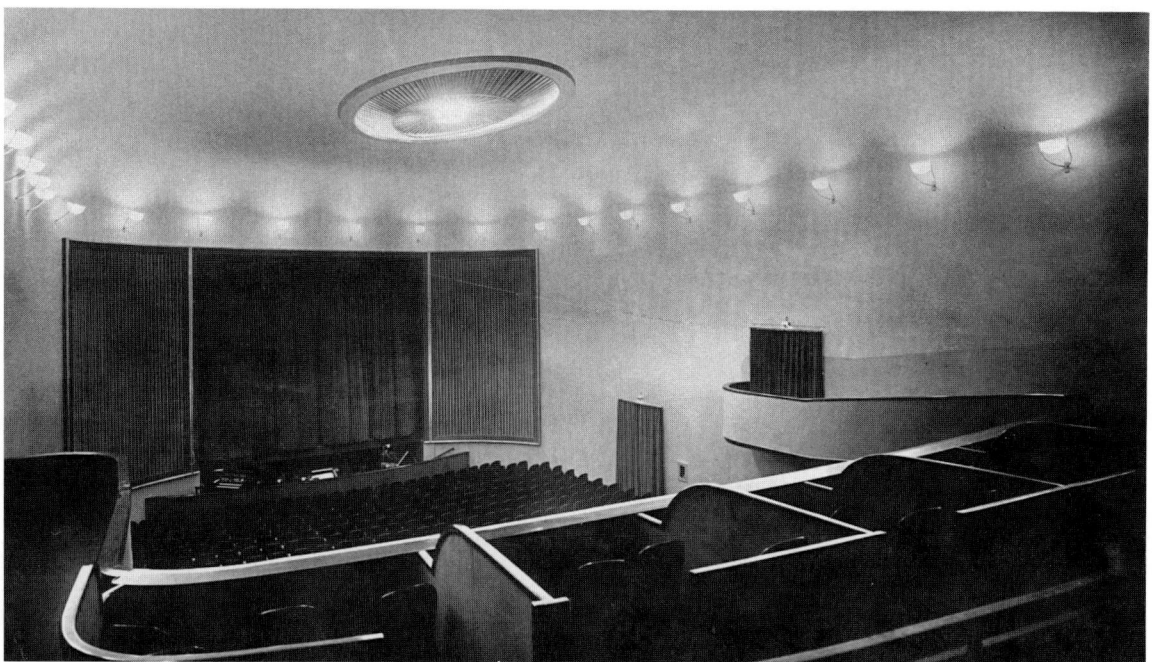

240 Hans Poelzig. Babylon Cinema, Berlin, 1928–29. Auditorium toward the screen. The openings on either side of the screen are for the organ.

241 Hans Poelzig. Babylon Cinema. Staircases.

lamps on the edges of the ceiling of the auditorium providing both direct and indirect lighting. This is a real cinema: It was not intended to look like a theater like the Capitol or be an "exciting" space like the Deli. One only has to compare the relationship between the projection screen and the organ screens in the two cinemas (see Figs. 235, 240). In the Babylon it could not be simpler. But who could deny that here a harmonious, "musical" space was created?

1930 Theater in Kharkov (Ukraine), project

Poelzig took part in an international competition for a theater in Kharkov in the Ukraine and submitted a scheme that he intended as a statement of principle. The main auditorium is parabolic and within it a large amphitheater rises up in steps (Figs. 242–244). The tip of the parabola was left empty for the stage; it penetrates into the large circle of the stage in which shallow parabolic scenery can be inserted. The

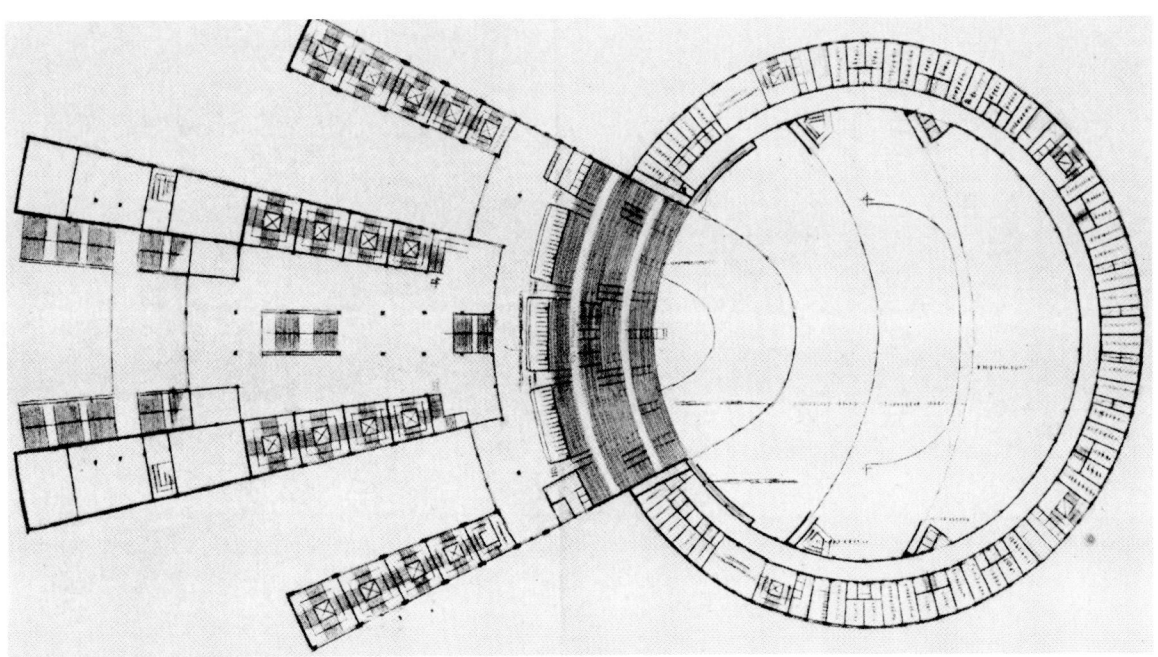

242　Hans Poelzig. Theater for Kharkov (Ukraine), 1930, project. Plan on the level of the third ring.

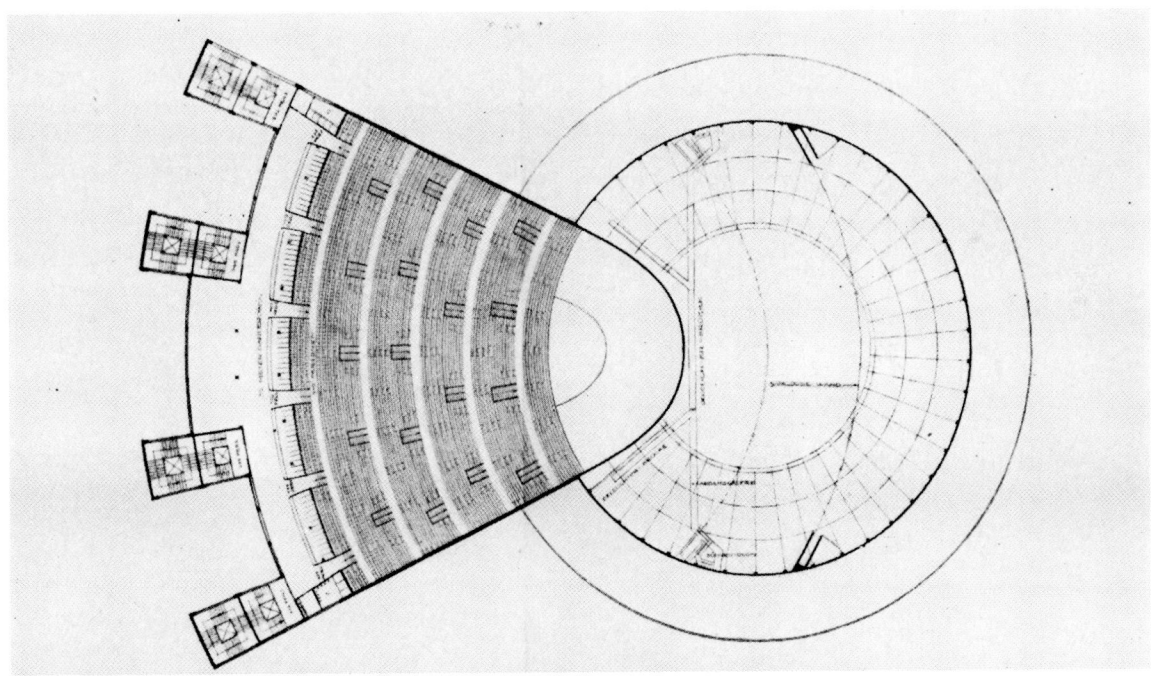

243　Hans Poelzig. Theater for Kharkov. Plan on the level of the fifth ring.

204 Hans Poelzig: Reflections on His Life and Work

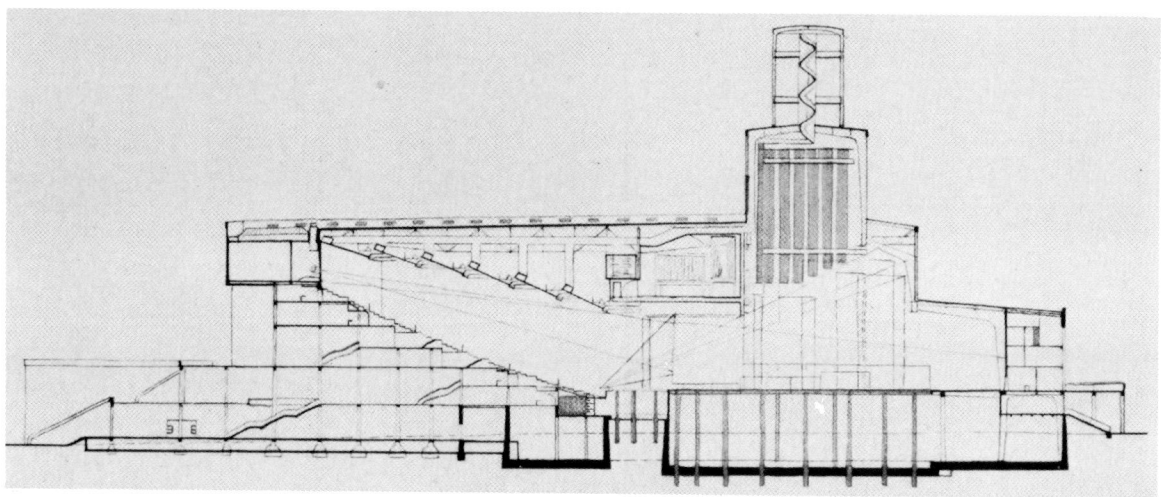

244 Hans Poelzig. Theater for Kharkov. Section.

245 Hans Poelzig. Theater for Kharkov. Perspective presentation.

246 (right) Hans Poelzig. Theater for Kharkov. Side elevation.

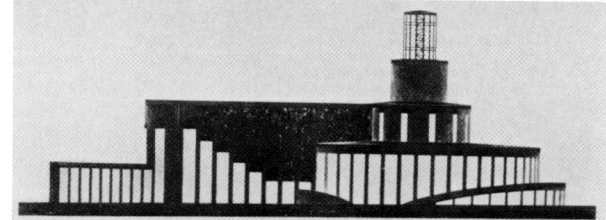

Works 1924–1931   205

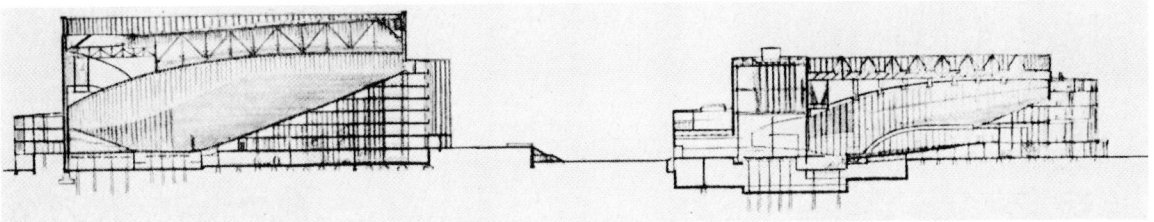

247 Hans Poelzig. Palace of the Soviets, Moscow, competition design, 1931. Sections.

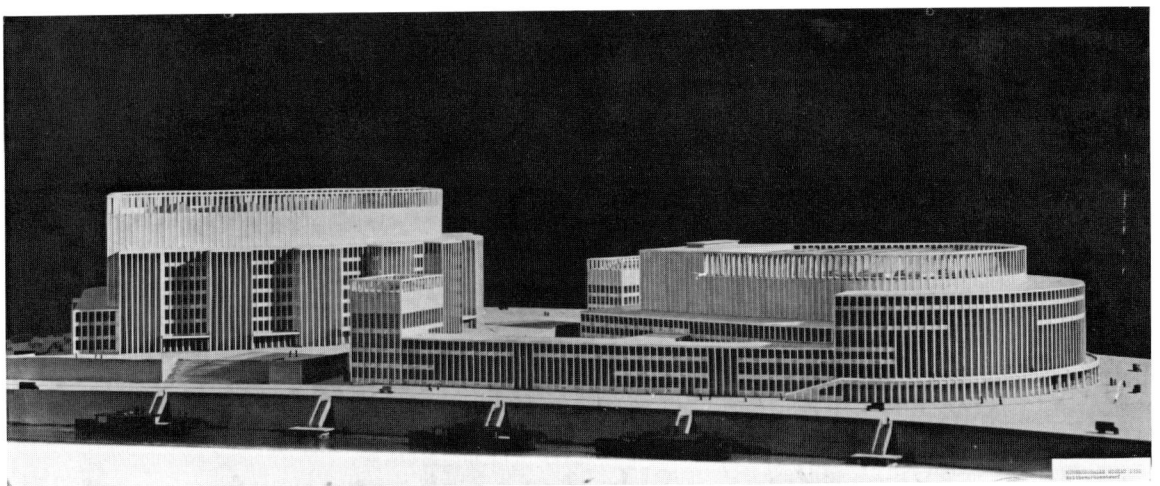

248 Hans Poelzig. Palace of the Soviets. Model.

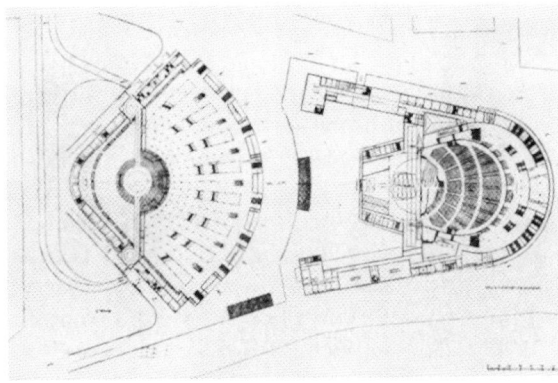

249 Hans Poelzig. Palace of the Soviets. Plan.

inner circle is in three steps: the upper stage, the flies, and a tower that is purely decorative. Around the stage are workshops, rehearsal rooms, dressing rooms. Flights of stairs give access to the amphitheater.

The theater was not intended to have many more seats than the Grosses Schauspielhaus. Yet it seems much more like a powerful machine for theater. The space is interpreted "mechanically": a large show apparatus. I assume that the fact that there is so much space above the auditorium has something to do with the desired volume: It would have been too complicated otherwise. But the descending windows in the stairwells and the unbroken expanse of wall above them seem strange (Figs. 245, 246). It looks almost as if the large ring of windows to the dressing rooms is the most important part.

250 Le Corbusier. Palace of the Soviets, competition design, 1931. Presentation drawing.

An attempt is made here to find an ideal solution: the parabola cutting through the circle. Perhaps it would have convinced the audience, but I have my doubts. The building became complicated, the stair motif is overemphasized.

ASSEMBLY HALLS

1927 Palace of the League of Nations, competition design;

1931 Palace of the Soviets, competition design

251 Erich Mendelsohn. Palace of the Soviets, competition design, 1931. Model.

After the Kharkov theater, it is logical to look next at two projects for large assembly halls. One of them is the building for the League of Nations in Geneva (1926–27), the other the Palace of the Soviets in Moscow (1931). Both are competition designs that were never built.

The two halls for Moscow can be seen as a true development of the Kharkov project, of course without the emphasized stage (Figs. 247–249; see Figs. 242–246). Stages were planned, and the circular one in the smaller building is not unlike the round inner stage of the Kharkov theater. As I see it, a great advantage here over Kharkov is that the stairs that provide access to the amphitheaters have been integrated into the shape of the buildings. Both volumes are simple and the larger building is even more compact than the smaller one with its two side wings. But even Theodor Heuss doubted the harmony of the way the two buildings are linked together. The stylistic coherence which the decidedly vertical articulation of the buildings was intended to give was not achieved in the composition of the whole.

Architects of renown, including Erich Mendelsohn and Le Corbusier to mention just two, took part in this famous competition. Le Corbusier's Constructivist project, in which the roof of the large building is suspended from a concrete parabola, became famous and rightly so (Fig. 250). By creating one stage that served both buildings Mendelsohn achieved a unique, wonderfully modeled building (Fig. 251). It is interesting that the way he arranges the circles in the large auditorium obviously draws upon Poelzig's third scheme for Salzburg (see Figs. 195–198). Projects such as these two show just how quickly architecture developed in the

252 Hans Poelzig. Palace of the League of Nations, Geneva, competition design, 1927, project. Perspective presentation.

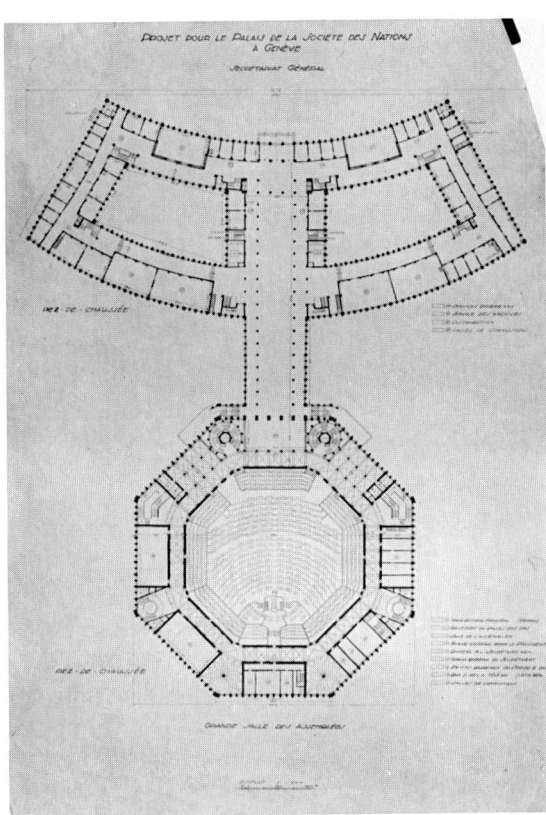

253 Hans Poelzig. Palace of the League of Nations. Plan.

twenties. Poelzig had no part in this development. His concern lay elsewhere; he was of a different generation.

The competition for the Palace of the League of Nations was also international and has remained famous. Here too Poelzig's work was confronted by a design by Le Corbusier and an even more progressive one by the Basle architects Hans Wittwer and Hannes Meyer. Both schemes are sufficiently well known so that there is no need to describe them here. But here, unlike in the Moscow competition, Poelzig's project can hold its own with these two projects (Figs. 252, 253). True, it is a product of the older generation but it is a very convincing piece of work. The building containing the main assembly hall, with the auditorium, a higher octagon, rising in the middle, is sited on the lakeside, in part even in the lake. The office wing, which forms a convex curve to the lake, is on land behind this building and rises up in three steps. It is linked to the octagon on the lake by a large covered way. If one asks today which building one would prefer to see built, Poelzig's scheme has a good deal to recommend it.

Maybe the assembly room itself is the least successful part of the project. It is an octagon with stalls sloping down to the stage, two circles going around the whole space, and a ceiling rising up in steps (taken from the first project for Salzburg). There is a conflict between the geometrical form of the auditorium and the way the stalls — that is to say the assembly seating itself — are arranged, a problem that Poelzig was not able to solve. It is said he sacrificed the practical to the symbolic aspects of the building. Symbolism dominates the shape of the exterior of the building. There is no doubt that it was the exterior form, the composition of the buildings, that interested Poelzig most, and it is in fact one of his finest ensembles.

No project from the modern school of architecture was ever built in Moscow and Geneva. In both places there was a return to formal architecture with columns and entablatures.

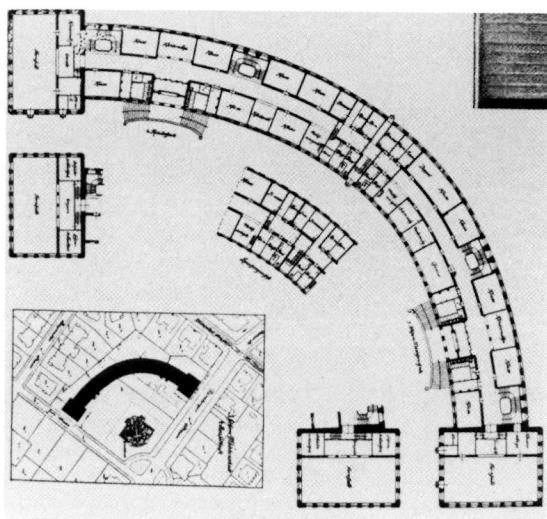

254   Hans Poelzig. School for Dresden, 1916, project. Plan and layout plan.

BUILDINGS IN GROUPS

1916–17 Two schools behind an existing church in Dresden, projects

This is one of the earliest groups of buildings planned for Dresden (Fig. 254). Poelzig drew both schools together in a composition that almost formed a quadrant. This provided a uniform background for the existing church; in other words, he planned the schools on *purely* urban design criteria. The planning was determined by the site and what Poelzig wanted to make it into. This may have been the most obvious solution in this particular case but even then, for school buildings too, functional planning existed, based on criteria such as the best possible lighting for the classrooms, most convenient access to the main hall, and so forth. This did not interest Poelzig. He evidently thought that for a schematic building — a row of classrooms, or, as we shall see, offices — functionality was not an issue; in other words, he thought on Beaux-Arts lines, or at any rate he *could* have thought like that.

Theodor Heuss never missed an opportunity to defend any building by Poelzig that was criticized for (God forbid!) being axial by saying that one should not be deceived: Poelzig's planning was *always* axial.[1] I would not say "always," certainly not in the early days in Breslau. But, as the overall form really did interest him more than function, he did, of course, use the simple ordering schemes of architecture — axes, dominants, and the like. Here it is the *other* building — the church — that is on the axis.

1927 Professional schools, Berlin-Charlottenburg, project

1928–29 Professional schools, Berlin (Kreuzberg), project

To stay with the subject of schools: There were two other projects for Berlin in 1927 and 1928, a college of higher education for Charlottenburg and one on the Urbanufer in southeast Berlin, the area that is now the Borough of Kreuzberg. The "feature" of the group in Charlottenburg is the short stretch of water, which branches off from the main river upon which the school was to be sited (Figs. 255, 256). In

Works 1924–1931   209

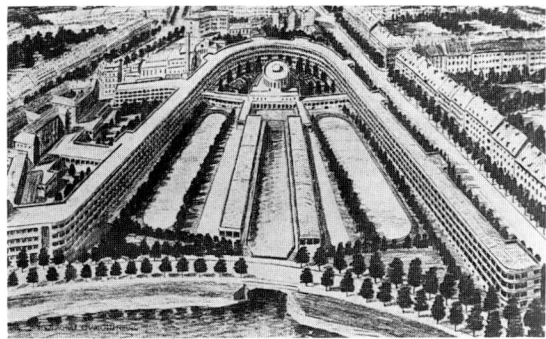

255   Hans Poelzig. Professional schools, Berlin-Charlottenburg, 1927, project. Perspective presentation.

256   Hans Poelzig. Professional schools, Berlin-Charlottenburg. Assembly hall building. Perspective presentation.

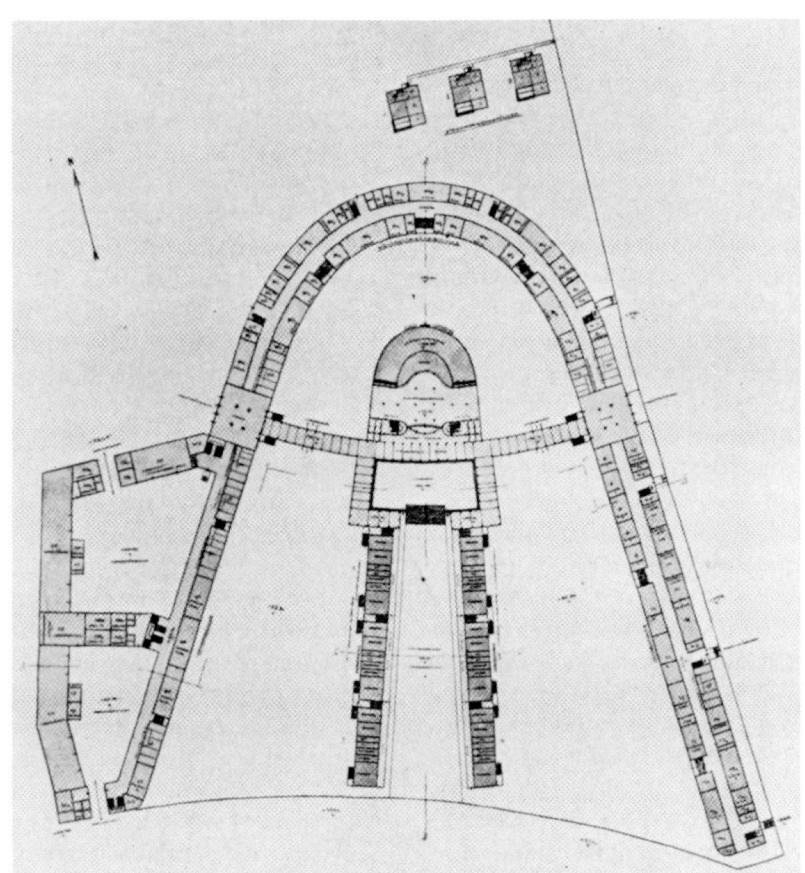

257   Hans Poelzig. Professional schools, Berlin-Charlottenburg. Plan.

Poelzig's scheme it is flanked by sports halls and leads to the focal point of the complex, the assembly hall, which is shared by the two colleges (Fig. 257). The curved shape of the girls' school, which links onto the boys' school at the eastern end, surrounds the assembly hall and forms a background to it (cf. the dual school in Dresden, Fig. 254). It is "balanced" on the western end by the straight arm of the craftsmen's school, which has only *one* row of classrooms and extends to the west with workshops. On the perspective the difference in width between the boys' school and the craftsmen's school is not visible. The workshops are given such cursory treatment that the first impression is that they belong to a different building. The school wings are in the overexaggerated shape of an (approximate) parabola that curves around the main hall at the head of the canal.

The assembly hall itself on the first floor is in the form of an ellipse. The entrance to it on the ground floor has a very strange shape. Depending on one's point of view, the ensemble is beautifully—or dreadfully—artificial.

The composition of the three colleges on the Urbanufer is similar, but smaller and without the watercourse in the center and the row of gymnasiums; it is in a semicircle, not a parabola, and has a much simpler, rectangular hall (Fig. 258). Nevertheless it is almost a replica of the group of schools in Charlottenburg.

1926 German sports forum in Berlin, competition design

The long stretched-out group culminates in the "Winter Stadium," an elliptical building at the head of a "Cour d'honneur" between a gymnasium and a "College for Gymnastics" (Figs. 259, 260). The scheme looks as if Poelzig would have liked to create an axial system for the whole project but the site was not right. The Winter Stadium was quite high. Poelzig obviously wanted to make this strangely shaped building the culmination, and it is the part of the project that most clearly bears his hallmark.

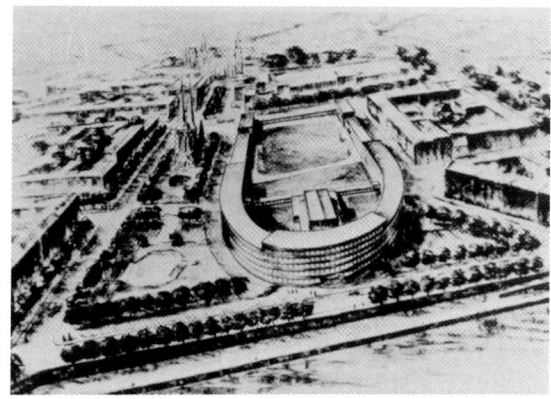

258   Hans Poelzig. Professional schools, Berlin. Urbanufer (Kreuzberg), 1928–29. Perspective presentation.

1926 Development of the Lehmann Cliffs in Halle, competition design

The two Lehmann Cliffs project from a plateau that rises up above the Saale Valley. The intention was to build a museum, an assembly hall to be called the Municipal Hall, and a building for "gymnastics" that is, a gymnasium and all that goes with it—on these cliffs. The hall, with a small stage, was to be used for concerts and occasional theatrical productions. A competition was advertised for architects resident in Halle and some well-known architects also were invited to take part. They were Behrens, Bonatz, Fahrenkamp, Gropius, Kreis, and Poelzig, all modern architects but not—with the exception of Gropius—the founders of modern architecture.

Poelzig saw the cliff formation above the river valley as a challenge. He put the oval hall on one of the cliffs and the museum on the other and then treated the building containing the hall as the main event in this landscape that would inevitably produce dramatic effects (Fig. 261). The museum, a low building with only one three-story wing, seems reserved beside it. The gymnasium is on the plateau farther away from the valley. At last Poelzig had a landscape to deal with comparable to the hill at Hellbrunn in Salzburg (see Figs. 189, 190). But again his

259 Hans Poelzig. German Sports Forum, Berlin, 1926, competition design. Cour d'Honneur.

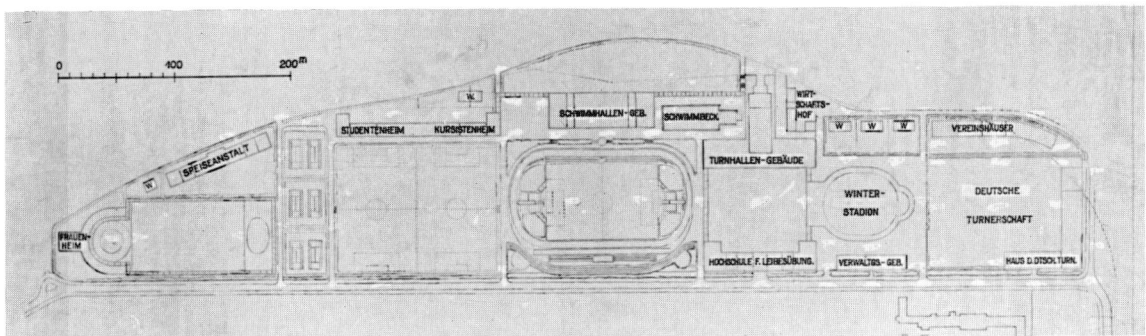

260 Hans Poelzig. German Sports Forum, Berlin. Layout plan.

261 Hans Poelzig. Group of buildings on the Lehmann Cliffs at Halle (Saale), 1926, competition design. Presentation drawing.

262 Hans Poelzig. Office and exhibition building for Hamburg, 1925, project. Perspective view from the city.

plans to use architecture to enhance a natural feature remained no more than plans.

Such were the most important aspects of the scheme. In plan, the oval building containing the hall is exactly what one would have expected from Poelzig, and the same is true for the access to it from the plateau, which slopes up to the edge of the cliff.

1925 Office and exhibition building in Hamburg, project

The scheme for an exhibition building in Hamburg with several large atriums and halls, including an exchange in the lower section, is the most extreme example of a terraced building (Figs. 262, 263). The design was done at the same time as the shop building with the Capitol Cinema, and, as I have already pointed out, Poelzig would have liked to introduce terraces into that building to enliven it but this was not possible (see Figs. 211, 212). One is tempted to say that he made up for this on a grand scale with the exhibition building in Hamburg, which incidentally shows no hint of axiality. The irregular site permits splendid chaos, and it is an integral part of this project that the building masses are in constant motion and do not even come to rest at the top. In this process the multitude of terraces rise up in front of the mass of a single curved twenty-three-story building — a sensation in 1925 — and then drop down again in steps at either end. This colossal building overlooks the railway, from where it would have been seen in all its glory. What actually went on inside the building is expressed dispassionately — just offices behind identical windows. The fact that the facade is not set back at the terraces emphasizes the coherence of the building. This is a composition of the kind Erich Mendelsohn had introduced and which in the 1950s was still considered "impossible" at an architecture school where I

263 Hans Poelzig. Office and exhibition building for Hamburg. Perspective view from the railway station.

taught in London. The draftsman who drew the perspective, which I have also reprinted here, must have thought the same, for he made the large wall look as if it *does* recede in terraces.

1929–30 Three building groups, competition designs:

Research Center for the German Aeronautical Research Institute, Berlin-Britz
Administration Building for the Nitrogen Syndicate, Berlin
Students' residence, Berlin-Charlottenburg

Around this time, Poelzig was working on his largest commissions: the building for I.G. Farben in Frankfurt, the buildings for the exhibition ground (Messegelände) in Berlin, and Broadcasting House, which was part of this exhibition complex. This did not prevent him from taking part in some of the competitions of the time. One reason for doing this was to provide employment for his office which was by now quite large.

These buildings are in the style of the time: flat roofs and ribbon windows or windows that are very close together. Poelzig had adopted this style but tried to raise the design from the banality of "accepted" architecture by one single strong effect or by grouping the buildings in

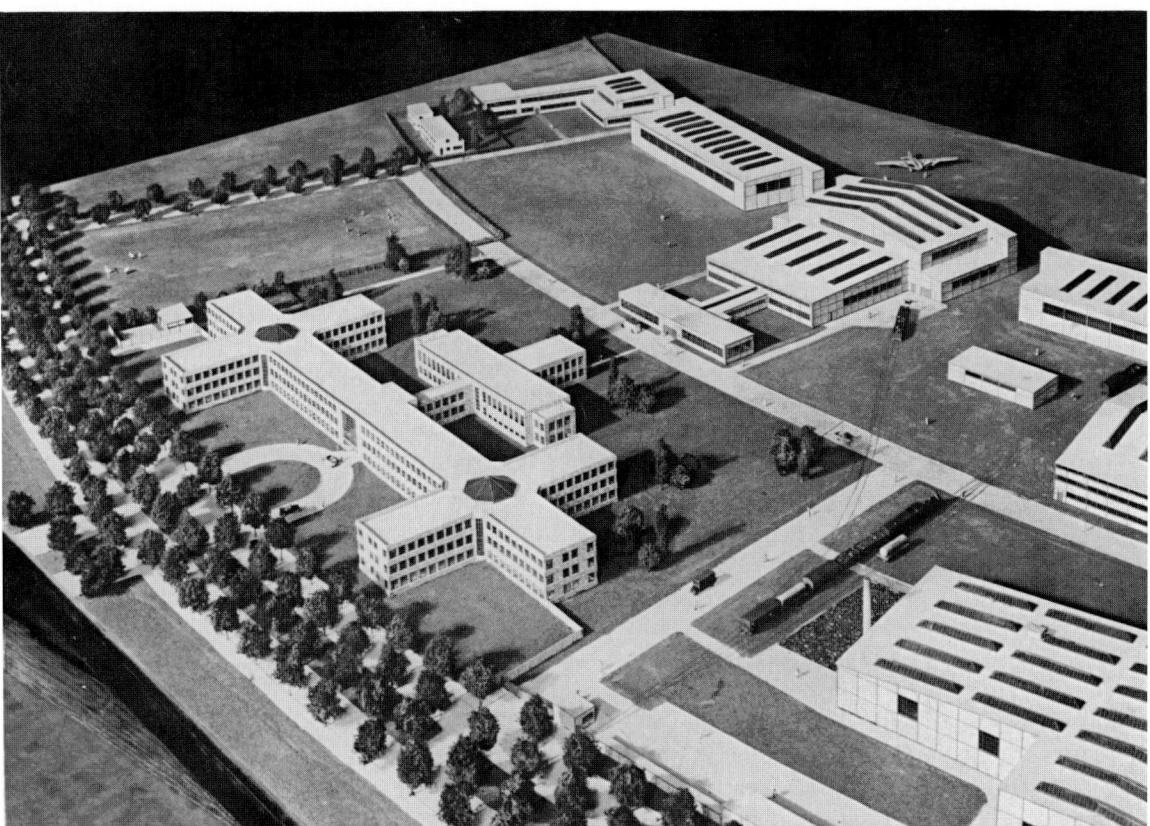

264 Hans Poelzig. Research Center for the German Aeronautical Research Institute, Berlin, 1929–30, competition design. Model.

265 Hans Poelzig. Administration building for the Nitrogen Syndicate, Berlin, 1929, competition design. Perspective presentation.

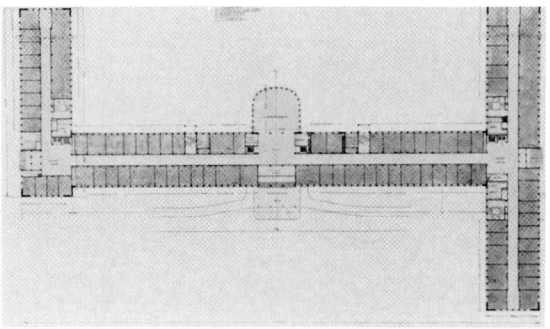

266 Hans Poelzig. Administration building for the Nitrogen Syndicate, Berlin. Plan.

a certain way, which sometimes went too far.

Exaggerated grouping can be found in the office building for the German Aeronautical Research Institute in Berlin-Britz (Fig. 264). In the office building for the Nitrogen Syndicate in Berlin Poelzig at least tried to interrupt the rear facade, which was far too long, by introducing a rounded "showroom" on the central axis (Figs. 265, 266). He repeated this composition to better effect in the strong articulation of the I.G. Farben building.

Finally, the main feature of the Students' Hall of Residence in Charlottenburg is the circular building in front of the assembly hall and the long glazed bay of the refectory, which is on the same axis (Figs. 267–269). Here on the ground floor, beneath the refectory and beneath the round space, there is a splendid axial access.

If one bears in mind that at this time, in 1929, Poelzig was not only working on his major building commissions and taking part in competitions but also had two teaching posts that he carried out with great energy—the master class and the class at the Technische Hochschule—one can picture his capacity for work at the height of his career.

267 Hans Poelzig. Students' residence, Berlin-Charlottenburg, 1929, competition design. Model.

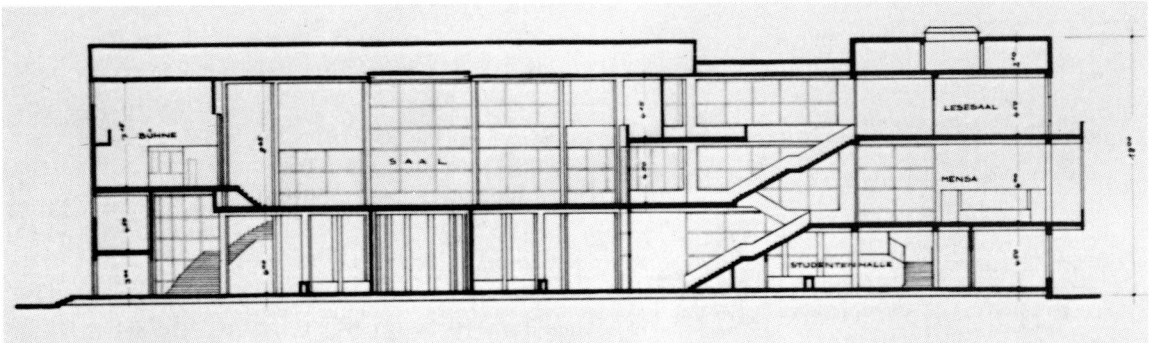

268 Hans Poelzig. Students' residence, Berlin-Charlottenburg. Section.

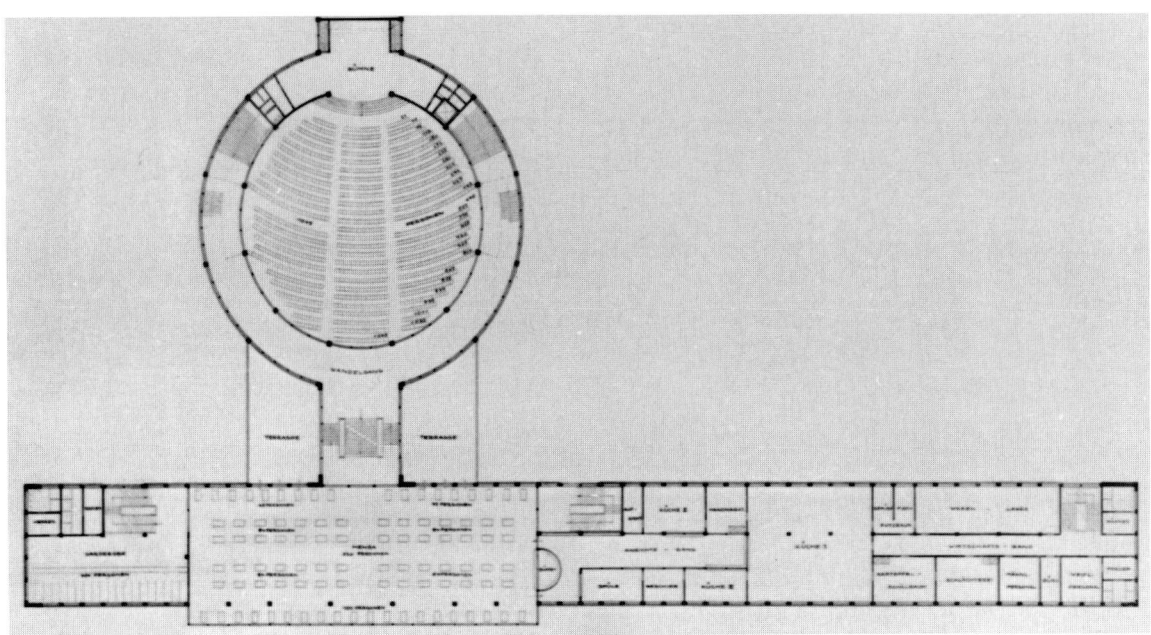

269 Hans Poelzig. Students' residence, Berlin-Charlottenburg. Plan.

URBAN DESIGN PROJECTS

1929 Extension to the Reichstag, Berlin, competition design

There is no fundamental difference between Poelzig's groups of buildings and his urban design projects. The emphasis in these projects was always on how to *design* for a particular situation in the city. Let us begin with the most extensive project, the one that was known as the extension to the Reichstag parliament building in Berlin. At the time, the Victory Column, the monument to Bismarck's three wars out of which the German Reich under the leadership of Prussia had been born, stood opposite Paul Wallot's Reichstag building on what was then known as Königsplatz and since 1918 has

270 Hans Poelzig. Library for the Reichstag, Berlin, 1929, competition design. Perspective presentation.

been called the Platz der Republik. The Reichstag was to have its own library in a separate building as well as a number of ministries, each one also in a separate building nearby. Poelzig's proposal of 1927 for the library building takes up again his 1922 design for a high-rise building at Friedrichstrasse station (Fig. 270; see Fig. 206). The triangular high-rise building with concave sides, sited very close to the strongly characteristic Reichstag building, on one corner of it in fact, could not relate to this form because it was not neutral enough. Poelzig grouped the ministries very schematically on the Platz der Republik.

In 1929 a second competition was held with only seventeen participants. Both the brief and the area affected were extended. Poelzig proposed demolishing the residential quarter enclosed by the bend in the River Spree to the north of the Reichstag in order to create a north–south axis that would run through the central point of this bend and would be marked by the Victory Column opposite the Reichstag. The idea of a north–south axis here had already been pursued by the town planner Martin Mächler. During the Third Reich, Albert Speer tried to implement it on a large scale. Poelzig's axis was meant to be a broad avenue that would continue the Victory Allée, a broad footpath leading to the Victory Column that Wilhelm II had laid out in honor of the House of Hohenzollern. On either side of this path through the Tiegarten the Kaiser had had a memorial erected to each of his ancestors. Unlike the town planners Mächler and Speer, Poelzig wanted to leave the Victory Allée intact. His intention was not to create a north–south axis for the city of Berlin but to improve the situa-

271 Additional buildings for the Reichstag, Berlin, 1929, competition design. Perspective presentation from the Spree River. In the background, the Victory Column.

tion around the Spree Bend close to the Reichstag. To achieve this it was necessary for the residential quarter that was there to be demolished. It was not just any residential quarter but one of the best in Berlin, an area where noble families like Count Barby's in Theodor Fontane's novel *Der Stechlin* lived.[2] The houses there dated from the late nineteenth century, a style that had come to be rejected, but they were nevertheless high-class houses whose quality cannot have escaped Poelzig's notice. Nevertheless, he proposed demolishing the quarter: This part of Berlin was to be the monumental embodiment of the political institutions of the Reich. Poelzig chose the most elemental way of expressing this idea architecturally by arranging the ministries radially on the bend of the Spree (Figs. 271, 272). He wrote himself about his proposal:

This proposal is like a great gesture. It would give Berlin the grand urban group in the center of the city that it is so noticeably wanting. It would also make the River Spree part of this townscape. It would certainly be adequate for the capital of the Reich. The whole complex would be an impressive symbol of just this idea: Berlin, the capital city. The price that would have to be paid would be the demolition of a whole quarter of the city, that is to say, a measure which for financial reasons is at present probably not within the realm of the possible.[3]

This may sound over-confident. Berliners would agree, however, that Poelzig's words were fulfilled in his plan. The site in the bend of the Spree still poses problems today. For several years urban planners have been concerned with this part of the city, which is known as the Central Area. None of the other proposals of 1929 approaches the monumentality of Poelzig's scheme. Also, what Poelzig says about incorporating the River Spree into the city is correct: The Spree flows through Berlin but at no point is it as significant for Berlin as the Seine is for Paris or the Thames for London. Strictly speaking, the Spree flows past Berlin.

Poelzig's proposal is of monumental simplicity. When I looked at it at the time I said, "How else could it possibly be done?" Only the library still looked a little lost, this triangular building on the corner of the Reichstag. I fear that the best thing one could have said about this building was that it destroyed the overall coherence only a little. The jury did not award the first prize to Poelzig. The competition brief had not

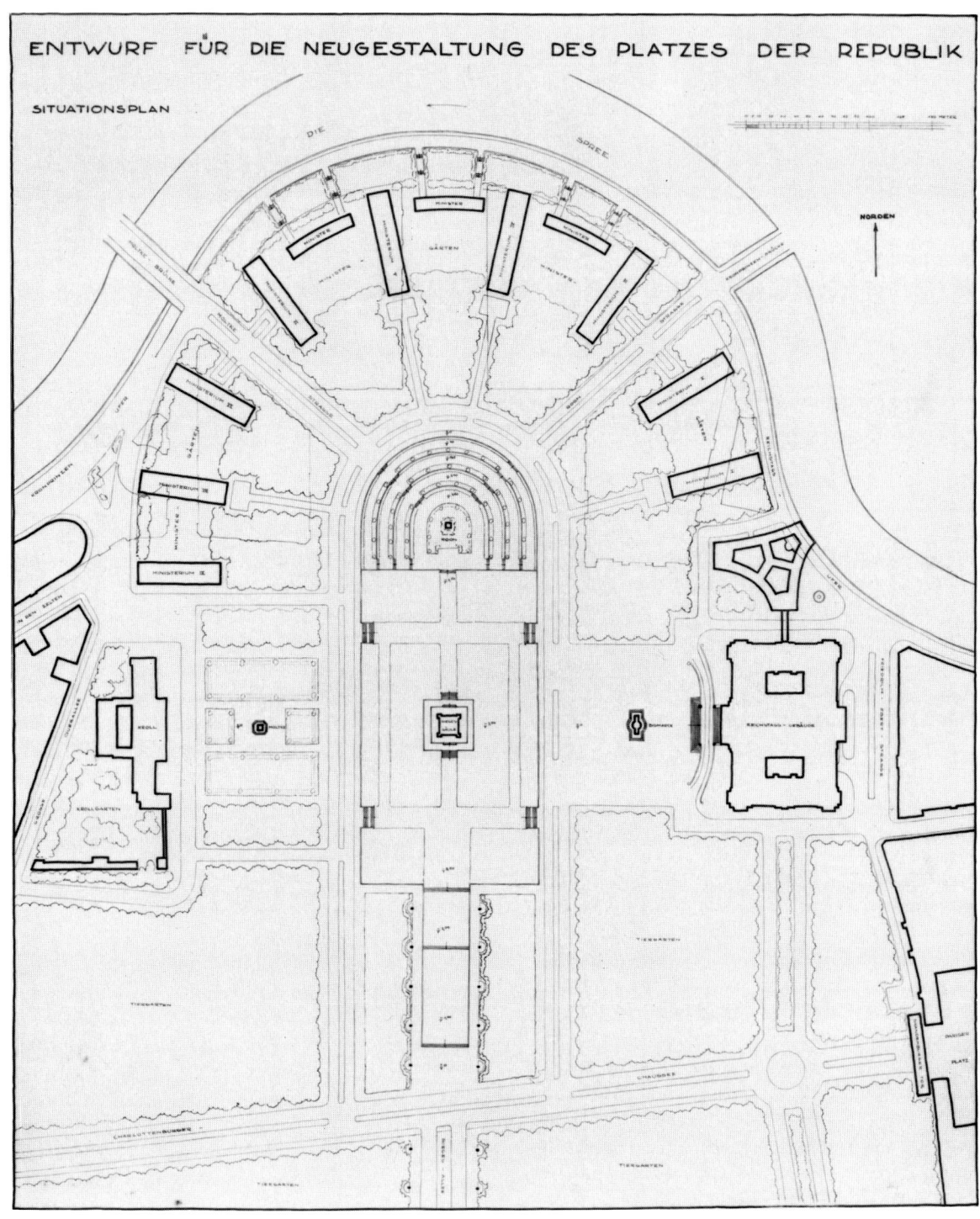

272 Hans Poelzig. Additional buildings for the Reichstag, Berlin, 1929. Layout plan.

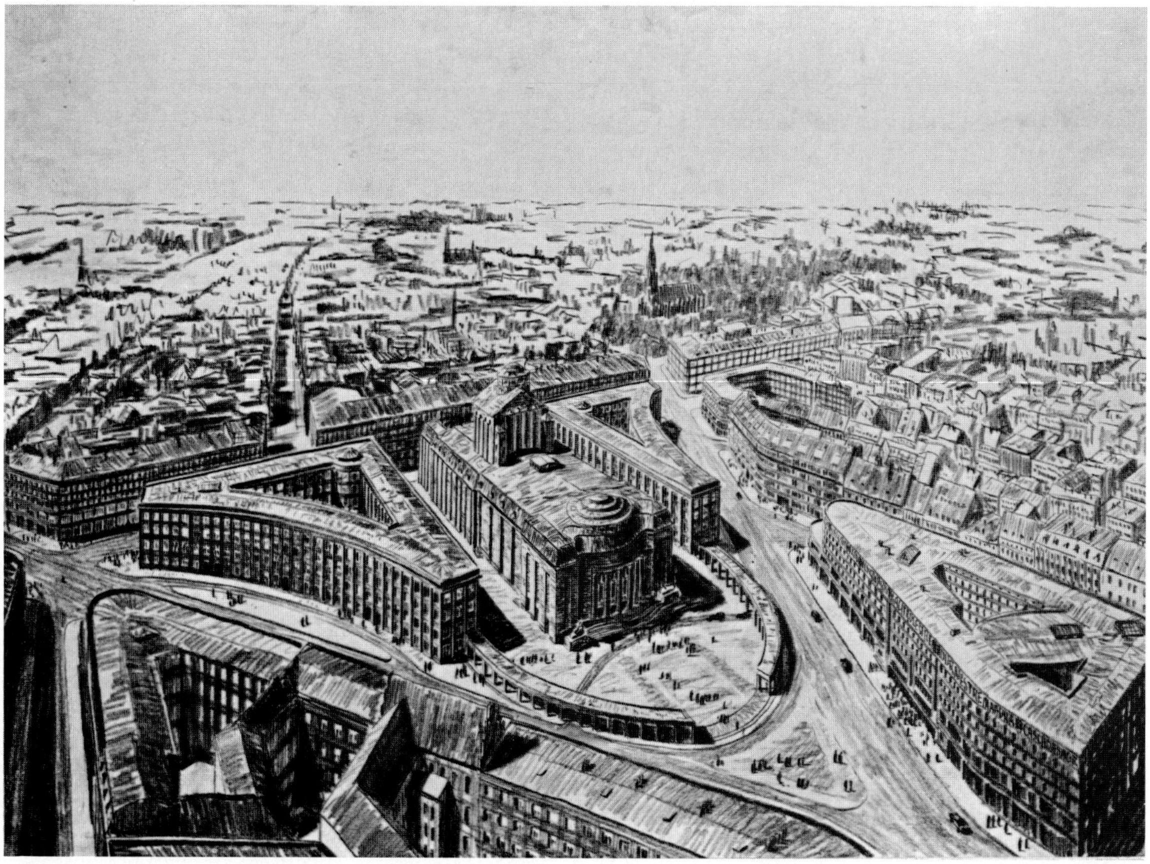

273 Hans Poelzig. Redesign of the Scheunenviertel, Berlin, 1927, partially realized. Perspective presentation. Proposed new buildings included offices, apartment houses, and the Babylon Cinema. Poelzig made Oskar Kaufmann's prewar Volksbühne theater the centerpiece of his design.

provided for demolishing the residential quarter in the bend of the river. The project was short-listed, however. If the prosperity of the Weimar Republic had lasted longer there might have been a chance of the project being built. But "Black Friday" on Wall Street in 1929 was already the beginning of the end of the Weimar Republic. It is important to bear these circumstances in mind because they were also responsible for the fact that Poelzig's other major project, the buildings for the Berlin exhibition ground in the west of the city, was only partially completed and, generally speaking, that Poelzig's work even in this period remained for the most part unbuilt.

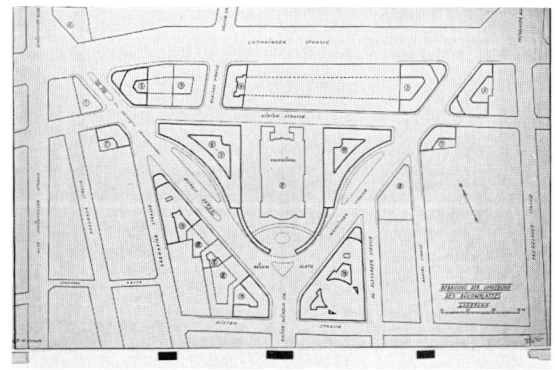

274 Hans Poelzig. Redesign of the Scheunenviertel, Berlin. Layout plan.

1927 Redesign of the Scheunenviertel in Berlin

The redesign of what is known as the Scheunenviertel, the quarter to the north of Alexanderplatz, the center of Berlin, was a direct commission, not the result of a competition. Since Martin Wagner had become city architect in Berlin, Poelzig's relationship to the city administration had changed radically. Relations between Poelzig and Wagner's predecessor Ludwig Hoffmann had been extremely bad. Hoffmann had been in office since 1896, which was too long. Poelzig had never had any sympathy for Hoffmann's historicism. Wagner, on the other hand, was one of his friends.

The Scheunenviertel, the area around Bülowplatz, was one of the underdeveloped parts of the inner city. In its center was a theater, the Volksbühne, designed by Oskar Kaufmann. It stood, as it were, in the open. I do not know what Poelzig thought of the architecture of the Volksbühne, but in any case he made every effort to create an architectural setting for it by siting buildings around it (Figs. 273, 274). He put triangular apartment blocks on both sides of the theater, and in front of the main facade of the theater he placed a parabolic space with a pergola along two sides. He planned more apartment buildings for the streets in the area. A few of them were built and one of them contains the Babylon Cinema (see Figs. 240, 241).

275 Hans Poelzig. City center for Hindenburg (Upper Silesia), 1928, project. Model.

Little was actually built and what was built is not particularly impressive. The important part of the scheme, at the sides and in front of the theater, was not built.

1928 City center of Hindenburg (Upper Silesia), project

Hindenburg was originally a village called Zabrze, which since the end of the eighteenth century had become an important coal-mining town; in 1905 it had over 50,000 inhabitants and in 1915 it was renamed Hindenburg in honor of the field marshal. It was a new town that needed a center created for it. In his plan, Poelzig surrounds a town hall with buildings containing shops and apartments (Fig. 275). To be more precise, he puts buildings with three stories over shops close to the town hall; on the other side of the curved street, which comes into the square in front of the town hall, there are four stories above the shops. This street climbs up from the town hall and the buildings are terraced accordingly. He plans a second square in this street in front of the theater. The apartment buildings are curved, have rounded corners and horizontal emphasis—reflecting the stories. The town hall is angular with vertical articulation. It is well worth looking at the project in detail on the model. The "city center ensemble" would most certainly have been very attractive. But this work was not built either.

1928–30 PLANNED AND BUILT

Radio Hall and other exhibition buildings for the Berlin exhibition ground

The Messegelände, the exhibition ground at the western entrance to the city of Berlin, was of megalomaniac proportions whose scale seems exaggerated not only in view of the rapid end of the "Weimar" prosperity. It was, in a way, the "favorite child" of the city architect Martin Wagner and the architect Hans Poelzig. Poelzig had, incidentally, already planned an exhibition hall beneath the Radio Tower in 1925, the "Radio Hall" ("Funkhalle") as it was called (Fig. 276). It was one of his most attractive projects, a good deal better than the stiff building (by Heinrich Straumer) that won the competition. The magnificent, broad-based building with a series of adjacent roofs each one higher than the next, could have been a work from his Breslau period. It cannot be compared with anything else he ever did.

The "Radio Hall" was abandoned in favor of the large exhibition ground project, which called for the existing Radio Tower to be replaced by two towers. The exhibition ground scheme, which the Berliners called the "Poelzig Egg," consists of an oval ring surrounded by an inner circle of wide exhibition halls and an outer circle of narrower halls that are linked to one another at regular intervals by transverse

276 Hans Poelzig. "Radio Hall" exhibition building, Berlin, 1925, competition design. Perspective presentation.

277 Hans Poelzig. Exhibition ground (Messegelände) for Berlin, with Martin Wagner, 1928–30. Model.

halls (Fig. 277). Alongside the inner halls there is a canal with numerous bridges crossing it on which the Berliners could have gone boating. The two main buildings are within this canal ring: the Congress Hall with its two pagoda towers and—at the opposite, narrower, end—the oval restaurant with six terraces.

The whole complex is very imaginative, one of Poelzig's dreams come true. Poelzig, moreover, repeatedly produced new sketches of fantastic details. For instance, for a time he planned to have an open dome, like a kind of spiral cage, on top of the oval Congress Hall of the second version (Fig. 278). A sketch of the first Congress Hall exists in which all the steps of the hall and the towers are decorated (Fig. 279). This shows, however, that it differed from the Salzburg project in that the decoration was not an integral part of the building or the architectural idea. Taking it away would not fundamentally change the building.

This project soon proved to be too expensive. A second version was planned, then a third, reduced version (Figs. 280, 281). The Radio Hall and Radio Tower remain. Where the broad oval "egg" should have been there is now an oval green space containing a smaller oval Congress Hall with a terraced restaurant in a semi-circle behind it. The canal remains, but the "egg" it encircles has been turned 90 degrees and has become a much smaller ellipse, a purely ornamental garden that no longer relates in any way to the exhibition halls. In the interior of this "egg" there is an oval sports ground.

224   Hans Poelzig: Reflections on His Life and Work

278   Hans Poelzig. Congress Building, Berlin exhibition ground. Sketch of an early version.

279   Hans Poelzig. Congress Building, Berlin exhibition ground. Decorated version, perspective presentation.

280 Hans Poelzig. Congress Building, Berlin exhibition ground. Final version, model.

281 Hans Poelzig. Exhibition ground for Berlin, final, reduced scheme, partially realized. Model. The Congress Building was not carried out. Poelzig's Broadcasting House is the triangular building on the right.

282 Hans Poelzig. Exhibition halls, Berlin exhibition ground, 1928–29. The hall in the background is typical, but only its upper part is visible.

The terraced restaurant spans the canal and extends over the steps of the central garden to the sports ground. There are exhibition halls beside the Radio Tower and on the other side of the oval. Avenues radiate from the oval into a park and for a time plans were considered for a second zoo there. Opposite the exhibition grounds, yet not on its axis, there was to be a Broadcasting House, which was in fact built as it appears on the model of the final version of the exhibition ground. The only exhibition buildings that were built were the halls; a garden vaguely reminiscent of the oval park but without the canal was also completed. The Congress Hall–restaurant ensemble was *not* built. The site where it would have been is now

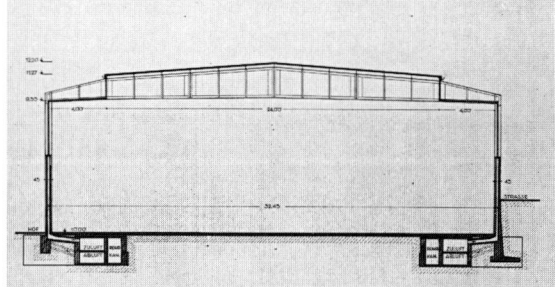

283 Hans Poelzig. Exhibition hall, Berlin exhibition ground. Section. Underground on either side are ducts for air exchange and channels for tubing.

284 Hans Poelzig. Typical exhibition building, Berlin exhibition ground. Interior.

the entrance to the exhibition ground in a building of the 1930s that is totally lacking in character, indeed ugly. The loss of the first large "egg" is easier to bear than the loss of the very carefully thought-out Congress Hall–restaurant ensemble. Had this been built it would have been a memorial to Poelzig. After all the cuts, the only major buildings by Poelzig still standing in West Berlin are a few exhibition halls and Broadcasting House (see below). Until recently the Grosses Schauspielhaus still remained in East Berlin, albeit very changed inside. It was not demolished until 1985 after it had been replaced by an entertainment palace in neighboring Friedrichstrasse.

The exhibition halls are designed in steel and lit by glass bricks in the upper section (Figs. 282–284). They have aged well and are still in use today. They are in fact all that remains of Poelzig's ambitious "egg project." In the meantime a congress center of colossal dimensions has been built near the Radio Tower, completely overshadowing the last remains of the Wagner-Poelzig era. An excerpt from Berlin's history between 1928 and 1980 can be seen in the exhibition and congress buildings.

1929–30 Broadcasting House, Berlin

The first project included two large broadcasting halls and between them on the axis a stairwell of very individual design (Fig. 285). The pointed part of the present building at the back was not there and the building was more cogent than it is now (Fig. 286). It is a great pity that the stairwell was not built. As it exists, the building has one large and two smaller main halls, a rectangular space with galleries around it, a glass roof, and two large lamps (Fig. 287). Stairs on both sides of that space link the

228 Hans Poelzig: Reflections on His Life and Work

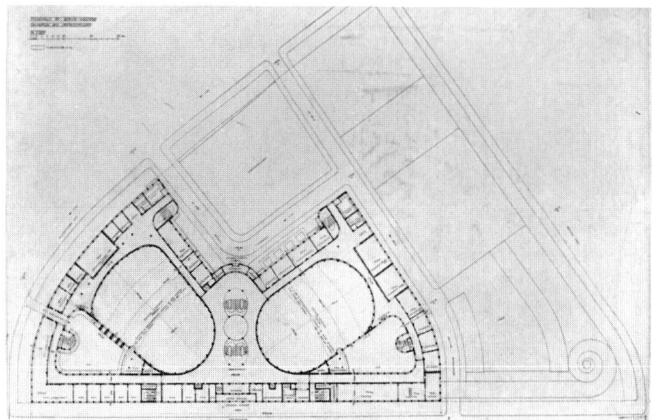

285 Hans Poelzig. Broadcasting House (Haus des Deutschen Rundfunks), 1929–30. First version, plan.

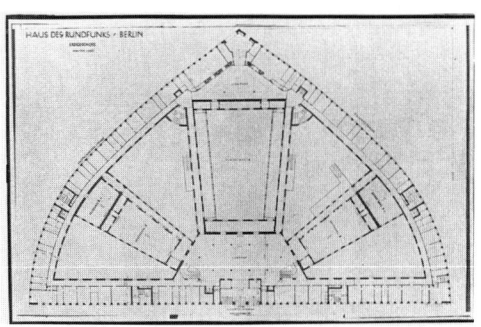

286 Hans Poelzig. Broadcasting House. Definitive version, plan.

287 Hans Poelzig. Broadcasting House. Great hall.

288 Hans Poelzig. Broadcasting House. Entrance.

289 Hans Poelzig. Broadcasting House. Aerial view.

ground floor to the first floor only. This cool, very beautiful space was disfigured by bad details after the end of the last war but it was recently (August 1987) restored; Max Berling, who worked with Poelzig on the construction of Broadcasting House, was in charge of the restoration.

The exterior of the first version was also changed—I believe for the better. The broad facade to the street, with its vertical articulation (opposite the entrance to the exhibition ground), is calmer than the one that had originally been planned (Figs. 288, 289). The building is in purple engineering brick, and the window and door surrounds are clad with ceramic tiles. This carefully chosen material is very beautiful. The windows are square, divided into four equal parts, with the central horizontal bar broader than the vertical. Pilasters are missing from the curved sides of the building.

Broadcasting House stands in this "exhibition" district of Berlin as a witness to what might have been built there. All the buildings which were built later—the entrance building to the exhibition ground, the congress center, the television center—seem to have been built for the sole purpose of proving the decline of quality in architecture.

1928–30 Administration Building for I.G. Farben, Frankfurt-am-Main

This group of buildings was also built not quite as Poelzig planned it. But he had reason to be content with the result and he was content: At last a large group of buildings had been *completed*. The change becomes clear if one compares the model with the site plan of the

290　Hans Poelzig. I.G. Farben administration building, Frankfurt-am-Main, 1928–30. Model of first version.

finished building (Figs. 290, 291). The slight curve in the seven-story-high office wing—which, as I have already mentioned, was the adjustment through which Poelzig "made the project his own—" was on the model reinforced in spatial terms by the broad side wings. They form an enclosed space on the northern side of the office wing, between it and the canteen. This was Poelzig's idea and it should not be forgotten, for although the I.G. Farben is a fine building, it is on first sight disappointing. Despite the curvature, despite the very subtle relationship to the canteen on the northern side, the building stands in its vast garden with no real setting. On the model, the curved paths, embankments, and rows of trees behind the canteen draw everything together to create a Poelzig form. That did not happen in the end. Although Poelzig was proud and pleased with what he achieved in Frankfurt, this group too remained a fragment.

I would like to add that the style of the building could have accommodated the broader massing seen on the model. This is a steel-frame building clad in travertine. Here too Poelzig uses extremely fine material, and the horizontal rows of windows in the main building, which works in fact as a link, are appropriate to the steel frame, which cannot quite be said of the strange frames surrounding seven rows of windows in the wings (Fig. 292). The detailing of the whole building is decidedly authoritarian. Now, after the Third Reich, I have heard it called "protofascist." At the time, just after the

Works 1924–1931   231

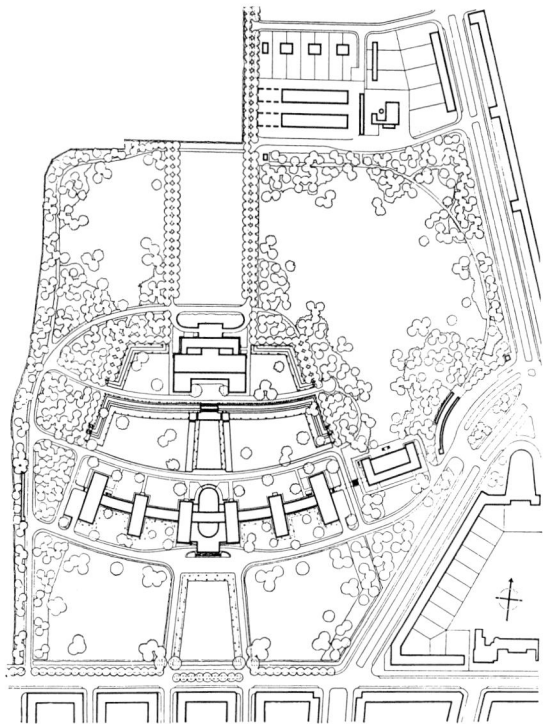

291 Hans Poelzig. I.G. Farben administration building. Final version, layout plan.

292 Hans Poelzig. I.G. Farben building. Part of entrance front.

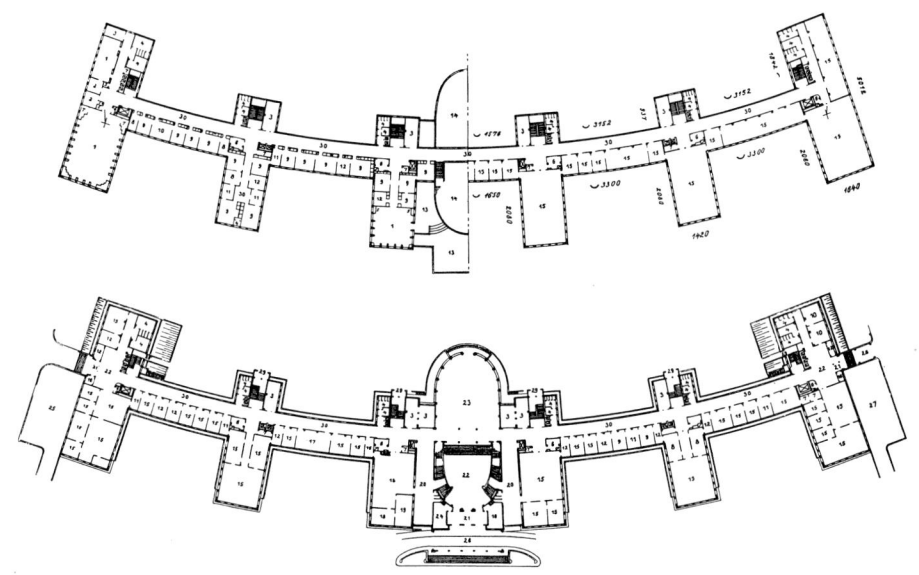

293 Hans Poelzig. I.G. Farben building. Plans of ground floor and upper stories.

294 Hans Poelzig. I.G. Farben building. Entrance hall.

295 Hans Poelzig. I.G. Farben building. Entrance building.

296 Hans Poelzig. I.G. Farben building. Staircase of entrance hall.

297   Hans Poelzig. I.G. Farben building. Open passage on first floor.

building was completed, a socialist critic rejected it furiously, saying it was a monument to capitalism. It can be interpreted at will. One can with justification ask how else the detailing in a large office block should have been if not large, simple, cool. The main effect here was meant to be not so much the detail as the overall form, which would have gained in breadth, compactness, even in softness, if the longer wings had been built.

One of the essential features of the plan was that the entrance to the building should be on its working side, that is to say, between the strongly projecting wings which contain the large offices and connect with the smaller offices in the link building (Fig. 293). There are only corridors on the north side of the link building and the short continuations of the wings that contain the large offices to the north have only stairs and service rooms, except for the two outside wings, which Poelzig made slightly longer so as not to lose completely the enclosing effect of the side wings. One more remark: The entrance to the building is on the convex side, which is unusual.

One passes through an entance building that makes a very formal impression, then proceeds through the curved space of the entrance foyer from where two very fine staircases on either side sweep up to the first floor (Figs. 294–298). Open corridors pass through the foyer, separating it from the space beyond, which is an exhibition space whose curved glazed facade projects far beyond the wings of the northern facade. With the progression of entrance hall, open corridors, and exhibition space, Poelzig

298 Hans Poelzig. I.G. Farben building. View from the windows of the exhibition room.

299 Hans Poelzig. I.G. Farben building. Exterior, upper part of entrance hall.

300 Hans Poelzig. I.G. Farben building. Stairs leading to the canteen.

was finally able to see one of his spatial sequences become reality. The way the rounded glass facade of the exhibition space protrudes in front of the concave, strongly articulated northern facade may raise a few questions, as may the way the semicircular entrance hall relates to the severe shape of the entrance building (Fig. 299). The precision — and softness — of the detailing, can be seen in the parapet walls of the staircase and the ramp up to the entrance building. It must be admitted, however, that the remark that the architecture was protofascist appears to be justified in regard to the entrance structure. The building now houses the American Military Administration.

All the spaces are broad, clear, and superbly detailed. This even applies to the corridors: The very fact that they are lit by windows is an indication of the generous planning.

The canteen, with its magnificent external stairs, its broad, light social room with its clarity of construction, is in keeping with the main building (Figs. 300–302). In this stage of his development Poelzig was finally able to achieve his full potential.

301 (top right) Hans Poelzig. I.G. Farben building. Social room.

302 (bottom right) Hans Poelzig. I.G. Farben building by night.

Works 1924–1931   237

238 Hans Poelzig: Reflections on His Life and Work

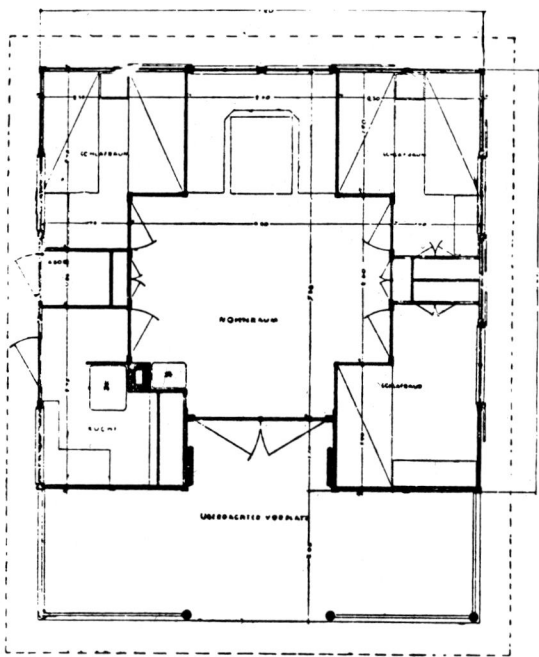

303 Hans Poelzig. Weekend house, 1927. Plan.

304 Hans Poelzig. Weekend house. Terrace and entrance.

DOMESTIC ARCHITECTURE

1927 Weekend house

Poelzig's designs for houses differed fundamentally from those for the large buildings I have talked about. I know of only one house design that is clearly symmetrical — a weekend house from 1927; it has a kitchen and miniature bedrooms for five people arranged around a central living room (Figs. 303, 304). But the living room here was not really meant to be used as such. It had to form a link; on three sides it had nothing but doors, and only in the background was there an alcove with a built-in bench around a table. It is an excellent plan for a weekend house and the fact that it is so comprehensible on first sight and convincingly symmetrical makes it particularly good.

1927–28 Housing estates: (1) Weissenhof estate, Stuttgart; (2) Im Fischtal estate, Berlin-Zehlendorf

Poelzig made a clear distinction between a weekend house, which had to provide accommodation for one or two nights, and a permanent home. At that time he built very few of the latter and they were designed in collaboration with his second wife, Marlene. It is only necessary to discuss two of them: the house in the Werkbund's Weissenhof estate near Stuttgart and the detached house and two-family houses on the "Im Fischtal" estate in Zehlendorf, Berlin.

To look first of all at the exteriors of the Weissenhof house and the detached house on the Im Fischtal estate. Although the two houses were built at virtually the same time, they could not be more different. The Weissenhof house has a flat roof with a roof garden and a remarkably lively volume, in view of its simple plan (Figs. 305–307). The house in the Im Fischtal estate is a closed volume with a roof with the 45-degree pitch laid down for the whole estate (Fig. 308; see also Fig. 219). (The Im Fischtal is the estate that was intended to be a counterdemonstration to "Onkel Tom," the modern estate designed by Taut, Häring, and Salvisberg [see Chapter 9; see also Fig. 18].) Admittedly, on closer examination one begins to ask which house is the more modern. The windows in the Im Fischtal house are broader than the ones in the Weissenhof, yet the elevation to the garden,

305 Hans Poelzig. One-family house, Weissenhof estate near Stuttgart, 1927.

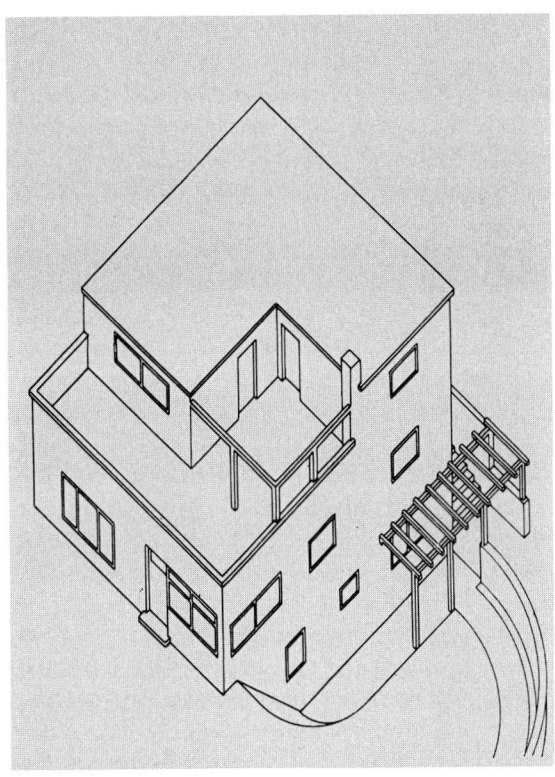

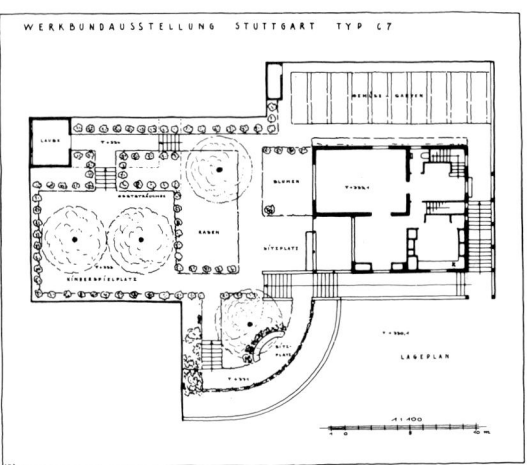

306 Hans Poelzig. House on the Weissenhof estate. Axonometry.

307 Hans Poelzig. House on the Weissenhof estate. Ground-floor plan.

240   Hans Poelzig: Reflections on His Life and Work

308 (left) Hans Poelzig. One-family house on the Im Fischtal estate. Berlin-Zehlendorf, 1927–28. Garden elevation.

309 (above) Mart Stam. Terrace houses in the Weissenhof estate, Stuttgart.

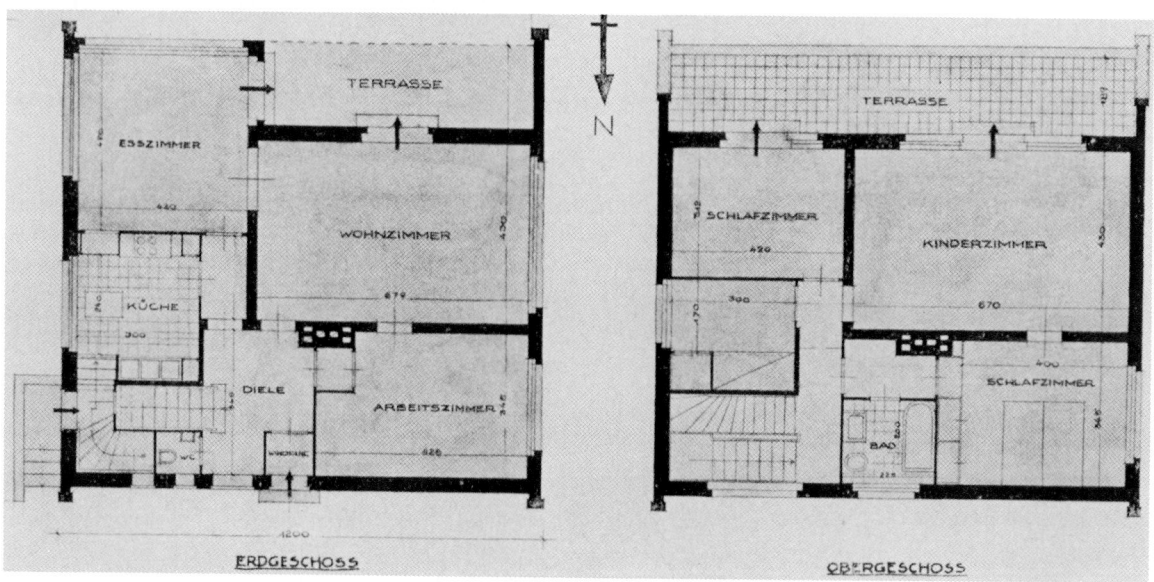

310 Hans Poelzig. One-family house on the Im Fischtal estate. Berlin-Zehlendorf. Plans of ground floor and first floor.

which is artificially held together by the two gables, is less well balanced than any of the facades in the Weissenhof.

In fact, Poelzig did not care in what style a house was or should be designed. If, as on the Weissenhof estate, it had to be "modern" Poelzig was perfectly capable of designing according to the rules of that game. If, as on the Fischtal estate, it was meant to be "traditional" he was just as capable of producing this style. It must be said, however, that although he played the game skillfully in both cases, it was not convincing because the player was not convinced. His house on the Weissenhof estate was never considered a clear demonstration of a new architecture. This claim actually could be made for both of Le Corbusier's houses and for the houses by Josef Frank and Mart Stam (Fig. 309). Similarly, Poelzig's Fischtal houses are unlike their neighbors designed by Tessenow,

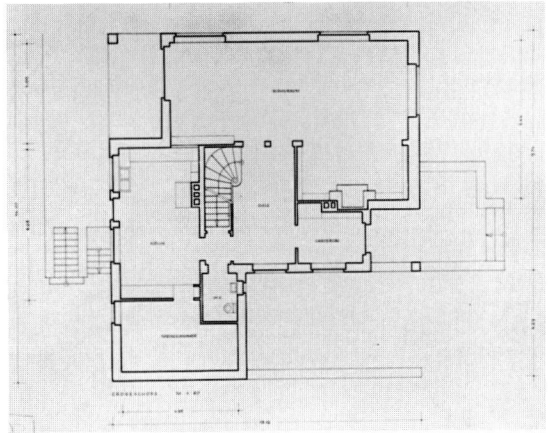 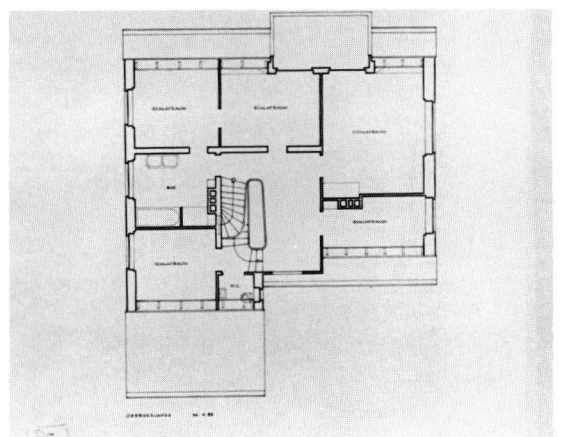

311a, b Hans Poelzig. One-family house at Kliedbruch near Krefeld, 1929. Plans of ground floor and first floor.

Schopohl, and Schmitthenner; they are not examples of traditional housing forms reflected in the design of the house itself. As I mentioned above, the garden elevations of these houses are *forced* under the roof by the gables. The windows are strikingly wide, and the free arrangement of the windows and doors on the street elevation does not match the degree of "niceness" of neighboring houses, for example, those designed by Schmitthenner (see Fig. 219). Both houses show how little interest Poelzig had for *this* question.

What did interest him was the planning of the house and the way its rooms related to each other (Fig. 310). And I must say that in this respect the Fischtal house is freer than the house on the Weissenhof.

The relationship between living room and dining room; the oblique view into the dining room, which is almost a loggia; the solid walls of the living room, which has its large window on the narrow side farthest away from the dining room: All this is excellent planning, "livable," one would say nowadays. On the bedroom floor it is striking that the children's bedroom is by far the largest; it is as large as the living room beneath. This is absolutely right, but which architect planned like that then — or now? Of all the houses on the Fischtal estate Poelzig's is the best as a family home.

Poelzig gave us the Fischtal program as a study project and began his crit with the following statement: "An architect can be faced with only two really difficult projects: a large theater and a small house. Of the two the small house is the more difficult."

1929 House in Kliedbruch near Krefeld

Although it cannot be called large this is quite a high-quality house. Poelzig made a very conscious planning decision to make one room, the living room, large (Figs. 311a, b). It has a corner window to the loggia on one side and in the other corner two large windows that let in light to a fireside alcove, which it would be more appropriate to call an annex with fireplace since it is as wide as the room itself. All the other rooms in the house are small. It is striking that the master of the house did not ask for a study for himself. The living room is *the* room.

I have not actually seen the house but there are to my mind a number of unsatisfactory points about its design: the way the balcony cuts into the curved roof; the glass wall of the

312 Hans Poelzig. House at Kliedbruch. From the garden.

313 Hans Poelzig. House at Kliedbruch. Entrance.

loggia close to the living room window; and particularly the way the broad curved roof over the window of the hall on the first floor merges with the roof above the garage, which slopes down to below the level of the ground floor (Figs. 312–314). It is an experimental house although it picks up again a very old Poelzig motif, the curved roof. One has the feeling that new tones are being struck here that might possibly have been developed further in later houses. But, apart from the house that Marlene Poelzig built for the Poelzigs in the Westend district of Berlin, there *were* no further houses. One can understand why the Weissenhof house did not satisfy him any more, and the Fischtal house may have seemed too artificial to him and at the same time too conventional—not yet the right form. In Kliedbruch an attempt is made to create the right form for a house. It is regrettable that Poelzig did not build any more houses after this one. Unlike the houses on the Weissenhof and Fischtal estates, where there are also two semi-detached houses, the house in Kliedbruch was planned for a specific client. Heuss says of Poelzig's late houses that he was planning for a *standard house*. The house in Kliedbruch is the exception in that he built if for a client. Most

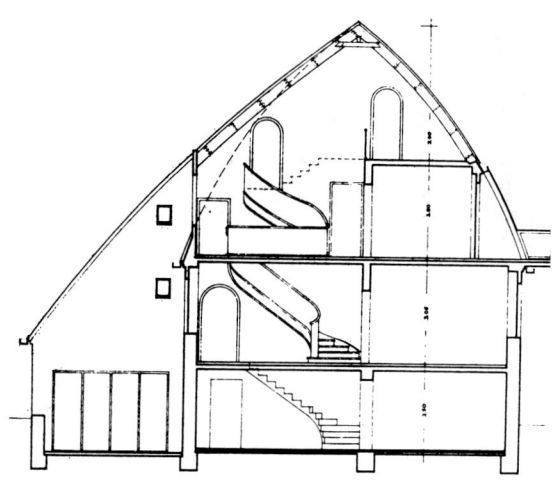

314 Hans Poelzig. House at Kliedbruch. Section.

certainly, other clients would have caused Poelzig to continue the experiment he began in Kliedbruch, as had happened in Breslau. Poelzig still believed that the client was necessary as the opposite pole to the architect. But he did not find any more clients.

315 Hans Poelzig. Church hall for the Evangelical community at Kammin, 1928–29. Front of the building.

OTHER WORKS OF THIS PERIOD

1928–29 Hall and parish rooms for the Evangelical church in Kammin
1931 Ship-lift in Niederfinow, project

To conclude this chapter I will look at two of Poelzig's works that were built at around the same time and yet are very different from one another.

The church hall is a brick building with small windows divided into four and an entrance porch with beautiful segmental arches (Fig. 315). A large expanse of wall surface is visible. The interior of the church hall has real wooden beams. It is almost as if Poelzig was "playing" Tessenow.

The ship-lift is a purely technical building, with an expressive, rhythmic concrete construction appropriate to its function, which is to lift ships from a lower to a higher level of the canal (Fig. 316). Each element of the construction is carefully shaped; the master who created the gasworks in Dresden-Reick (see Figs. 138, 139) has surpassed himself in this building. What the church hall and the ship-lift have in common is their rhythm. What is very different is their character: in the former, decidedly heavy and calm; in the latter, just as decidedly tense, on edge, light.

As I said, the two were designed almost at the same time. They show to just what extent Poelzig was outside the battle over traditional and

244 Hans Poelzig: Reflections on His Life and Work

316 Hans Poelzig. Ship-lift, Niederfinow, 1931, project. Presentation perspective.

modern architecture that was being fought in those years. It is as if he were trying to say that he would accept and try to do justice to every brief, whatever that meant in each particular case. This was how he saw the role of the architect. No matter what means the architect uses, the scheme can be said to be good if the end product is true architecture.

CHAPTER ELEVEN
The Final Years 1932–1936

AT THE BEGINNING of the 1930s Poelzig was at the height of his prestige and success. On his sixtieth birthday, 30 April 1929, colleagues, critics, and art writers, the young generation of architects, one could say Germany's leading cultural figures, had paid homage to him. Important designs of his had been built. He was a leading celebrity on the Berlin scene: No one would dream of missing the "Poelzig Party" in February, a grand masked ball. The great attraction was the man himself, "the Master," drinking champagne and laughing heartily. Everyone knew the name Poelzig.

But this was not only a source of pleasure. It also meant that everyone wanted something from him. He was seen as the great mediator who could arbitrate in any crisis, such as the one in the art school, the "Academy," which had been caused by the resignation of Bruno Paul who had been its director for many years. Poelzig was asked to take Paul's place, which he did. He wrote to the sculptor Theodor von Gosen, his friend from Breslau days: "It's really funny that in recent months I often had a dream that I would take over an academy again and now the dream has become awful reality."[1]

He was also invited to become vice-president of the Prussian Academy of Arts and at the beginning of 1933 this position caused him to become involved in a real scandal. He was slandered by the press and could not understand why. The subject of the dispute—that the Academy planned to put on an exhibition of Belgian art at a time when German nationalists were protesting against the treatment of German minorities in Belgium—left him completely cold. He did not see that present-day Belgian politics could have anything to do with Memling or Van Eyck. But he was hurt that having been celebrated so recently he was now being harassed. What is more, the arguments put forward in his defense were even more stupid than the ones used against him. As he put it himself: "A dog pisses on my trouser leg and somebody comes along with a cloth and wipes it all over my trousers."[2]

What had happened since 1930 that could have changed his position in public life so drastically? Two things had happened, two catastrophes. One of them was the economic collapse on Wall Street in 1929 which triggered a world-wide depression and put seven million people in Germany out of work. The other was a political catastrophe: In 1930 the National Socialists gained their first overwhelming election victory. The brownshirts moved into the Reichstag and ruled the streets. There is a connection between these two events. For Poelzig, the economic collapse meant that no new commissions followed the major commissions, which he continued to work on in the early thirties. In 1930 he must have hoped that he had finally entered a phase where his projects would be built, but this hope turned out to be an illusion. From 1932 onward almost all the entries in his list of works are unbuilt projects. The prosperity of the Weimar Republic had come to an end and with it the Republic itself. The government had already eliminated the influence of parliament and was ruling the country by means of "emergency decrees." The situation was economically and politically so desperate that I heard even calm people shouting, "We need a coup, it doesn't matter whether it comes from the left or the right, but we cannot go on like this."

The coup came from the right and a kind of civil war came from the left which was liquidated bloodily. A man like Poelzig, who as recently as 1931 had announced his creed as an artist and a man in his speech "The Architect," could only look on aghast. Both movements, the extreme right and the extreme left, were alien to him.

At least neither movement penetrated into his classes. This was no coincidence. The students who came to Poelzig were those who wanted to find out whether they were talented as architects. They had not been able to establish this in the first part of their studies. It had been like being at school, nothing but "subjects" and examinations. Nor would they ever be able to find out from *those* professors, for whom the world had come to a standstill in 1918. Nor would they find out from a man like Tessenow, who insisted that his students adopt one particular philosophy, one particular style. There really was only *one* liberal seminar and that was Poelzig's. That is why the students who came to Poelzig were liberals, they were interested in new things, were left-wing in the cultural sense. People soon started to talk about the "black-haired Poelzig students," although Jews were certainly in the minority in Poelzig's seminar. Poelzig's students were looking for inspiration and he wanted to inspire. He once said that an architect can never have enough education, and so he supplied us with inspiration from all aspects of European culture.

This was grist for the mill of those who had assumed power and already considered Poelzig to be "unreliable," if not worse. And *was* he not unreliable? Had he not planned the Grosses Schauspielhaus in collaboration with the Jew Max Reinhardt? Were not "the dregs of the degenerate Weimar society," the disrespectful, the reformers, gathered around him? Was not something growing here which had to be halted, even destroyed, in the name of tradition? In reality, Poelzig was less "unreliable" than his Nazi critics suggested. I have pointed out that there was a distance between him and the advocates of modern architecture, and this distance was important to him. Furthermore, he was, and remained to the end, very conscious of German culture. When I went into exile in Paris he warned me about the "French slickness," which would be of no use to us Germans. Poelzig's sense of the slightly odd, the rough-and-ready, the individual, the nonclassical, in a word, all that was German, which he talked about so eloquently in the Salzburg speech, never left him. And as his feelings about this were fed by a deep conviction, he simply could not understand the insults that were fired at him on the occasion of the "Belgian scandal" in 1933 and on other occasions.

Was Poelzig one of the people who put up active resistance? It cannot be claimed that he did. He had no interest in the matter; it was alien to him, at any rate in the form it took. He even thought it inexcusable for artists to get involved in politics. In 1933 two members of the Prussian Academy of Arts, Käthe Kollwitz and Heinrich Mann, had signed a manifesto of the "People's Front" which was the amalgamation of the Social Democrats and Communists. Bernhard Rust, the Prussian "Minister of Culture," who was of course a Nazi, demanded that they be expelled from the Academy. Poelzig, who was vice-president, put forward the theory that the Academy was an institution for the arts and not for politics, by which obviously he meant that, since they were artists, those two should never have involved themselves in a political act. Martin Wagner, the city architect and a colleague of Poelzig's from the days of the "Egg" for the Berlin exhibition ground, turned Poelzig's words around and said that the Academy was an institution for the arts and was therefore obliged to resist any interference by politicians. He was right, of course, and what is more, he took the only logical step and resigned from the Academy. He nevertheless remained Poelzig's friend, I imagine because he knew the man so well that he understood what Poelzig meant by art and what he meant by politics.

This is not intended as an attempt to justify Poelzig's behavior. On this occasion it cannot be justified. Part of the reason for his behavior was that he was quite simply apolitical. Poelzig had a middle-class, national consciousness. The question remains as to whether he had sympathies for any of the underlying values of the politics emerging in these years. I touched upon this question at the beginning of this book.

I have pointed out that he felt very uneasy about the emerging influence of technology. He feared for what would become of art if artists and architects looked to technology for inspiration. In Stuttgart in 1919 he had spoken about craftsmanship or rather about his idea of craftsmanship (see Chapter 6, Doc. 6B). What he said sounded a little out of touch with reality. But from the outset Poelzig always appreciated things that were well built and powerful: the wall with rough joints, the arch thrusting against the weight of the wall. Nazi architects such as Paul Schmitthenner, the head of what was known as the Stuttgart School, repeatedly stressed the importance of good craftsmanship. They also spoke of the fact that science and research were intruding into the planning process and standing in the way of creativity. I remember a speech in which Schmitthenner introduced some of his houses with the remark, "Built, gentlemen, built — not researched!" The remark was intended as a dig at the Reichsforschungsgesellschaft, the Construction Research Company of the Reich. "Built — not researched" — this could have been said by Poelzig. But Poelzig must have thoroughly disliked the houses of Schmitthenner and the Stuttgart School. Schmitthenner spoke of craftsmanship, and as we know Poelzig also spoke of craftsmanship. It may be true that Schmitthenner knew more about it than Poelzig; he was the architect of the well designed, appropriate detail and taught on these lines in Stuttgart. But these good, craftsman-built houses were retrograde architecture, precisely what Poelzig had never subscribed to. They represented a "make-believe architecture" — making believe that nothing in architecture or in society had changed. This gave it the perfect qualifications needed for Nazi architecture, and, it hardly needs saying, Schmitthenner was a convinced National Socialist. I think the distinction between this architecture and Poelzig's can best be illustrated by the following anecdote. In 1927 Schmitthenner had designed some rather agreeable houses for the Im Fischtal estate, which was built next to the "Onkel Tom" estate of Taut, Häring, and Salvisberg as a kind of protest against their flat-roof architecture (see Figs. 219, 308, 310, 18). One day, two of Poelzig's students, Walter Segal and myself, went along to look at the Im Fischtal "counter-estate." We did have some liking for the houses; even Poelzig had built three houses there. I have already pointed out that Poelzig was quite critical of modern architecture, and so we were smiling expectantly as we went into one of Schmitthenner's houses and looked at it closely. After ten minutes Walter Segal came out, put his head between his hands, and said with a sigh: "Posener, give me Gropius at his harshest!" He had recognized how false it all was, an idyll that sent a shudder down one's spine. Today, after the event, it is clear to everyone just how much justified that shudder was. Walter Segal actually felt it physically. And I cannot imagine that someone who felt the difference between what was real and what was a fake as strongly as Poelzig did, did not also shudder. He really disliked Schmitthenner's style, to what extent can still be seen today if one compares the houses that he himself designed on the Im Fischtal estate with those by Schmitthenner (see Figs. 308, 310, 219). The Poelzig houses stand out on this counter-estate. They do not look as though nothing had happened since 1760.

There were also visible differences between the work, ideas, and teaching of Poelzig and that of Heinrich Tessenow, his colleague at the Technische Hochschule, although it was Poelzig who had gone to the trouble of having Tessenow appointed to the school a year after he had taken up his own teaching post. Poelzig and Tessenow remained on good terms as colleagues, and even as friends. Yet at the same time they were in competition with each other, fighting, as it were, over the new generation of architects. And although Poelzig never said anything against Tessenow in front of students, he could occasionally be heard to murmur as he looked through the students' examination projects, "When it comes to tackling a brief on their own, mine are the best." Tessenow, incidentally, was not a National Socialist like Schmitthenner. The Nazis thought he was; they never thought that of Poelzig.

Although Poelzig may have had some affinity for the fact that the National Socialist philosophy valued craftsmanship and tradition, that it rejected pure reason, the intellect, saying it was un-German and Jewish — stressing instead the importance of "the Muses" (the word they used was "musisch"), he must have had reservations when he realized that this philosophy restricted the freedom of creative activity. To have expected Poelzig, the antirationalist, the poet of the solid building, the advocate of a craftsmanship that was very close to art, to welcome National Socialism, at least as a critic of the Bauhaus and its offshoots, would have been seriously to misjudge him. He could not welcome what was emerging then, but he did not put up any resistance to it either. Anyone who expected him to do *that* would also have been misjudging him. It cannot have been his personal circumstances that prevented him from doing so. It was rumored that his father was a Jewish doctor. Whether his father, whom he did not know and to whom he attached the not-so-friendly description "coachman," was a Jewish doctor or an English aristocrat was of little interest to Poelzig. When the Nazi press

317 Hans Poelzig. World War Memorial to be housed in Schinkel's Neue Wache (New Guardhouse), Berlin, Unter den Linden, 1930, competition design.

called him Poelzig the Jew, I asked him, "Are you, Master?" to which he replied,

"No Jew ever thought I was a Jew, and the Goyim have no idea about these things."

No, Poelzig never felt "racially" uncertain; the race question did not concern him. He did not put up any resistance because he never felt obliged to make a public statement. He insisted on the apolitical nature of art — and the artist. He did not have left-wing opinions like his friend Martin Wagner. Poelzig was looking for a space for what he wanted with his whole soul: a creative culture that had its roots in traditional German culture but embraced new influences. The scope for this was decreasing rapidly. In the early twenties it had seemed to be an attainable objective. The emergence of modern architecture in the mid-twenties may have made it slip farther away with each passing year; technology became an ever-greater obstacle in its path, but National Socialism made it definitively unattainable. So far, I have mentioned only those aspects of the National Socialists' attitude to architecture that Poelzig could have agreed with. But what Schmitthenner wanted was completely alien to Poelzig,

The Final Years 1932–1936   249

318   Heinrich Tessenow. World War Memorial in the Neue Wache, 1930–31. Interior.

319   Hans Poelzig. World War Memorial at Berka (Thuringia), 1932, project.

who had, of course, talked about crafts; but for him crafts essentially meant art under another name. He never became obsessed with the minute details of a window, nor did he ever want to build houses that looked as if they had been built in the eighteenth century. He had little time for the lifeless Neo-Classicism of architects like Albert Speer. And if overtones of Neo-Classicism can be detected in some of the later works, such as the theater design for Dessau (see Fig. 332), it can probably be ascribed to the tiredness that overcame him in the end.

There was, however, something in his way of working that could have allowed him to identify with what emerged in the 1930s: his sense of the dramatic. I have examined one extremely dramatic work from his early years, the two schemes for a Bismarck Memorial above Bingerbrück-am-Rhein (see Figs. 50, 105–107). Poelzig's feeling for the dramatic did not make National Socialism accessible to him, but he may have felt in tune with the atmosphere of the years that prepared the ground for it. I describe the time like this because the sudden growth of the movement in the years leading up to 1933 did not take place in a vacuum. National Socialism—or should I say, an atmosphere related to it—was one of the decisive factors that shaped public life in those years.

The war memorials can be cited as just *one* striking manifestation of this atmosphere. Until shortly before 1930 no one wanted to be reminded of the lost war. But one fine morning in 1929, when I went to see what time it was, I found that the big clock in the atrium of the Technische Hochschule had been replaced by a war memorial bearing the inscription: *Invictis victi victuri* (To the unconquered the conquered who will conquer). This shows at what an early date people started to erect war memorials and turn their thoughts to the next war.

The competition for a war memorial in Berlin, to be housed in Schinkel's "New Guardhouse" ("Die Neue Wache") on the Unter den Linden, was advertised in 1930. An open courtyard to serve as a memorial was to be created in

320 Hans Poelzig. "Schauburg" ("Show Castle"), 1932, project. Interior toward stage.

321 Hans Poelzig. "Schauburg," project. Auditorium.

322 Hans Poelzig. "Schauburg," project. Back of building.

the New Guardhouse. In it a monument to the heroes of the World War was to be erected but, as I said, the courtyard itself was meant to be the memorial. Poelzig took part in the competition and adhered strictly to these stipulations. The courtyard he designed had concrete columns that, together with the slightly set-back concrete beam, formed a row of crosses around a simple soldier's grave; it would have been impressive and dramatic in an appropriate way, one could say (Fig. 317). But, as is sometimes the case with competitions, the jury changed its mind about the stipulations, on the basis of the designs submitted by the big names, including Peter Behrens, Mies van der Rohe, Tessenow. The jury recommended that Tessenow's scheme be built, although it did not include a courtyard but, rather, a covered space with a circular top light (Fig. 318). It was a quiet, undramatic space that was superior to all the other designs. Poelzig protested and took part in the competition for another "Memorial to the War" to be erected near Berka in the wooded, hilly landscape of Thuringia, in central Germany.

Heuss commented on this. Poelzig proposed a memorial garden rising up the hillside in terraces (Fig. 319). The only provision for ceremonial occasions was an open-air space in the entrance area. The spirit of this memorial is different from the one Poelzig designed for the Neue Wache. It is an extremely fine design. Heuss wrote:

He has submitted a scheme which is a large walled garden in terraces, a precinct which neither invites nor tolerates masses but is meant to promote silence and prayer.... But that was just a way out.... [By "a way out," Heuss means that this enabled Poelzig to avoid the actual subject of the memorial. —Au.] In the end Poelzig abandoned it and on the suggestion of a friend [Heuss?—Au.] he created a work of great architecture, which was also intended to be a memorial.... It no longer had anything to do with "being quietly alone" but was a place where the people celebrating en masse could understand their history, realize who they were.

This "Festival Theater" is clearly affected by what had begun to emerge as a new quasi-religious style developed to meet the new need for processions with flags, massed choirs of singers or speakers, mass orchestras playing powerful music.[3]

Poelzig's design, which he called the *"Schauburg"* ("Show Castle"), was a building to accommodate 20,000 people; the five house-high arches behind the stage could be opened on to the countryside (Figs. 320, 321). But, as Heuss continued, "The moment when he published his plans, — summer 1932 — was not congenial to them." By which Heuss means that the National Socialist period during which he was then writing *would* have been congenial.

It may be said that Heuss could not have written a book about Poelzig in 1939 without *in some way* applauding the regime, without an assurance that what he was writing concorded with the spirit of the regime. Writing the book at all was a risk. But Heuss sounds convinced here, and I am quite sure that Poelzig himself designed the "Show Castle" with true conviction. This also means that it was with conviction that he abandoned the quiet memorial, the garden, in favor of this highly dramatic hall.

In this work Poelzig returned to the forms he used in the third version of the fire station for Dresden (Fig. 322; see Fig. 144). As far as I know, it was the only time that he reused forms and structural methods from the Dresden period, such as piers and arches. But it is interesting that only the outer parts of the building are "built" in this way, as well as the solid wall between which stairs ascend to the colossal amphitheater — these being, incidentally, the best part of the design (Figs. 323–325). The five large arches behind the stage, which could be opened, are a great technical achievement. The ceiling, which Heuss describes as being "quite flat," is not in fact flat but is a sort of "larger than life" ceiling with "beams" hung on deep steel joists.

Anyone wanting to characterize the design of the "Schauburg" as National Socialist is not considering its forms. They are Poelzigesque

323 Hans Poelzig. "Schauburg," project. Stairs.

forms taken from the period in his work *before* the successful years in Berlin. The fact that he returns to them may say something about this point in his life but also about this moment in history. It is a rejection of the time of prosperity during the Weimar Republic, in which Poelzig had achieved his greatest successes, a rejection of the new architecture that had developed during those years, which, as I have pointed out, Poelzig viewed critically. The drama of the design is *mass drama*. Of course, the Bismarck Memorial was also planned for "the people" who would have assembled there (see Figs. 50, 105–107). But this space was not just designed for assemblies but also for processions, marches, flags.

Finally, tendencies that are not so alien to National Socialism can be discerned in the "Schauburg." I am thinking of the role technology is forced to play here: It is used—but it is hidden behind Roman arches and a "beamed ceiling." All this does not make it a work of National Socialist architecture, however. It remains a work of Hans Poelzig. I would, though, like to add some remarks about the role of technology in this project.

Highly sophisticated technology is used in the "Schauburg" to make the larger-than-life doors slide behind masonry piers and to close the very wide span of the assembly room. But the machinery is hidden behind a rough kind of masonry and "beams" that look traditional, not in keeping with advanced technology.

This is how the Nazis treated technology. It had no place in their ideology, just as it had no place in Poelzig's. They used it without acknowledging it. Occasionally they went so far

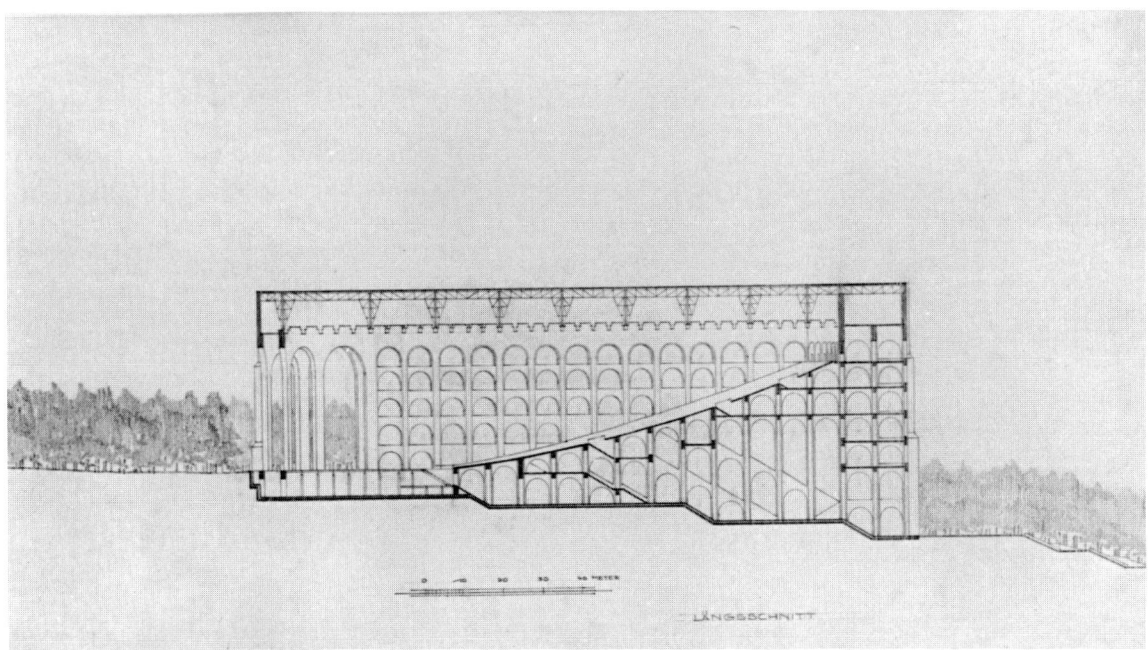

324 Hans Poelzig. "Schauburg," project. Section.

as to *replace* building technology with craftsmanship, even in large structures. Speer's gigantic dome, the culmination of his plan for Berlin, was meant to be vaulted. That was, I would say, the Nazis' ideal: to push the old crafts techniques to inconceivable dimensions and thus declare modern technology to be redundant. *This* ideology was not however universally recognized and certainly not the universal practice of the Third Reich. The possibilities offered by industrial building technology were used but they were hidden behind constructions that looked as if they were the work of craftsmen, and maybe they even were, but craftsmen could never have produced the *whole* building. The reader will note that this seems familiar, that since Poelzig had left Breslau he had given technology a similar role because it meant so little to him as an element in architecture. What could be seen in his "Schauburg" project was the logical consequence of his antitechnology stance.

A general remark may be in order here. The avant-garde—Gropius and Mies—insisted upon their architecture reflecting technological progress. Nazi architecture tended to deny technological progress. Poelzig in his architecture of the late twenties followed what may be called a middle course. The I.G. Farben building, to take a typical instance, does not actually reveal its structure, which is a steel frame, although its appearance does suggest some kind of framed construction. The "Schauburg," however, is close to Nazi architecture, its construction being hidden throughout.

Nevertheless, this "Show Castle" stands alone in Poelzig's *oeuvre*. Poelzig did not become a National Socialist architect as he could well have done. No one can say he belonged to the group of architects who offered their services enthusiastically, to the many who said that National Socialism was just what they had been waiting for. He stayed in the background and became more and more withdrawn. His behavior during the Nazi regime casts a somewhat different light on the "Schauburg."

Poelzig eventually considered emigrating. His old friend Martin Wagner arranged for him

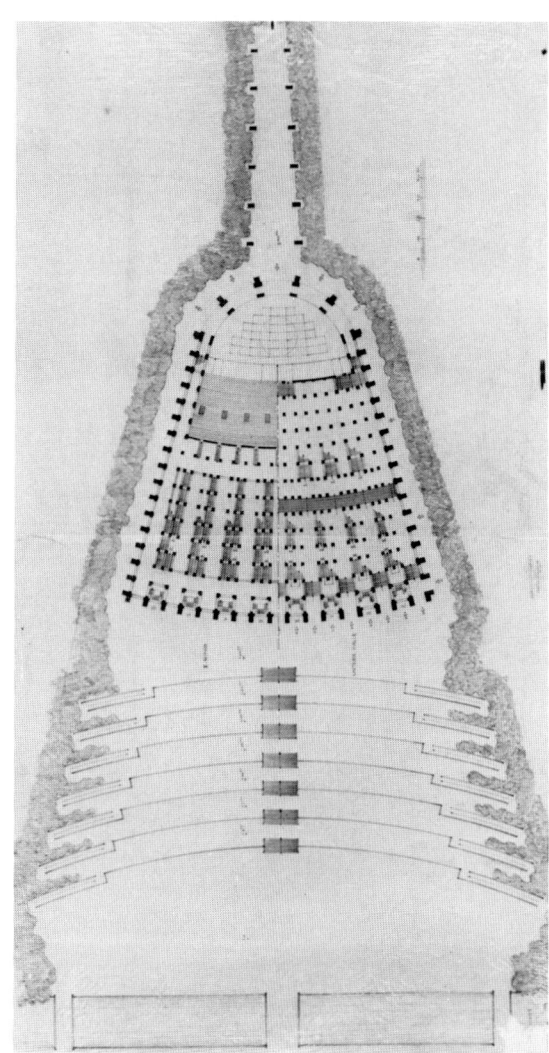

to take up a teaching post at the Academy in Istanbul after his contract at the Technische Hochschule expired. Poelzig even traveled to Istanbul; he returned bitterly disappointed. He was a sick man but it is hard to say what he was suffering from. When he died in 1936 he was only sixty-seven. (See Heuss's comments on this in the documentation section of this chapter.) Poelzig suffered from the fact that his ideas were out of place now in Germany—and that *he* was out of place outside Germany. Heuss put it like this: "He took his departure very seriously and died."[4] There is nothing I wish to add to that.

325 Hans Poelzig. "Schauburg," project. Plan of the levels.

Chapter Eleven: Documentation

Document 11

At the close of the chapter I quoted a remark, a very true remark, made by Theodor Heuss on the death of his friend Poelzig. I believe it is appropriate to hear more from Heuss about these final years. I am sure there was no one else who knew him as well. It is, however, important to remember that Heuss published his book on Poelzig in 1939. There is actually no trace of caution in his description of the end. Heuss writes quite openly. To what extent he had the political situation of the time in mind, which he did not openly oppose and which he may have believed in with certain reservations, is another question which I do not wish to discuss here.

Doc. 11* Theodor Heuss, in *Hans Poelzig. Bauten und Entwürfe*, 1939

Things touched him, tortured him, more than he showed at the time. It was not his way to let himself be baffled or discouraged. Although he did not seek dispute, he met opponents openly. But friends who knew him long enough and knew that he could usually cope with any situation, no matter how varied, found him for the first time helpless in the face of attack. He launched himself once more into his work at the Technische Hochschule. It gave him great satisfaction that he had had his contract extended by a year after reaching retirement age in 1934 and that, over and above this proviso, he would also be able to see some students through to their examinations. But he had practically no commissions at all. Once more he took out his huge canvasses and added to the old paintings: Putting his own stubborn patience to the test, he sought the key to the secret of the relationship between harmony and contrast and then sank again into black demonic moods, black shreds of paint lead the eye into landscapes with flowers and blue skies....

He was supposed to emigrate in the spring of 1936. As early as the summer before he must have begun to have doubts as to whether his health would stand up to the difficult new beginning ahead of him; deep exhaustion had left him with vision problems. These, however, had rectified themselves. But he looked to the day of his departure with increasing unease. He puts his house in order, postpones his departure, he knows he must go but cannot find the strength.

His friends observed this tragic play of wanting to go and not being able to go with deep spiritual perturbance and understood its symbolic significance. What a misguided stroke of fate, that this man of exceptional talent, a talent that in its instincts and responsibility was so completely linked with the German people and Germany, should be expelled on an adventure into intellectual and cultural exile! A sense of responsibility and desire to be creative called this untiring spirit to his new life. But was this to be the last twist of fate in the life of a great man—to go and teach the Turks something about good architecture? Was not the very point of his being born in Germany at this point in history that he was a revolutionary and a conservative, both teaching and personifying in his own life courage and respect? His honest temperament made him a rebel and his appreciation of true and eternal values made him a conservative. He took his departure very seriously and died. He died on 14 June 1936....

One of his lifetime companions said of his death, "In my mind I had the image of a strong deer, who retreats into his lonely thicket in order to remain at one with himself." Rudolf G. Binding, who had become close to Poelzig during his last years, wrote, "Germany has lost one of its best men, one of the best of his kind, and so truly German, although no one realizes it."

---

* Theodor Heuss, *Hans Poelzig. Das Lebensbild eines deutschen Baumeisters. Bauten und Entwürfe*, Berlin, 1939; reprint, Stuttgart, 1985, pp. 77–79.

CHAPTER TWELVE
The Late Designs 1932–1936

THERE ARE ONLY a few designs from the later years that remain to be discussed. Of these, the designs for housing estates are the most interesting because they show Poelzig tackling a new subject. It must be admitted that the other designs he did during this period are disappointing. Architects who worked in his office during this time recount that Poelzig was no longer full of excitement about his work, as he had always been before. Apparently he entrusted far more to his staff than he had done previously. Poelzig's designs reflect the threat that hung over those years, the economic misery which had an all-pervading influence, his growing uncertainty about what role he and his work could have in a country that had undergone a political transformation in 1933, or alternatively what he could contribute to the development of architecture in another country, such as Turkey. The designs are important in that they bear witness to a condition from which Poelzig could ultimately find no way out.

1932 "Growing House," project

Poelzig took part in the competition on this topical subject of the day and in the exhibition that followed it. Some of his former students also entered the competition and exhibited "growing houses," and Poelzig's school—if a "school of Poelzig" did, in fact, exist—made an appearance on this occasion. The idea behind the competition was to make it possible for less-well-off families to be able to build a minimal house which they could then easily extend later when they had the money to do so. The idea was not pursued further during the Third Reich. The exhibition, "The Growing House," held at the exhibition ground in Berlin, was one of the last manifestations of the Weimar Republic and the social democratic administration in Berlin.

Poelzig presented a scheme for the simplest possible form of a "growing house" (Fig. 326). The curved louvre roof meant that the attic could easily be converted into living space. By putting the staircase on one side of the original house Poelzig made it simple to add rooms to both stories. The house would have increased by its own width.

1932 Housing estate in Dahlem, Berlin, project

This is one of a number of housing projects from this time. Poelzig made little attempt in his planning to become involved in "urban design," to make picturesque or monumental-looking streets and squares. He simply grouped

326 Hans Poelzig. "Growing House," exhibition building, Berlin, 1932.

327 Housing estate in Dahlem, Berlin, 1932, project.

standard houses of different sizes close together in such a way that each one had a modest-sized garden and was at a reasonable distance from its neighbor (Fig. 327). Some of the houses are quite large. All of them are flat-roofed bungalows. In a housing estate like this one the street seems to have been of particular interest to Poelzig, and in this respect his projects are progressive. The greatest problem in estates of detached houses is the street, which is why Camillo Sitte, the urban designer who had the greatest influence on projects in Austria and Germany at the beginning of the century, was of the opinion that a suburb made up of detached houses is not a subject for urban design. Poelzig tried to make it into a subject for urban design by using walls to link the individual houses to each other. In this way he created streets, or rather lanes, which give a sense of space. He made these lanes pleasant by creating deep flower beds at the foot of the houses and the linking walls.

To my knowledge no estates of this kind were built, certainly not in Berlin. They were planned for slightly more discriminating residents, and by 1932 it was already too late to build a middle-class estate of this kind.

Wherever the topography of the site offered the opportunity, Poelzig used the variation in level to arrange the estate in terraces, similar to those in the competition for the "memorial" in Berka (see Fig. 319).

Hans Poelzig: Reflections on His Life and Work

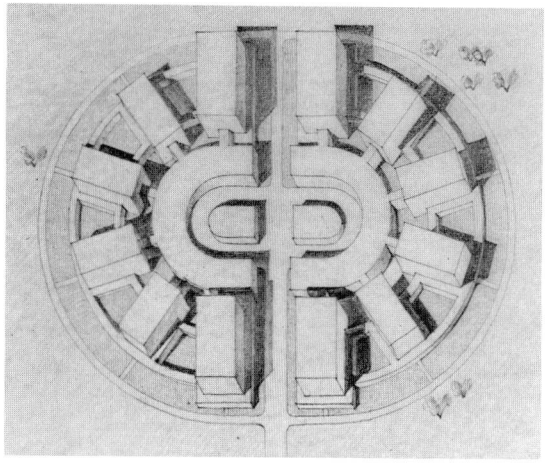

328 Hans Poelzig. Film studios, Gatow near Berlin, 1930, project. Layout drawing.

1930 Film studios in Gatow, near Berlin, project

The radial arrangement of the film studios in two semicircles seems on first sight to be extremely practical, given a large enough site (Fig. 328). It may be due to the perspective drawing that one is reminded of the radial composition of the ministries in the Spree Bend, the competition scheme for the extension to the Reichstag in 1929 (see Figs. 270–272). In this case, however, the composition is a little too monumental for the brief—that is, film studios.

1933 Extension to the Reichsbank, competition entry

Architects of renown, including Mies van der Rohe, took part in this limited competition. Poelzig's scheme, in the form of a wagon wheel with six spokes, looks a little schematic (Fig. 329). For the internal circulation of a building like this such a severely geometrical organization does not have the effect one might imagine of creating order. On the contrary, it causes confusion as it is impossible to know exactly where one is. The large cylinder was also criticized from an urban-design point of view, not without justification. A shape like this does not fit into any urban context; it stands alone, is

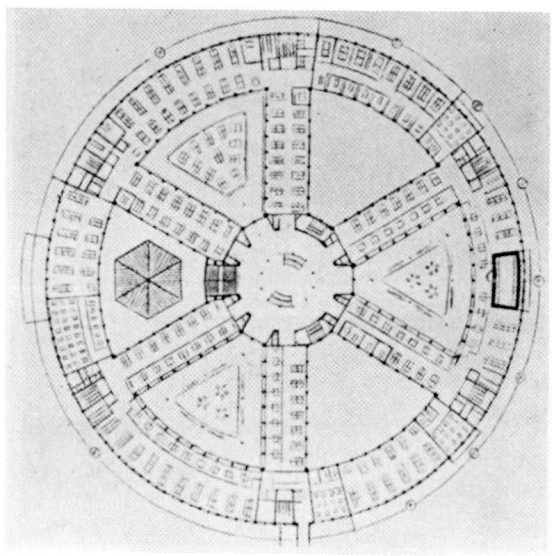

329 Hans Poelzig. Extension to the Reichsbank (German State Bank), Berlin, 1933, competition design. Plan.

330 Hans Poelzig. Reichsbank extension. Perspective presentation.

dismissive of its surroundings (Fig. 330). Incidentally, it is unique in Poelzig's *oeuvre*, although it could be said that his two triangular buildings with concave sides—the high-rise building at Friedrichstrasse station and the library for the Reichstag—are of a similar kind (see Figs. 206, 207, 270–272).

The Late Designs 1932–1936

Platz

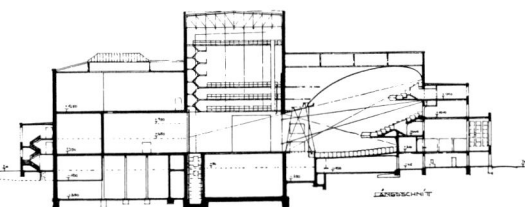

Schnitt

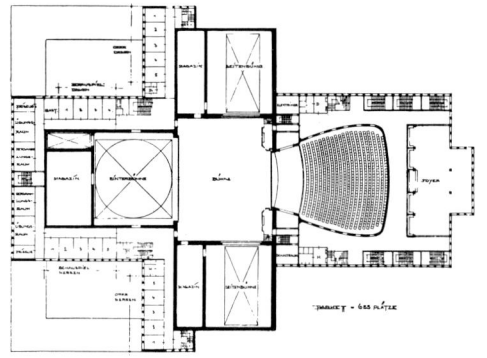

331 Hans Poelzig. Theater in Dessau, 1935, competition design.

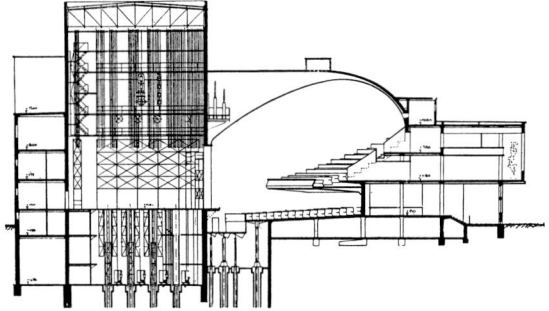

332 Hans Poelzig. Theater and music school for Istanbul. First version, section.

333 Hans Poelzig. Theater and music school for Istanbul. First version, model.

THREE DESIGNS FOR THEATERS

1934–35 Theater and music school in Istanbul, competition scheme

1935 Theater in Dessau, competition scheme

1935–36 Theater and music school in Istanbul, final scheme

The three theaters are of comparable size. They are also comparable in that they are more conventional than the other theaters designed by Poelzig. The most Poelzigesque feature in all of them is the shape of the stalls—they are wonderfully broad and integrated with the stage.

The building for Dessau has a strangely cubic severity; even the part housing the auditorium is a pure cube (Fig. 331). This gives the exterior form of the building a certain logical consistency. The auditorium itself is relatively high and has two circles—something quite rare in Poelzig's theaters.

On plan, the stalls section of the theater in the competition scheme for Istanbul is the broadest of all the projects and most "integrated with the stage" (Fig. 332). One must not be deceived by the plan, however; the auditorium has a very deep, amphitheater-like circle that projects over

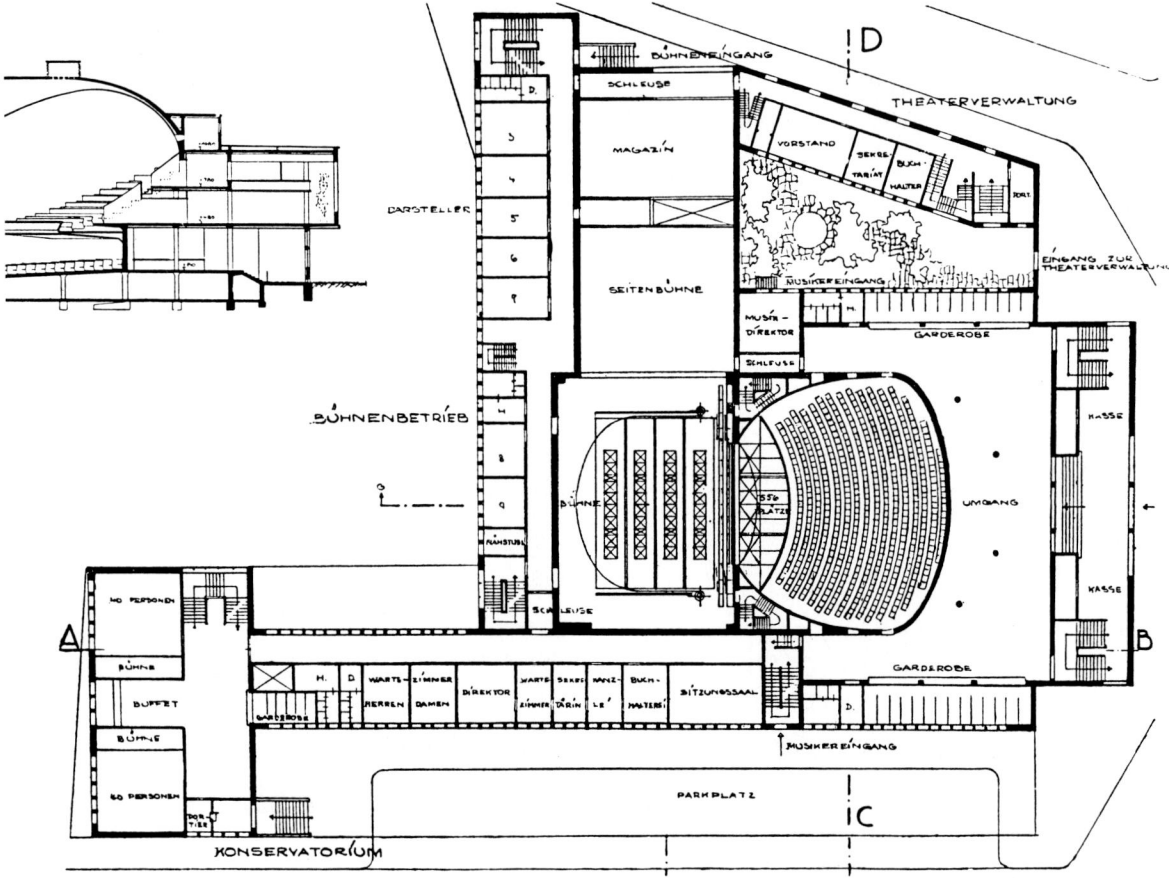

334 Hans Poelzig. Theater and music school for Istanbul, 1934–35 project. Plan of first version.

almost the whole of the stalls (Fig. 334). It has already been pointed out that Poelzig avoided this fairly common arrangement in the Capitol Cinema (see Figs. 211–218). One can see the shape of the roof on the photograph of the model (Fig. 333). In reality it would have been possible to see the roof only from quite a distance. The exterior form is not as clear as in the theater for Dessau.

In the final scheme of the theater for Istanbul the form of the auditorium is expressed in the exterior (Fig. 335). To be precise, it is a symbolic round form. Ideas of Poelzig's that are familiar can be recognized in this shape and in the sweeping stairs on both sides of the deep foyer. The advantage of this auditorium over the competition design is that the circle, as in the Capitol Cinema, has been pulled back.

It is impossible to look at the three designs without a feeling of regret. They are tame and not very interesting compared with earlier designs for theaters and cinemas. The Master does not seem to have been able to get very involved in these projects.

1935–36 House for diplomats in Ankara, project

Poelzig did two schemes for this building, too, as the site changed (Figs. 336, 337). From a distance both schemes look familiar. In its composition, the first is reminiscent of the de-

The Late Designs 1932–1936   261

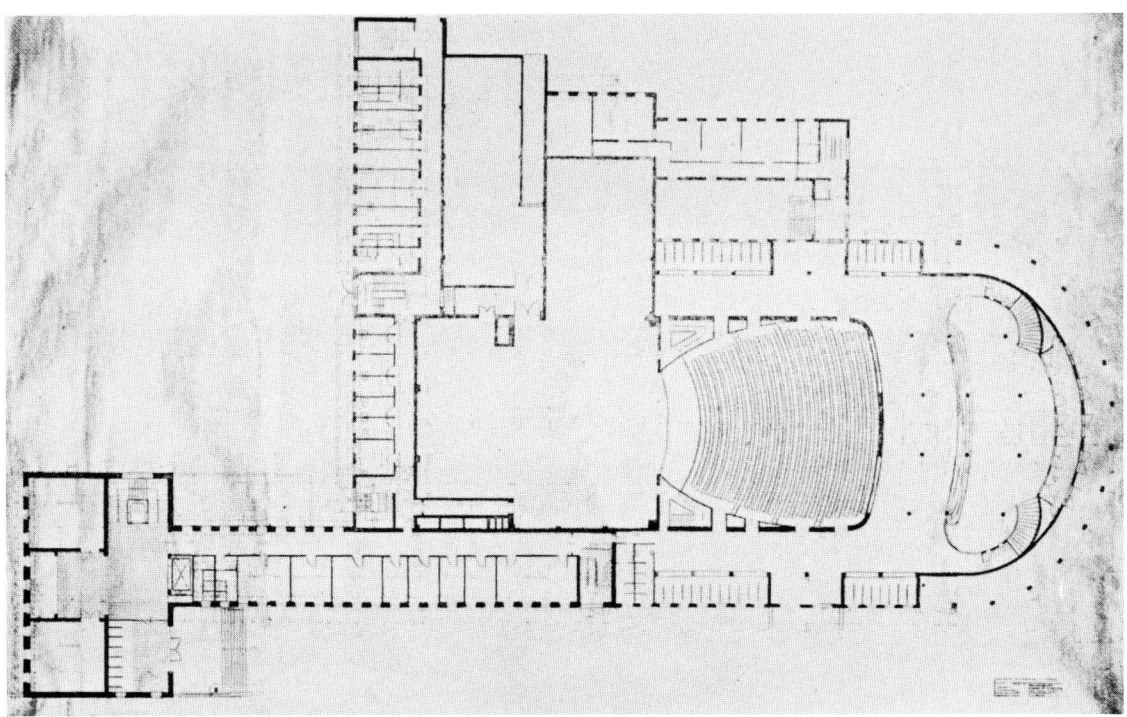

335 Hans Poelzig. Theater and music school for Istanbul, 1935–36. Final version, plan.

336 Hans Poelzig. House for diplomats, Ankara, 1935, project. First version, perspective presentation.

337 Hans Poelzig. House for diplomats, Ankara, 1935–36, project. Second version, perspective presentation.

sign for the Palace of the League of Nations in Geneva, except that here the terraced section is the main part of the building (see Fig. 252). The other scheme is reminiscent of the "House of Friendship" that he designed in 1916 (see Figs. 155–166), except that the outside walls of the house, which rise up in six terraces, are not as solid as in the "House of Friendship"; they have a much more lively articulation, which means that this scheme does not have the same uncompromising quality as the famous scheme for Constantinople. The most remarkable feature of both schemes is the room sequence: stair hall, corridor, banqueting hall.

CHAPTER THIRTEEN
Reflections

ANYONE WRITING A BOOK about an architect of our century is bound to be asked why he has chosen this particular moment. There is no doubt that there is considerable general interest in Expressionism at present. It has something to do with the move away from what was known as "modern architecture," that is, the architectural movement that began in the mid-twenties, particularly in Germany, and was interrupted by National Socialism but taken up again after 1945. It is linked with names such as Gropius, Mies, Le Corbusier. The move away from this modern architecture is not a recent development and should not be confused with Post-Modernism. It can be found as early as the 1960s, and it is accompanied by a rediscovery of the trends that were prevalent before modern architecture emerged and continued to exist parallel to it in the twenties. It is only natural that Expressionist architecture, which seemed to have been obliterated by modern architecture, is one of the most exciting of these rediscoveries. Wolfgang Pehnt's book, *The Architecture of Expressionism*, was published in 1973. Pehnt begins his book with Poelzig; the drawing of the round foyer in the Grosses Schauspielhaus adorns the cover, a magnificent Poelzig sketch introduces the foreword, and the first chapter is entitled "Instead of a definition: The theatre of the five thousand."

Next to it is a quotation from Poelzig's speech to the Werkbund in 1919: "Let us even be impractical if in doing so a ray of our creativity will shine into the human soul." This is the language of Expressionism, and in my account of Poelzig I have left no doubt about the fact that at the time—during and immediately after the First World War—Poelzig was an Expressionist. He was perhaps even the leading Expressionist architect.

But here the first seeds of doubt appear. If one thinks today about Expressionist architecture in those turbulent years other names immediately spring to mind: Bruno Taut and members of the Glass Chain; Scharoun and the Luckhardt brothers; also members of the Working Council for Art, such as Erich Mendelsohn. These were younger architects; they were born in the 1880s, whereas Poelzig was born before 1870. They can be said to have made their architectural debut with Expressionism, whereas in Poelzig's career it was preceded by a phase that was concerned with the objectives of the Werkbund, which had been founded in 1907. Poelzig's architecture in Dresden in the years following 1916 and in Berlin after 1919 *was* Expressionist. But after the design for Salzburg, or even while he was working on it, a new phase began in Poelzig's work which can no longer be termed Expressionist.

Due to this change in his work, Poelzig has been called a Proteus. There is some truth in this, but not in the sense that he adapted to every changing mood of the times. He was Protean in that he tried to make each design truly different and indeed was able to do so. Quite often he would produce "variations" on the same theme. He also incorporated the changes taking place at the time into his work. Since the changes that took place in the years between 1900 and 1933 were, or seemed to be, radical, the change in the appearance of Poelzig's designs also was radical, or seemed to be. (I will come back to this qualifying remark, "or seemed to be.")

It will be seen that the historical events that left their mark on the architecture of this period were not quite as far-reaching as one might suppose. It is, of course, impossible to look at Poelzig's work without at the same time paying some attention to the developments and changes that occurred in architecture during his lifetime. That may be a platitude: *Every* biographer should look beyond the artist he is writing about, and this is particularly true in a period with such distinctly different phases as this one. It would seem appropriate here to compare the reactions of Poelzig's contemporaries to the same changes in order to see how they differ from Poelzig's reaction. I have outlined the role of his direct contemporary Peter Behrens and shown that Behrens started out as an unequivocal advocate of the Jugendstil, then developed an architecture that I have called "essentially Neo-Classical," that after 1918 he became decidedly Expressionist, and later became just as decidedly modern. Poelzig also lived through these changes, but he did not identify to the same extent with the rapid succession of philosophies—or fashions—of the time. I have claimed that he was Protean, someone who is changeable. But this is not the same thing as someone who constantly adapts to the times. Changing is in the very nature of Proteus; he remains Proteus, indeed becomes Proteus, by changing. It was always possible to recognize Poelzig in his changes, even if they were quite significant. We have also encountered certain limitations in his attitude, which are very clearly illustrated, for example, in the role he was prepared to give technology in architecture. These things, too, are Poelzig.

But what does that mean—"Poelzig"? This is a second point of interest: Can this quality be defined? Or can it only be accepted as if it were simply a personal aura? If this were the case, would it be worth publishing a book about Poelzig? Is anyone interested in hearing about "how someone clears his throat and spits,"[1] or does this person Hans Poelzig mean something that affected others besides those people who were lucky enough to have been close to him?

We have seen that in his early works in Breslau he adhered quite closely to those theories that at the time were thought to be the basis of a new architecture. The theories of the time, which were also subscribed to by the Werkbund, were reactive, by which I mean they reacted against the misconception that "architecture" meant the application of style forms. The members of the Werkbund had set themselves clearly defined aims which they hoped to achieve in a short time. They wished to educate people to better understand the essence of architecture. It was tantamount to educating people to be decent or rational. It was akin to lessons in how to acquire good taste. They knew they would not be able to achieve this quality which they had learned to call "culture." They had defined their whole idea of culture on the basis of a lack which they felt emotionally and recognized intellectually. They were identifying what they did *not* possess, or rather what they no longer possessed and did not yet possess again. And they knew that they and their contemporaries would not be given the opportunity to shape the culture of the future. It was at that time that the expression "cultural fertilizer" (*Kulturdünger*) was coined. This referred to the contemporary generation or generations that would sacrifice themselves for a future culture. This was actually asking a great deal, more than someone with Poelzig's talent and temperament would have *wanted* to take on. More too, I believe, than he *did* take on. The attitude or mood I am alluding to, and it was not only Poelzig's, can be described as follows: People knew that they were not yet able to create what was really essential, but flattered themselves with the thought that they had occasionally achieved it. The hallmark of something genuine, capable of giving birth to culture, and in the end worthy of the name "culture" was the consciousness that we encounter so often in Poelzig's work and words, the consciousness that felt at one with history.

What did the history of architecture mean to architects at this time? What *could* it mean to them? They saw it in a different way from the eclectics—that is, it was no longer a succession of periods characterized by a particular style such as Romanesque, Gothic, or Renaissance. Around 1900 they did not want to see the history of architecture as a succession of forms but rather as an evolution of methods. Poelzig—and he was not alone in this; Perret and others too had said the same thing—thought that methods remain in essence constant while forms change. *For this reason* Poelzig had recourse to functional buildings, because in them the fundaments of architecture in the true sense of the word—that is, *building,*—could be seen. This "essential building" was what mattered, not the variety of faces a building might assume when different styles are applied to it—in many cases to its detriment.

This is why Poelzig, and Perret, sought an analogy with the old methods: They thought that architects must work in their day with steel and concrete the way previous generations had worked with wood and stone. I have shown how Poelzig tried to do just that, with some degree of success in the case of the Posen tower (see Figs. 26, 27, 93–98). But the fact that I mention the Posen tower so often shows that Poelzig must have done something there other than simply adapt these universally valid methods to the ways of building, to the materials and technology of his time. Sometimes he also adopted the forms that the old methods produced because he loved them and may have felt that it was not possible to improve on them. There was a conflict within him: On the one hand, he approved of dematerialization, and yet at the same time he loved material.

Before 1914 yet another theory, which for reasons of simplicity can be called the functionalist theory, was popular in the Werkbund: This claimed that form was a result of function. This perception, if it can be called that, was widely publicized. It was a perception that many architects of the time wanted to be true. One could imagine an artist, an architect, who regrets the fact that form depends on function, or at best can accept it as an unfortunate fact about the nature of architecture. When Poelzig said he worked on an object until nothing remained but form he spoke as an artist of this kind, and indeed as one who is determined to overcome what he sees as a shortcoming, and has obviously succeeded in overcoming it. Those, however, who saw this "shortcoming" as something positive claimed it was this very relationship that gave form its significance. It has been referred to as an epic quality.

The *epic* is the genre of poetry that transfigures the mundane by the very fact that it does not elevate it but, on the contrary, gives it full recognition for what it is. The epic shows us a chair in such a way that we cry out, "Why, yes, that *is* a chair! Until now we did not know what a chair is!" We are all familiar with epic objects; everyone can think of something he treasures particularly highly. I personally have Japanese ceramics, pitchers, dishes, beakers in mind that embody so completely the spirit of these articles that they are "pitcher," "dish," or "beaker" pure and simple and yet they also transcend this plane. If one considers that the epic effect of these objects stems from their form, that it is the form—of course, in conjunction with the treatment of the material and the technique—that enables us to recognize that we are looking at the essential pitcher, one could assume that this is what Poelzig meant when he said he worked on an object until nothing remained but form, that at any rate he was referring to this aspect of form. I doubt, however, that this was Poelzig's view. He never expressed it in so many words and I cannot imagine that this is what he meant.

Let us recall the factory in Luban, perhaps his

most "objective" building (see Figs. 24, 25, 85–90). Its whole effect stems from the purest expression of the two kinds of construction he used, the brick load-bearing wall and the brick curtain wall in Prussian bond that is hung in front of a frame construction. But this effect did not suffice for Poelzig. The small square windows in the curtain wall are arranged in patterns. I do not know if it was necessary to use the striking staggered pattern of which so many photographs have since been published; and I have pointed out that he introduced an historical motif that seems out of place in this context: the stepped gable. If he had tried to take his orientation from the needs of the production process and derive the form from them and from the dictates of the construction method, he would not have employed these forms. It seems to me that Poelzig did not mean by "form" the epic, pure expression of a useful object: spoon, chair, window, stove, house, factory, or whatever it might be. His idea of form was something different.

How can this idea be reconciled with the plans and the exterior form of some of his houses? I am thinking primarily here of his one-family house on the Im Fischtal estate in Berlin-Zehlendorf (1927; see Figs. 308, 310). How is this idea reconciled with the lively interest he had in everyday things, which he also tried to inspire in his students? The question is not easy to answer. If one compares the plan and the external form of the Fischtal house it will be seen that the epic quality is in the plan (see Fig. 310); as I have pointed out, the exterior form is somewhat artificial. A house is meant to accommodate a process: The house and the process of living in it are not the same thing. This process cannot be expressed only by way of spatial relationships, in this particular case, in the diagonal relationship between the living room and the square dining room which is almost a veranda. This is a relationship that influences the inhabitants of the house. One could even go so far as to say that here a spatial composition inspires a particular use. Some people have inverted Sullivan's aphorism "form follows function" and said that there are forms—or, to be more precise, relationships between forms or spaces—that inspire function. At any rate, it is in these spatial relationships that Poelzig's work comes closest to having an epic quality. Let us admit that these relationships are not found very often in his work, or rather, they are more frequent than it would at first appear but you have to look for them. An architect simply does not work with abstract forms but with forms that have an inherent meaning. Poelzig knew that, and one could even go so far as to say that wherever it was possible he made the meaning an integral part of the form. If he had not done that he would not have been a true architect.

It is nevertheless legitimate to say that abstract form was important to Poelzig. If it had not been for the war, the defeat, and the period of poverty that followed, he might have developed the relationship between pure form and specific form, as this form that is related to purpose may be called. But these events did occur and Poelzig reacted to them by starting to divorce form from purpose. The fire station for Dresden is a brilliant scheme, a highly impressive form, or rather two impressive forms—he also produced a third scheme which might have made it possible to build the second, more extreme, scheme (see Figs. 141–144). Both schemes are quite far removed from the idea of a fire station. And although the design for Salzburg once again unites form and content, it does so by formalizing the content (see Figs. 177, 189–192, 194–198). He talks of Mozart, of Mirabell and the Hellbrunn park, the site that sent the architect "into a frenzy." He talks of the German Baroque too. He talks so seldom of the Festival Theater in practical terms that the architect, and the client, seem to have completely forgotten the need for the ancillary facilities, without which a festival theater sited outside the city cannot function.

I think this is another conflict Poelzig lived with, and was able to live with, because he was not an analyst who thought in categories such as pure form and specific form. He was someone who designed, and once he had achieved the degree of significance with which he was able to endow a particular form or design or spatial relationship, he did not—in fact, *could not*—spare the matter another thought. He did sometimes impose a form onto buildings, such as the professional schools in Charlottenburg and Kreuzberg (see Figs. 255–258) and even the I.G. Farben building as it appears in the first model (see Fig. 290). It is no coincidence, and certainly not the result of ignorance, that he liked to define the craftsman as someone "who creates forms." He needed this philosophy, if not to say illusion, just as he needed the other illusion he had, about the fundamental inability of technology to create form because its form is a by-product of the manufacturing process and thus would be made "outdated" by progress. He needed these illusions, which he admittedly did not see as illusions, in order to preserve the connection with history that gave his forms, be they pure forms or specific forms, legitimacy in his eyes. This continuity with history, which in fact was also an illusion, was deeply rooted in him and was more important to him than the conflicts in his own work that I have enjoyed discovering and that he had an inkling of but refused to define or even discuss.

On the basis of these premises it is possible to define his work in the following phases: in Breslau, virtual congruence of history and gradual development of content and form; in Dresden, the divergence of content and form, of concept and built reality—this is the moment that can be termed Expressionist; and finally, in Berlin, the attempt to defend continuity *and* form from the intrusion of technology which as an agent of rationalism would lead to false forms. (I shall come to his confrontation with National Socialism later.) These are different phases in Poelzig's basic philosophy. I have pointed out, however, as I am sure the reader remembers, that the changes in German architecture between 1900 and 1935 were perhaps not as radical as they may have appeared to be and as they wanted to be—if I may use this rather unusual expression. Any examination of the architecture of those thirty-five years that is at all accurate shows that whenever a new development began, the principles of the one preceding it continued to be considered valid, as did numerous hybird forms, compromises, and quasi-innovative forms. Similarly, it may be said that the volte-face, a favorite German occupation, had actually begun years earlier. One need only think of what an architect like Schmitthenner was doing *before* 1933. The events were not as far-reaching, nor did they bring about as radical a change as they pretended to. This is evident in Poelzig's works. Consider the latent Expressionism of his Breslau period and the clarity and calm of an "Expressionist" design like the "House of Friendship," which is a far cry from a "star dome" (see Figs. 14, 153–166, 140). Poelzig's idea of what architecture is runs through the whole of his work as a constant factor, even if the formal language of the buildings changes. I have repeatedly drawn attention to signs of this constancy, which was his true strength. It even includes the limitations and misconceptions of his philosophy, which I have also discussed. He needed them, they were part of his concept of architecture, which *fundamentally* did not change. (This is why he was able to teach during all the phases of his development, and his teaching remained constant.)

I say this despite the fact that in an essay on the modern factory written in 1911 Poelzig expressed an opinion about the relationship of the artist to technical progress that is totally different from what he said on this cardinal topic in any of his speeches or articles after the war (see Chapter 2, Doc. 2B). The role of the artist remains the same. The difference is that, whereas in Breslau Poelzig allowed technical progress to inspire him, after the crisis of 1916 he rejected it out of hand. He had become suspicious of the new powers, which had not been the case in Breslau. After the war one repeatedly encounters the very same expressions he had coined in Stuttgart in 1919. They appear again in his speech "The Architect" which he gave in 1931 (see Chapter 9, Doc. 9C). He used these ideas to counter the powers he was suspicious of, not just the power of technology of which he spoke so frequently but also the trend toward the impersonal. One need only think of how in

1931 (and later) he was still talking of the relationship between the architect and the client without which a work of architecture could not be created. At this time this relationship had already become an exception and most of the works that were created had to be created without it. Poelzig simply needed this idea.

Poelzig countered the developments that were beginning to emerge with his whole body and soul and with his concept of the artist, the architect, or—as he would have preferred to call him—the master builder. I believe that he would not have been able to withstand these powers in the long run. National Socialism prevented the conflict from being resolved. In this new German environment Poelzig was overcome by an increasingly strong feeling of claustrophobia. But he did not feel it was his destiny to fight it, and the realization that he was helpless overcame him in the end. He did not participate in *this* struggle. He fell on the wrong battlefield. Perhaps this was for the best; he was spared the obligation to resolve the conflict he really cared about. This also rescues the picture of him that has been handed down to posterity. We have been given a strangely unanimous view of him. The partial eclipse of the sun that occurred in 1933, the darkness that enveloped this figure whom we remember as someone of immense power, concealed the fact that the sun's light was actually beginning to fade. This did not become apparent until later, and we are the first to have to come to terms with it.

I said earlier that anyone publishing a book about an artist will have to answer the question as to why he has chosen this particular moment.

Am I trying to put Hans Poelzig forward as a model for us to follow today? He was an outsider even in his own time, as early as his Breslau days, because he went so far beyond the Werkbund theories that he subscribed to at the time; as has become evident, he became more and more an outsider. He did, however, succeed in sending out signals to those around him, in emanating a power that lived on for a long time after his death through those who had been his students. It would be wrong to imagine that he realized that the scope of his influence was constantly declining. External events, the economic crisis, the Third Reich, hid the real truth from him. Again and again he was able to draw on his innate power and his consciousness of his artistic freedom and creativity to give him faith in the power of hope, although, as Heuss shows, at the end of his life he was plagued by doubts and despondency.

Today we have a different view of Poelzig's situation and of Poelzig himself. As I said, the sun's light has faded, we no longer have the confidence and optimism that the avant-garde of the time, people such as Gropius, had. On the contrary, we see them as having contributed to the impersonal, uncaring architecture we are afflicted with. This was not the intention of these men and they did not see the danger. We recognize that the things they pronounced to be positive—progress, rationality, understanding of tangible problems—also have a negative side. In this situation the image of a *man* such as Poelzig may be able to give us hope. In the end Poelzig failed. In this world truly great people often fail. But they bring a glimmer of hope to the world.

Postscript

WHILE I WAS WRITING THIS BOOK, over 1,150 drawings from Poelzig's office were found in the Hamburger Bahnhof, one of Berlin's disused railway stations which, incidentally, was serving as a museum of transport and civil engineering. The drawings had been there for decades without anyone realizing it. The reason for this was the division of Berlin, which meant that the Hamburger Bahnhof, like other facilities that belonged to the "Reichsbahn," the East German Railways, was under East German jurisdiction and therefore not accessible to people living in the western part of the city. The recent breakdown of the political division allowed this extensive material from Poelzig's *oeuvre* to come to light. Matthias Schirren collected, sorted, processed, and analyzed the material. He organized an exhibition in the Museum for Transport and Technology and I was invited to give a talk at the opening. He was then commissioned by the museum to produce a book titled *Hans Poelzig. Die Pläne und Zeichnungen aus dem ehemaligen Verkehrs- und Baumuseum in Berlin* (Hans Poelzig. The Plans and Drawings from the Former Transport and Civil Engineering Museum in Berlin).[1]

Schirren's book is much more than a catalogue of the material that was found. It opens up a whole new perspective on Poelzig. Schirren himself wrote two introductory articles and very informative texts to accompany the thirty-seven entries in the catalogue. Wolfgang Pehnt, known especially for his book on Expressionist architecture that begins with a study of Poelzig,[2] also contributed an essay which he called, "Ein Kerl wie Poelzig. Skizze eines Architektenlebens" (A Chap Like Poelzig. Sketch of an Architect). It is a particularly admirable contribution because here Pehnt concentrates on how Poelzig fitted in to this time of great change; he makes a clear distinction between Poelzig and the architects of the younger generation—Taut and Gropius, for instance. In doing so he quotes a statement from Poelzig that makes this difference very clear: "The actual spokesmen of a revolution are the weak. The strong are always revolutionary but in another sense. They protest against the tendency of tradition to produce standardization but instead of trying to ignore tradition, they oppose it and then pass beyond."[3]

Schirren's book also contains an essay by Dieter Bartetzko, a study of Poelzig's most famous building, the administration building for I.G. Farben in Frankfurt-am-Main. Bartetzko calls his study "Between Freedom and Constraint—Fossilized Modernism in Hans Poelzig's I.G. Farben Building." This analysis

270 Hans Poelzig: Reflections on His Life and Work

338 Hans Poelzig. Sports Hall, one of the buildings planned for the Berlin Fair of 1928–30 by Poelzig together with Martin Wagner, city architect of Berlin. Project. From Matthias Schirren, *Hans Poelzig. Die Pläne und Zeichnungen aus dem ehemaligen Verkehrs- und Baumuseum in Berlin*, 1989.

also aims at making a distinction between Poelzig and the younger generation, the modern architects.

These essays introduce the main part of the book, the catalogue of Poelzig's work discovered in the Hamburger Bahnhof. A fair number of those projects were hitherto unknown, certain others had received scant mention. I have asked myself which of these newly discovered aspects of Poelzig's work ought to figure in the present book. Three of the drawings seemed particularly appropriate. With the kind permission of the publisher, Ernst & Sohn, I have added them in conjunction with the relevant text (Fig. 338; see also Figs. 59, 68).

Hans Poelzig: Buildings and Projects

1897–98
Town hall. Schinkel Prize Competition of the Architects' Association, Berlin, for 1898. Competition design.

1899
Memorial hall. Monthly competition of the Architects' Association, Berlin, January 1899. Competition design.

1900
BARTH: Memorial chapel. Monthly competition of the Architects' Association, Berlin, May 1900. Competition design.

1901
BRESLAU: Spire of court church.
TREBNITZ (Silesia): Church organ.

1902
BRESLAU: Organ and other furnishings for the university auditorium.

1903
OELS (Silesia): Alterations to church.

1903–6
LÖWENBERG (Silesia): Additions to the town hall.

1904
BRESLAU: One-family house at the Exhibition of Applied Art.

1905
WÜLTSCHKAU (Silesia): Alterations to the Protestant church.

1906
LEERBEUTEL (nr. Breslau): House of Hans Poelzig.
BRESLAU: "Werdermühle" factory. Project.
MALTSCH: Protestant church.
ZIEGENHALS (Silesia): Altar of the Catholic church.

c. 1906
BRESLAU: Dining room and billiard room in the apartment of Herr von Loebecke.

1907–12
BRESLAU: Apartment houses.

1908
KLINGENBERG (Saxony): Dam.

1909
KÖNIGSBERG (East Prussia): Bridge leading to the palace. Project.

1910
HAMBURG: Water tower on the Sternchanze. Competition design.
LÖWENBERG: Zwirner house (residence and youth hostel).
BRUSTAWE (Silesia): Palace. Project.
WASHINGTON, D.C.: German embassy. Project.

1911
POSEN: Upper Silesia Tower (water tower).
COLOGNE: Bridge and bridgehead. Project.
BRESLAU: Office building on the Junkernstrasse.
BINGERBRÜCK: Bismarck Memorial. Project in two stages.

1911–12
LUBAN (nr. Posen): Chemical factory and workers' housing.

1912
BERLIN: Opera house. Project.

1913
BRESLAU: Buildings at the Centennial Exhibition.
CAROLATH (Silesia): Palace chapel. Project.
RÜSTRINGEN: Redesign of town center. Competition design.

1913–14
RADLIN (Silesia): "Römergrube" mine. Administration and shaft buildings.

1913–15
PSCHOW (Silesia): "Annagrube" mine. Three factory buildings.

1914
RADLIN: "Emmagrube" mine. Public hall and bachelors' house. Projects.
BRESLAU: One-family house for the Garden City Society of Brockau.

1915
GLATZ (Silesia): Franciscan monastery. Project.

1916
RADLIN: Workers' housing. Project.
DRESDEN: Gasworks at Reick.
CONSTANTINOPLE: "House of Friendship." Competition entry.
DRESDEN: Fire station. Project in three versions.
DRESDEN: Two school buildings. Project.

1917
DRESDEN: Gas storage tower. Project.
DRESDEN: Town hall. Project.
DRESDEN: Group of two museum buildings. Project.
DRESDEN: Town planning scheme. Project.

1918
DRESDEN: Bridge over the Elbe. Project.
DRESDEN: Concert hall. Project.

1919
BERLIN: Grosses Schauspielhaus.

1920
DRESDEN: Porcelain Pavilion for 1921 exhibition.
BERLIN: Film set for *Der Golem*.

1920–22
SALZBURG: Festival Theater. Project in three versions.

1921
DRESDEN: Bank building. Project.
DRESDEN: Majolica Chapel. Project.
MANNHEIM: Exhibition of decorative objects (and designs) in porcelain; with Marlene Moeschke, later Poelzig. (Marlene Moeschke also participated in the design of the decorative columns in the Grosses Schauspielhaus, and she designed the Poelzigs' house in Berlin after 1930. The full extent of her work is not well documented.)
DRESDEN: Hotel. Project.
HELLERAU: Wooden houses. Project.

BERLIN: High-rise building near the Friedrichstrasse station. Project.
BERLIN: War memorial at Siemensstadt. Project.
COLOGNE: Merchants' Building. Project.
DRESDEN: Majolica fountains; with Marlene Moeschke.

1923–24
HANNOVER: Mayer Brothers administration building at Vinnhorst.

1924
HANNOVER: Storage building for Mayer Brothers.
RHEYDT: Theater. Project.
CHEMNITZ: Hotel Atlantic. Project.

1924–25
BERLIN: Alterations to a commercial building near the zoo.
BERLIN: Building incorporating shops, offices, and the Capitol Cinema.

1925–27
CHEMNITZ: Göritz factory.

1925
BERLIN: Exhibition building of the *Frien Sezession*. Project.
UNTERSCHREIBERHAU (Silesia): Tomb of Karl Hauptmann.
BRESLAU: Alterations to concert hall.
BERLIN: "Radio Hall." Project.
HAMBURG: "Messehaus" (office and exhibition building). Project.
COLOGNE: Bridgehead. Project.

1926
BERLIN: Remodeling of the Parkhotel, Kantstrasse. Project.
BERLIN: Two-story addition to the Hotel Kaiserhof, Wilhelmstrasse. Project.
BERLIN: Street telephone posts.
DRESDEN: Mosaic fountains.
BRESLAU: Deli Cinema.
BRESLAU: Sports building and students' residences. Project.

1926–27
BERLIN: Sports Forum. Competition design.

1927
HALLE: Buildings on the "Lehmann Cliffs." Project.
LEIPZIG: Augustus Square. Project.
BERLIN: Group of professional schools, Charlottenburg. Project.
BEUTHEN: Alterations to concert hall.
BERLIN: Weekend houses.
STUTTGART: One-family house in the Weissenhof Estate.
BERLIN: Additional buildings for the Reichstag on the Platz der Republik. Project.
GENEVA: Palace of the League of Nations. Competition design.
BERLIN: New street joining the Tiergarten and Wilhelmstrasse. Project.

1927–28
BERLIN: Petrol stations for Reichssprit GmbH.
BERLIN: "Thermenpalast" (sports building); with J. Goldmerstein and Karl Stodieck. Project.
SCHULAU: Power station; with Werner Issel.

1927–29
BERLIN: New district plan for the Scheunenviertel.

1927–30
BERLIN: Master plan for the "Messegelände" (exhibition ground); with Martin Wagner, City Architect. Project.

1928
HINDENBURG (Silesia): Plan for the city center. Project.
BERLIN: Apartment buildings in the Scheunenviertel.
BERLIN: Store for the Adam company. Project.
BERLIN: One-family house and two semidetached houses for the Gagfah Estate (Im Fischtal), Zehlendorf.
SPEYER: Bridge over the Rhine. Project.
MAXAU: Bridge over the Rhine. Project.
MANNHEIM: Friedrich-Ebert Bridge. Project.

1928–29

BRESLAU: Department store for L. Tietz AG. Project.
BERLIN: Exhibition and office building near the zoo.
BERLIN: Babylon Cinema in the Scheunenviertel.
BERLIN: Cable factory for Dr. Cassirer & Co. in Spandau.
BERLIN: Group of professional schools in the Urban district.
KAMMIN: Church hall of the Evangelical community.

1928–30

FRANKFURT-AM-MAIN: Administration building for I.G. Farben.

1929

KASSEL: Old people's home and welfare center for the Aschrott Foundation. Project.
BERLIN: Exhibition halls for the Berlin Fair.
BERLIN: Additions to the Reichstag at the Spreebogen. Project.
BERLIN: Students' residences at Charlottenburg. Project.
BERLIN: Administration building for the Nitrogen Syndicate. Project.
KLIEDBRUCH (nr. Krefeld): One-family house.
BRESLAU: Addition to the zoo. Project.
LUDWIGSHAFEN: Bridge over the Rhine; with Gollnow & Son. Project.

1929–30

BERLIN: Research Center for the German Aeronautical Research Institute in Britz. Project.
BERLIN: Broadcasting House.

1930

HAMBURG: War memorial; with Marlene Moeschke Poelzig. Project.
BERLIN: "Reichehrenmal" (war memorial) inside Schinkel's Neue Wache. Project.
BERLIN: Exhibition pavilion of the Deutscher Stahlbauverband at the 1931 building exhibition. Project.
BERLIN: Film studio at Gatow. Project.

1930–31

KHARKOV: Theater. Project.

1931

BERLIN: Exhibition pavilion for the Adolf Lauster Travertine works at the 1931 building exhibition.
MOSCOW: Palace of the Soviets. Project.
WOLGAST: Savings society building.
NIEDERFINOW: Ship-lift. Project.

1931–32

BERLIN: One-family house for the competition "Das wachsende Haus" (The Growing House).

1932

BERKA (Thuringia): War memorial in garden form. Project.
THURINGIA: "Schauburg" (festival theater). Project.
BERLIN: Housing estate in Dahlem. Project.
BERLIN: Housing estate in Eichkamp. Project.
BERLIN: Housing estate near the Waldfriedhof cemetery. Project.

1932–33

Houses of standardized design for use on housing estates. Project.

1933

BERLIN: Building for the Reichsbank. Competition design.
ROSTOCK: Town hall. Project.

1934

HÖCHST: Transport building for I.G. Farben, Frankfurt. Project.

1934–35

ISTANBUL: Theater and music school. Project.

1935

DESSAU: Friedrich Theater. Project.
ANKARA: Diplomats' housing. Project.
BERLIN: Building for the Luftkreiskommandos II (Air Command). Project.

STAGE DESIGNS

1920
DRESDEN: *Der König,* by Hanns Johst. Sächsische Landesbühne.
BERLIN: *Hamlet,* by William Shakespeare, directed by Max Reinhardt. Project.
BERLIN: *Faust,* by J.W. von Goethe, directed by Max Reinhardt. Project.

1922–23
BERLIN: *Die Räuber,* by Friedrich von Schiller. Centraltheater.

1923
BERLIN: *König Lear,* by William Shakespeare. Grosses Schauspielhaus.
BERLIN: *Don Giovanni,* by W.A. Mozart. Staatsoper.

1924
BERLIN: *Gilles und Jeanne,* by Georg Kaiser. Dramatisches Theater.

1926
HEIDELBERG: *Munken Vendt,* by Knut Hamsun. Stadttheater (Festspiele).

HEIDELBERG: *Ein Sommernachtstraum,* by William Shakespeare. Schlosshof. With Ludwig W. Schmieder and Marlene Poelzig.
HEIDELBERG: *Urfaust,* by J.W. von Goethe. Bandhaussaal. With Ludwig W. Schmieder.

1929
BERLIN: *Ödipus,* by Sophocles and Lipmann. Staatliches Schauspielhaus.

FILM SETS

1920
BERLIN: *Der Golem.* Buildings carried out with Kurt Richter.

1923–25
BERLIN: *Lebende Buddhas.* Poelzig with Botho Höfer and Berti Rosenberg.

1925
BERLIN: *Zur Chronik von Grieshuus.* Poelzig with R. Herlth and W. Röhrig.

Notes

The following abbreviations are used in the Notes.

Arch d'Au *L'Architecture d'Aujourd'hui*

Heuss Theodor Heuss, *Hans Poelzig. Das Lebensbild eines deutschen Baumeisters. Bauten und Entwürfe,* Berlin, 1939; reprint, Stuttgart, 1985

Posener Julius Posener, ed., *Hans Poelzig. Gesammelte Schriften und Werke,* Berlin, 1970

FOREWORD

1. Julius Posener, "Hans Poelzig and the Architecture of Expressionism," in *From Schinkel to the Bauhaus: Five Lectures on the Growth of Modern German Architecture,* London, 1972, p. 25.
2. Ibid., p. 29.
3. Julius Posener, *Fast so alt wie das Jahrhundert,* Berlin, 1990, chap. 3, p. 49.
4. Ibid., Epilogue, p. 312; also referred to as "Master," chap. 9, p. 170, and "our Master," chap. 5.
5. My conversation with Julius Posener, fall, 1990.
6. Ibid., and Posener's letter to me, 26 June 1991.
7. Rémi Baudoui, "Dittier à Aujourd'hui," Arch d'Au, no. 272, December 1990, p. 63.
8. Ibid., p. 66.
9. Julius Posener, "Erich Mendelsohn," Arch d'Au, no. 4, 1932, p. 7.
10. Julius Posener, "L'Exposition: Soleil, Air, Maison Pour Tous, Berlin, Eté, 1932," Arch d'Au, no. 6, 1932, pp. 25–32.
11. Ibid., p. 26.
12. Jean-Louis Cohen, *Architectures modernes, relations internationales* 2 . . . , École d'Architecture Paris-Villemin, Paris, 1988, pp. 71–98.
13. Posener, "Mendelsohn," pp. 7, 13.
14. Jean-Louis Cohen, "Judéo-Soviéto-Boche," Arch d'Au, no. 272, December 1990, p. 65.
15. Taut was in large part responsible for the incorporation into Berlin's School of Fine Arts (Hochschule der Bildende Künste) of the department of architecture, which Posener was asked to join.
16. Julius Posener's letter to me about his post-1961 years, undated [early 1991].
17. Fritz Neumeyer's letter to me, 9 February 1991.
18. See Document 9C.
19. Posener's letter to me.
20. Ibid.

CHAPTER ONE

1. Joan Campbell, *The German Werkbund. The Politics of Reform in the Applied Arts,* Princeton, 1978.
2. Gustav Wolf, *Die Schöne deutsche Stadt. Mitteldeutschland,* Munich, 1912, p. 130.

3. Karl Scheffler, "Das Grosse Schauspielhaus," *Kunst und Künstler* 18 (1920), pp. 231–41.
4. I would like to make an exception for Peter Behrens's office block for the dyeworks in Höchst (near Frankfurt). The central hall there is one of the few Expressionist spaces that were ever built, a room of festive quality, executed with great splendor down to the last detail—an outstanding work. Of course, one wonders about the meaning of this space in the office block of an industrial company. To be blunt, what is it doing there, as it has a decidedly sacred quality?
5. Walter Gropius, "Programme des Staatlichen Bauhauses in Weimar, 1919," in Ulrich Conrads, ed., *Programme und Manifeste zur Architecture des 20. Jahrhunderts*, Berlin/Vienna/Frankfurt, 1964; English ed., *Programs and Manifestoes on 20th-Century Architecture*, Cambridge, Mass., 1971.
6. Walter Gropius, "Grundsätze der Bauhausproduktion" (Dessau), 1926, in Conrads, op cit., pp. 90–91 (excerpt).
7. Walter Gropius, paper given in 1911, mentioned and quoted in Helmut Weber, *Walter Gropius und das Faguswerk*, Munich, 1961, p. 24.
8. Sigfried Giedion quotes Vierendeel's criticism in *Raum, Zeit, Architektur*, Ravensburg, 1965 (first published as *Space, Time, and Architecture* in Cambridge, Mass., in 1941), p. 193. The comment quoted by Giedion is extremely interesting: "The fact that it is out of proportion in this way produces a very bad effect: the beam is not weighted, it has no seating, the eye is not reassured. The curve of the arch is also very lacking from an aesthetic point of view. It begins too low down. The imposts in the Palais des Machines also are not right—they look too hollow."
9. Henry van de Velde, "Aperçu en vue d'une synthèse d'art," Brussels, 1895, in *Henry van de Velde. Zum neuen Stil*, a selection of his writings with an introduction by Hans Curjel, Munich, 1955, pp. 39–40. In this article, van de Velde says: "Industry has subjected the arts, which until now were diverging in the most different directions, to uniform standards and laws and in doing so has given them a common style."

CHAPTER TWO

1. Pol Abraham, *Viollet-le-Duc et le rationalisme médiéval*, Paris, 1934.
2. Hans Poelzig, "Der Architekt," published with a foreword by Theodor Heuss, ed. Eugen Fabricius, Tübingen, 1954. The speech actually was given at the Federal Assembly of the Bund Deutscher Architekten (B.D.A.) in Berlin on 4 June 1931. Reprinted in Posener, p. 229.
3. Eugène Viollet-le-Duc, *Histoire d'une maison*, Paris, 1873.
4. Hans Poelzig, "Der Architekt," in Posener, p. 231.
5. Hans Poelzig, "Der neuzeitliche Fabrikbau," *Der Industriebau* 2 (1911), no. 5, pp. 100–106.
6. Hartmut Frank, "Ein Bauhaus von dem Bauhaus. Die Ausbildungs reform an des kgl. kunst und Kunstgewerbe in Breslau," *Bauwelt*, November 1983, pp. 1640–53.
7. The letters, in the possession of the Pallat family, have not yet been published. Poelzig enjoyed letterwriting and a large number still exist and would be well worth publishing.
8. During his years in Breslau, Poelzig designed other furniture besides that for Pallat, including several groups for the family of Oscar and Hedwig Brieger (see Figs. 134–136).
9. Theodor Fontane, *Frau Jenny Treibel*, 1888–91.
10. Hermann Muthesius, *Das Englische Haus*, 3 vols., Berlin, 1904; English ed., *The English House*, in 1 vol., London, 1979.
11. Vincent Scully, *The Stick Style and the Shingle Style*, New Haven, 1955; rev. ed., New Haven, 1971.
12. Gustav Wolf, *Die Schöne deutsche Stadt. Mitteldeutschland*, Munich, 1912, p. 130.
13. Franz Geiger, "Mühle und Lagerhaus," *Die Raumkunst*, Munich and Darmstadt, 1908, pp. 93–95.
14. Cf. n. 5. "Der neuzeitliche Fabrikbau" is reprinted in Posener; quotations on p. 42.
15. Charles-Edouard Jeanneret, *Etude sur le mouvement d'art décoratif en Allemagne*, La Chaux-de-Fonds, 1912.
16. William Shakespeare, *King Lear*, Act 1, Scene 4.
17. Theodor Heuss, "Poelzig," *Die Neue Rundschau*, 47 (1936), no. 9, pp. 938–61. Reprinted in Posener, pp. 22–23.

18. Theodor Heuss, "Poelzig," in Posener, p. 22.
19. Ibid.

CHAPTER THREE

1. Heuss, p. 20.
2. Friedrich Ostendorf, *Sechs Bücher vom Bauen*, Berlin, 1913–20.
3. Geoffrey Scott, *The Architecture of Humanism*, London, 1914.
4. Heuss, p. 23.
5. Hans Poelzig, "Der Architekt," speech to the 28th Federal Assembly of the Bund Deutscher Architekten on 4 June 1931. Published with a foreword by Theodor Heuss, ed. Eugen Fabricius, Tübingen, 1954. Reprinted in Posener, pp. 229–46.
6. *Die Kunst in Industrie und Handel. 1913*, Yearbook of the Deutsche Werkbund, Jena, 1913.
7. Walter Curt Behrendt, "Hans Poelzig," *Kunst und Künstler* 12 (1913), no. 1, pp. 55–61. Reprinted in Posener, pp. 63–65; quotation on p. 64.
8. The granite and porphyry monuments of Egypt exercise an incredible power on the spirit. What is the essence of this magic power? In part it is certainly that they are the neutral ground, where the hard, resisting material and the soft hand of man with his simple tools (hammer and chisel) meet and make a pact which says "So far and no further, this way and no other!" That has been their unspoken agreement for thousands of years. Their magnificent calm and solidity, the somewhat angular fineness of their lines, the moderation in the treatment of the difficult material, which shows itself in them, their whole way of being, are beautiful qualities of style which, now that we can cut the hardest stones as if they were bread and cheese, have to some extent become redundant.

    Gottfried Semper, *Wissenschaft, Industrie und Kunst. Vorschläge zur Anregung des nationalen Kunstgefühls*, Braunschweig, 1852 (written in London in 1851). Reprinted in Gottfried Semper, *Wissenschaft, Industrie und Kunst*, ed. Hans Wingler, Mainz and Berlin, 1966, pp. 25–79. Quotation on p. 36. Semper, like Poelzig after him, approved of progress in building technology. Also like Poelzig, he realized that "the overabundance of technical possibilities is a great danger, which art will have to face" (ibid., p. 35).
9. Henry van de Velde, "Die Belebung des Stoffen als Prinzip des Schonheit," in *Henry van de Velde. Zum neuen Stil*, ed. Hans Curjel, Munich, 1955, p. 176.
10. Walter Gropius, "Der stilbildende Wert industrieller Bauformen," *Der Verkehr, 1914*, Yearbook of the Deutsche Werkbund, Jena, 1914, p. 31.
11. Hans Poelzig, "Der neuzeitliche Fabrikbau," *Der Industriebau* 2 (1911), no. 5, pp. 100–106. Reprinted in Posener, p. 40.
12. The architect Oskar Kaufmann built the Krolloper inside the Kroll entertainment establishment which had been built in 1843 by two architects of the Schinkel school. The competition for an opera house on this site, held in 1912, envisaged the demolition of the Kroll establishment.
13. Hans Schliepmann, *Neue Entwürfe zum Berliner kgl. Operahaus*, Berlin, 1913. *Allgemeiner Wettbewerb von 1912*, special issue of *Berliner Architekturwelt*, Wasmuth, 1913, pp. 45–132.
14. Arthur Moeller van den Bruck, *Der Preussische Stil*, 1916; rev. ed., Breslau, 1931, p. 194.
15. Letter to Theodor Heuss written in 1924, that is, almost ten years later. The letter, which also speaks of the fact that Poelzig "to a certain extent sought a confrontation with antiquity," seems, despite its late date, to reflect quite precisely the spirit in which Poelzig approached this commission, which is an exception in his *oeuvre*. See Heuss, p. 28.
16. Willy Hahn, *Baurundschau*, Hamburg, 1913, pp. 372–77.

CHAPTER FOUR

1. Inaugural address at the Werkbund meeting of 1908 in Munich. In D.W.B., *Die Veredlung der gewerblichen Arbeit im Zussamenwirken von Kunst, Industrie und Handwerk*, Leipzig, 1908.
2. Julius Posener, *Berlin auf dem Wege zu einer neuen*

Architektur. Das Zeitalter Wilhelms des Zweiten, Munich, 1979, p. 32.
3. Heuss, p. 66.

CHAPTER FIVE

1. Wenzel Holek, autobiography: vol. 1, *Lebensgang eines deutsch-tschechisehen Handarbeiters,* Jena, 1909; vol. 2, *Vom Handarbeiter zum Jugenderzieher,* Jena, 1924. On Hellerau, see pp. 119–22, 124–28, 141, 142.
2. This was how the architect Fritz Schumacher referred to the economy in his speech on the founding of the Werkbund in Munich in October 1907: "And thus art is not only an aesthetic but a moral force, and these two forces produce in the end the most important force of all: economic force."

CHAPTER SIX

1. Julius Posener, *Berlin auf dem Wege zu einer neuen Architektur. Das Zeitalter Wilhelms des Zweiten,* Munich, 1979, p. 443.
2. Erich Mendelsohn, "Das Problem einer neuen Baukunst," speech to the Working Council for Art, Berlin, 1919. Reprinted in Erich Mendelsohn, *Das Gesamtschaffen des Architekten. Skizzen-Entwürfe-Bauten,* Berlin, 1930, pp. 7–21. Quotation on p. 18.
3. The Grosses Schauspielhaus stood in what was until recently East Berlin.
4. Karl Scheffler, "Das Grosse Schauspielhaus," *Kunst und Künstler* 18 (1920), pp. 231–41. Also in Posener, op. cit., p. 442.
5. Posener, op. cit., p. 443.
6. Hans Poelzig, "Der Bau des Grosse Schauspielhaus. Das Grosse Schauspielhaus," *Schriften des Deutschen Theaters,* ed. Max Reinhardt, Berlin, 1920, pp. 119–22. Extract in Posener, pp. 123–24.
7. Letter of 24 April 1921.
8. Speech to the Werkbund, Stuttgart, 1919, *Mitteilungen des Deutschen Werkbundes* (in-house publication of the Deutsche Werkbund), Berlin, 1919, no. 4. Reprinted in Posener, pp. 111–12.

CHAPTER SEVEN

1. Letter from Poelzig of 20 April 1921. He wrote: "I am thinking of founding a secret nationalist club." Quoted in Heuss, p. 38.
2. Johann Wolfgang von Goethe, *Faust,* Part 2, Act 1, "Finstere Galerie":
   Mephisto. Kein Weg! Ins Unbetrente
   Nicht zu betretende; ein Weg ans Unerbetene,
   Nicht zu Erbittende. Bist Du bereit?
3. Hans Poelzig, "Festspielhaus in Salzburg," speech given at a meeting of the Salzburg Festival Theater Association in 1921. In Posener, pp. 142–51; quotation on p. 144.
4. Hans Poelzig, letter to Theodor Heuss, November 1920. In Heuss, p. 48.
5. Hans Poelzig, "Festspielhaus in Salzburg," in Posener, p. 142.
6. Ibid., p. 150.
7. The circles in this auditorium are part of the dome, which begins on the floor of the stalls. In the first scheme, the boxes, too, continue into the dome. It is interesting that Erich Mendelsohn adopted the ordering of the circles in Poelzig's third Salzburg scheme in his design for the Palace of the Soviets (1929; see Figs. 195–198, 251).

CHAPTER EIGHT

1. Adolf Behne, *Max Taut. Bauten und Pläne. Neue Werkkunst,* Berlin/Leipzig/Vienna, 1927.
2. In conversation with the author.

CHAPTER NINE

1. Hermann Muthesius, "Die Neue Bauweise," review of the Weissenhofseidlung in the *Berliner Tageblatt,* 1927. Also in Julius Posener, *Die Anfänge des Funktionalismus,* Berlin/Frankfurt/Vienna, 1964, p. 229.
2. Hans Poelzig, speech as president of the Deutsche Werkbund at Stuttgart, 1919, *Mitteilungen des Deutschen Werkbundes,* 1919, no. 4, pp. 109–24. Also in Posener, pp. 111–21; quotation on p. 113.
3. Hans Poelzig, "Der Architekt," speech at the

28th Federal Assembly of the Bund Deutscher Architekten on 4 June 1931. Published with a foreword by Theodor Heuss, ed. Eugen Fabricius, Tübingen, 1954. Reprinted in Posener, pp. 229–46; quotation on p. 231.
4. Hans Poelzig, "Vom Bauen unserer Zeit," *Die Form,* 1922, no. 1. Also in Posener, pp. 170–86.
5. Walter Riezler, "Uber des Veralten technischer Formen," *Die Form,* 1922, no. 2, p. 31. Reprinted in Posener, p. 188.
6. Johann Wolfgang von Goethe, *Xenien,* "Revolutionen":

> Was das Luthertum war, ist jetzt das Franztum in diesen
> Letzten Tagen, es drängt ruhige Bildung zurück.

7. Hermann Muthesius, *Handarbeit und Massenerzeugnis,* Berlin, 1917, pp. 29ff.
8. Ibid., p. 16.
9. Ibid., p. 13.
10. Hans Poelzig, "Der Architekt," in Posener.
11. Heuss points to the difficulties the architect encountered: "The sketch shows that he intended to blend into these surroundings [which were pseudo-Romanesque in style—J.P.] a building with a strong character of its own. He did not succeed. He was fighting energetically, yet in vain. He had to abandon his basic concept. And yet the Capitol Building became for Poelzig himself, and also for those who tried to follow him, a very important work." Heuss, p. 73.

CHAPTER TEN

1. Theodor Heuss, p. 52.
2. Theodor Fontane, *Werke,* jubilee edition, Munich, 1968, vol. 11, *Der Stechlin,* pp. 402–800. For the description of the Barby house, see chap. 12, pp. 517ff.
3. From the description of the competition scheme. Cf. Heuss, p. 61.

CHAPTER ELEVEN

1. Letter of 9 January 1933. In Heuss, p. 76.
2. In conversation with the author early in 1933.
3. Heuss, pp. 61–62.
4. Ibid., p. 79.

CHAPTER THIRTEEN

1. J.C.F. von Schiller, *Wallensteins Lager,* Scene 6:
   Wie er räuspert und wie er spuckt
   Das habt ihr ihm glücklich abgeguckt.

POSTSCRIPT

1. Matthias Schirren, *Hans Poelzig. Die Pläne und Zeichnungen aus dem ehemaligen Verkehrs- und Baumuseum in Berlin,* Berlin, 1989.
2. Wolfgang Pehnt, *Die Architektur des Expressionismus,* Stuttgart, 1973; English edition, *Expressionist Architecture,* New York, 1973.
3. Hans Poelzig, quoted by Pehnt, op. cit., p. 26.

Index

Figure numbers appear in italics following page numbers.

A
Abraham, Pol, 22–23
Academy (school of fine arts), Berlin, 45, 138, 179, 245
Arch +, x
Art Nouveau, 3, 6–7, 132, 173, 183, 190, 191; *1, 2.* See also Jugendstil
arts and crafts movements, 6, 7, 26, 29, 102, 134, 173, 176
Arts and Crafts Workshops, Hellerau, 102, 173, 176; *137*
Avenarius, Ferdinand, 51, 98–99

B
Bähr, Georg: Frauenkirche, 110; *148, 149*
Baroque style, 87, 110, 119, 136–37, 152, 154, 158
Bartetzko, Dieter, 269–70
Bartning, Otto, vii, xiv
  "Sternkirche," project, 110; *147*
Bauhaus, 11, 26, 119, 171
Behne, Adolf, 158
Behrendt, Walter Curt, 72
Behrens, Peter, viii, xiii, 3, 6, 8, 12, 17–18, 42, 93, 97, 112, 127, 132, 171, 210, 251, 263
  A.E.G. Montaghalle, 70; *83*
  A.E.G. Small-Motors Factory, 70, 72; *84*
  A.E.G. Turbine Factory, 3, 13–15, 18, 42, 69, 72, 132; *19, 20, 22, 23*
  concert hall, Dresden, 3; *6*
  crematorium, Hagen, 3, 18; *5*
  embassy in St. Petersburg, 84; *112*
  Höchst office building, 110, 158, 277 n. 4
  "House of Friendship," project, 112; *153*
  Jugendstil house, Darmstadt, 3; *2*
  lamp in Jugendstil, *1*
  Obenauer house, 3, 30; *3, 4*
Berg, Max: Jahrhunderthalle, 87, 99; *120, 121*
Berlin villas; style of, 28–29
Berling, Max, 229
Bernoulli, Hans, 95
Bestelmeyer, German, 112
Binding, Rudolf G., 255
Bismarck, memorials to, 39–40
Bonatz, Paul, 210
Bund Deutscher Architekten, 187

C
Cahen, Marcel-Eugène, viii
Centennial Exhibition, 1913, Breslau, 87–93; *120–129*
Cézanne, Paul, 8
Chiaveri, Gaetano: Hofkirche, Dresden, 110
Choisy, Auguste, 23, 24
classicism, 23, 24, 68, 87, 91, 93, 99, 112, 132, 153, 184–85, 191, 250
concrete construction, 64, 78, 87, 99, 103, 171, 181–83, 243
Constantinople, 10, 93, 110–18, 117–18. See also Istanbul
Coudenhove-Calergi, Nicholas, Count, 195

"country-house style," 30, 42, 60, 69
craftsmanship, 6, 11, 19–20, 24, 126–27, 154, 247, 250, 252

D
Deutsche Werkstätten für Handwerkskunst, 102, 173, 176; *137*
Deutscher Werkbund, xiii, xiv, 6–10, 24, 32, 39, 40, 46, 47, 72, 78, 96, 102–3, 112, 126–27, 129–34, 135, 171, 174, 175, 176, 186, 238, 263, 265, 279 n. 2
    Cologne exhibition of 1914, 9, 91, 93, 103, 112; *12*
    yearbook, *225–229*
Die Baugild, viii
Die Bauwelt, viii
Die Form, 175, 180, 186
Don Giovanni, 139, 160, 275; *179, 181*
Dresden Opera House (1835), 86; *116, 117*
Drexler, Dolly, 45, 179
Dutert, C.L.F.: Galerie des Machines, 13–14; *21*

E
Eiermann, Egon, 44
Endell, August, 119
Expressionism, vii, xii, xiii, 8–11, 19, 30, 35, 108, 110, 123, 131, 133, 137, 148, 171, 183, 187, 189, 263, 269, 277 n. 4

F
factory architecture, 47–50, 70, 73, 181
Fahrenkamp, Emil, 210
    Shell Building, Berlin, 171; *220*

Finsterlin, Hermann, ix, 21, 158
Fischer, Theodor, 6, 42, 93, 96, 112
Fontane, Theodor, 28
Frank, Hartmut, xi, 25, 26
Frank, Josef, 240
Frauenkirche, Dresden, 110; *148, 149*
Friedrich Wilhelm IV, 86
functionalism, 23

G
Geiger, Franz, 31–32, 35
Gessner, Albert: apartment house, Berlin-Charlottenburg, 60; *69*
Giedion, Sigfried, 277 n. 8
Glass Chain, 58
Gollnow & Sons, 84
Gosen, Theodor von, 245
Gothic architecture, 22–23, 152, 154, 158, 182, 183, 190
Gropius, Walter, viii, 11, 14, 19, 26, 42, 77–78, 93, 110, 119, 126, 158, 177, 187, 210, 253, 263, 268
Grosses Schauspielhaus. *See under* Poelzig, Hans: works and projects
Gurlitt, Cornelius, 77

H
Hahn, Willy, 94
Hämer, Hardt Waltherr, x
Hamlet, 139, 275; *185*
Häring, Hugo, 12, 172, 238
Hauptmann, Gerhard, 25
Hauptmann, Karl, 25
Hellbrunn park, 142–43, 150–51, 157, 266; *180*
Heuss, Theodor, 41, 44, 45, 50–51, 56, 69, 70, 98–99, 103, 112, 116, 117–18, 150, 208, 251, 254
Hochschule der Bildenden Künst, Berlin, ix, x

Hoffman, Josef, 142
Hoffmann, Ludwig, 187, 221
Hofkirche, Dresden, 110
Höger, Fritz: Chilehaus, 11, 158, 183; *16*
Horta, Victor, 29
housing estates, 171, 172, 238, 240–42, 256–57, 266; *219, 305–308, 310, 327*

I
Im Fischtal housing estate, 172, 238, 240–41, 247–48, 266; *219, 308, 310*
International Style, 11–12. *See also* modern architecture
Istanbul, 254, 259–60; *332–334*. *See also* Constantinople

J
Jugendstil, 3, 6–7, 17, 29, 132; *1, 2*. *See also* Art Nouveau

K
Kahn, Louis I., ix
Kaufmann, Oskar, 278 n. 12
    Cines Cinema, 170, 200; *238, 239*
    Komödie Theater, 148; *193*
    Volksbühne theater, 200, 220, 221; *273*
King Lear, 139; *184*
Kirchner, Ernst, 8
Kollwitz, Käthe, 246
Kramer, Ferdinand, 171
Kramer, Piet, 171
Kreis, Wilhelm, 40, 82, 210
Kühn, Hermann, 26
Kuhnert, Nikolaus, x
Kunstwart, 51

L
Laprade, Albert, ix
L'Architecture d'Aujourd'hui, viii–ix

Lauterbach, Heinrich, 46
  house, 60–63; *70–71*
Le Corbusier, 42, 171, 187, 240, 263
  Palace of Justice, Chandigarh, 106; *145*
  Palace of the League of Nations, project, 207
  Palace of the Soviets, project, 206; *250*
  Savoye House, viii
Lethaby, William, 44
Liebknecht, Karl, 135
Loos, Adolf, 29
Luckhardt brothers, 158, 263
Lurçat, André, viii
Lutyens, Sir Edwin, 29
Luxemburg, Rosa, 135

M

"machine for living," 191
Mächler, Martin, 217
Maffei locomotive, 176; *225*
Mann, Heinrich, 246
mass production, 176–77
Mattern, Hermann, x
May, Ernst, 171
Mebes, Paul, 29
Mendelsohn, Erich, vii, viii, ix, 8, 10–11, 19, 20–21, 108, 110, 123–24, 159, 167, 212, 263
  Palace of the Soviets, project, 206, 279 n. 7; *251*
  Schocken department store, 64; *74*
  sketches, *15, 152*
Messel, Alfred: department store, Wertheim, 42, 63; *73*
metal construction, 13–15, 23–24, 72–73, 77–78, 99, 181–83, 184, 186
Meyer, Hannes, 42, 207
Michelangelo, 184
Middleton, Charmian (Mrs. Julius Posener), viii

Mies van der Rohe, Ludwig, vii, xii, 42, 161, 187, 251, 253, 258, 263
  Barcelona Pavilion, 172, 174
  high-rise building nr. Friedrichstrasse station, project, 165; *208*
  Tugendhat House, 172
modern architecture, 11–12, 136, 172–74, 187, 189–91, 196, 210, 248, 263
Modersohn, Paula, 25
Moeller van den Bruck, Arthur, 87
Moeschke, Marlene (2d Mrs. Hans Poelzig), 41, 44, 122, 138–39, 238, 242
Möhring, Bruno: Berlin opera house, project, 86; *118*
Morris, William, 6, 7–8, 23, 98
Mozart, W. A., 157
Müller-Rehm, Claus, ix
Muthesius, Hermann, vii, viii, 6, 8, 29, 42, 68, 69, 77, 93, 102, 113–14, 126, 127, 130, 173–74, 176–77
  Cramer house, x
  De Burlet house, *6*
  von Seefeld house, 30; *34*

N

Neo-Classicism, 3, 6, 153
Neumann, Balthasar, 23, 137
Neumann, Ernst, 176; *229*
Neumeyer, Fritz, x, xi
"New Objectivity" *(Neue Sachlichkeit)*, 189, 192
November Group, 158

O

Olbrich, J. M., 29
"On Architecture in Our Time" (Poelzig), 180–86
Onkel Tom housing estate, 12, 172, 238, 247; *18*
Ostendorf, Friedrich, 68

Osthaus, Karl Ernst, 127
Oud, J.J.P., 171
  row houses, Hook of Holland, *223*

P

Palace of the League of Nations, 189–90. *See also under* Poelzig, Hans: works and projects
Pallat, Ludwig, 25, 26–27, 98
Paul, Bruno, 93, 112, 245
Pechstein, Max, 8
Pehnt, Wolfgang, 263, 269
Perret, Auguste, xii, 44, 265
Pinthus, Kurt, 10
Piranesi, 160
Poelzig, Hans: life
  at Academy, Berlin, 45, 138, 179, 245
  address to Deutscher Werkbund in 1919, 129–34
  affected by collapse of Weimar Republic, 246, 256, 268
  appearance of, 44; *Frontispiece*
  on architectural training and profession, 153, 187–96. *See also below* on teaching
  on art, 177, 181, 182–83, 185, 190–92, 195–96
  artistic preferences of, 137
  on artistic taste, 131
  attitude toward avant-garde, 174, 183
  Baroque elements in his work, 119
  "Belgian scandal," 245, 246
  buildability of his projects, 108, 148, 158
  ceramicwork, 41, 138, 158; *178*
  chronology of work and projects, 271–75
  on client-architect relationship, 187, 192, 193, 194, 195, 242, 268

Poelzig, Hans: life *(continued)*
color, use of, 123, 133
on craftsmanship, 27, 126–27, 129–34, 154, 174, 176, 247, 250, 267
death of, 22, 255
design process of, 44–45, 56–57, 179
domestic architecture, approach to, 172, 191–92, 238–42, 256–57, 266
drawings recently found, 268–69
as Dresden city architect, 28, 103–10, 119
education, 22–23, 24, 52
on engineering, 48, 189, 190
as Expressionist, 10–11, 30, 39, 41, 76, 82, 95, 103, 108, 110, 118, 123, 126, 128, 131, 147, 158, 170, 183, 263, 267
extreme designs of, 108, 110
on factory design, 47–50
family background, 22
as film-set designer, 141–42, 150, 159, 160, 275; *186–188*
on "form," 265–66
as furniture designer, 98; *134–136*
on German art, 151–53
on Gothic architecture, 190
and Jugendstil, 17–18
letters to Ludwig Pallat, 26–27
on mass production, 8, 127, 131–32
and metal construction, 23–24, 35, 47, 49, 50, 78, 181–83, 184, 253, 265
on modern architecture, xiii, 189–91, 196
on Neo-Classicism, 153
on ornament in architecture, 189, 192
as painter, 40–42, 50–51, 140, 159; *54*

personality of, 42, 44, 50–52, 245
political stance of, 135–36, 247, 248
in Potsdam, 138, 179
at Prussian Academy of Arts, 245, 246
on role of civil-service architects, 193–95
as stage-set designer, 139–41, 159, 160, 275; *179, 181, 184–188*
as teacher, viii, xii, xiii, 24–28, 44–46, 103, 119, 126, 137, 179, 195, 246, 248, 254
on technological progress, 11–12, 46–50, 64, 77, 98, 103, 131, 132–33, 156, 174–78, 181–83, 184, 187, 190–91, 247, 252–53, 267
on theater architecture, 154, 155
on tradition, 183–85
on "type forms," 127, 131, 174–77, 194–95
windows as used by, 35, 39, 50, 60, 99
See also Poelzig, Hans: works and projects
Poelzig, Hans: works and projects
Annagrube, 36; *45*
apartment house, Breslau, 60–63; *67, 68*
Babylon Cinema, 200, 202, 221; *240, 241, 273*
bank building for Dresden, project, 80, 84, 165; *108*
Berlin exhibition ground (Messegelände), 213, 220, 222–27
Congress Hall and restaurant, projects, 223–27; *277–281*

exhibition halls, 226–27; *282–284*
Radio Hall, project, 222; *276*
Bismarck Memorial, project, 39–40, 76, 80–82, 99, 104, 106, 165, 250, 252; *50, 105–107*
bridge for Königsberg castle, project, 82; *109*
Broadcasting House, 95, 213, 227–29; *281, 285–289*
Capitol Cinema, 149, 165–70, 178–79, 197, 200, 212, 260; *211–218*
Centennial Exhibition buildings (1913), 87–93, 99, 103; *122–29*
Historical Exhibition Building, 91; *125–128*
Pergola, 91; *122, 124*
Weinhaus, *129*
chapel for Dresden ("Majolica chapel"), project, 161; *204*
chemical factory at Luban, 15, 18, 24, 35, 42, 47, 70–72, 99, 265–66; *24, 25, 42, 85–90*
church, Maltsch, 8, 57–60; *10, 60–66*
church alterations, Wültschkau, 57
church hall, Kammin, 243; *315*
concert hall for Dresden, project, 108, 146, 148; *192*
Deli Cinema, 199–200; *235–237*
diplomats' residence for Ankara, project, 260–62; *336, 337*
Elbe River bridge, project, 161; *203*
embassy in Washington, project, 84; *110, 111*
film studios, Gatow, project, 258; *328*

Index   285

fire station for Dresden, project, 104–6, 128, 149, 158, 251, 266; *141–144*
Franciscan monastery, project, 67–69, 91, 95, 99; *79–81*
gas storage tower for Dresden, project, *202*
gasworks in Dresden-Reick, 35, 103, 243; *44, 138, 139*
German Aeronautical Research Institute research center, project, 213–15; *264*
Göritz factory, 36–39, 176, 178; *46–48*
Grosses Schauspielhaus, conversion, 11, 119–29, 145, 146, 147, 155, 160, 170, 246, 263; *167–176*
"Growing House," project, 256; *326*
Hamburg exhibition and office building, project, 212–13; *262, 263*
Hamburg water tower, project, 39, 47, 76–79, 80; *49, 100–102*
high-rise building nr. Friedrichstrasse station, project, 161, 163, 165, 217, 258; *206*
Hindenburg city center, project, 94, 222; *275*
hotel for Dresden, project, 165; *209*
house in Breslau, 128; *32*
"House of Friendship," project, 10, 93, 110–18, 136, 262, 267; *14, 155–165*
house for Im Fischtal estate, 172, 238, 240–41, 242, 266; *308, 310*
house in Kliedbruch, 241–42; *311–314*
house at 1904 Exhibition of Applied Art, 28, 29–30, 53, 56, 65, 98; *30, 32, 33, 133*
house for Weissenhof estate, 238–41, 242; *305–307*
housing estate in Dahlem, project, 256–57; *327*
I.G. Farben headquarters, 12, 45, 47, 179, 213, 229–37, 253, 267, 269–70; *17, 231, 290–302*
Junkernstrasse, Breslau, commercial buildings, 63–65; *72, 75*
Klingenberg dam, 76; *99*
Lauterbach house, 60–63; *70, 71*
Lehmann Cliffs development, project, 210–212; *261*
Löwenberg town hall extension, 8, 26, 27, 30, 65–67, 91, 126; *9, 29, 35–37, 76–78*
Majolica chapel, project, 161; *204*
Majolica fountain, 161
Mayer Brothers administration building, 161; *205*
memorial at Berka, project, 251; *319*
memorial in the Neue Wache, project, 250–51; *317*
memorial to the Wars of Liberation, project, 68
Merchants' Building, Cologne, project, 165; *210*
miscellaneous sketches, 140–41, 160; *179, 180, 182, 199–201*
Nitrogen Syndicate administration building, project, 213–15; *265, 266*
opera house for Berlin, project, 84–87; *113–115*
organ, University of Breslau, 3; *7*
Palace of the League of Nations, project, 206–7, 262; *252, 253*
Palace of the Soviets, project, 206–8; *247–249*
Poelzig house in Leerbeutel, 53, 128; *55, 56*
Porcelain Pavilion, 161
Posen (Upper Silesia) Tower, 17, 24, 42, 72, 73–76, 176, 265; *26, 27, 93–98*
professional schools for Berlin-Charlottenburg, project, 208–10, 267; *255–257*
professional schools for Berlin (Kreuzberg), project, 208–10, 267; *258*
Radio hall, project, 222; *276*
Reichsbank extension, project, 258; *329, 330*
Reichstag extension, project, 163, 216–20, 258; *270–272*
Römergrube, 35, 72–73; *43, 45, 91*
Rüstringen town center, project, 93–95; *130–32*
Schauberg (Show Castle), project, 251–54; *320–325*
Scheunenviertel (Berlin district) redesign, partially built, 221–22; *273, 274*
Schinkel Prize Competition design, 24–25; *28*
schools for Dresden, projects, 208; *254*
ship-lift, project, 243–44; *316*
sports forum for Berlin, project, 210; *259, 260*
sports hall for Berlin (with M. Wagner), project, *338*
students' residence for Berlin-Charlottenburg, project, 213, 215; *267–269*
theater and music school for Istanbul, project, 259–

Poelzig, Hans: works and project *(continued)*
  60; *332–335*
  theater for Dessau, project, 259–60; *331*
  theater for Kharkov, project, 202–6; *242–246*
  theater for Rheydt, project, 197; *232–234*
  theater for Salzburg Festival, project, 11, 108, 119, 136–37, 142–56, 157, 158, 165, 177, 206, 223, 266; *180, 183, 189, 194–198*
  weekend house, 238; *303, 304*
  Werdermühle, project, 31–35, 69–70, 72, 126; *38–41, 82*
  Zwirner house, 56–57, 128, 187; *57–59b*
Pöppelmann, M. D.: Zwinger, 108, 110
Posener, Julius, vii–xiv
Post-Modernism, 263
Prior, Matthew, 29
Prüss construction, 15; *87, 88*

R
Radicke, Dieter, 95
Reichstag, 163, 216–20, 258; *270–272*
reinforced concrete. *See* concrete construction
Reinhardt, Max, 119, 120, 122, 146, 246
Riemerschmid, Richard, 6, 93, 102, 112; *137*
Riezler, Walter, 175, 186–87
Rilke, Rainer Maria, 25
Roller, Alfred, 142–43, 151, 153, 155, 156
Ruskin, John, 7, 23, 77
Rust, Bernhard, 246

S
St. Peter's basilica, 184
Salvisberg, O. R., 12, 172, 238

apartment block for Weisse Stadt estate, *224*
Salzburg, 156, 157, 266. *See also* Poelzig, Hans: works and projects: theater for Salzburg Festival
Schäche, Wolfgang, xi
Schäfer, Karl, 22, 23–24, 188
Scharoun, Hans, ix, 8, 11, 146, 158, 161, 165, 263; *11*
Scheerbart, Paul, 9
Scheffler, Karl, 11, 125–26, 128, 145, 176
Schinkel, Karl Friedrich, vii, xi, 193
  Neue Wache, 250; *317, 318*
  "Old Museum," Berlin, 86; *119*
  Schauspielhaus, Berlin, 86
Schirren, Matthias, 269–70
Schliepmann, Hans, 86
Schmidt, Hartwig, xi
Schmidt, Karl, 102–3, 119, 127, 173, 176
Schmidt-Rottluff, Karl, 8
Schmitthenner, Paul, ix, 12, 241, 247, 248, 250, 267
  house for Im Fischtal estate, 171, 172; *219*
Schmitz, Bruno: Battle of the Nations monument, 40; *51, 52*
Schopohl, Fritz, 172, 240–41
Schumacher, Fritz, 130, 279 n. 2
Schwarz, Rudolf, 44
Scott, Geoffrey, 69
Scully, Vincent, 29
Segal, Walter, 44, 247
Semper, Gottfried, 24, 77, 155
  Dresden Opera house (1835), 86; *116, 117*
Shakespeare, William, 137
Shaw, R. Norman, 23
Siclis, Charles, viii
Sitte, Camillo, 257
Sombart, Werner, 26
Speer, Albert, 217, 250, 253
Spengler, Oswald, 180

Stam, Mart: houses for Weissenhof estate, 238; *309*
"Star dome," *140*
steel construction. *See* metal construction
Straumer, Heinrich, 222
structuralism, 23
Studio, 29
Sullivan, Louis, 23, 172, 266
  Guaranty Building, 165; *207*

T
Taut, Bruno, vii, viii, xiv, 11, 19, 20, 98, 106, 112, 123, 126, 263
  "Alpine Architecture" (sketches), 9–10; *13*
  "Domstern" (Star dome), 110, 158, 267; *140*
  cinema on Kottbusserdamm, 170
  Glass Pavilion, 8–9, 42, 91, 103, 158, 171, 172; *12*
  "House of Friendship," project, 112, 113; *154*
  Onkel Tom estate houses, 12, 171, 238; *18*
Taut, Max, ix, 158, 170
  Book Printers' Trade Union building, 171; *221, 222*
  Trade Unions building, 171
  water tower at Nauen, 78; *103, 104*
Technische Hochschule, Berlin, viii, x, xii, 22, 44, 45, 103, 138, 179, 248, 250, 254, 255
Tessenow, Heinrich, ix, xii, 102, 119, 127, 159, 172, 240, 243, 246, 248
  Bismarck Tower, project, 40; *53*
  house, 172; *230*
  war memorial in the Neue Wache, 251; *318*
"The Architect" (Poelzig), 103, 175, 187–96, 245, 267

The Golem, 141–42, 150, 160, 275; *186–188*
"The Modern Factory" (Poelzig), 24, 35, 46–50, 267
Transport (1914 Werkbund yearbook), 175–76; *225–228*
"type-forms," 98, 126–27, 131, 176–77, 186–87, 194–95

V
Vago, Pierre, viii
Valéry, Paul, 196
van de Velde, Henry, 18, 77, 185
Van Gogh, Vincent, 8
Vers Une Architecture (Le Corbusier), 171

Vierendeel, A. J., 13
Viollet-le-Duc, E. E., 22–23, 24
Vogler, Heinrich, 25
Voysey, C.F.A., 29, 69
  country house, *31*

W
Wachsmann, Konrad, 44
Wagner, Martin, 95, 171, 195, 221, 222, 246–47, 248, 253–54; *338*
Wallot, Paul: Reichstag building, 216
Wandervogel, 137
Wechsler, Alfred, 136

Wegener, Paul, 141–42, 150
Weissenhof housing estate, 171, 238–41; *305–307, 309*
Werkbund. *See* Deutscher Werkbund
Wittwer, Hans, 207
Wolf, Gustav, 30
Working Council for Art (Arbeitsrat für Kunst), 158, 263

Z
Zimmermann, Erich, 45
Zweig, Arnold, 129
Zwinger, Dresden, 108, 110, 152